PERTINENT PLAYERS

PERTINENT PLAYERS

ESSAYS ON THE LITERARY LIFE

by JOSEPH EPSTEIN

W. W. NORTON & COMPANY
NEW YORK
LONDON

The text of this book is composed in ITC Galliard, with the display set in Michelangelo and Garamond Old Style. Composition and manufacturing by The Maple-Vail Book Manufacturing Group.

The essays in this volume originally appeared in the following publications: *Commentary, The New Criterion,* and *The Hudson Review.* They are reprinted here with the kind permission of the editors.

Library of Congress Cataloging-in-Publication Data
Epstein, Joseph, 1937–
    Pertinent players : essays on the literary life / Joseph Epstein.
        p.   cm.
    I. Title.
    PS3555.P6527P47   1993
    809'.03—dc20   92–40860

ISBN 0-393-03519-0

W. W. Norton & Company, Inc., 500 Fifth Avenue, New York, N.Y. 10110
W. W. Norton & Company Ltd., 10 Coptic Street, London WC1A 1PU

1 2 3 4 5 6 7 8 9 0

For my dear Annabelle,
new life.

Contents

Introduction

I COULD NOT have been less than eighteen-years old
when I first took notice of the word *literary,* but I
liked it straightaway, the sound and even the look
of it. Ever since that time I have liked it, and still do. The
word, I recognize, is not everywhere in good repute, but I take
it as an honorific and always shall.

The Oxford English Dictionary finds the word first to have
been used by Sir Thomas Browne in 1646. Various dictionar-
ies offer slightly varying definitions, the standard ones referring to possessing humane learning, or being well-read or
bookish. I prefer my own, which holds that a literary man or
woman is someone who is not only steeped in literature but
has made this immersion into literature part of his or her own
life, so that the experience of books has been integral with the
experience of life and therefore strongly influences his or her
general point of view. At its worst, this can issue in comic if
not pathetic pretension, whose main effect is to remove the
literary man or woman from real life. But at its best, to be
literary results in a way of looking at the world not quite like
any other—in seeing the world in a greater richness than non-
literary people are likely to do.

As someone whose own education has been literary, someone who as a university teacher takes a small hand in the liter-

ary education of the young, I have often wondered what is at the heart of this kind of education. To say that what is at its heart is literary works—novels, poems, plays, essays—is both obvious and inadequate. If you have read a vast number of works of literature, what, when you come down to it, do you know? I have myself never been quite certain. If you have devoted a good part of your days to acquiring a fair amount of literary history—a history of the lives and conditions of writers and of the progress of literary forms and genres—what, really, do you have? All of it is pleasing to know, but so is the history of aviation and so, too, I suppose, is the behavior of penguins.

The usefulness of knowing many works of literature becomes even more questionable as you grow older and find you retain less and less of what you read and, worse news still, lose in the bogs of memory more and more that you had read earlier. Generations of literary men and women earlier than mine committed a good deal of poetry to memory, could quote Shakespeare by the acre, were erudite in three or four languages. I can do none of these things, nor have I any of these admirable abilities. I am merely someone who has read a reasonably large number of serious books by imaginative writers, which has been a pleasurable way to pass my days, but beyond having pleasured myself, as the Quakers say, to what does all this soaking in literature amount?

Desmond MacCarthy once said that it is the business of literature to turn facts into ideas. By this he meant that literature works by means of inductive reasoning: the facts first, Ma'am, we'll get to the ideas later. (Oddly, this is the way the scientific method is supposed to work, though many savvy scientists tell you that it never does—that scientists, the well-advertised scientific method to the contrary notwithstanding, work chiefly by hunches.) Milan Kundera has referred to the novel as one of the great inventions of the modern world: up there with the telescope and the microscope, an invention that makes possible other significant discoveries. It is literary method that makes for discovery. The writer, by scrupulously studying the facts, letting them speak for themselves, extends his (and our) knowledge. The sense in which writing becomes an act of discovery was perhaps best captured by Robert Frost, who said that whenever he wrote a poem whose ending he knew in advance, it inevitably turned out to be a damn poor poem.

At the same time that the business of literature is turning facts into ideas, different sets of facts are regularly being set out by other writers that can contradict, delimit, heavily qualify, even destroy the first set of ideas. In the study of literature, no ideas are locked in; nearly everything is in flux. Tolstoy said that all happy families are alike but every unhappy family is unhappy in its own way. As a literary man, my guess is that Tolstoy was only half right about this; every happy family is probably happy in its own way, too. Literature is inexhaustible data, endless stories that, taken together, add up to—what?

I have come to believe that one of the things that the reading of endless stories, poems, and plays adds up to is an abiding scepticism about general ideas, systems, and theories. When T. S. Eliot said of Henry James that "he had a mind so fine no idea could violate it," what he meant was not that James neither knew nor cared about ideas, but instead that, as a literary man, which of course Eliot himself was too, James believed that the most interesting truths about life for human beings were to be found above the level of ideas. What the instincts, the feelings, the heart in conflict report—these are the truths that form the quarry that literature operating at its highest power seeks to mine. That this quarry seems boundless, filled with surprises, and somehow magically self-renewing, with new writers turning up all the time, is one of the many rewards of literary study.

One of the things a literary education does is teach a scepticism about ideas in the name of a belief in the richness of life—a richness that, in the end, will always mock any attempts to schematize it. Life, dear intractable life, is always tossing up exceptions that prove no rule; it turns out to be more various than any philosophy has ever dreamed or any set of ideas can hope to encompass. Literature, when it is doing what it is supposed to be doing, through an act of reinforcement, reassures us that this is so. The result of a literary education, of long exposure to works of the imagination, is a literary point of view, which sees the world as sad, comic, heroic, vicious, dignified, ridiculous, and endlessly amusing—sometimes by turns and sometimes all at once.

The disadvantage of a literary point of view is that those who seek it—or are stuck with it—give up the notion of ever possessing a small body of mastering ideas that might explain the world for them. (This, of course, has come to seem less a disadvantage as, at the end of the twentieth century, such ideas—among them Marxism, Freudianism, variants of Structuralism—are today, if not totally bankrupt, at least in Chapter Eleven.) A serious literary education, breeding the useful doubt it does, makes life under the sway of such ideas unthinkable. The advantage of a literary point of view is that, once one grants life's resistance to being captured by a few ideas, one is regularly amazed and amused by it. I, at any rate, always have been.

The essays in this volume, all of them about writers and intellectuals, demonstrate something of the impressive range of human types and possibilities, even among people in roughly the same line of work, that the world provides. When I am asked to write about a writer or intellectual figure, I find myself, as I read through his work and through what others have written about him, asking, what is his story? How did he achieve what he did—against what odds, with what secret resources. (In some cases, it works the other way round: How did he fail as he did—despite such magnificent advantages?) But each life is a story, each different from all others, each with its own strange, sometimes mystifying pattern. Life and literature, from the literary point of view, aren't all that far apart.

The answer to the question of why I have chosen to write about the figures I have written about in this book is in part because they fascinate me, in part because in some instances I was asked to write about them, and in part because I enjoy writing about other people's lives generally, especially when these are lives that are intrinsically interesting. In this, my third such book of essays on literary subjects, I note that I have begun to write more and more about writers from earlier centuries: specifically, in this volume, this includes Chamfort, Sydney Smith, William Hazlitt, Robert Louis Stevenson. This may have a good deal to do with my growing older and finding that, after working at writing for more than thirty years, I more readily see strong connections between the lives of writers born two hundred years ago and writers of our own day, myself included.

I was drawn to write about other figures in this book because the shape of their careers outside literature impressed, or surprised, or saddened me. Thus I found myself writing about such extra-literary figures as Sidney Hook, Ben Hecht, and Robert Hutchins. Others—Italo Svevo, Desmond MacCarthy, Maurice Baring—I wrote about because I felt they were neglected and didn't deserve to be. Not that I think my writing about them will resuscitate their reputations, but it is useful to remind others, as well as myself, about writers who, though still rewarding, seem to have slipped out of sight. I wrote about Henry James because he is a hero of culture for me, and writing about him gives me the excuse for rereading him and recalling the exaltation that the literary life is capable of providing. With most of the writers and intellectuals in this book I feel an affinity—with the exception of Carl Sandburg, whom I wrote about as an interesting case study in the history of publicity and quickly faded reputation.

Many years ago, I heard the English humorist Stephen Potter give a lecture in a university setting. I recall almost nothing about the lecture, except that afterwards a graduate student arose and, with grim earnestness and availing himself of just about every stiff academic locution I have ever heard, asked Potter how it was that he, an established Coleridge scholar, had come to write such extraordinary books as *Lifesmanship* and *Gamesmanship*. Potter, after an excruciating pause during which he coughed and harrumphed and did other peculiar things in his throat, finally replied: "Out of work, you know."

One of the nice things about the literary point of view, about writing, about the literary life itself, is that, even when unemployed, you are never really out of work.

PERTINENT
PLAYERS

The Mere Common Sense of Sydney Smith

ODD THAT IT should be called "common sense," when the quality that those words have been appointed to describe is itself not only uncommon but extremely rare. Everyone will have his own notions of what constitutes common sense, and mine include an ability to tote up accurately the debits and credits that any complex decision presents; sufficient detachment to be able to remove one's own emotions and personal interests in order to gain maximum lucidity in understanding; a gift for grasping and articulating the obvious point that eludes everyone else; and, above all, a superiority of perspective that permits one to realize how issues and questions that agitate minds and stir hearts today will appear five and ten and fifty years from now. "Mere common sense," we say, but so unusual is it that we might as well say "mere transcendent beauty" or "mere wisdom."

Common sense has not been notable among German philosophers, French literary critics, professors of all nationalities, psychotherapists, and most people who earn their livings with their minds. Not that it is the preserve of the working classes or common people. It pops up with a randomness Darwinism cannot account for or common sense itself quite comprehend. A French diplomatist might have it, or a Texas politician, or a Jewish grandmother. How charming that it should have shown up, in heightened form, in a portly English clergyman born in 1771 who bore the name of Smith—though Macaulay, when told that a man named Smith was awaiting him, realizing that the man was Sydney Smith, referred to him as "the Smith of Smiths."

Where he is known at all, Sydney Smith is today best known for his aphorisms and comic *mots*. "Those two women will never agree," he once said of two women screaming insults at each other from their apartments across a narrow street in Edinburgh. "They are arguing from different premises." He is also known as one of the founders of the *Edinburgh Review,* the great Whig journal to which he contributed chiefly polemical articles during its first three decades. Queen Victoria laughed heartily at his sayings, as reported to her by Lord Melbourne; Dickens claimed that the praise of Sydney Smith meant more to him than that of anyone else; and Abraham Lincoln read him regularly and quoted him often. If one has to have a small, select audience of admirers, here are three names well worth including in it.

One gets, I believe, a nice sense of the general tone of Sydney Smith in a letter of 1807 that he wrote to Francis Jeffrey, the editor of the *Edinburgh Review,* in which he avers: "I have three motives for writing reviews: 1st the love of you; 2nd the habit of reviewing; 3rd the love of money—to which I would add a fourth, the love of punishing fraud or folly." I was much impressed by this letter when I first came across it twenty-odd years ago quoted in John Clive's *Scotch Reviewers: The "Edinburgh Review" 1802–1815,* and now after thirty years in the business—"and still wearing a cardboard belt," as Zero Mostel says in *The Producers*—I remain impressed with it for both its precision and its comprehensiveness as an account of why one writes for intellectual journals. No one but Sydney Smith, I think, would have included motive number two, sheer habit, in such a list, but then part of his skill was to say the obvious thing that is only obvious after he has said it.

"No man but a blockhead ever wrote, except for money," wrote Dr. Johnson, rather blockheadedly, in my view, for Hobbes scarcely wrote his *Leviathan* for cash or Tom Paine *The Rights of Man* with, specifically, subsidiary rights in mind. But Sydney Smith was a man in need of money in all but the last years of his life, and no doubt without the need for money he would have written less. His moderate penury was owing to his father, a rash man who bought and sold several houses— roughly nineteen of them, by his granddaughter's count— altering and spoiling each and then selling it for a loss. Sydney's father, according to Alan Bell in his 1980 biography, "was an ill-tempered man, who treated all his children badly, and Sydney, his most famous son, worst of all." Sydney was the second born of four sons (there was also a last-born child, a daughter). Two of the sons went to Eton; Sydney and one of his younger brothers went to Winchester. He hated public school—where, as he later wrote in an *Edinburgh Review* essay, "every boy is alternatively tyrant and slave"—but this hatred did not deflect him from winning a fellowship at Oxford. Sydney's older brother read for the bar, and later, through connections, became Advocate General at Calcutta, where he arranged for jobs for the two younger brothers. Sydney would have preferred to study law, too, but his father, concerned about the expense, discouraged him and urged on him instead a career in the Church. Without great enthusiasm, Sydney acquiesced. It was a decision that kept him worried about money for most of his life.

The constant concern about money, the sadness of carrying around the secure knowledge that one's father was distinctly not on one's side—such things have permanently thrown lesser men. Sydney Smith, however, was not to be thrown. He determined not to be and, therefore, wasn't. Locked into a clerical living in the fastness of Yorkshire, one that paid poorly and was well beneath his talent and kept him from the London society in which he shone so lustrously, he nonetheless wrote to his friend Lady Holland, who he had heard laughed at reports of his contentment in the country:

> In the first place whether one lives or dies I hold and always have held to be of infinitely less moment than is generally supposed; but if life is the choice then it is common sense to amuse yourself with the best you can find where you happen to be placed. I am not leading precisely the life I should chuse, but that which (all things considered, as well as I could consider them) appeared to be the most eligible. I am resolved therefore to like it and to reconcile myself to it; which is more manly than to feign myself above it, and to send up complaints by the post, of being thrown away, and being desolate and such like trash. I am prepared therefore either way. If the chances of life ever enable me to emerge, I will shew you that I have not been wholly occupied by small and sordid pursuits. If (as the greater probability is) I am come to the end of my career, I give myself quietly up to horticulture, and the annual augmentation of my family. In short, if my lot be to crawl, I will crawl contentedly; if to fly, I will fly with alacrity; but as long as I can possibly avoid it I will never be unhappy.

Sydney Smith was thirty-eight when he wrote that, a fine time to feel melancholy about the absence of progress in one's life. But he had his wife, their children, his books, his intellectual curiosity, his ever refreshed amazement at the world's apparently endless peculiarity—and it was sufficient until something better turned up. "Genius," said Ortega, "is the ability to invent one's own occupation," but at the level of common sense I wonder if it doesn't require something very akin to genius to find happiness at an occupation not of one's choosing.

If with no strong sense of either special aptitude or spiritual vocation Sydney Smith became a clergyman, his doing so was not entirely anomalous, for it is well to recall that late in the eighteenth and in the first half of the nineteenth century an intelligent young man of literary leanings could still find the clergy a fit profession. In the Church of England, Swift became a dean, and Laurence Sterne a canon. Like the Church of Rome before it, the Church of England, as Richard Monckton Milnes noted, "participated in all the intellectual as well as spiritual movements of mankind. . . . It thought it no derogation to be a valuable branch of the civil service, to guard the morality and guide the education of the people." Nor were its members above political bias, and most clergymen tended toward Toryism at least insofar as they were preponderantly opposed to change. Part of the distinction of Sydney Smith is that he was lined up on the other side, a Whig with strong Whiggish connections, a member of an established church who nevertheless considered few social arrangements permanently locked in.

Sydney Smith is distinctive, too, in having a reputation far from, nor even chiefly, founded on his purely literary work. Something of the same might be said of Samuel Johnson, whose standing for certain readers owes much to the impressive persona created for him through the pages of Boswell's biography. But Johnson was, after all, a poet, critic, essayist, journalist, lexicographer—in short, a powerful writer who gave his name to an age. Sydney Smith was mainly a polemical essayist and occasional satirist, the vast quantity of whose work appeared in one journal, the *Edinburgh Review*. He was also a charming letter writer, and the two-volume edition of his letters edited by Nowell C. Smith, filled with delightful wit, wisdom, and plainspoken good sense, comprises one of the great collections of nineteenth-century letters. Yet letters are literature only by the way, or after the fact. In his own day, Sydney Smith was most famous as a talker, a fount of bonhomie and uproarious laughter. Testimony to how good the flow of his talk must have been is provided by the large fund of his jokes, puns, aphorisms, and drolleries that has been preserved, often in other people's diaries and memoirs, where accounts of his social performances pop up with some regularity. "I sat next to Sydney

Smith," noted a young Benjamin Disraeli, "who was delightful. . . . I don't remember a more agreeable party." Similar
quotations are not difficult to find.

As writer, talker, correspondent, clergyman, husband, and
father, Sydney Smith's life, in all its aspects and facets, was so
much of a piece as to appear a seamless performance. There
was something at once formidable and informal about Sydney
Smith; reverend though he was, no one less required reveren-
tial treatment. A devastating polemicist and hence not a man
one would want for an enemy, he was nonetheless referred to
almost universally as "Sydney"—as one thinks of another writer
in the same line, Max Beerbohm, as "Max"—and he referred
to his own wife, in correspondence with others, as "Mrs. Sydney." In a "Narrative for My Grandchildren," written after his
death, she noted: "I do not believe that anyone filling only a
subordinate rank in life ever past thro' it more universally
beloved, more sought after for his brilliancy and wit, his honorable bearing, his masterly talents, his truth, his honesty."

Although Mrs. Sydney never had any doubts about her husband's winning through—in the "Narrative for My Grandchildren" she cited his "bold and fearless love of truth" and "ardent
love of human happiness that no feelings of selfish prudence
could ever control"—Sydney Smith's eventual triumph owed
much to his connection with the *Edinburgh Review,* the journal
of which he is now commonly reckoned to have been the chief
progenitor. He found himself in Edinburgh to begin with only
because he and the son of a well-to-do squire, to whom he had
signed on as a tutor, felt it unsafe to travel to Weimar with war
then raging in Europe and so settled instead in Edinburgh in
1798. Of his years in Edinburgh, which ran from 1798 to 1803,
he later wrote: "Never shall I forget the happy days passed
there, amidst odious smells, barbarous sounds, bad suppers,
excellent hearts, and most enlightened and cultivated under-
standings."

Along with its libraries, interesting architecture, terrible sewerage system, and "large healthy virgins with mild pleasing countenances and white swelling breasts" (in the young Reverend Smith's careful description), Edinburgh was the site of several small dining clubs and debating societies made up of young lawyers and litterateurs as well as scientists and scholars from the University of Edinburgh. With his wide intellectual interests and conversational suavity, Sydney Smith smoothly inserted himself among the habitués of these groups, and to five or six of the most impressive intellectual figures in Edinburgh he proposed that they join to put out a journal to review both domestic and foreign books of serious intent.

In the language of the Chamber of Commerce, the *Edinburgh Review* not only put the city of Edinburgh intellectually "on the map" but did something similar for serious journalism. George Saintsbury, in his essay on Francis Jeffrey, remarks that "the reviews of the time had got into the hands either of gentlemen and ladies who were happy to be thought literary, and only too glad to write for nothing, or else into those of the lowest booksellers' hacks, who praised or blamed according to orders, wrote without interest and without vigour, and were quite content to earn the smallest pittance." The *Edinburgh Review* paid its contributors, and paid them well enough to hold them up to standards of quality. In a letter outlining the original plan for the journal, Sydney Smith wrote that "the rocks and shoals to be avoided are religion, politics, excessive severity, and irritable Scotchmen." Except perhaps for the irritable Scotchmen, it was precisely among these rocks and shoals that the *Edinburgh Review* sailed most successfully. As Saintsbury notes, "the *Edinburgh*, whatever it pretended to be, was violently partisan, unhesitatingly personal, and more inclined to find fault, the more distinguished the subject was."

Before it was done, the *Edinburgh Review* could claim many a political prize for its trophy case. In ways that cannot be precisely calculated but that are nonetheless generally acknowledged, the journal, through arguments conducted in its pages, contributed importantly to the emancipation of Catholics, the representation by counsel for anyone accused of a capital crime, the abolition of the death penalty for stealing, the establishment of parliamentary representation in Scotland, the closing off of the slave trade, and much more. As Sydney Smith wrote to Jeffrey in 1826, twenty-four years after the founding of the *Edinburgh Review,* "it must be to you, as I am sure it is to me, a real pleasure to see so many improvements taking place, and so many abuses destroyed;—abuses upon which you, with cannon and mortars, and I with sparrow shot, have been playing for so many years."

After Sydney Smith left Edinburgh, Francis Jeffrey, a lawyer by training, became the *Edinburgh Review*'s full-time editor at a full-time salary (commercially, the journal was an immediate success). From London and from his subsequent parsonages in Yorkshire or Somersetshire, Sydney wrote to Jeffrey to request new books to review and offered him straightforward criticisms of each issue. About writing of any kind, he said, "I never deceive." Scrupulous financial accounts were kept; with four children on a not very ample church living, Sydney had good use for the money he earned reviewing. All contributions to the *Edinburgh Review* were unsigned, though Sydney's must have been unmistakable for their playful wit—not that he couldn't, playfully, knock an author's head off or, wittily, eviscerate a work of extravagant pretensions.

But no editor-writer relationship, no matter how much affection is felt on both sides, is without its prickliness. Before long Sydney is complaining to Jeffrey about editing: "I think," he writes in 1807, "you have spoilt many of my jokes; but this, I suppose, every writer thinks, whose works you alter; and I am unfortunately, as you know, the vainest and most irritable of human beings." As Sydney becomes more famous, he becomes touchier about editorial tinkering: "while I write," he reports to Jeffrey, "I must write in my own way." He agrees to revise an article, but cannot resist adding: "If you mean that

my article itself is light and scanty I agree to that, reminding
you that lightness and flimsiness are *my line of reviewing.*"
Meanwhile, he does not hesitate to tell Jeffrey that too many
pieces in the *Edinburgh Review* are too long, or that Jeffrey
should knock off his own criticisms of Wordsworth. (Poor
Francis Jeffrey, a splendid editor and for the most part a fine
critic, has gone down in literary history as the man who could
not have been wronger about Wordsworth.) "Do not be hurt
by my critiques on your criticisms," he writes to Jeffrey, "you
know (if you know anything) the love and respect I have for
you; this is not enough—add also, the very *high admiration.*"

Sydney Smith was one of those altogether agreeable men
who absolutely know their own worth and he was, consistent
with his desire to remain agreeable, not to be pushed around,
taken advantage of, or otherwise trifled with. He was an habi-
tué of Holland House, the most brilliant of Whig salons, where,
according to David Cecil, biographer of Lord Melbourne, Smith
was "the most humane of clergymen, crackling away like a genial
bonfire of jokes and good sense and uproarious laughter." I
am sure it was so, but it won't do to overplay Sydney Smith as
the jolly jokey clergyman. Lady Holland, hostess of Holland
House and a woman to whom he wrote some of his tenderest
and most solicitous letters, once, at table at Holland House,
asked him to ring the bell for a servant, to which he replied:
"Certainly. And shall I sweep the floor as well?"
Sydney Smith was a witty man who could also be passionate. The passion appears in his writings where it combines with
wit, often to devastating effect. Sydney Smith has been called,
after Swift, England's most powerful satirist. His best early
work in this line is to be discovered in *The Peter Plymley Letters,*
which he began publishing pseudonymously in the autumn of
1807, on behalf of Catholic Emancipation. Roman Catholics
in England at that time could not (until 1829, when full rights
were granted them) vote for candidates for public office, sit in

Parliament, or take commissions in the military, and their free-doms were restricted in other ways. *The Peter Plymley Letters,* of which Sydney published ten in all, were addressed to their pseudonymously named author's putative brother, a bumpkin Church of England parson named Abraham who held all the stock prejudices about Catholics of the day, prominently included among them a terror that the Pope was perpetually on the verge of invading England. ("God bless you, reverend Abraham," ends the first letter, "and defend you from the Pope.")

Although Sydney only much later owned up to the author-ship of *The Peter Plymley Letters,* everyone seemed to have agreed that the work had too many fine Smithian touches to have been written by anyone else. The satire is said to have kept him from ever gaining a bishopric; certainly the enemies it made him—the Tory Prime Minister Canning and his Foreign Sec-retary Perceval among them—remained enemies for life. But, as Sydney Smith himself put it, "If I could see good measures pursued, I care not a farthing who is in power; but I have a passionate love for common justice, and for common sense, and I abhor and despise every man who builds up his political fortune upon their ruin."

Sydney Smith, it must be understood, had no particular love for Catholics. He never attacked Catholicism, though, no doubt because the civic position of adherents of that religion in England was so vulnerable. But he did blast away at those Christians who set out to convert the Hindus in India, and for the Methodist notion that God intervenes to distribute perfect justice in the life of every man or woman he had the keenest contempt, which he didn't in the least mind expressing. "The honest and orthodox method is to prepare young people for the world, as it actually exists; to tell them that they will often find vice perfectly successful, virtue exposed to a long train of afflictions; that they must bear this patiently, and look to another world for its rectification."

Wherever or whenever common sense is outraged, so is Sydney Smith, and so he is entirely out of sympathy with the pleasure-hating element of Methodism, or for that matter of any other religion. "*Ennui,* wretchedness, melancholy, groans and sighs, are the offerings which these unhappy men make to a Deity, who has covered the earth with gay colours, and scented it with rich perfumes; and shown us, by the plan and order of his works, that he has given to man something better than a bare existence, and scattered over his creation a thousand superfluous joys, which are totally unnecessary to the mere support of life." Sydney viewed religion as a source of comfort and hope, which filled the heart with charity and gentleness for others. He thought religion provided a means for current contentment and future salvation, when rightly practiced—which is to say, when practiced with benevolence and good sense. But even when wrongly practiced—when demons and witches were brought into play, when God was thought to dispense penalties and rewards for discrete human acts or held to approve human miseries and privations—he nonetheless felt that even such religion deserved toleration, if no dispensation from ridicule, which, as he wrote on one occasion, "is excusable, when there is no other [way] that can make fools tremble."

The Lord, in his abundance, provided fools aplenty outside the realm of religion. Most of Sydney Smith's writings in the *Edinburgh Review,* apart from those on religious subjects, were on political and social matters. As in religion, so in politics, his was the line of common sense. That he was all his days a Whig made him, mutatis mutandis, what in our day would be a liberal, but without any of the contemporary liberal's terror of seeming unvirtuous by finding himself on the wrong—which is to say, not the Left—side of any political issue, question, or cause. W. H. Auden, citing Sydney Smith as "an example of English Liberalism at its best," went on to say that he was never doctrinaire. Auden illustrates his point by setting out examples, both from religion, in which Sydney was in one case

favoring reform and in another opposing it. But examples elsewhere are not at all difficult to find. He was, to mention one
such example, against early self-government for Australia on
the grounds that the Australians, in 1823, are still "too young,
too few, and too deficient for such civilized machinery at present." Always specific, he set out his reasons:

> "I cannot come to serve upon the jury—the waters of Hawkes-
> bury are out, and I have a mile to swim—the kangaroos will
> break into my corn—the convicts have robbed me—my little
> boy has been bitten by an ornithorynchus paradoxus—I have
> sent a man fifty miles with a sack of flour to buy a pair of breeches
> for the assizes, and he is not yet returned." These are the excuses
> which, in new colonies, always prevent Trial by Jury; and make
> it desirable, for the first half century of their existence, that they
> should live under the simplicity and convenience of despo-
> tism—such modified despotism (we mean) as a British House
> of Commons will permit, in the governors of their distant col-
> onies.

Close though he was to the Whigs through his Holland
House connection and his friendship with Lord and Lady Grey,
Sydney was at once a firm party man and, within party circles,
someone who insisted on the rights of criticizing his party and
viewing it through the lens of superior perspective. Not few
were the social and political abuses of Sydney Smith's day, and
several were the defenders of those abuses, and sundry those
who stood to gain from their perpetuation. With his common
sense and power of ridicule, Sydney was beautifully equipped
to chide, mock, and scorn the party in power. As the punish-
ment ought to fit the crime, so ought the talent the time, and
given Sydney's talent and the time in which he lived, he could
only have been among the Whigs. As George Saintsbury says:
"Except that the sentimental side of Toryism would never have
appealed to him, it was chiefly an accident of time that he was

a polemical Liberal. He would always and naturally have been on the side opposite to that on which most of the fools were." Sydney Smith was of that permanent minority, the party perpetually out of power, the Party of Common Sense.

"The whole of my life has passed," wrote Sydney Smith, "like a razor—in hot water or a scrape." (Nobody better than Sydney at what one might call the delayed punch-line simile: "Correspondences are like smallclothes before the invention of suspenders," he wrote, "it is impossible to keep them up.") In an age ruled by patronage and preferment, the expression of strong opinion was free in name only; in fact, if one were on the wrong side, there was a price to be paid. It was, wrote Sydney, "an awful period for those who ventured to maintain liberal opinions; and who were too honest to sell them for the ermine of the judge, or the lawn of the prelate." Those who felt themselves compelled to issue such opinions could look forward to "a long and hopeless career in your profession, the chuckling grin of noodles, the sarcastic leer of the genuine political rogue; prebendaries, deans, bishops, made over your head; reverend renegades advanced to the highest dignities of the Church, for helping to rivet the fetters of Catholic and Protestant Dissenters; and no more chance of a Whig administration than of a thaw in Zembla."

Yet if the penalties are plain, why take up the certain risk of incurring them? Life is short, the afterlife from such sketchy reports as we have tremendously long, and in politics, unlike in physics, great causes tend to have very small effects; and all this being so, why not cultivate one's garden, do what one can to advance one's career, take the money and run, or, in the case of a talented cleric like Sydney Smith, the bishop's miter and walk? In 1824, when Sydney Smith was fifty-three years old, something like this question was put to him by his friend Lord Carlisle. Carlisle wrote to him to recount how many enemies his writings had made, and to remind him to "for God's sake consider that what often is forgiven from the *tongue* is not endured from the *pen*." Carlisle concluded on an admonitory note: "Retire from the dangerous enterprise. Why prepare for yourself a bed of thorns for that hour when one of down might hardly invite repose?" To Lord Carlisle's quite sensible question of why make enemies when there is not an absolute need to—it is a question that everyone who writes must ask himself—Sydney's response seems to me bang on the money. Assuming, he replies, that his attacks are made with "a mixture of argument and pleasantry which commands attention and produces a strong effect—what are the advantages to the writer?"

> The successful exercise of power in the promotion of truth and justice: the advancement of good principles and the destruction of bad ones; emersion from darkness and obscurity; the sincere friendship of many good men, who agree with his opinions, honour his courage, respect his honesty and are grateful to him for the triumphant statement of their own argument and the successful development of their own thoughts.

Sydney concluded his answer by remarking that, but for the writing that so alarms him at the moment, Lord Carlisle should never have known him in the first place, nor should he, Sydney Smith, be "writing familiarly to a nobleman of the most cultivated talents and of the highest rank, about myself and my own concerns."

Sheer ebullience might be all the cause and motive required to explain Sydney Smith's need for the regular assertion of his opinions. It was from this ebullience, his almost endless flow of lively conversation, that Sydney Smith's reputation as one of the great English talkers derived. Even considering the main competition—the thundering pronunciamentos of Samuel Johnson, the metaphor-strewn periods of Edmund Burke, the oratorical pyrotechnics of Lord Brougham, the elegant epigrams of Oscar Wilde—Sydney Smith's talk sounds as if it might have given the greatest pleasure of all. Laughter was the intention of most of his talk, and laughter it usually achieved: "It is his condition to be witty," said Guizot, "as it is that of Lady Seymour to be beautiful."

"The fanciful and inexhaustible humorous drollery of his conversation among his intimates can never be adequately rendered or reproduced," Fanny Kemble claimed. As a talker, Sydney apparently did more than merely scatter *mots* about the room, though his *mots* have been remembered in ample number: there are fifty-three Sydney Smith items in the most recent *Oxford Dictionary of Quotations,* some drawn from his writings but many recollected later by friends and memoirists in social tranquillity. Much of what he said reflected his own unmitigated worldliness, such as his remarking that "if a messenger from heaven were on a sudden to annihilate the love of power, the love of wealth, the love of esteem, in the hearts of men, the streets of London would be as empty and silent at noon as they are now in the middle of the night." Nor did he dominate by garrulity, as did Macaulay, whom Sydney once called "a book in breeches"; another time, finding Macaulay still in bed, he said of his conversation that it contained "some gorgeous flashes of silence." Sydney never set out to monopolize conversation; it rather monopolized him, as Richard Monckton Milnes reported, for his reputation as a wit, like his increasingly spreading stomach, preceded him. So great was this reputation that while he was about there was very little inclination on anyone else's part to talk. With George Gershwin in the house, who, after all, would have had the nerve to sit down at the piano?

Sydney Smith's conversational style apparently resembled what we should nowadays call "being on a roll." Someone would say something that struck his fancy, and he would be off, building a vast conceit upon it composed of anecdotes, puns, wild observations, oddities of language, all ending in a delightfully comic piece. One of his contemporaries, a Mrs. Brookfield, claimed that, along with Sydney's avoirdupois, he had "a mouth like an oyster, and three double chins." The diarist Charles Greville noted: "His appearance, voice and manner added immensely to the effect, and the bursting and uproarious merriment with which he poured forth his good things, never failed to communicate itself to his audience, who were always in fits of laughter." About the laughter, there was no question; the poet Thomas Moore, comparing another wit of the day, Henry Luttrell, with Sydney Smith, remarked that "after the former, you remember what good things he said, and after the latter you merely remember how much you laughed."

"If there was a fault in it," Charles Greville noted in his diary shortly after Sydney Smith's death, "it was that it was too amusing." Greville himself had "very little doubt that Sydney often felt oppressed with the weight of his comical obligations, and came onto the stage like a great actor, forced to exert himself, but not always in the vein to play his part." Whether or not this is true is difficult to gauge. For a natural entertainer the only thing worse than to be asked to sing for his supper is not to be asked to sing at all. Some artists aim for prosperity and others for posterity, but Sydney Smith's chief aim, at least in his talk, was to bestow pleasure. "I talk only the nonsense of the moment for the good humour of the moment," he wrote in his seventy-second year to one of his many female correspondents, "and nothing remains behind, no more is known of the Constitution of the Germanic Empire, than if I had never dined there."

Sydney Smith was an apostle, a positive ideologue of good cheer. He was, in this aspect of his life and career, a subtler and wittier version of Benjamin Franklin, a writer he much admired. In his perhaps most famous letter—and he had occasion to indite various versions of it to others—he provided Lady Georgiana Morpeth with twenty quite specific steps for throwing off the heavy harness of depression. These run from

"1st. Live as well as you dare" and "2nd. Go into the shower-bath with a small quantity of water at a temperature low enough to give you a slight sensation of cold, 75° or 80°" to "8th. Make no secret of low spirits to your friends, but talk of them freely—they are always the worse for dignified concealment" and "17th. Don't be too severe upon yourself, or underrate yourself, but do yourself justice." The most notable, and perhaps the most helpful, item, however, is "4th. Short views of human life—not further than dinner or tea." This excellent letter, it is well to remember, begins, "Nobody has suffered more from low spirits than I have done—so I feel for you."

"Take short views"—that sentence pops up more than once in Sydney Smith's letters and in his journalism. It was advice he had need of in his own life, which knew no paucity of reversals. As a young clergyman, he was, in the root sense of the word, rusticated to backwoods parishes—"twelve miles from a lemon," as he described one. He lived most of his days under the lash of financial worry. When the Whigs came briefly into power, he was overlooked for a bishopric, which he claimed did not bother him, though clearly it did. His youngest son, Wyndham, turned out a ne'er-do-well. Most shattering of all, his most talented child, his son Douglas, died when he was in his early twenties and Sydney and his wife in their late fifties. He wrote the following inscription for the young man's gravestone: "His life was blameless. His death was the first sorrow he ever occasioned his parents, but it was deep and lasting." To the London hostess Maria Kinnaird he wrote, apropos of his son's death: "I am very unhappy, and quite beaten but I shall get better."

And he did soon get better, on his prescription of taking short views and not forgetting that happiness depends mainly on little things: enjoying specific pleasures ("a comfortable house is a great source of happiness. It ranks immediately after health and a good conscience"); finding delight in the present moment (while visiting historical sites when abroad, he claimed "the aujourdhui of Life is enough for me"); never neglecting animal spirits ("I am convinced digestion is the great secret of life"); and adoring life ("I have a contempt for persons who destroy themselves") while not anticipating too much from it ("the whole of Life is a trumpery business—do not expect any great things from it, it will deceive you if you do"). Sydney was a parson who practiced what he preached. "Our house," he wrote five years before his death to Mrs. Grote, wife of the great historian, "is full of beef, beer, young children, newspapers, libels, and mince pies, and life goes on very well, except that I am often reminded I am too near the end of it." But his guiding principle appears to have been: "Pleasure is very reflective, and if you give it you will feel it." He gave it in vaster quantities than any man of his time.

Does Sydney Smith continue to give pleasure in our time? Sad to report that his formal writings do not provide the same delight in our day than they must have done in his own. In large part, this is owing to his subject matter and the nature of his intentions. Much the greater part of his writing was given over to polemic—to arguing, to making a case, to banging heads—and polemic on subjects of once great but now merely antique interest. One of his most perfectly executed essays is "Spring Guns and Man Traps," in which he sets out to show the inhumane villainy of squires positioning guns to go off automatically to prevent poaching on their lands. "The best way of answering a bad argument is not to stop it," Sydney writes in that essay, "but to let it go on its course till it leaps over the boundaries of common sense," which is what he artfully does. It's a fine little piece of work, this essay; and one can recommend it without hesitation to anyone amongst one's friends who is currently having problems with poachers, if you take my point.

The polemical tradition is not without its glittering names: Richard Hooker, Swift, Milton (in some of his prose works), and, closer to our time, George Orwell. Just about every other English and American prose writer who was in the least *engagé*—Hazlitt, Macaulay, Carlyle, Matthew Arnold, J. S. Mill, Thoreau, and T. S. Eliot, among others—has in his career felt the need to write polemic. But those who write polemic nearly exclusively face the danger of their own writing dying along with the issues that brought it forth. This, regrettably, has happened to much of Sydney Smith's writing. One of his most smoothly executed, liltingly argued, lengthy pieces of work, for example, is *Letters to Archdeacon Singleton,* which is about the proceedings and constitution of the Ecclesiastical Commission on reform of church organization. Too much of Sydney's work is similarly hostage to dead subject matter. Throughout everything he wrote one finds delicious passages, touches, turns, ornamentation in sufficient quantity to decorate the Christmas tree at Rockefeller Center, but now hung, in his three volumes of collected writings, for the most part on quite bare boughs.

This explains why Sydney Smith is less and less frequently anthologized. Instead his name, inscribed under charming remarks notable for their commonsensicality, appears in collections of aphorisms, books of quotations, slender volumes of wise and witty sayings. His essays may even have passed outside the wide range of interest of Samuel Johnson's and Virginia Woolf's honorifically named Common Reader. These essays may now be readable only for that band of readers absorbed by questions of literary style. For those who care about style—sheer style, yes, style even detached from content—Sydney Smith's writing remains immensely readable.

Style was always of the keenest concern to Sydney Smith. "It is more tolerable to be slovenly in dress than in style," he wrote to Miss Georgiana Harcourt. "Dress covers the mortal body, and adorns it, but style is the vehicle of the spirit." Style and wit and common sense were all intertwined in him. "The pleasure arising from wit," he wrote, "proceeds from our surprise at suddenly discovering two things to be similar, in which we suspected no similarity. [Aristotle claimed the same pleasure for metaphor.] Practical wit discovers connection between actions, in which duller understanding discovers none." He was himself powerfully adept at arguing by analogy, parable, fable, quietly demonstrating the fundamental good sense of his own side by setting out the absurdity of the other, making seemingly whimsical connections that were at bottom usually quite serious. In *The Peter Plymley Letters,* for example, he noted that it struck him as foolhardy to antagonize the Catholics and that perhaps England would do better to find a weaker group to pick on. "Cruelty and injustice must, of course, exist: but why connect them with danger? Why torture a bulldog, when you can get a frog or a rabbit?" One of his analogies, likening an English housewife (whom he named Dame Partington) mopping her stoop during a ferocious storm to the efforts of the Tories to hold back parliamentary reform, made its way into the *Times* and was said to have contributed to the passage of the Reform Bill of 1832.

Sydney Smith's fecundity in this line is most impressive. But then anyone who relies on common sense inevitably falls back upon analogy. Presented with an assertion or even a fairly elaborate argument, a commonsensical thinker asks how does this compare with that; isn't this rather as if . . .; if that is the case, doesn't it follow that . . .; and isn't what is being said here really like . . . ? If the commonsensical thinker is also imaginative, he fills in those ellipses with strikingly homely analogies. "If men had made no more progress in the common arts of life than they have in education," Sydney wrote, "we should at this moment be dividing our food with our fingers, and drinking out of the palms of our hands." And if the commonsensical thinker has into the bargain a sense of style and an eye for comic elaboration, he is likely to hit upon tropes such as Sydney came upon in describing a verbose historian: "He has not the talent of saying what he has to say quickly; nor is he aware that brevity is in writing what charity is to all other virtues.

Righteousness is worth nothing without the one, nor author-ship without the other."

Along with Sydney Smith's gifts of clear common sense and inventive wit ran a happy taste for whimsy and nonsense. Strong common sense, after all, confers an immediate penetration into nonsense; and wit turns it all to charming advantage, generally in the form of whimsy. "Lucy, dear child," he writes to the daughter of friends, "mind your arithmetic. You know, in the first sum of yours I ever saw, there was a mistake. You had carried two (as a cab is licensed to do) and you ought, dear Lucy, to have carried but one." But he does not restrict whimsy of this kind to children. Of his hay fever, he reports to his physician son-in-law: "The membrane is so irritable, that light, dust, contradiction, an absurd remark, the sight of a dis-senter,—anything, sets me a sneezing and if I begin sneezing at 12, I don't leave off until two o'clock—and am heard dis-tinctly in Taunton when the wind sets that way at a distance of 6 miles." When Malthus, the population man, pays a visit, he, Sydney, writes to Lady Holland:

> I got an agreeable party for him of unmarried people. There was only one Lady who had had a Child, and for her I apologised, saying nothing of a recent misfortune; but he is a very good natured man, and if there are no appearances of approaching fertility is civil to every Lady.

A Sydney Smith letter must have arrived like a gift. Each conveys not solely information but a touch or two of gratu-itous delight. Few fail to contain a joke. Certain themes recur, such as the interest of clerics in digestion, or his boredom with the country, which he considers "a sort of healthy Grave." Even his complaints are charming. Suffering from gout, that malady that awaited every heavy victualizing eighteenth- and nine-teenth-century Englishman, he describes it as akin "to walking on your eyeballs" and writes that "it is the only enemy I do not

wish to have at my feet." When four first cousins who are visiting fall ill and stay with the Smiths for three weeks, he reports,
" 'Oh that those first Cousins were but *once removed*' was my
constant exclamation." An amiable generosity lies behind these
little constructions; made to give pleasure to others, they
doubtless also gave great pleasure to the man who fabricated
them.

But the effect of reading Sydney Smith, in his essays and
letters, and of contemplating his life, goes beyond pleasure alone.
While under the spell of his immensely commonsensical charm,
the desperate doctrines of Rousseau, Nietzsche, Marx, and other
intellectually rambunctious thinkers seem so much unfortunate lunacy. They are not lunacy, of course, not completely at
any rate, but it is useful to consider them in the clean, clear
light of common sense to get them in better focus. It is useful
in the same way that it was useful to have Max Beerbohm, after
acknowledging D. H. Lawrence's power as a novelist, go on
to say: "He never realized, don't you know—he never suspected that to be stark, staring mad is somewhat of a handicap
to a writer." Beerbohm, on his seventieth birthday, upon
rereading some of his own writing, remarked that "what especially struck me was that I had always had a great deal of common sense. It is a far less noble, but a far more useful thing
than wisdom." Not only is common sense useful, but without
it life quickly comes to seem blurred, misshapen, more than a
little monstrous.

For Sydney Smith, who was never without common sense
in the highest degree, life, no matter what setbacks it provided,
always seemed full of interest, amusement, delight. Knowing
always where he stood, he knew always what to laugh at, and
had the sweet talent to make others laugh along with him.
How splendid it would be today to hear him on such subjects
as the female clergy, the politics of the Church of England,
contemporary academics, television journalists, and much
modern psychotherapy!

In Sydney Smith's late years, he came into a large inheritance from one of his brothers, and acquired a very handsome ecclesiastical living when appointed Canon of St. Paul's. As he grew old, his health inevitably declined and with it his energy— "I am seventy-two years of age," he wrote to Harriet Martineau, "at which period there comes over one a shameful love of ease and repose, common to dogs, horses, clergymen, and even to *Edinburgh Review*ers"—but large reserves of wit remained. In response to a French-Belgian poet named Eugène Robin, who was preparing what we should nowadays call a profile of him for the *Revue des deux mondes*, Sydney wrote:

> I am seventy-four years of age; and being Canon of St. Paul's in London, and a rector of a parish in the country, my time is divided equally between town and country. I am living amongst the best society in the Metropolis, and at ease in my circumstances; in tolerable health, a mild Whig, a tolerating Churchman, and much given to talking, laughing, and noise. I dine with the rich in London, and physic the poor in the country; passing from the sauces of Dives to the sores of Lazarus. I am, upon the whole, a happy man; have found the world an entertaining world, and am thankful to Providence for the part allotted to me in it.

Less than a year later, on February 22, 1845, Sydney Smith died, peacefully, in his house on Green Street in London, the city he once referred to as "the Spot I am convinced where all the Evils of Life are soonest forgotten and most easily endured." These evils must have seemed less easily endured to his friends with Sydney dead. Thinking about him today, the lightness of being becomes, somehow, quite bearable. Life, most assuredly, is no joke; but consider what, one imagines Sydney Smith readily rejoining, life without a joke would be like.

Messrs. Fowler & Gowers

I N THE PREFACE to a small but impressively lucid book on punctuation written in 1939 and entitled *Mind the Stop,* the author, an Englishman named G. V. Carey, reserved his last sentences for what he called "a spasm of self-consciousness." Given the year of publication, with England having just entered upon a cataclysmic war with Germany, Carey felt that he ought to register the fact that "the mind of one who happens to have an eye for a comma is not necessarily incapable of comprehending larger issues or embracing wider interests." Yet no disclaimer, however mild, needed to be entered. One of the reasons that nations go to war is so that men like G. V. Carey, in immaculately setting out the subtleties of the semicolon, can carry out the daily work of civilization. Today, more than fifty years later, when the art of careful punctuation threatens among the young to become as widespread as that of intaglio, a book such as Carey's seems rather more significant. But then those who have taken it upon themselves to be guardians of the language must alternate almost hourly in their feeling about their work between certainty of its fundamental importance and an at least equal certainty of its complete hopelessness.

All guardians of the language resemble a little the village idiot in the shtetl of Frampol who was given the job of standing at the village gates in wait for the coming of the Messiah. The pay was not high, he was told, but he didn't ever have to worry about running out of work. The guardians of the language need similarly never worry about running out of work. Like Heraclitus's famous river—"Upon those who step into the same river different and ever different waters flow down"— the river of language continues to flow along, never remaining the same, changing every foot of the way. Heraclitus spoke of his river being in perpetual flux but never of its muddying, whereas in the river of language flux frequently does issue in mud, garbage, and other detritus. To change classical references, the task of the guardian of language can be likened to cleaning out the Augean stables with the horses still in them. This, for reasons needing no explanation, is not everybody's idea of a good time.

What may need explanation is the motivation of those who go in for it. As a university teacher, I find myself, among my students, from time to time wielding a small Augean broom. Why do I bother? It won't do to say, à la John Wayne in the role of federal marshal, "Cause it's my job, ma'am." It is closer to the truth to say that woolly circumlocutions, psychobabblous phrasings and sentiments, and language used as if it were a game of horseshoes (in which one expects points for being close) offends me. What it offends is my sense of decorum. When a student, asked about the quality of the character Verloc's relationship with his wife, Winnie, in Joseph Conrad's *The Secret Agent,* answers, "At this point in time, a caring person would not consider it meaningful, at least hopefully not," I find I cannot let it pass—especially at these prices. It offends me that such wobbly language is being tossed around by a fairly high-IQ kid in a hall of learning where the annual cover charge is roughly twenty thousand dollars a head. Such language also makes it impossible, of course, to talk about literature or anything else above the level of yogurt.

People who take pains with their language are not just now

in danger, through their vast number, of bringing about a population explosion. They are instead a bit difficult to find; you won't, certainly, find them concentrated in any one place. You won't find many of them among the professoriat; in fact, much of the dreariest abstract language we now have was first put into circulation by social scientists, though nowadays historians, philosophers, and literary scholars are hot on the social scientists' gummy heels. But today no social class is notable for correct or interesting speech. It used to be said that the working class provided pungent and solidly concrete additions to the language and the upper class provided standards of correctness. No longer.

Once upon a time, though not so recently as all that, careful English was part of the patrimony of the well-born. Edith Wharton, in her memoir *A Backward Glance,* noted that a strong element in her upbringing was "a reverence for the English language as spoken according to the best usage," and this despite the fact that her parents read little and had scarcely any intellectual interests. "Usage, in my childhood, was as authoritative an element in speaking English as tradition was in social conduct," she writes. The kind of English Edith Wharton was taught to speak was "easy, idiomatic English, neither pedantic nor 'literary' "; and while her parents' sensitivity to careful English remained a mystery to her, they always wanted their children's English to be better, "that is, easier, more flexible and idiomatic." English like that ain't spoke here no more.

English is still spoke, of course, but it is rarely bespoke, as one imagines it was in Edith Wharton's New York, or at Henry Adams's Harvard. Language today seems chiefly to come off the rack, no matter what social class is speaking or writing it. Not that there aren't people who make very deliberate efforts to say precisely what they mean; or that there aren't writers—novelists and critics, essayists and poets, historians and philosophers, the occasional scientist—who command styles of true power, real elegance, and general felicity. There are, but their number and social provenance are not—probably cannot be—known. They have determined to take pains. But why do they bother? Why, now that the way one uses language has scarcely any effect on one's financial fate or social standing, does anyone any longer bother?

Although the honors list of those who have taken up the cause of good linguistic hygiene has over the centuries included Confucius, Cervantes, Swift, Samuel Johnson, William Hazlitt, and George Orwell, the same cause, it must be allowed, has attracted prigs, pedants, intellectual bullies, and snobs. "She is, I am sorry to have to say," a woman I know reported to me of another woman, "one of those people who is always misusing 'hopefully.' " More recently, I met a man who told me that, in the middle of delivering a wedding toast, he was corrected for incorrectly using the word "fulsome." No doubt there were people in fifth-century-B.C. Athens who discovered solecisms in Pericles's funeral oration as there were those in twentieth-century London who discovered solecisms in Winston Churchill's World War II broadcasts. Purists have always existed who write and speak with the linguistic equivalent of their little fingers crooked above the cup of language, people—they, I suspect, would prefer the word "persons"—of whom H. W. Fowler once remarked, "There speaks one of those friends from whom the English language may well pray to be saved, one of the modern precisians who have more zeal than discretion." In the lengthy saga that one thinks of as the perpetual decline of the English language—it has been going on for nearly a thousand years—the current villains are well known: the perpetrators of the hopelessly abstract, the devotees of the too precise, the schoolmasters who invent unnecessary rules, the populists who cry out against the need for any rules whatsoever.

The heroes of this saga are those extraordinary writers who in every age demonstrate that more can be done with the language than might hitherto have been thought. Some among them, viewing the world in ways no one before them has done, forge new styles to give expression to their new views; others work within traditional styles, but through their individuality develop them to a higher power. Avant-garde or traditional, together such writers, whose unshakable assumption is that everything in the world can be rendered in words, freshen and regularly refreshen the language, saving it from ossification and from rot.

On occasion such writers have themselves complained of the spoliation of the language. Jonathan Swift, writing to his prime minister, held that "daily improvements [in English] are by no means in proportion to its daily corruptions; that pretenders to polish and refine it have chiefly multiplied abuses and absurdities; and that in many instances it offends against every part of grammar." In his now famous essay "Politics and the English Language," George Orwell, in plain Orwellian fashion, set out the possibilities for deep corruption when politicians go to work on language. Evelyn Waugh, the most elegant and efficient of twentieth-century prose writers, used to fume against the horrendous lapses in English usage he claimed to find all around him—further evidence, of course, of the general degradation of the modern world that seemed so to please him. Edmund Wilson was not shy about returning certain of his correspondents' letters with his corrections of their grammar, syntax, and semantics indelicately scrawled in the margins.

Apart from demonstrating how language ought to be used through their own writing and sending up occasional wails about its debasement by politicians, social scientists, advertising men, and other linguistical thugs, writers have not generally been much interested in fighting the trench warfare of language. This has been left to such foot soldiers as lexicographers and linguists, many of them academics but perhaps the most impressive among them not. The English have been particularly strong in this line, a line that begins with James Murray (1837–1915), who personally edited roughly half the great *Oxford English Dictionary;* Henry Watson Fowler (1858–1933), who with his brother Frank edited the *Concise Oxford Dictionary* and alone wrote *A Dictionary of Modern English Usage;* Eric Partridge (1894–1979), whose many lexicographical works include the *Dictionary of Slang and Unconventional English, Usage and Abusage,* and *Origins: A Short Etymological Dictionary of Modern English;* and Sir Ernest Gowers (1880–1966), who revised Fowler's *Dictionary of Modern English Usage* and produced two remarkable brief books of his own entitled *Plain Words* and *The ABC of Plain Words,* which, taken together, have appeared in various editions as *The Complete Plain Words.*

All four men were born while Queen Victoria ruled, all had what one has come to think of as nineteenth-century energy, all had the quite sensible Victorian belief in self-improvement. K. M. Elisabeth Murray, in *Caught in the Web of Words,* has chronicled her grandfather's, James Murray's, prodigious efforts in the composition of the *OED.* Of Eric Partridge, who was born a New Zealander and whose death occurred roughly fourteen years ago, nowhere near so much is known, or at any rate has been revealed. Rather more is known of H. W. Fowler, who was in so many ways an extraordinary character, and I shall get to some of it presently. Sir Ernest Gowers is a man about whom very little is known, and this by design, for he was an English civil servant—a "public servant," in the older and better phrase—and as such felt altogether content with anonymity. His, as we shall see, was a quieter but no less impressive contribution.

Although Henry Fowler was born twenty-two years before Ernest Gowers and Gowers died thirty-three years after Fowler, and although the two men never met, one tends to think of them as a tandem. Gowers, of course, performed a singular service in revising Fowler's *Dictionary of Modern English Usage,* tactfully bringing it up to date without allowing any serious loss in its idiosyncratic character. Gowers, in "H. W. Fowler: The Man and His Teaching," has written the most intelligent essay on Fowler. But above and beyond these services that the younger man performed for the older, Gowers seems to complement Fowler as Fowler felt the word "meticulous" should have complemented the word "punctilious," "the two covering between them the positive accuracy that omits no detail and the negative accuracy that admits no error."

As befits a man who took it upon himself to shape up the English language, H. W. Fowler kept himself in top physical trim. Until nearly the end of his life, he was a runner and a swimmer; he ran to his swim, swam, and then home he ran. A photograph of Fowler that appears in *The Oxford University Press: An Informal History* shows him outside his cottage in Guernsey, bald, goateed, in shorts that fall just below the knees and in an English football jersey, holding a towel that he will doubtless use after his swim. He is a shortish man, well set-up physically—neither muscle-bound nor thin but without any trace of softness or fat, compact—with a confident smile that seems to come easily to him. Short, solid, humorous, H. W. Fowler may be said to resemble nothing quite so much as one of his own entries in *A Dictionary of Modern English Usage*.

How does one happen to set oneself up as arbiter of the entire English language? In H. W. Fowler's case the answer is that he had first to fail at a number of much smaller tasks. The son of a schoolmaster, Fowler, after winning a scholarship to Balliol College, Oxford, failed to get a first and had to settle for a second-class degree in Moderations and in *Litterae Humaniores*. Upon Fowler's leaving Oxford, the master of Balliol, Benjamin Jowett ("There's no knowledge, but I know it"), gave him the following characteristically curt recommendation:

> I have a very high opinion of Mr. H. W. Fowler. While at Balliol College he has made himself respected. He is quite a gentleman in manner and feeling and has good sense and good taste.

He is a very fair scholar and has, I think, a natural aptitude for the profession of Schoolmaster.

A schoolmaster Fowler became, first teaching at a school in Scotland and then settling in at a quite good public school called Sedbergh in the northwest corner of Yorkshire, where he remained for seventeen years. Shy and fastidious as a young man, he had not the gift of easy intimacy, and consequently was a teacher of the kind that his students did not adore but came eventually—sometimes even in later life—to admire. Fowler left Sedbergh over a religious dispute with the head-master, who asked that his housemasters put their students through confirmation, which Fowler, who was up for a house-mastership, felt himself unprepared and unwilling to do. When the headmaster remained adamant on the point, Fowler wrote to him: "the choice is between acquiescence and resigning my post, and the latter is what I now feel compelled to do. . . . It is better to recognize that we have a perfectly friendly, but irreconcilable difference of opinion, and to regard the matter as settled." Along with keeping himself in physical trim, Fow-ler, as this incident reveals, liked to keep himself in moral trim.

Fowler was forty-one years old when his teaching career was finished. He next turned to journalism. He moved to London and attempted to write for the British weeklies. He did publish in the *Spectator,* though not frequently enough to be thought a regular contributor. According to G. G. Coulton, upon whose lengthy memoiristic account of H. W. Fowler I have been drawing, he put together two volumes in typescript of essays he had written, but no publisher was interested in them. He did bring out one of these volumes, which he entitled *More Popular Fallacies,* at his own expense. Of this volume, Coulton remarks: "It fell flat: being neither good enough nor bad enough for popular success." Doubtless the difficulty was in part owing to Fowler's style. Gowers, in his essay on Fowler, notes that

"Fowler's style is mathematical rather than literary," adding: "His first concern was precision not elegance, and, as we all know, it is not easy to combine the two."

When Fowler was attempting to make his way as a journalist, the *Spectator* accepted one of his essays, but, having long delayed its publication, informed him that it would no longer be able to run it, though its editors enclosed a check for full payment. Fowler, with no spite but only his customary moral scrupulousness intended, returned the check. In 1915, with England at war, Fowler, at age fifty-seven, enlisted, claiming to be forty-four. (His brother Frank, at forty-five, also enlisted.) Given his own program of physical fitness, Fowler apparently found military training no hardship. What he did find a hardship was that, when his battalion was sent to France, he and his brother were not permitted to fight but instead were given various dogswork—dishwashing, coal-heaving, porterage— which caused him to write a formal letter owning up to his true age and requesting that he either be permitted to do real soldiering or be discharged. In the event, he and his brother were discharged, but the incident once again illustrates H. W. Fowler's scrupulosity, his moral fastidiousness.

Much earlier, in 1903 in fact, Fowler departed London to live in Guernsey. There he built a cottage fifty yards' distance from his brother Frank's cottage and roughly a mile from the sea, which made possible a daily swim and a two-mile run. It also made possible editorial collaboration with Frank, whose training in classics was quite as good as Henry's and whose intellectual interests were congruent with his older brother's. Their first combined enterprise was a translation, in four volumes, of the Greek writer Lucian (c. A.D. 117–180) which appeared under the authoritative imprint of the Clarendon Press, of the Oxford University Press. Before the *Lucian* appeared, Henry Fowler inquired of his editor at the Oxford University Press about his interest in his and his brother's next project:

> We have just begun to collect materials for a little book which
> we think might serve a useful purpose, but which would per-
> haps not be in your line. This is a sort of English composition
> manual, from the negative point of view, for journalists and
> amateur writers. There is a vast number of writers nowadays
> who have something to say and know how to make it lively or
> picturesque, but being uneducated cannot write a page without
> a blunder or cacophony or piece of verbiage or false pathos or
> clumsiness or avoidable dulness. . . . It might possibly, we think,
> be mildly entertaining as well as serviceable.

Charles Cannan, the editor of the Oxford University Press,
replied that "we in the office would welcome an antibarbarus,"
and went on to explain that there were two possible publics
for such a book: "one is the schools which desire something in
the nature of a Rhetoric (in the old sense). The other is that
which you have in mind: the editor of the *Spectator* and the
people who write in the *Times*." The book was eventually published, in 1906, under the title *The King's English* by H. W.
Fowler and F. G. Fowler. Peter Sutcliffe, the author of the
informal history of the Oxford University Press, writes, correctly, that the Fowlers' book "was never really suitable for
schools, and it was taking a narrow view to suppose that it
would serve as a guide for journalists." Nor did the book receive
a hardy critical welcome. Desmond MacCarthy, whom one tends
to think a generous critic, wrote of *The King's English* that "it
is clear that such rules must often involve the consideration of
barely perceptible subtleties which waste the writer's time."
The greater significance of *The King's English,* however, is that
it formed the base on which Henry Fowler, after his younger
brother's death, would write *A Dictionary of Modern English
Usage.*

A Dictionary of Modern English Usage is one of a shelf of fifty
or so great books written in English in this century. It is

immensely helpful, happily memorable, and endlessly rereada-
ble; it stands in a splendidly synecdochic relation to the culture
that produced it: from the part that is this book one can infer
the entire tradition of correctness, lucidity, and wit that once
seemed emblematic of English intellectual life at its best. *A
Dictionary of Modern English Usage* is also clearly the book that
all Fowler's previous experience led him to write. As for how
the book came into being, after working on *The Concise Oxford
Dictionary* and *The Pocket Oxford Dictionary,* both bearing the
names of the two Fowler brothers (Frank died in 1918), Henry
Fowler announced that he had grown tired of straightforward
lexicography. He thought about turning to a dictionary that
would leave out the obvious words and concentrate instead on
idioms and other aspects of language that exist in a state of
jumbled inexactitude in the minds of even the most highly
intelligent people. Fowler thought of it as his "Idiom Dictionary," though at Oxford University Press one of the principal
editors referred to it, in a letter to Fowler, as "A Utopian dictionary [that] would sell very well—in Utopia." But Fowler,
as Englishmen of his own day might have said, pressed on,
finishing the work, which was given the title *A Dictionary of
Modern English Usage,* in 1925. It was reprinted four times the
year of publication, 1926, along with a special impression for
the United States of fifty thousand copies.

Whenever a serious book becomes a best-seller, even a modest best-seller, an explanation is required. The most cogent
explanation for the success of *A Dictionary of Modern English
Usage* is to be found in the character of its author. Pedagogue,
lexicographer, essayist, late Victorian—all the elements in
Fowler's character conjoined to make this remarkable book, a
product of his intellectual maturity, the capstone to his career.
Sir Ernest Gowers felt that the appeal of *Modern English Usage*
"lies partly in the way the author reveals his idiosyncrasy to the
reader," taking his definition of "idiosyncrasy" from Fowler's
own entry on the word in *Modern English Usage:*

Its meaning is peculiar mixture, & the point of it is best shown in the words that describe Brutus: *His life was gentle & the elements So mixed in him that Nature might stand up and say to all the world, "This was a man."*

No supposed reference work has ever been more suffused by the spirit of a single man than H. W. Fowler's *Dictionary of Modern English Usage,* including Samuel Johnson's *Dictionary.* In this wondrous work, Fowler, freed from the stringent demands of straight and strict lexicography, let fly, never restraining his wit or whimsy or opinionation. Every writer seeks his true form, and Fowler's was evidently the dictionary article, which one scarcely considers a literary form at all, though he was able to turn it into one. Even in Fowler's hands, an odd form it is; it is a form with a beginning, which usually formulates the problem; a middle, which provides illustrations of error occasioned by ignorance of the problem; and generally no end whatsoever, for the article frequently trails off after the final illustration with no summarizing statement from the author. The wit and whimsy, the point and pique, are found at the front, as in this opening for the article "Sturdy Indefensibles," which sounds the characteristic Fowlerian note:

Many idioms are seen, if they are tested by grammar or logic, to express badly, even sometimes to express the reverse of, what they are nevertheless well understood to mean. Good people point out the sin, & bad people, who are more numerous, take little notice & go on commiting it; then the good people, if they are foolish, get excited & talk of ignorance and solecisms, & are laughed at as purists; or, if they are wise, say no more about it & wait. The indefensibles, sturdy as they may be, prove one after another to be not immortal.

No one, I more than suspect, would ever think to look up such material in an entry with the title of "Sturdy Indefensibles," or look to "Elegant Variation" to deal with the problem of repetitions, or expect to find abbreviations under "Curtailed Words." Many items in *Modern English Usage*, to be sure, are precisely where one would expect to find them—"Split infinitive," "Participles," "Subjunctives"—as are entries on specific words that are not always used with sufficient distinctiveness: "barbarian," "barbaric," "barbarous," for example. But who would have thought to look up the vaguely archaic language of certain nineteenth-century novels under "Novelese," or would search out the wish to avoid perfectly useful common words under "Novelty Hunting"? The entry "Superiority" turns out to be about apologizing for using slang in one's prose, and has the following extraordinary beginning:

> Surprise a person of the class that is supposed to keep servants cleaning his own boots, & either he will go on with the job while he talks to you, as if it were the most natural thing in the world, or else he will explain that the bootboy or scullery-maid is ill & give you to understand that he is, despite appearances, superior to boot-cleaning. If he takes the second course, you conclude that he is not superior to it; if the first, that perhaps he is.

Owing to this often slightly bizarre arrangement, *A Dictionary of Modern English Usage* is a book best approached serendipitously (see the Fowler entry "Love of The Long Word"). It is a particularly fine volume to wander around in. When not going to the book for help with a particular problem—I looked a while back to see if Fowler had anything to say about the word "pique," which I used a few paragraphs before; apart from brief advice on pronunciation, he didn't—I tend to roam around in its pages, usually stopping at an entry on a word I have myself used but never with full confidence. Such a word I recently looked up in Fowler is "palpable," which he says provides a useful illustration "of the need of caution in handling dead metaphors." He then tells exactly what the word does mean, even in a generous definition, and closes with the admonition that "P. is one of the words that are liable to clumsy treatment of this sort because they have never become vernacular English, & yet are occasionally borrowed by those who have no scholarly knowledge of them."

I enjoy Fowler when he is dispensing not merely instruction but advice, particularly of a moralizing kind. I enjoy the Fowler who begins his entry "French Words" by remarking, "Display of superior knowledge is as great a vulgarity as display of superior wealth—greater, indeed, inasmuch as knowledge should tend more definitely than wealth towards discretion & good manners. . . . To use French words that your reader or hearer does not know or does not fully understand, to pronounce them as if you were one of the select few to whom French is second nature when he is not one of those few (& it is ten thousand to one that neither you nor he will be so), is inconsiderate & rude." *Modern English Usage* is a chest filled with such didactic gems. "Men, especially," wrote Fowler in his entry "Didacticism," "are as much possessed by the didactic impulse as women by the maternal instinct." The Victorian schoolmaster in Fowler was never for long in abeyance. If his *Modern English Usage* is in effect a book of instruction in manners—in how to conduct oneself on the page—it is also a book of moral instruction. For the Victorians, as their historian Gertrude Himmelfarb has convincingly argued, the separation between manners and morals did not exist; manners were morals, morals created manners, and with impressively salubrious result.

In a dispute over the grammatical construction that Fowler termed the "fused participle," Otto Jespersen, the Danish philologist, called H. W. Fowler an "instinctive grammatical moraliser." Sir Ernest Gowers, in his essay on Fowler, tells us that Fowler resented the attack but not the epithet. Gowers nicely deals with the charge of "instinctive grammatical moralising" when he writes: "The prime mover of Fowler's instinctive moralising was not grammatical grundyism; it was intellectual fastidiousness. He had the soul of a craftsman and could not bear slovenly work." Fowler detested affectation and empty authority. He was ever the critic of the slipshod journalist, the pompous scholar, the precious aesthete. His hatred of humbug could on occasion take a moral turn, but he was inevitably moral on the side of good sense.

It may well be that the moral tone in Fowler, combined with the frequency with which he uses such words as "barbarous" and "vulgar," have lent *A Dictionary of Modern English Usage* the reputation of a crotchety work composed by a heavy-breathing reactionary. Such a reputation, along with being unearned, couldn't be wronger. Nor will it do to score Fowler off as an amiable pedant with a penchant for moralizing and an agile wit. In a way that Fowler himself would no doubt have found amusing, he has come to stand, in matters having to do with English usage, for the stodgy, the staid, the stuffy. In point of plain fact, H. W. Fowler was in his day a radical. "Here," as Sir Ernest Gowers writes, "was an emancipator from the fetters of the grammatical pedants that had bound us for so long."

It was Fowler who first held that it was better to split an infinitive than when not to do so was to lapse into a sentence that sounded barbarous. (His entry on "Split infinitive" begins: "The English-speaking world may be divided into (1) those who neither know nor care what a split infinitive is; (2) those who do not know, but care very much; (3) those who know & condemn; (4) those who know & approve; & (5) those who know and distinguish.") It was Fowler who held that the world knew greater crimes than ending a sentence on a preposition, that *different* need not always be followed by *from,* that it was permissible to use *whose* with an inanimate antecedent, that common words had an impressive dignity of their own. Everywhere Fowler worked to destroy the blind reverence for literary fetishes and to increase the respect for clear common sense. As Gowers rightly remarks: "Fowler's true place is among the first of the rebels rather than among the last of the die-hards."

Gowers ends his essay by asserting that "I do not see how in its essentials Fowler's teaching can ever be out of date." A brave assertion, but is it true? I think it is true while at the same time I think the audience for Fowler's teaching continues to diminish. Higher education was supposed to cause that audience to grow larger. "The spread of education," Fowler began his entry "Illogicalities" by writing, "adds to the writer's burdens by multiplying that pestilent fellow the critical reader." Pestilential some readers may be, yet, despite the vast spread of not only education but so-called higher education, epidemic their numbers have failed to become. Fowler could not have been unaware of this prospect, or of the fact that his was a valiant yet all but lost cause. "In this era of democracy," he wrote, "it can hardly be expected that the susceptibilities of so small a minority should be preferred to the comfort of the millions, and it is easier for the former to dissemble their dislike of barbarisms than for the latter to first find out what they are and then avoid them."

The need for such a book as Sir Ernest Gowers's *The Complete Plain Words* is in itself evidence sufficient to prove H. W. Fowler's dour prophesy. It is a book originally written for public servants by a public servant. It was begun in the late 1940s at the invitation of the British Treasury, which was concerned about the quality of prose written by British officials. Now, the British civil service, at least in those days, was not like the American, where your Uncle Louie may have been able to get you a job because he had an in with a guy named Vito down at city hall. The British civil service, at any rate in its higher grades, was chiefly staffed by men who had gone to public schools, had had to pass extremely difficult examinations, and (certainly when the British Empire was still a going concern) were often given immense responsibilities at an early age. It was for these men, as well as for military men, local government officials, and the staffs of public bodies (such as the rail-road), that *The Complete Plain Words* was written. It was written because, it was felt, they badly needed it.

The man chosen to write it, Ernest Gowers, was himself a public servant, and a high exemplar of the type. Gowers was especially exemplary in his propensity for self-effacement. "I know of no one in any walk of life who so dislikes and distrusts publicity as Sir Ernest Gowers," wrote Ivor Nicholson in *Pall Mall Magazine*. Although ostensibly a profile of Gowers, Mr. Nicholson's article does not tell much about him, apart from such facts as his having gone to Rugby, thence to Cambridge (earning a first in the classical tripos), thence into the civil service, where among other early jobs he served as principal private secretary to Lloyd George, who was then Chancellor of the Exchequer. The *Dictionary of National Biography* entry on Gowers—written by R. W. Burchfield, the current editor of the *Oxford English Dictionary*—notes: "Gowers may be regarded as one of the greatest civil servants of his day." Certainly the résumé of his jobs is immensely impressive; it includes the chairmanship of the Inland Revenue Department (England's IRS), London Regional Commissioner for Civil Defence (he was responsible for the defense of London during World War II), and the chairmanship of the Coal Mines Reorganization Commission (later known as the Coal Mines Commission). Gowers was, according to Lord Nugent, the chairman of more public inquiries and royal commissions than any other man of his day. "In fact," Lord Nugent writes, "his political convictions were unshakeably conservative, but his reputation for impartiality and integrity, combined with a penetrating intellect, were such that any Report from a Royal Commission or Public Enquiry which he produced was certain to win public confidence." R. W. Burchfield adds: "His courtesy, his fine sense of humour, and his unfailing clarity of expression explain why his services were so frequently sought."

Gowers was six feet three, blue-eyed, and a man of gentle

but compelling charm. He had the enviable reputation of not suffering fools gladly yet of being a man of unstinting courtesy and unending patience. He had what sounds a happy home life. He was a good pianist and took great pleasure from music. His daughter, Mrs. Eileen Duveen, has recounted how, during the war, when Gowers was "Regional Commissioner for London, as an antidote to going round the bomb sites and dealing with the crises of a London under siege, he would go to his local church where he had been given permission to play the organ, and for half an hour or so, relax with music." He was penetrating about politics, in which his was an insider's view, for he had known and worked with nearly all the great English political figures of the century. He kept up his reading in the classics and, Lord Nugent reports, "kept in touch with changing modern trends by reading the plays of modern playwrights—however awful he found some of them!"

Not least impressive of Gowers's achievements was his revision of Fowler's *A Dictionary of Modern English Usage,* which he began at seventy-five and completed at eighty-five, a year before his death. Since Gowers's *Plain Words* is a book greatly respectful of Fowler, and one that strongly showed the influence upon it of *Modern English Usage,* it is scarcely surprising that the editors of the Oxford University Press chose Sir Ernest Gowers to revise it. Without divesting Fowler's book of its original author's strong character, Gowers streamlined the book, cutting out no longer relevant entries, trimming away references and illustrations that might make it seem antique, adding material that took account of such phenomena as the rise of sociology, which took place after Fowler's death, modernizing generally.

Where Gowers added an entry, it invariably seems sensible for him to have done so. Some of the additions are brilliant, such as "Worsened Words," which takes up "changes in the meaning of words, and still more in their emotional content, [that] often reflect changes of opinion about the value of what they stand for," and which accounts for the slippage in prestige of such words as "colonial," "imperial," "academic," and "appeasement." Even though Gowers was a more understated man than Fowler, he could turn out a more than fair imitation of the master in his best whiplash mode, as in this passage from an article he added entitled "Abstractitus":

> A writer uses abstract words because his thoughts are cloudy; the habit of using them clouds his thoughts still further; he may end by concealing his meaning not only from his readers but also from himself, and writing such sentences as *The actualization of the motivation of the forces must to a great extent be a matter of personal angularity.*

Usage does not change as rapidly as fashion in clothing, but over the long haul it does change as inexorably. To write a book on the subject is to court revision; or, more precisely, to hope that one has written something good enough to be found worthy of revision. But if your subject is usage, the need for revision is your fate. As Gowers revised Fowler, so now Gowers's *The Complete Plain Words* has itself been twice revised. Gowers's book is nowhere near so ambitious a book as Fowler's; it began life, after all, as a pamphlet. Where Fowler took as his subject all that was in disarray in English usage, Gowers's more modest aim was to aid officials to write with greater clarity. Fowler's book is essential for all who take writing as their craft—writers, editors, teachers—as well as for those who, as Thomas Mann puts it in *Doctor Faustus,* find it "interesting to see how man can use words and what he gets out of them." Gowers's book addresses itself more directly to the questions of how to avoid awkward writing and how to evade lapsing into grammatical errors.

Gowers is less crackling and uncompromising, more measured and reasonable, than Fowler. He supplies therefore less fun but more perspective. He tells a reader what he needs to know, and tells it with an impressive sense of limitation. In the original *Complete Plain Words,* for example, Gowers allows that much has been written on the art of paragraphing, then adds: "But little of it helps the ordinary writer; the subject does not admit of precise guidance." He then goes on to tell his reader what little can be usefully said on the subject: that paragraphs oughtn't to be too long, that they should be unitary in subject matter and sequential in treatment, and so forth. In his Epilogue, he writes that his book runs the risk of making things look worse than they are, adding: "The true justification for such a book is not so much that official English is specially bad as that it is specially important for it to be good."

Gowers's good sense, reasonableness, and superior perspective can be a helpful brake on the runaway fanaticism that seems to set in among those of us who have decided to take a small part in that best of all lost causes, the battle for good usage. Gowers does not lead one to want to give up the battle, but only to be more judicious in picking one's targets and more careful not to squander one's ammo. The first point he reminds one of is that the English language is not cast in marble, *per omnia saecula saeculorum.* He writes:

> English is not static—neither in vocabulary nor in grammar, nor yet in that elusive quality called style. The fashion in prose alternates between the ornate and the plain, the periodic and the colloquial. Grammar and punctuation defy all the efforts of grammarians to force them into the mould of a permanent code of rules. Old words drop out or change their meanings; new words are admitted. What was stigmatised by the purists of one generation as a corruption of the language may a few generations later be accepted as an enrichment, and what was then common currency may have become a pompous archaism or acquired a new significance.

It is salutary to remember that two such smart fellows as Joseph Addison and Jonathan Swift objected to the emergence of the useful word "mob" (which derives from "mobile"). No doubt others have looked down upon "gazebo," "gismo," and "go-go." A new word is a fine thing when it is vivid and crisp and amusing and needed. New formations of old words, the most common mechanism of which derives from turning old nouns into new verbs ("finalize," "prioritize"), has to be viewed with the gravest suspicion, but at the same time it is useful to recall, as *The Complete Plain Words* reminds us, that this is the way the words "diagnose" and "sterilize" entered the language. Mike Tyson, the boxer, speaking of his wife's initial distrust of boxers, once remarked that this changed when she met him: "I took her off her feet," he said. "I suaved her." As a verb, "suave" is mildly amusing, but even now I see the word's ruination in an advertising campaign: "Suave her with Soave Bolla."

The problem is that it is difficult to object to most new words, or terms, or even trends, on principle. Usually there is no principle involved. One despises a new word because it sounds barbarous; yet once that word "barbarous" is past one's lips, the game is up—the charge of snobbery has already been entered. I do not mind the charge all that much myself, but I prefer to argue from solider ground. Too often the ground in these matters slides away from under one. The argument from etymology, for example, is not usually convincing. I am someone who uses the word "presently" in the sense of "soon" or "by and by" and not, as it is nowadays more often used, as a synonym for "currently." I have all along been doing so under the assumption that I had the authority of etymology on my side. Wrong. The Gowers-revised Fowler entry on "presently" has it that the word originally meant "instantly," and so its etymology is really closer to "currently" than to my usage. I shall continue to use the word in the way I have, but henceforth with a slight suspicion that I may merely be suaving myself.

When I say that it is difficult to object to new words, terms, or trends on principle, what I mean, more precisely, is that it is difficult to object to them on general principles. One has, as in traffic and divorce courts, to take each case as it comes, arguing the demerits of every separate entry. I do not like the word "arguably," for example, as it is used in the sentence "Anthony Powell is arguably one of the great English novelists of the twentieth century." I think that in this usage—in which the word "arguably" means "a respectable argument for the case could be made"—it is a weasel-word, which allows one to get around answering the question of whether Powell is or isn't one of the century's great English novelists. I am not much for the word "intriguing" either, as in the sentence, "I find women of her kind intriguing." I cannot see what advantage "intriguing" in this usage has over "interesting" or "fascinating," except perhaps to make the person who uses it himself sound, you should pardon the expression, "intriguing." Fowler says of the word used in this sense that "it is one of the Gallicisms, & Literary Critics' Words, that have no merit whatever except that of unfamiliarity to the English reader, & at the same time the great demerit of being identical with & therefore confusing the sense of a good English word." I would only add that, so often has the word come to be used in the way I have described it, it no longer has the merit of unfamiliarity.

In his day, Sir Ernest did not have to deal with the vexing problem of ethnic sensitivities, where even the nomenclature of groups is regularly changing, so that one cannot know if, say, a word such as "Chicano" is or is not in good form on a given day. He also escaped the earth before the most recent wave of feminists arrived with the demand that language be "desexitized." In my view the problem of sex and language cuts much deeper than such superficialities as "chairman" versus "chair" or "mankind" versus "humankind." It is much better engaged at the level where one can no longer think of a man as "enraged," while a woman at the same pitch of anger is declared "hysterical." It is better engaged at the level where one no longer thinks of certain work, or subjects, or points of view as belonging exclusively to one or the other sex.

Which brings me to another category of words I think fit for outlawing. These are words that once seemed quite all right, but have now to be turned in for overuse and ill use. "Experience" used as a verb is such a word: "Kent," the cigarette ad runs. "Experience it!" (Death, the surgeon general adds, risk it!) "No problem" is a phrase that has had it, especially with the ejaculatory "hey" before it; "no problem" is also coming, in the United States, to replace "you're welcome." "Special" as an adjective has long been at the Hallmark-greeting-card level of language, particularly when it is followed by "person." A "special person" usually turns out to be a "caring person," as one need scarcely add. "Community"—as in the poetry, arts, or even homeless community—has been vastly overworked. Well, one could go on, and I doubtless shall, the flecks of foam forming at the corners of my mouth, but not here and not now.

Many have been the events and moments in recent history when one has wished that certain figures from the past had been alive to comment upon them. How fine to have had H. L. Mencken's report on the creationism-evolutionism controversy, or A. J. Liebling on the gloating of the press around the time of Watergate, or Max Beerbohm on the Pop Art movement, or Edmund Wilson on any of the past ten years' meetings of the Modern Language Association. As for H. W. Fowler and Sir Ernest Gowers, they, were they alive today, would find plenty to keep them busy. Fowler, after sampling some of the work of contemporary academics, would doubtless wish to begin his *Dictionary of Modern English Usage* over from scratch. Gowers would readily see the need for another *Plain Words,* this one written for literary critics. Funny business, language—like the man said, the pay may not be high, but you're never out of work.

Italo Svevo,
the Good-Natured Pessimist

A S A YOUNG MAN, the Triestine novelist Italo Svevo's favorite author was Schopenhauer. "The whole of Svevo's life shows traces of the deep impression left on his mind by 'the philosopher of pessimism,' " writes John Gatt-Rutter, in his carefully researched and richly detailed biography of Svevo, "but his application of Schopenhauer was not the usual one." A good thing, too, for it was Schopenhauer who wrote that we must "regard man first and foremost as a being who exists only as a consequence of his culpability and whose life is an expiation of the crime of being born." It was Schopenhauer, again, who set out the bleak terms under which, in his view, we all play the hopeless game of life:

> The vanity of existence is revealed in the whole form existence assumes: in the infiniteness of time and space contrasted with the finiteness of the individual in both; in the fleeting present as the sole form in which actuality exists; in the contingency and relativity of all things; in continual becoming without being; in continual desire without satisfaction; in the continual frustration of striving of which life consists.

Italo Svevo believed all this, but he also believed that embedded in the tragedy of existence there was comedy. Man may be tragic in the long view but in the short view he was more often ridiculous; and this ridiculousness, along with making him comical, made him, in the work of the mature Svevo, sympathetic. This general view makes Svevo himself what the Italians call a *pessimista bonario,* or good-natured pessimist.

Attributing a strong, unitary influence of any thinker on the work of any serious artist is always risky business. Svevo liked to tell the story about Wagner writing to Schopenhauer to inform him how profound an effect the philosopher's thought had on his music, and Schopenhauer replying that the composer whose music seemed best to fit his philosophy was Rossini. Svevo had a true taste for life's contradictions, a positive passion for paradox. "Life leaves no space for illusion," he said, yet in his masterpiece, *Confessions of Zeno,* he has his autobiographically based character Zeno Cosini reflect: "I honestly believe that I have always needed to be in the middle of an adventure, or of some complication that gives the illusion of one."

No room for illusions in life, Svevo might say, except who can live without them? Tell Svevo that the shortest distance between two points is a straight line, and he would likely have responded that it strikes him there are more than two points out there, he doesn't have a ruler, and besides yesterday he broke his last pencil. Perverse though this general view sounds, it nonetheless had behind it an epistemology, a theory about the nature of knowledge. "Truth," the extraordinary fellow who called himself Italo Svevo once wrote in a book review, "is a lady who gives the finger to whoever excitedly runs after her, while she surrenders herself, indeed, imposes herself, on the man who does not seek her."

Svevo's real name was Ettore Schmitz, and behind the pen name of Italo Svevo there is a history and a geography and a psychological condition to consider. Italo Svevo translates to Italus the Swabian, or the Italian-Swabian, after the German district of Swabia. Ettore Schmitz was born in 1861, the fifth of eight children of a Jewish glassware merchant in Trieste. He was brought up speaking Italian while holding Austrian citizenship and having German ancestry. Schmitz later attributed his pen name, which he took up with the publication of his first novel, *A Life* (1892), to his German education, which was a commercial one and not very good. The Trieste in which he lived was populated by a mixture of Italians, Austrians, and Slavs. The city's politics, given its place as a pawn piece in the intricate chess game of the Austro-Hungarian Empire, require a more patient intelligence than mine and a thicker book than you are now reading to describe adequately. A city dominated by commerce and finance—Stendhal once claimed that its only religion was money—Trieste was largely indifferent to a dreamy literary man of the type of the youthful Ettore Schmitz.

A dreamy type Schmitz clearly was, and would remain through all his life. What he dreamed about was becoming a famous writer. He dreaded the business career his father had planned for him—a career made all the more necessary when his father, having suffered serious financial setbacks, lost his nerve and hovered near breakdown. Svevo's first serious job out of school was as a clerk in the Trieste branch of a Viennese bank. He alternated between bouts of excruciating boredom and dreams of saving the bank through some fantastical act of financial heroism. "A poet," the Russian proverb has it, "always cheats his boss." A novelist is generally not much better. Schmitz, though, was not yet a novelist, nor did he even aspire to be. He did some reviewing for the local press, he started various plays, most of which he never completed, he daydreamed about playing heroic roles in a world in which he sensed that he was never likely to play more than a bit part. He was, in other words, already well launched on that career of abulia—an acute sense of loss of willpower—that would not only haunt him his life long but provide one of the great subjects for his art.

Loss or lack of will ought not to be confused with laziness, of which Schmitz could never be accused. While laboring away at his dreary tasks at the Unionbank in Trieste, he taught courses at the local Istituto Superiore Commerciale Revoltella, worked part-time on a local newspaper, and read widely in continental philosophy and literature. He served a year's compulsory duty in the Austrian army. (He liked to tell about following an imperious Austrian officer up an escarpment: the officer, turning back, said to him, "See that you don't bite my behind," to which Schmitz responded, "Don't you know Jews don't eat pork?") A full-time job-holder, a part-time litterateur, a man with several interests but no great promise in any one line, he believed himself, not unreasonably, a dilettante, with the instincts of an artist but none of the requisite originality. A man with so strong a feeling for his own limitations slips easily into irony, that mode of speech and writing in which one never quite means what one says or ever quite says what one means.

Svevo's irony is gentle yet pervasive, and not in the least bitter. His is the irony appropriate to a man bemused by the world yet at the same time entertained by his own bemusement. "How astonishing reality was!" says a character in Svevo's second novel, *As a Man Grows Older* (1898). That exclamation, with its perpetual note of surprise, could stand as an epigraph to all that Svevo wrote. His writing has a quality of amused astonishment, as if he wrote with both eyebrows raised and a sly smile upon his lips. If the effect seems comical, so do most photographs of Svevo reveal a comedian's face. He had a large head, dark languorous eyes, and, it is reported, a deafening laugh. The youthful Svevo resembles an Italianate Charlie Chaplin; later he comes across as Ben Blue wearing Buster Keaton's pancake boater; and finally, in his last years, he could pass for a smaller version of a Keystone Kop. But any resemblance of Italo Svevo to a silent film star is put to rout by his relentless self-analysis and endless loquacity. Asked to account for the twenty-five year hiatus between his second and third novels and how he was able to abstain from writing for so long, Svevo explained, "I talked a great deal."

Svevo delighted in the mysteries of human personality, beginning with his own. His novels and stories are filled with such amusing notes of wonderment as his asking why "good talkers never have luck with women," or why "whenever two Italians are at the same table each of them is burning to get away from the other so as not to have to listen to him." But not all is at this level of charming kibitzing. "It is in illness that animals most resemble men," wrote Svevo in his story "Short Sentimental Journey." "It isn't race that makes a Jew," he noted elsewhere, "it's life."

Life's astonishments, one's inability to mold it to one's desires—let us not begin to speak of conquering it—these were things Svevo was well set up to understand from the very beginning. He believed that some people in life were better fitted for living; in some loose Darwinian sense, they were further evolved; they had more energy, were more beautiful or handsome or talented; they were less burdened by a nagging consciousness of life's perils. Svevo knew himself not to be among these lucky ones, gifted of the gods. In *Confessions of Zeno*, the hero reflects: "At that time [on my honeymoon] I was attacked by a slight illness from which I was never to recover. It was a mere trifle; the fear of growing old, and above all the fear of death." Such fears can only conduce to detach one from life, however much one wishes to take an active hand in one's own destiny. They tend, too, to relegate people, as Edouard Roditi once put it in describing Svevo's characters, to "the margins of social and economic activity where, instead of acting, they generally dream, analyze and comment [on] the actions of others or the workings of chance."

Novels with congenitally passive heroes—always acted upon, never propelling themselves into action—are not everybody's idea of a good time. Marinetti, author of the Futurist manifesto, said that in reading Svevo "I got the impression I was eating chocolates. I am a lion and do not eat chocolates." This was in 1930, two years after Svevo's death. The year before

Svevo died, a young critic named Guido Piovene, writing in the aftermath of the discovery of Svevo by the modernist cognoscenti in Paris and during the time of Mussolini, took out after him with the critical equivalent of a rubber truncheon:

> Italo Svevo, a Triestine merchant, author of mediocre novels, viewed among us with the indifference he deserves, finds himself suddenly proclaimed a great writer by a decadent Irish novelist living in Trieste, Joyce; by a decadent poet from Paris, Valéry Larbaud; and by a critic, Benjamin Crémieux, who, because he is competent in matters of French literature, passes in France for a connoisseur of Italian literature, of which he has some notions among people who have none. What are the merits of Svevo? The fact that more than any other Italian he has espoused a passive and analytic treatment which reached its peak with Proust, and which will be considered a decadent art as long as it is held that art must be the work of living and active men, and that a painter is more deserving than a mirror.

With the notable exception of Eugenio Montale, who early recognized his quality, Italians generally tended not to be enamored of Svevo. In Italy his books were put down when they weren't ignored. Benedetto Croce makes no mention of Svevo; Pirandello never commented on a play that Svevo once sent him (as Freud never wrote to acknowledge the copy of *Confessions of Zeno* Svevo sent along to him). Svevo's books, rather modest in scope and almost entirely self-reflexive, must have confused an Italian readership heated up by the strenuous grandiosities of D'Annunzio. His books were no doubt an affront to those who believed in the puffed-up caricature of Italian manliness. "We are," Svevo once wrote, "a living protest against that ridiculous conception of the Superman, which has been so much drummed into us (particularly us Italians)." During his lifetime, Svevo was never widely appreciated in Italy; and despite his late-life *succès d'estime* in Paris, literary capital of the world, he had to struggle to get his early novels re-issued in the country of his birth.

Although I have just enough Italian to board the wrong train for Milan out of the rather dreary *stazione* at Bologna, people who really know Italian and its various dialects always remark on Svevo's language, which did not in the least aid his reputation with the Italian critics of his day. Sometimes termed "Triestine merchant's Esperanto," this language fell far short of what then was thought "good Italian." As Svevo himself wrote to the editor of the Italian journal *La Voce*, "Perhaps it is obvious that I have written only one novel in my whole life. All the less pardonable that I always wrote it badly." At other times, Svevo defended his language as the only one that was alive and natural to him, arguing that to have attempted to avail himself of the floridities of literary Italian would have resulted in dismal artificiality. In English translation, Svevo reads well and sounds altogether modern. François Bondy, writing in *The Hudson Review* more than twenty years ago, noted: "Today, the 'incorrect' style of Svevo passes for a model of writing. It has loosened the tongue of a whole new Italian literature—I am thinking of Pavese, of Vittorini, and even of Silone—which unmasks rhetoric and has only an ironic rela-tionship to the great sonorous flights." The lesson here to young and old is clear enough: one may write as "poorly" as one likes, so long as one has genius.

A genius, even a modest one, is the last thing Svevo ever felt himself. Never having been taken quite seriously as a writer by anyone else, he had scarcely anything but doubts about his own writing. He had to contribute to the cost of publication of all three of his novels, the first two of which created barely a ripple. His wife, as Professor Gatt-Rutter remarks in his biography, "tolerated his literary and philosophical interests as a more or less harmless and rather superior pastime." Svevo himself alternated between feeling lashed to his writing—"the only business in which I can take pleasure," he called it—and treating it as if it were a vice he had to break himself of, like his endless smoking.

In nearly all photographs of him, Svevo has a cigarette going. His diary makes frequent mention of yet another of his resolutions to quit smoking; he was always in search of the perfect day on which to do it. "I'm smoking like a mobilized Turk," he once wrote to his wife while travelling on business, "and so I cough busily away, especially in the morning." Colleagues recall him characteristically smoking and joking. He quit almost daily but never truly stopped. Near the end of his life he was smoking thirty or forty cigarettes a day. P. N. Furbank, in his 1966 study of Svevo, recounts how, on his deathbed, Svevo, seeing his physician-nephew Aurelio light up a cigarette, asked for one himself. When refused, he is said to have murmured, "That really would have been the last cigarette."

What a splendid vice smoking is for a Schopenhauerian! Few habits teach us so much about the place of will—and especially will-lessness—in life; few make a greater comedy of human resolution. Few things, too, give more pleasure than contemplating ceasing to smoke, so long as a freshly lit cigarette is in one's hand, a wreath of blue smoke gathering about one's head. Svevo understood all this perfectly, but his was an understanding that passeth all resolution. As he wrote in "The Last Cigarette," the opening section of *Confessions of Zeno:*

> In order to make it seem a little less foolish I tried to give a philosophical content to the malady of "the last cigarette." You strike a noble attitude, and say: "Never again!" But what becomes of the attitude if you keep your word? You can only preserve it if you keep on renewing your resolution.

Svevo also understood the link between smoking and dreaming. An early essay of Svevo's entitled "Il fumo" notes:

> The smoker is first and foremost a dreamer. . . . The dreamer is never consistent because dream carries you far away and not in

a straight line. . . . The true dreamer . . . always leads a double
life and both his lives are equal in intensity. . . . Thus his inspiration has two sources: pure observation and dream, dream which
is distorted by corrupted nerves.

Smoking aids dreaminess, and his habit of dreaming, Svevo
once averred, "is really what gives me my almost continual
serenity"—not excluding his dream of one day successfully
quitting cigarettes.

As for the double life of the dreamer, all of us, I believe, at
least partially lead that, divided in our thought between the
lives we lead and the lives we might sometimes wish we led.
In Svevo's case, this sense of a double life was intensified with
his marriage to Livia Veneziani, daughter of a successful paint
manufacturer in Trieste. She was his cousin and thirteen years
younger than he, who was thirty-five when he married. She
was a good wife and mother—they had one child, a daughter
Letizia—though apparently little interested in her husband's
interior life. Owing to this marriage, Svevo eventually went
into the family business, whose specialty was producing paint
that wore especially well on the hulls of ships; he agreed to
have himself baptized a Catholic—though he continued to think
of himself as an atheistic Jew—and told himself that he had
put aside his hope for literary glory.

Although through the paint business Ettore Schmitz would
become a reasonably wealthy man, the notion of his having
knuckled under, or sold out, or otherwise betrayed his art
doesn't, in my view, really come into play. Had his first two
novels met a kindlier fate, earning him some measure of money
or distinction, perhaps he would have tried to work full-time
at literature. But life, plainly, had other things in store. "Mid-
way through life's journey," wrote Svevo in an essay entitled
"Optimism and Pessimism," "we shut our eyes in slumber to
shattered delusions, forgotten desires, renunciations forced upon
us by the imperious claims of our milieu, of people, of time."

Suffering, we know, is not absolutely compulsory in life, for the wicked and the silly sometimes flourish like crabgrass, but Svevo could never have become the writer he was to become had his way been made smooth.

You can't, after all, be a pessimist and expect perfect justice, too. Nor can you hope to write Svevian novels after a lifetime of sunny-skied, rosy-cheeked success—going, as the Victorians were wont to say, from strength to strength. Svevo, like most of the characters in his fiction, went instead from doubt to doubt. These characters are for the vast most part autobiographical, if not in minute detail then in general spirit. The Svevo fictional hero tends to be a secondary character, a sideline figure, nobody's main man. One might call him a failure except that he is never really in serious contention for success. Had Italo Svevo written *Hamlet,* it might today be called *Yorick.*

Un inetto ("A Failure") was Svevo's original title for his first novel, which was published in 1892, when he was thirty-one years old, under the publisher's suggested title of *Una vita,* or *A Life.* It is the story of a young man come from the provinces to an unnamed city (obviously Trieste), there to fail miserably. It is an old story, a Stendhalian and Balzacian story, except that Svevo's young hero, Alfonso Nitti—no Julien Sorel or Lucien Chardon—could scarcely be accused of giving it his best shot. Alfonso is a dreamer, as every seriously ambitious young man tends to be, but his dreams give him perhaps too much pleasure. "He himself when he felt at his most wretched," Svevo writes, "took refuge in unrealizable dreams." And even when Alfonso's dreams come true—as they do in one key incident in the novel—the reality proves more than he can handle. The crucial difference between the normal person who has his dreams and the case-hardened dreamer is that the latter really prefers not to be wakened.

Alfonso Nitti works in a bank—as did the young Ettore Schmitz—where his principal task is to copy out documents.

The excruciating dullness of the work gives him ample room to slip away into his various fantasies, which include: doing something heroic to aid the bank in crisis and thus be recognized for the brilliant and resourceful young man he is; achieving literary glory for an original philosophical book he is at work on in his hours away from the bank; and conquering the love of Annetta Maller, the rather haughty daughter of the owner of the bank where he serves as an obscure clerk. Svevo is impressively efficient on the fantasy of his young hero's book, on which Alfonso is said to "work well but very little," so that after months all his efforts come to "three or four short pages of preface, which promised to do and attempt much while nothing was actually done or attempted at all." Such paucity of production was "equivalent to a tacit renunciation of all ambition." But then Svevo also tells us that "anything at all doubtful eventually became important for Alfonso."

A Life is one of those novels in which not much happens, but very slowly. The dreariness of Alfonso's work in the bank is set out in exhaustive detail; his not much jollier life at the Lanuccis, the lower-middle-class family with whom he boards and is viewed as a potential husband for their hopeless daughter, is firmly established in all its grayness. Between the pillar of boredom and the post of despair, Alfonso lives his negligible days, refreshed chiefly by the imaginary breezes provided by his fantasies of literary, commercial, and romantic conquest. All his relationships are superficial; and, within, inertia struggles (not, to be sure, very fiercely) with doubt for his soul. The heavy aroma of failure, with a faint hint of oregano, hangs over all.

The central event in *A Life* is Alfonso's seduction of Annetta, a dilettante with literary aspirations. He spends much time collaborating with her on a novel of apparently boundless vacuity. The seduction has only to be effected for Alfonso to lose interest, feel restless and disgusted. When it is time for him to solidify his gains by turning his conquest into marriage, thus lifting himself up from his current obscurity, he leaves town to return to his village, where he discovers his mother is dying. Told he must return immediately or lose Annetta, he naturally delays. Annetta decides to marry someone else. When he does eventually return, he learns that he is to be demoted at the bank. Worse, Annetta's brother challenges him to a duel. It is all really too much for Alfonso, who determines to commit suicide—"never in his daydreamer's life had he been so completely possessed by a dream." In a somewhat muddled Schopenhauerian abnegation of will, he turns on the gas and has done with it.

One of the advantages in having written a masterpiece is that one's earlier works are re-examined in the search for premonitions of what is to come. Late in life Svevo wrote to a French critic that if, as James Joyce and others had said, every writer really has only one book in him, with all books that follow being essentially embellishments and twists and turns on that one book, his, Svevo's, one book would be *A Life*. "Except," he added, "that it is written so badly (far worse than the other two) that I ought to rewrite it." Certainly *A Life* is the dimmest of Svevo's novels. In it his comic powers are still only incipient. *A Life* owes its own life, insofar as the life of a book is measured in the interest it can command, to the novels that will follow.

These did not come quickly. Svevo did not begin his second novel, *As a Man Grows Older* (*Senilità* in Italian), until fully four years later, in 1896, the year, in fact, of his marriage. Two years after that, when this second novel was published, it received six for the most part rather niggling reviews, the most depressing of which had to have been the following single-sentence slap in a Milanese socialist newspaper: "Italo Svevo's analytical novel of passion, which indulges in the details of the psychology of love, would gain from greater attention to form and from reducing its largess of striking phrases." Svevo was thirty-seven, a married man, the father of a two-year-old daughter. Enough of literary games. He accepted his mother-in-law's invitation to join the Veneziani family underwater paint business.

Svevo later claimed, in an autobiographical essay, that he tried to give up writing, but, nothing if not a slave to habit, he found it no more easy to stop writing than to stop smoking. Even so, however halfheartedly he may have entered the paint business, he worked at it full-time. He divided his work day, which began at seven in the morning, between the Veneziani factory and office. He was vouchsafed the family's secret paint formula and supervised the brewing of paint. He was in charge of the factory work force, and was apparently, according to Professor Gatt-Rutter, very good at dealing with the workers. He handled, in fact, every aspect of the business, and at one point was sent to England to open a new factory. Meanwhile, he lived with the habits and among the full trappings of the typical bourgeois: a good cigar and a comfortable armchair at home after lunch, theater- or opera-going in the evening; he was the dutiful father, the loving husband. When a critic named Ida Finzi at one point asked about his writing, Svevo replied, "Oh, I'm deep in underwater paint." But the writer within him was not so easily drowned.

Still, the dreary reception accorded *As a Man Grows Older* (the novel was given its English title by James Joyce) must have stung. After it Svevo wrote, "In this world one is compelled to write but not to publish." There is nothing callow about Svevo's second novel, which is a remarkable book and the work of a mature artist. Like *A Life, As a Man Grows Older* is about the fantasies of the weak, but it adds to these high-minded self-justification and cunning self-deception, so that the fantasies take on a complex life of their own and a richer interest all round. "No fool like an old fool" is an often-enough repeated maxim, yet Emilio Brentani, the hero of *As a Man Grows Older,* is only thirty-five, which only goes to show that, in this amazing world, there is precocity even in foolishness.

Brentani is a writer who has published a single, now nearly forgotten, novel and who holds a subordinate post in an insurance society the salary from which supports him and his younger, though already old-maid, sister. He has ceased to write out of inertia, but this does not prevent him from continuing to take himself as an artist. His ample self-esteem is crucial to his (from the outset) fraudulent relationship with Angiolina, a daughter of the lower working class, "a tall, healthy blonde, with big blue eyes and a supple graceful body, an expressive face and transparent skin glowing with health." Angiolina is a young woman with a vast enthusiasm for life and its simple rewards and also a woman with a certain reputation—she is, not to put too fine a point on it, an amiable and faithless slut. All Brentani has in mind is to have a brief fling with her. Being an intellectual, whose experience comes chiefly from books and who has little appetite for facing facts in life, however, he is able to make himself miserable in no time at all. But then any man who wishes to educate a woman, as Brentani does Angiolina, is in for a grim education of his own. In a nice reversal of the legendary King Pygmalion, Brentani really wishes to turn a live woman into a statue.

As a Man Grows Older is a novel about a state of mind. When Svevo entitled it *Senilità* he had in his own mind the notion of creating a character of spiritual if not physical senility, someone who lives passively and in confusion wandering about without a firm hold on reality. As the critic Beno Weiss puts it, "Unlike Alfonso [in *A Life*], Emilio's conflict is no longer with society or with his work, but rather with his own personality and the dual reality of his life, being and appearance." In his second novel, Svevo is a much more confident writer than he was in his first novel, more penetrating psychologically, richer and denser and defter with detail, a serious craftsman, an artist.

Emilio Brentani is a man who filters all experience through his sensibility. This means that he imposes his often parboiled ideas on such reality as he encounters. He is blind to obvious truths that do not immediately affect him, such as, for example, the hopeless dreariness of his sister's life. He turns the lives of others into material that will comport well with his own fantasies. He is always making Angiolina into something she is not, teaching her things that simply aren't so. Emilio is vaguely a socialist, or at least, as Svevo writes, "in the past he had indulged in socialistic ideas, of course without ever stirring a finger to realize them." When he explains his dream of a socialist future to Angiolina, telling her that a time will come when capital will be abolished, working conditions improved, and woman "the equal of man and love a mutual gift," she replies: "If everything was to be divided there wouldn't be much left for anybody. The working-classes are jealous good-for-nothings and will never succeed, however much you do for them." But nothing finally stops Emilio in his determination to shape Angiolina into the stuff his dreams are made of. Years later, long after Angiolina has run off with an embezzling bank clerk, Emilio somehow conflates his memories of her with those of his sister who has died of a broken heart, so that "she stood for all that was noble in his thought and vision during that period of his life." The astonishments of reality are simply unavailable to Emilio Brentani, who, despite his elevated view of himself as a cultivated gentleman, is merely another of the vast majority who cannot stand too much reality.

After the general incomprehension and disdain that greeted *As a Man Grows Older,* the public literary ambitions of Ettore Schmitz, as we now must once again think of Svevo, died. Privately, though, the flame never went out. Sometimes he gave way to despondency; sometimes he chastised himself for being unable to think without a pen in his hand—that is, for not being more of a man of action. Writing to his wife, he complained about "the violence I did myself in making such a clean leap into this new line of business," then added: "Inside my brain there must be a cog that won't stop churning out those novels that no one would read, and rebels and goes on spinning crazily whether you're there or not." When his wife at one point asked that he destroy her letters to him, he shot back: "Why are you so scared that *other people* might read your writings! I who have published novels know that *other people* are extremely discreet." He took up the violin, which he played passionately but apparently not well (he had difficulty with tempo), and played—naturally—second fiddle in an amateur string quartet. He was becoming a wealthy man; the entire British navy was gray with Veneziani paint, thanks to a surprisingly easy deal that, Professor Gatt-Rutter reports, Schmitz himself negotiated. As late as 1912, he announced that he had given up his pen name of Italo Svevo and any further hope of "a little proud literary fame," but he continued to read modern literature and could not stop the ideas for plays, stories, and essays that swirled in his mind.

In 1905 there arrived in Trieste a slender, ill-sighted Irishman with an ego as big as the Ritz and a revolutionary literary talent to match whose name was James Joyce. Joyce had not yet published any of the books that would make him famous, but he already carried himself as if he had. He had come to Trieste with his family to teach English at the Berlitz School there, which he did until he was released because the school was overstaffed. After a spell in Rome, a city that he hated, Joyce returned to Trieste, earning his living by, among other jobs, giving English lessons privately. Schmitz needed English to facilitate his running the Veneziani factory in England, and hired Joyce to teach him and his wife—he was to call Joyce *il mercante di gerundi,* the purveyor of gerunds. Thus began one of the rare sweet symbiotic relationships in modern literature.

Schmitz was twenty years older than Joyce—they were, respectively, forty-five and twenty-five when they first met— but the younger man, despite his largely unsettled condition in life, was much the more confident. During one of the thrice-weekly lessons that Joyce provided for Schmitz and his wife, he brought along and read his recently completed story "The Dead." Schmitz's wife was so moved by it that she repaired to the garden of their villa to gather a bouquet to present to Joyce in honor of his story. Schmitz meanwhile was moved to tell Joyce that he, too, had once written, having years before published two novels to resounding silence. Joyce took copies of these novels home with him that evening. At his next lesson, as Richard Ellmann recounts in his biography of James Joyce, Joyce told Schmitz: "Do you know that you are a neglected writer? There are passages in *Senilità* that even Anatole France could not have improved." Joyce then quoted a few, from memory. Schmitz was stunned, delighted, exhilarated. Joyce's opinion enabled him to take himself seriously again as a writer in a way he had not allowed himself to do for years. Later, Joyce's intervention was crucial to the success of *Confessions of Zeno*.

What did Joyce get from Schmitz? First, the thing that Joyce seemed to ask from all friends and acquaintances: money. Schmitz lent Joyce money in Trieste and he later sent him money in Ireland. Joyce often applied to Schmitz for aid, and once he left his dog Fido in Schmitz's family's care. Schmitz sent business clients Joyce's way for English lessons, and his father-in-law briefly hired Joyce as a correspondence clerk in 1914. Joyce pumped Schmitz for information about the Jews, which he used in the composition of his character Leopold Bloom in *Ulysses*. Although Schmitz was not the precise model for Bloom, Richard Ellmann claims that he was "almost certainly" the prototype. Joyce also borrowed Schmitz's wife Livia's name, and her long, reddish-blonde hair, for Anna Livia Plurabelle in *Finnegans Wake*. P. N. Furbank quotes Joyce's letter to Schmitz on this point: "Reassure your wife with regard to Anna Livia. I have taken no more than her hair from her and even that only on loan, to adorn the rivulet which runs through my city, the Anna Liffey." Joyce and Schmitz were never intimate friends—

intimacy was not Joyce's specialty—but each man, the prudish bohemian and the exuberant bourgeois, liked and amused the other. Furbank tells the story about Schmitz once telling an off-color joke to Joyce, who reproved him for having done so, remarking that "I never say that sort of thing, though I write it." Schmitz's comment on this was, "It would appear then that his works are not ones that could be read in his own presence."

Writing to his wife from England, Schmitz once noted: "A beaten footballer still has his self-respect; a failed writer is merely ridiculous." Nevertheless, fight against it though he did, the appetite for literary glory rose up in him once more, and by 1919 he had set to work on *Confessions of Zeno*. Naomi Lebowitz, who wrote with balance and penetration on Svevo in her 1978 study of the writer, remarks that there are three specific events that "help us to chart the motivating influences behind Svevo's third novel: the meeting with James Joyce, the reading of Freud, and the sequestered leisure imposed upon him by the war." Of the three, perhaps the event that best explains the leap from the grayness of *A Life* and the deep brown of *As a Man Grows Older* to the rich and brightly colored palette of *Confessions of Zeno* is the author's encounter with the writings of Sigmund Freud.

Schmitz's first encounter with the doctrines of psychoanalysis came through a friend of his brother-in-law's, a Triestine psychoanalyst named Edoardo Weiss. Weiss sent this brother-in-law, who sought a cure for his homosexuality, to Victor Trausk, an early member of Freud's Vienna circle. (No cure was effected.) In 1911, Schmitz himself met another member of the Freudian circle, Wilhelm Stekel, while he was on holiday in Bad Ischl. In his book, Beno Weiss sets the date when Schmitz began reading Freud seriously at 1916. In 1918, it is known, he began to work, in collaboration with his physician-nephew, on a translation into Italian of *The Interpretation of Dreams*. How much of Freud Schmitz read is not known. What is certain is that he took to Freud like a fat boy to a candy store.

Little wonder, for Ettore Schmitz was a Freudian delight, a walking laboratory of hesitations, symptoms, odd tics. On his own, he could have kept three couches busy. He suffered persistent needless jealousy, hypochondria, melancholia, you name it. Nor did he wish to be fully engaged by life, as this entry from the diary that he kept for his wife before their marriage shows:

> My indifference towards life is still there: even when I'm by your side enjoying myself, there is something inside me that isn't sharing my enjoyment and that says to me: "Watch out, it's not as you think it is, it's all a comedy, the curtain will come down in the end." Besides, indifference towards life is the essence of my intellectual life. Whatever's worth-while in my own talk comes from irony, and I'm afraid lest the very day you managed to make me believe in life (but you never will) I should find myself diminished by doing so. I'd almost beg you—almost— to leave me as I am. I have a great fear of happiness making me stupid.

A man who cultivates indifference and detachment, who prefers to filter life through the fine mesh of irony, who daydreams unduly, who feels preternaturally old and has had a vivid presentiment of his death from his earliest days, who can't (never really could) enter fully into the steam of life, yes, Doctor, the pieces begin to sort themselves out, a syndrome emerges, our patient has what looks suspiciously like the disease of being a modern writer. In Schmitz's case, the disease was intensified by his doing very little writing. A quarter of a century elapsed between *As a Man Grows Older* and *Confessions of Zeno,* which was completed in 1922 and published in 1923. Italo Svevo, as he now once again became, was sixty-one when he finished the novel, and with the passing of years had acquired an increased amusement, tolerance, and heightened recognition of the rather comic helplessness against which most of us struggle when faced with life. If Svevo suffered from the disease of being a modern writer, there is in his final novel an absence of alienation, depression, and defeat, and an impressive aura of comedy, ebullience, and endlessly fascinating complexity. *Confessions of Zeno* is one of those rare modern novels that make one happy.

Yet the novel has often been described, mistakenly in my view, as a psychoanalytic novel. Beno Weiss, for example, writes that *Confessions of Zeno* "is the first Italian psychoanalytic novel," and in his criticism of the novel he expends great energy fitting its plot and characters to Freudian schema (". . . when we try to identify the etiology of Zeno's illness, we must go beyond the oedipal question since everything seems to revolve around the father figure [yawn] . . ."). It seems to me that while the sources of Svevo's novel are psychoanalytic—the novel is written in the form of a diary written for Zeno Cosini's psychoanalyst—the intention of the novel is, among other things, to mock psychoanalysis, with its confident labeling, its lockstep determinacy, its seemingly comprehensive explanations for all human behavior. "We novelists," Svevo wrote about Freudianism, "are wont to play with great philosophies and are certainly not fitted to clarify them: we falsify them but we humanize them." In the novel, Zeno remarks upon his psychoanalyst's solemn comments: "I prefer laughing about these asininities to discussing them." And when the psychoanalyst, discovering that Zeno wishes to make love to two different beautiful women, asks himself why would a man wish to do such a thing, Zeno thinks, "Who but he could have invented questions like that?" Or, as Svevo put it to an admirer who was considering undergoing psychoanalysis, "Freud was a great man, but more for us novelists than for the ill."

Italo Svevo's acquaintance with Freud's writing stimulated him not so much to submit to Freud's ideas but to test their truth through counterposing his own ideas in the only way that novelists legitimately can—through the intricate dialectic of narrative. In Svevo's case, the confrontation between novelist and thinker is more direct than it generally is, owing to the psychoanalytic setting of *Confessions of Zeno*. The novel is divided into six main sections: on Zeno's smoking problem, on his complicated relationship with his father, on his proposal to his wife, on his marriage and his mistress, on his business partnership with his brother-in-law, and finally on his observations about his own psychoanalysis. Each section is free-wheeling, highlighting the paradoxical elements in life—Zeno's wife, for example, isn't his first or even his second choice, yet she turns out to be the perfect mate—and the whole is obliquely comical.

From the start we know that a game is being played when the novel begins with a preface written by the analyst who was working with Zeno Cosini and who blames him for having "suddenly thrown up his cure just at the most interesting point, thus cheating me of the fruits of my long and patient analysis of these memoirs." The name Zeno, too, is a giveaway, for the two famous Zenos in classical history are Zeno of Elea (born c. 490 B.C.), inventor of the dialectic and of Zeno's paradox, and Zeno of Citium (335–263 B.C.), founder of the Stoic school of philosophy. Zeno Cosini, a fifty-six-year-old Triestine businessman, husband and father and bourgeois par excellence, will pose paradox and stoicism against the mighty engine of psychoanalytic doctrine. It doesn't sound at all like a fair fight but for Cosini's (really Svevo's) secret weapon—a devastating sense of humor.

In one of its aspects *Confessions of Zeno* is a comedy about human resolution—"delicious resolutions," as Zeno Cosini at one point calls them. Zeno is always resolving to quit smoking, to leave his mistress, to treat his brother-in-law fairly, to gain control over his business, to cease being the nearly negligible character whom no one—scarcely even himself—can take quite seriously. He expends vast energy making an abundance of resolutions, which leave him rather exhausted. "If you use up all your energy in making resolutions you have no time for anything else," he writes, "for it takes a Julius Caesar to be able to do two things at once." At one point in his early manhood, Zeno wrote out in advance on the walls of his bedroom the dates on which he planned to quit cigarettes, but he changed these dates so often that he eventually ran out of wall space and had to move. But this is sick, you might suggest. "Perhaps so," Zeno would doubtless reply, "perhaps so," and then ask to borrow a cigarette from you.

"Sickness is a conviction," Zeno notes early in the novel, "and I was born with that conviction." Zeno admires the healthy, and one of the great divisions among characters in all Svevo's novels is that between those who are naturally healthy and those who are otherwise. Admirable, fortunate, happy though the healthy may be, there are drawbacks, in Zeno's view, even to their condition: "Health cannot analyze itself even if it looks at itself in the glass," Zeno writes. "It is only we invalids who can know anything about ourselves." Svevo himself suffered many a *maladie imaginaire,* and he awarded some pips in this line to Zeno: a limp, a stabbing pain in the side, and so tender a conscience that "I was always trying by my present behavior to diminish the remorse I must feel in the future." (Svevo joins Kafka and Proust in being among the great hypochondriacs of modern literature, though it is well to remember—à la Delmore Schwartz's famous remark about even paranoids having real enemies—that even hypochondriacs have real illnesses, for both Kafka and Proust died young.) It will be one of the conclusions of this rich novel that, within limits, sickness may be underrated—may even be indivisible from one's own special power.

An amusing moment occurs roughly halfway through *Confessions of Zeno,* when Zeno Cosini, departing the apartment of his working-class mistress, with whom he has just made physical love for the first time, reports:

> As I hurried home, I was even bold enough to begin attacking our social system, as if that were responsible for my shortcom-

ings. I thought it ought to be so arranged as to allow one to have intercourse occasionally with other women without having to fear the consequences. Even with women one could never love.

Zeno goes on to make plain that man's weakness has nothing to do with any social system, nor can it be remedied by psychological cure. "Therefore," he continues, "I don't think that remorse springs from regret for having done something wrong, but rather from a recognition of one's own sinful nature. The higher part of one's body bends down to observe and judge the lower, and finds it monstrous." At the same time, the paradox-loving Zeno reports that this love affair has been very good for his marriage. It has made him appreciate his wife all the more, made him all the more affectionate to her, which has in turn made her all the more loving toward him. "I had not," Zeno concludes, "felt so innocent for a long time."

Svevo is skeptical not only of criticisms of the social system and of elaborate intellectual systems but even of writing itself. In a lovely letter to his then ten-year-old daughter (the letter is quoted in full by P. N. Furbank), who was evincing an interest in writing poetry, the novelist tells her about two different men, one who makes beautiful wardrobe cabinets and the other whose job it is to describe beautiful wardrobe cabinets. "And so they went on," Svevo writes, "the one making wardrobes and the other describing them." Then, later in the letter, after recounting how the describer of wardrobes continually adds little flourishes and touches that change the nature of what he is describing, he adds: "I am sure you can see what a stupid creature that describer of live wardrobes was. But it wasn't really his fault, you know. If you go on describing, day in and day out, you are bound to end up describing all wrong." This was written before Svevo had regained his confidence in his own writing, but nonetheless, as any describer of wardrobes has in his heart to concede, there is much truth to it.

Toward the close of *Confessions of Zeno,* Dr. S., Zeno's psychoanalyst, informs him that he has been suffering from an Oedipal conflict, of which, while he may not yet realize it, he is now cured, though more work by way of re-education is needed. Zeno receives this information with nonchalant incredulity, believing neither in the Oedipal conflict nor in its cure. What he does believe is that even disease brings its own odd kind of strength. Besides, as he notes on the novel's penultimate page, "Life is a little like disease, with its crises and periods of quiescence, its daily improvements and setbacks. But unlike other diseases life is always mortal. It admits of no cure. . . . We need something more than psychoanalysis to help us." This ought to make for a dark ending, but, somehow, it doesn't.

Although Svevo must have known that in *Confessions of Zeno* he had written an extraordinary book, for a time it appeared that he would have to stand by and watch it, too, sink without trace. Reviews in the Italian press treated it as negligible; the *Corriere della Sera* in Milan summarized the book as "a somewhat ramshackle and fragmentary novel, perhaps over-prolix, but not without psychological interest." The year before the publication of *Confessions of Zeno,* in 1922, James Joyce had published *Ulysses* and was already well on his way to becoming a heroic figure in modern literature. As Professor Gatt-Rutter puts it, "At last Joyce was in a position to help [Svevo]."

Svevo had sent Joyce a copy of his novel. Joyce wrote back to say that the novel gave him great pleasure and instructed him to send copies to T. S. Eliot, Ford Madox Ford, Gilbert Seldes, and two French writers with a special interest in Italian literature named Valéry Larbaud and Bernard Crémieux. It was Larbaud and Crémieux who were to prove the making of Svevo by devoting a special issue of the magazine *Le Navire d'Argent* to Svevo and his novel. Meanwhile, in Italy, a future Nobel Prize winner, Eugenio Montale, wrote an introductory essay in praise of Svevo for a little magazine. Now, at last, in his middle sixties, a decent modicum of fame was to come Svevo's way. Professor Gatt-Rutter measures the extent of this fame with precision: "Svevo was not to win a wide readership success until long after his death, either in Italy or abroad, but the *succès d'estime* which he won in 1926 took his books (as soon as they became available) straight into the European literary consciousness."

Having waited so long for literary glory, Svevo, when it arrived, lapped it up with uncomplicated pleasure. Giani Stuparich, a writer from Svevo's circle of friends in Trieste, wrote that "perhaps there really never was a writer who so reveled in fame and remained so uncorrupted and untroubled by it." At a PEN Club dinner given in his honor in Paris—other honorands included Ilya Ehrenburg and Isaac Babel—Ehrenburg remembers Svevo smoking one cigarette after another. "Then I remembered *Zeno,*" he writes, "and smiled involuntarily." Svevo was all for receiving more praise and was full of literary ambition. He turned out some remarkable stories and began the uncompleted book that bears the English title *Further Confessions of Zeno;* he had a play produced in Rome. When he was traveling under the name Schmitz, he was asked by a stranger, who had learned that he was from Trieste, whether he had ever met the writer Italo Svevo. After a lifetime of writing in obscurity, this was strong stuff.

An automobile accident, alas, put an end to it all. Driving from Borimo to return to Trieste, the car the family was driving in swerved in the rain into a tree. Svevo appeared only to have injured his leg, but he had suffered from high blood pressure and the accident provided a shock from which his heart never recovered. He was sixty-seven. Doubtless he should have preferred to hold the dice much longer, but at least he died after receiving some literary fame and with his powers undiminished, and there are worse times to depart.

In later years, Svevo's reputation as a writer was always a bit muzzy, and he was talked about as, variously, the Italian Kafka, or the Italian Proust, or the Italian Thomas Mann. He was, finally, the Italian Svevo. As a fellow Triestine, who knew Svevo for decades, wrote to Eugenio Montale, who had written an homage to Svevo after his death, there was a danger of over-interpreting him and turning his life into a legend. "All he had was genius," wrote the man, "no more." This genius, in the event, has proved sufficient to make Italo Svevo a writer of compelling interest today, more than sixty years after his death.

Behind Italo Svevo's genius was his refusal to accept clichés, lofty abstractions, literary and pseudo-scientific constructs—in short, all the standard explanations—as solutions to the profound puzzle that is life. There is something heroic, inspiring even, about a writer who, without reducing life's complexity or denying its terrors, never loses his delight in it. Italo Svevo, the good-natured pessimist and admirer of Schopenhauer, was such a writer. Simply because life is impossible, his writing implies, is no reason not to enjoy it. The good-natured pessimist laughs in the dark, and we, laughing with him, feel, however fleetingly, that we can glimpse the light.

Ben Hecht, the Great Hack Genius

Nowadays, as the media boys down at the ad agency are likely to tell you, the name Ben Hecht doesn't have much carry. Ben Hecht, Ben Huebsch, Ben Hur, one can easily imagine a crossword-puzzle or Trivial Pursuit addict struggling to get the name straight. Persons now of a certain age will recall Hecht as the co-author, with Charles MacArthur, of the play *The Front Page,* subsequently made into three different film versions. The movie-minded will remember that Ben Hecht was perhaps the foremost Hollywood screenwriter of his day: "the giant," as Degas said of Meissonier, "of the dwarfs"—a sentiment with which Hecht himself would probably have agreed. Fewer people figure to remember that Ben Hecht was a uniquely blacklisted screenwriter: unique in that the films he worked on were blacklisted not in America but by the British. In his day Ben Hecht was also a journalist, novelist, poet, autobiographer, and movie director, ran a television talk show, and in his spare time was a fairly serious woman chaser.

No one could ever accuse Ben Hecht of concentrating his efforts, husbanding his substance, spending his talent wisely and well. Profligate in the root and every other sense of the word, Hecht was a man whose failures are perhaps more instructive than his successes, and who—one may as well admit it at the outset—was a good deal more interesting than significant. But interesting he genuinely was. "He was a pretty devious guy with lots of different sides to him," said the movie director Howard Hawks. Hecht turned out a vast quantity of garbagey commercial writing yet seemed not particularly driven by greed or delighted by the rewards brought by money. He was never taken in by the radical politics of the 1930s—"Once a revolutionist," he noted, "always a hack"—yet risked his reputation and his earning power by openly supporting the Irgun in Mandatory Palestine from the 1940s onward (which is what gained him the enmity of the British). He was until late in life an agnostic yet was obsessed by, sometimes brutal toward, and often sentimental about, his fellow Jews.

From Ben Hecht's earliest adult years there was about him the aura of the legendary. As a young journalist in Chicago, he was a relentless scoopster, and later, he famously brought the use of novelistic detail to the newspaper column. As a short-story writer, he contributed to Margaret Anderson's *Little Review* and H. L. Mencken's *Smart Set* and *American Mercury;* the critic Harry Hansen called him "the Pagliacci of the fire escape"; and the expatriate American poet Ezra Pound, when asked why he chose not to return to his native country, replied that "there is only one intelligent man in the whole United States to talk to—Ben Hecht." Both the French director Jean-Luc Godard and the American producer David O. Selznick claimed that as a screenwriter Hecht was the best in the business, ever; and the film critic Pauline Kael, after Hecht's death, remarked that he had had a hand in roughly half the most entertaining movies produced in Hollywood. Of such stuff are legends made.

Now a biography of Ben Hecht has appeared, written by William MacAdams, a journalist who specializes in the movies, and it does indeed carry the subtitle *The Man Behind the Legend.* One is reminded of the story the pianist Oscar Levant told about meeting Greta Garbo after his friend the playwright S. N. Behrman had told her about Levant's legendary wit.

Thrown by so glamorous a movie star, Levant, upon introduction, burbled something about not quite catching her name. At this Greta Garbo, turning to Behrman, remarked, "It is better that he should remain a legend." Is the same true of Ben Hecht? Will modern biography, with its propensity for digging up hallowed ground, reveal him to have been a greatly overrated, or dreary, or finally quite disgusting character? Will it prove better that Ben Hecht, too, should remain a legend?

Hecht's parents emigrated to New York from Minsk, in southern Russia, in 1878. Joseph Hecht worked as a cutter in the garment district; in 1899, when Ben was six, the family moved to Chicago. Four years later, Joseph Hecht took his family to Racine, Wisconsin, where he began manufacturing his own line of women's dresses, which he not only designed but pushed as a salesman on the road. His wife, Sarah, sold these dresses in a shop she ran in downtown Racine. In *A Child of the Century,* his autobiography, Ben Hecht reports that his father was a delusionist. "He savored success before it came. He rolled in millions when only pennies were in the safe. . . . He never had any profits to share with his family, except for the happy smile of his daydreams."

But business failure did not issue in family unhappiness. Hecht grew up loving his parents and his large, extended, nutty Jewish family of wild uncles and half-mad aunts, among them Tante Chasha, who advised the young Benjamin to "shun small women because they had large vaginas." The central, the essential character in Hecht's youth was his mother. She, he writes, "disdained sentimentality, bristled at flattery, sneered at hypocrites, and God—Whom she respected—was less to her than honesty." It must have been from his mother that Hecht's high opinion of himself derived. "She never sought to instruct me or improve me. She deemed me moral and upright as herself, as a queen might deem her son to be of royal blood." A man confident of his mother's love, said Freud, is a conqueror. He might also, Freud neglected to add, have to become a con man. Hecht continues: "I never gave her even a hint of what sort of unroyal fellow I actually was. She would probably have loved me no less had she known. But that sort of gamble was beyond me in the boyhood days when I fashioned myself into a liar for her sake."

If con came readily enough to Hecht, so did confidence, for which throughout his life he never wanted. For some people the world represents terror, for others adventure. Ben Hecht was one of the others. To him security was never a serious concern, or even a legitimate category, and he appears never to have done anything with it in mind. He walked away from a university education, for example, having lasted three days at the University of Wisconsin; he claimed to have read most of the books in the school's Arts and Sciences prospectus, which might even have been true, since he was an omnivorous boy reader who had made his way through nineteenth-century novels, Shakespeare, world histories, and other steaming literary dishes from the autodidact's table.

As it turned out, Ben Hecht had no real need of a university. Four years in such an institution might have sufficed to kill off all that was most original and vital in him. Instead he went to that other, perhaps greater, university—let us call it, in lowercase letters, city college—the American newspaper. Apart from those who came from well-to-do, or possibly socially nervous, families, most of the best American writers of the time, from Theodore Dreiser through Ernest Hemingway, acquired their education this way. H. L. Mencken, whose family did have the money to send him to college and who was a good and conscientious student, chose instead to work on a Baltimore daily. He said the choice was between covering murders, fires, and raids on bordellos, and sitting in the stands of a stadium on a cold day in a raccoon coat waving a pennant—not, as Mencken saw it, much of a choice.

Hecht's first newspaper job was on the *Chicago Daily Jour-*

nal. He was seventeen when he began, but he already knew that he was where he was meant to be. Journalism provided, he would later write, "a world that offered no discipline, that demanded no alteration in me. It bade me to go out and look at life, devour it, enjoy it, report it. There were no responsibilities beyond enthusiasm." Hecht's initial assignment on the *Journal* was that of picture-chaser, whose task it was to come up with photographs of the recently scandalized, the violated, or violently dead: the divorced, the raped, the murdered. Since families of these victims were not generally keen to have such photographs in the press, the job of picture-chaser called for ingenuity—and a pretty good set of burglary tools. Hecht brought both to the job, along with much youthful energy. Once he smoked a family out of its house in winter by sealing off the chimney, then proceeded to enter and begin his search. Another time he shocked even his case-hardened employers by stealing a four-foot-square oil painting of a murdered Pole. "I'd go a little easy if I were you," the assistant city editor instructed him.

Before long the young Ben Hecht was made a reporter and given journalistic run of Chicago. This meant that he covered whorehouses and madhouses, courtrooms and poolrooms, hangings and fires, riots and theatricals. When he couldn't find a story, he made one up. He worked among men with odd erudition and even odder appetites who filled him in on how the world worked. He much admired Sherman Duffy, then the sports editor of the *Journal,* a horticulturalist specializing in irises, a Phi Beta Kappa, and the paper's most capacious drinker. "Socially, a journalist fits in somewhere between a whore and a bartender," Duffy once pronounced, "but spiritually he stands beside Galileo. He knows the world is round." Under men like Duffy, Hecht learned this, too. He also learned, in those early Chicago days, that he loved life—a love he could never shake. "Now after long immersion in the brutishness and lunacy of events and with the vision in me that tomorrow is a hammer swinging at the skull of man," he would write in *A Child of the Century*, "I still glow with this first love."

Although Hecht spent most of his childhood in Wisconsin, and much the greater part of his adult life in New York and Hollywood, he continues to be thought of as a Chicago writer. True enough, his years in Chicago—he worked there from 1910 until 1924, with a year out as a correspondent in Germany—did seem to form him. Chicago in those days presented the grand spectacle of the nation's most cynical politics, endless opportunities for big financial scores, and assorted social classes, ethnic groups, hustlers, marks, freaks, dorks, and yokels going at one another nearly full-time. Such a spectacle would tend to leave its imprint on a young man, especially one paid to write about it and make it seem even more lively than it already was. Chicago stirred both Ben Hecht's cynicism ("You'll find out that's the easiest thing people can do," his mentor Sherman Duffy said, "change into swine") and his sentimentality ("There was no money in his pocket, no food in his stomach," Hecht wrote in one of his many columns about the defeated in Chicago, "no hope in his heart").

Not only the city of Chicago but its newspapers were wide open: one could still print, over the story of a dentist arrested for rape, the headline "Dentist Filled Wrong Cavity"; one could still quote a man, asked on the gallows if he had anything further to say, answering, "Not at this time." Through energy and skill, Hecht was eventually promoted from reporter to columnist. His column, appearing in the *Chicago Daily News* under the rubric "One Thousand and One Afternoons," was a great success in its day. In ours the best that can be said is that it still has its moments. If much of the material now seems cliché-ridden, one does well to recall that Hecht invented many of those clichés. The work-worn mother of the young whore, the con man down on his uppers, the busted-out man of letters, the heavily hit-upon manicurist, the foreign-born laborer whose wife has deserted him—Hecht did what used to be called "human interest" (is there another kind?). He served it up, in the literary pre-cholesterol era, with plenty of schmaltz. And yet he could ruminate on why people who look too long at Lake Michigan tend to grow sad, or how Michigan Boulevard ("this Circe of streets") allows Chicagoans to dream of a more heroic life than was (or remains) available on the city's commercial streets, and do so in ways that make a pleasing ping on the truth gong even today.

Ben Hecht not only had a strong appetite for life, an abundant flow of energy, and a high threshold for chaos, such as only the top journalists possess, but he could write. He loved words; he could construct interesting sentences. He also knew that "phrases, not ideas, are the tools for recreating life." That he had also acquired a strong penchant for overwriting, let pass for now.

But then newspapers were more literary in those days. When *The New Yorker* started up in 1926, it was staffed chiefly by people—James Thurber, E. B. White, Katherine Angell, its editor Harold Ross himself—whose experience came chiefly from newspapers. The Chicago Renaissance, the curious gathering of writers that led H. L. Mencken in Baltimore to call Chicago "the literary capital of the U.S.," was made up almost exclusively of newspapermen (with the exception of Sherwood Anderson, who was first in the paint and then the advertising business). Floyd Dell, Carl Sandburg, Maxwell Bodenheim, Vachel Lindsay all put in their time on newspapers; so did such lesser-known figures as Vincent Starrett, Harry Hansen, Francis Hackett, and Burton Rascoe. Literary historians have set different dates for the Chicago Renaissance, but most agree that it began roughly with the founding in Chicago of Harriet Monroe's *Poetry, A Magazine of Verse* in 1912 (Margaret Anderson's *Little Review,* the first American magazine to run fragments of James Joyce's *Ulysses,* was also published in Chicago until it was moved to New York in 1916 and thence to

Paris in 1919, where it folded) and closed with Ben Hecht's departure for New York in the spring of 1924.

A false rebirth, the Chicago Renaissance did not come to much—"Would that our writing had been as fine as our lunches" was Hecht's own final word on the phenomenon—but while it lasted it must have been a hell of a lot of fun. It was bohemian in style and avant-garde in spirit. During these years Hecht, while continuing his newspaper job, wrote a number of novels and much poetry that took their aesthetic lead from Imagism, German Dadaism, and other European imports. All are today quite unreadable. Always prolific, always in need of a few extra bucks—he had married in 1915, at the age of twenty-two, and soon acquired the habit of living grandly—Hecht also pumped out a large number of stories for H. L. Mencken at the *Smart Set*. At the Dill Pickle Club, scene in Chicago of poetry readings, one-act plays, and other excruciating evenings of advanced culture, Hecht once engaged to debate Maxwell Bodenheim over the question "That People Who Attend Literary Debates Are Imbeciles." Hecht began by announcing that the affirmative side rested, Bodenheim followed with "You win," and the two men walked off with the evening's receipts.

One of Hecht's novels, *Fantazius Mallare* (1922), had the good fortune to be censored for obscenity and to become thereby a *cause célèbre*. It was defended (unsuccessfully) by the famous lawyer Clarence Darrow—a man who seems to have lost an inordinate number of cases—and the episode ended with Hecht being fired from his newspaper job. He next began, with Maxwell Bodenheim as associate editor, a larky, bohemian-spirited paper called the *Chicago Literary Times,* though in the last three months of its roughly sixteen-month existence it was known as *Ben Hecht's Chicago Literary Times*. Hecht and Bodenheim would also use each other as characters in novels. Bodenheim, in his, wrote of his Hecht character:

He wanted to be an affluent, luxurious, commercial panderer, tossing off flashy bilge with his tongue in his cheek, and also an unruly, brilliant, slashing intellect in more serious talk and creations . . . he wanted to be supreme in both camps, commercial and artistic, without pledging allegiance to either one. . . .

It was only after Hecht left Chicago for New York that this split in him between the serious and the commercial—the one writing for the show, the other for the dough—became an issue in his career. The need for money was now there. He had shed his first wife in Chicago, and taken the woman who would be his second (and final) wife with him to New York. He had debts, fairly large ones, and a taste for high living; at a minimum he had no wish to be mindful of those small expenses— for rent, clothes, food, and drink—over which most people are bound to spend their lives worrying. By now, after producing six novels, he knew that he could not score with a best-seller, and so he turned his supple talent to the theater.

Did he also know that he simply was not a very good novelist? *Erik Dorn* (1921) is Hecht's best-known work from his Chicago years, and it is a mess, a compendium of its author's strengths and more voluminous weaknesses. Hecht's epigram-making power is among his strengths—he would always be adept at one-liners—and it is nicely displayed in this novel. " 'The press,' Dorn once remarked, 'is a blind old cat yowling on a treadmill.' " And: "It's the only art we've developed in America—overdressing." And (Dorn speaking again): " 'I advise you to complicate life with ideals. . . . A conscience is an immediate annoyance, whereas ideals are charming procrastinations.' " Although the character Erik Dorn is given the same physique and job as Hecht's friend Sherman Duffy, he is otherwise clearly intended autobiographically; and being the autobiographically based character of a somewhat overheated writer in his late twenties, Dorn is also, as who will be surprised, the epitome of an *Übermensch*.

The novel has no shortage of overwriting (snow is "a thick white lattice [which] raised itself from the streets against the darkness"); hernia-causing heavy thinking ("The race can survive only as long as its weakest survive"); hopelessly ornate vocabulary ("the love affair of a Baptist angel and the hamadryad daughter of a Babayaga"); and an inflation of the chief character that results in unconscious comedy (" 'You are too big for love to hold,' " says Dorn's ever obsequious lover). No need to summarize the plot of *Erik Dorn,* for there really is none. Instead there is a rather unpersuasive, self-justifying account of the breakup of Dorn / Hecht's marriage and another of Dorn / Hecht's days as a correspondent in Germany after the war. " 'I admire revolution,' " says Dorn in this portion of the book. " 'Why? Because it diverts.' " Maybe for Dorn, but not, sad to report, for the reader.

What is of interest in *Erik Dorn* are the occasional remarks on what I take to be Hecht's own self-acknowledged shortcomings as a serious writer. Many of these are made by means of the contrast between Dorn and Warren Lockwood, a character based on Sherwood Anderson, of whom Dorn says: " 'The fellow's content to write. I'm not. He's found his way of saying what's in him, getting rid of his energies and love. I haven't.' " Lockwood says of Dorn: " 'He's the kind of man who knows too damn much and don't [*sic*] believe anything.' " And Dorn later says of himself: " 'My damned cleverness puts me beyond artists who find a destination for their energies in the struggle to achieve the thing with which I began.' "

But outside books, in so-called real life, Sherwood Anderson was not buying any of this. In a letter to Hecht, quoted in William McAdams's biography, he wrote:

> . . . why do you have to bluff and bluff and impress me. Why are you so unsure of yourself. You can write man. You don't have to convince me of anything.

Return now to Maxwell Bodenheim's novel *Duke Herring,* where of his Ben Hecht character Bodenheim writes:

> His favorite boast was that he intended to accumulate a million dollars in the following year, and though this goal had eluded him so far, he did amass thousands of dollars annually through the sale of meretricious short stories, shallowly clever plays with short runs, and epileptic novels, whose malicious brilliance always held one eye cocked toward the adding machine in the publisher's office.

Bodenheim's portrait is far from free of malice, but it does underscore the issue around which people have always considered Hecht's career. This issue can be formulated simply enough: was Ben Hecht a sellout? The term "sellout" has a dishonorable history. It originated in the enclosed, always at least slightly paranoid, world of American Communism, where any divergence from the party line sent from Moscow was felt to constitute a desertion, or selling-out, of true principles. Transferred to the realm of art, the term meant betrayal of one's talent for the sake of either money or popular success or both. The assumption was that buyers were everywhere: Hollywood and Henry Luce, Edmund Wilson remarked in the 1930s, were the two great enemies of talent in our time.

The notion inevitably lent a strong note of inner drama to artistic careers. Anyone who wrote for the movies, or Broadway, or the news magazines, or at one point *The New Yorker* (where Edmund Wilson himself eventually found a financially comfortable home), or later television, had to consider the possibility that he was selling out. It was of course also and always a self-congratulatory possibility, implying that one had something high and fine and serious in oneself to sell. Writers pumping out zippy prose for *Time,* or pilots for television sitcoms, could think that but for their staggering alimony payments or their children's private-school bills they might be devoting themselves to the deep art (great novel, elegant book of poems, powerful play) that lay buried within them. Such was the interior scenario that permitted one to cry—or, in some instances, drink—all the way to the bank.

But the line between what passed for selling out and what for artistic purity began in time to blur. The year 1964 may have been a watershed, when Mary McCarthy, with *The Group,* and Saul Bellow, with *Herzog,* both formerly small-public writers, had novels on the best-seller list. Soon authors one was accustomed to read exclusively in *Partisan Review, Kenyon Review,* and other intellectual journals began to appear with some regularity in *Esquire, Playboy,* even *Vogue,* where for a time the historian Arthur Schlesinger, Jr., served as movie critic. Writers of the most extravagant intellectual pretensions—Harold Rosenberg, Susan Sontag, George Steiner—became frequent contributors to *The New Yorker.* Others went off to Hollywood without bad conscience, and why should they have done otherwise during a period—the middle sixties through the middle to late seventies—when movies were themselves awarded great (if finally false) intellectual prestige? As the distinction between highbrow and middlebrow art, along with that between elite and mass culture, itself began to blur, the entire notion of selling out began to seem questionable. Not that genuine talent, of literary and other kinds, did not continue to be deflected by the palmy prospects of big money and popular success. It did and does. Only nowadays no one seems much to notice.

In Ben Hecht's day people noticed—and perhaps few more so than Hecht himself. Through his work there runs an almost continuous criticism of the kind of writing he spent the better part of his own career doing, and this criticism contains more than an implicit suggestion of self-contempt. Soon after Hecht arrived in New York, for example, he began writing for the Broadway stage. At first he did so with moderate success; and then, in *The Front Page* (1928), with smashing success. Yet in a most peculiar novel entitled *A Jew in Love* (1931), Hecht could say the following about Broadway writers little different from himself:

> These Jews [who dominate the night life of Broadway], decadent, humanless, with minds sharp and strident as banjos, offer through the mask of their perversities the last blatant sob of Jewish culture. They sing of mothers, babies, faraway homelands, of breaking hearts and lost joys, but to this eternal scenario of middle-class art they add a set of histrionics filched from the dwindling synagogues. Their songs quiver with self-pity, are full of the unscrupulous wailings of ancient Jew grief tricked out in Negro, Russian, and Oriental rhythms, and pounded home with the rabbinical slobber of an atonement prayer.

Further qualification does not make it better. Maybe rather worse:

> Their wit, sterile with disillusion, cackling, derisive, full of epithet, proclaims them clowns and from behind their clownish front they sell Jewish tears at a fancy profit; weep into the coffee cups and wine glasses of the Gentiles and label the performance Broadway. Their doltish amours, their slapstick repartee and ragbag talents are chronicled by scores of journalists who follow them around like a procession of Pepyses.

Hecht spent still more of his life working on movies, about which he had even darker views. The movies, in his opinion, were quite simply the enemy of art; they were for the people, and the People (Hecht used a capital P), from the Renaissance on, always knew that Art (with a capital A) wasn't for them. "When you think of all the books, statues, paintings, oratorios, symphonies, cantos, etcetera that the People have never been able to enjoy, you can begin to understand their excitement over the Movies [caps again]," Hecht wrote in a story, "The Missing Idol."

> The Movies are their Cellinis and Angelos, their Shakespeares and Shelleys. They control all the plots and elect their own geniuses. And, like some international Lorenzo the Magnificent, they distribute rewards undreamed of by their ancient enemies—the Artists.

In yet another story, "The Heavenly Choir," this one about a man who makes a fortune by recognizing and then realizing the potential of radio for selling products, Hecht considers the advantages of so potent a mass medium for conveying the beauties of art to the beastly masses. Could not radio bring about "the long-awaited liaison between Beauty and the Beast"? Not, it turns out, in Hecht's view—not radio, nor the movies, nor any other medium. When Beauty lay down with the Beast, he notes, "it was not the Beast that underwent any marked alteration, but, as always, Beauty. For Beauty lying down with the Beast too often grows a bit cockeyed and contemptible herself." The attitude expressed here is rather more like T. S. Eliot than like the man who churned out more than seventy-odd credited and uncredited movie scripts.

Although Hecht was to write for Broadway sporadically over the years, it is his work for the movies that has been best remembered. Or perhaps it is more accurate to say, for which *he* is best remembered. Given the zany nature of collaboration in Hollywood, it is not always easy to know who wrote what. Of the producer in his story "The Missing Idol," Hecht observes: "Some eight different scripts were prepared by a dozen different authors, all of them of considerable renown (for it was Mr. Kolisher's principle to discard only the best)." This same Kolisher, an amalgam of the Jewish mogul-tyrants of the early Hollywood years, actually cuts out a scene from the movie he has produced on the life of Jesus that was inserted into the film by God Himself.

Hecht seems to have taken little pride in most of the work he did for Hollywood, apart from the extraordinary speed with which he could turn it out and the size of the fees he could demand for it. That he is best remembered for the work about which he cared least is an irony unlikely to have escaped him.

But then much having to do with Ben Hecht's career in Hollywood is suffused with irony, ambiguity, comedy, mis-understanding. Even Hecht's Hollywood beginnings had a touch of madcap comedy about them. "Will you accept three hundred per week to work for Paramount Pictures?" Herman Mankiewicz wired him. "All expenses paid. The three hundred is peanuts. Millions are to be grabbed out here and your com-petition is idiots. Don't let this get around." Before joining the Hollywood gold rush, Mankiewicz had been a second-line drama critic for the *New York Times* and, as befitted a man who had put in his time at the round table at the Algonquin, had famously remarked that "Los Angeles is a great place to live if you're an orange." (Mankiewicz's own claim to fame is the screenplay for *Citizen Kane,* though there is controversy over how much of it he actually wrote.) It was Mankiewicz who, serving briefly as Hecht's screenwriting tutor, explained to him that in a novel "the hero can lay ten girls and marry a virgin for a finish," whereas in the movies "the hero, as well the heroine, has to be a virgin."

Not that Hecht, a quick study if ever there was one, needed a tutor for long. His first screenplay, *Underworld,* written for a movie directed by Josef von Sternberg, won one of the sixteen Oscars presented at the first Academy Awards ceremony in 1929. Hecht claimed that when he first saw what Sternberg had done to his script he felt as if attacked by *mal de mer,* but he none-theless accepted his Oscar and the higher fees that winning it brought. In *Talking Pictures: Screenwriters in the American Cin-ema,* Richard Corliss writes that not only was Ben Hecht typical of Hollywood screenwriters; he was, in effect, *the* Hollywood screenwriter:

> Nearly every facet of that talented and haunted breed—from the streetcorner wit and inexhaustible articulateness to the sense of compromise and feelings of artistic frustration—can be found in Hecht's dazzlingly contradictory career. Indeed, it can be said without too much exaggeration that Hecht personifies Hollywood itself: a jumble of talent, cynical and overpaid; most successful when he was least ambitious; often failing when he mistook sentimentality for seriousness, racy, superficial, vital, and *American.*

The legendary Ben Hecht stories have to do with making large sums for little labor, or taking on big jobs without anything like serious preparation—and just because the stories are legendary does not mean they are untrue. He worked on the screenplay for *Gone with the Wind,* for example, without having read the novel; other people summarized it for him as he went along. To two stenographers he dictated a full screenplay for the producer Samuel Goldwyn in a single day, for which he (and, on this project, his partner Charles MacArthur) received $25,000 and 3.5 percent of the gross. He worked on the script of *Scarface* for Howard Hughes (then running a Hollywood studio) for $1,000 a day; since Hughes's solvency was then in doubt, Hecht added a provision that he be paid after each day's work, sharply at six o'clock, and he was. Throughout his career he did a vast amount of script doctoring, usually for heavy fees, since he was generally called in at a point of crisis. ("Whenever my father was in trouble," Sam Goldwyn, Jr., told the biographer A. Scott Berg, "he went to Ben Hecht.") David O. Selznick said: "Ben in my opinion was the greatest of all scenario writers." This is an opinion with which Joseph Stalin, apparently, would have agreed. After seeing Hecht and Howard

Hawks's movie about Pancho Villa (*Viva Villa!*), William McAdams reports, Stalin "was prepared to send a battleship to fetch Hecht back to the USSR but Hecht refused when he learned that the film Stalin wanted to make would only be shown in the USSR." The stuff of which legends are made.

Hecht had few illusions about the standing of writers in Hollywood. According to an unnamed screenwriter quoted in Neal Gabler's *An Empire of Their Own*, "Jews are the writers of the business and writers are the Jews of the business." Hecht noted that "at a Hollywood party, there would be forty or fifty celebrities, but I don't think you'd find any writers, possibly one, at the most two. They were never invited out in mixed company. They were treated much like butlers, socially." The service writers provided for the powerhouse studio owner, according to Hecht, was to make him feel, through his power, somehow cultured: "The higher the class of talent he could tell what to do and how to do it, the more giddily cultured he could feel himself." Yet Hecht also understood that these often coarse men (one of them, Harry Cohn, used to say that he had "a foolproof device for deciding whether a picture is good or bad—if my ass squirms, it's bad; if my ass doesn't squirm, it's good") were not without their own strange but real talents. Samuel Goldwyn, though often inarticulate, could be oddly stimulating: he "filled the room with wonderful panic and beat at your mind like a man in front of a slot machine, shaking it for a jackpot."

But the main point, which Hecht rightly seems never for a moment to have forgotten, was to get as much money out of these men as one could. And there was lots to get. In an amusing story entitled "Concerning a Woman of Sin," Hecht sets out to explain why in Hollywood so many mediocre people are paid so much money. It is owing, he claims, to the agent, "for it was the agent who first uncovered the Basic Principle of Hollywood":

This is that the Pharaohs who run the studios measure their own greatness by the amount of money they are able to spend. There is, in fact, no other activity open to them. The Pharaoh who can spend the most money on stars and geniuses becomes automatically the most dazzling figure in the cinema capital. Thus the competition to run the studios into bankruptcy is an extremely hot one. That all the studios are not quickly ruined by these royal extravagances is due to a single fact out of their control. . . . The popularity of the movies has become almost equal to that of sex.

In the same story, Hecht has a Hollywood Pharaoh, one Jerome B. Cobb—a character modeled, it was said, on Louis B. Mayer, who never forgave Hecht—buy and invest millions on a screenplay that he does not know has been written by a nine-year-old girl bred on *True Confessions* and *True Love Stories*. " 'God, I love this town,' " says the agent who sells the screenplay.

Yet there is evidence that, despite his contempt for the chances of producing even halfway serious work in Hollywood, Hecht more than once made the effort. On a few occasions, he was even able to direct his own scripts, using the artful cinematographer Lee Garmes; and in one instance, *Angels over Broadway* (1940), he served as writer, director, and producer. I have never seen this movie, but even fanatical moviegoers do not rate it all that highly. Leonard Maltin gives it two and a half stars, saying that "it's just too offbeat (and pleased with itself about it)"; Richard Corliss advises, "Read the script, don't see the movie."

Those who study movies with an intensity worthy of oncological CAT scans profess to see many a hallmark, even a comprehensive vision, in a Ben Hecht script. They speak of the gusto, style, satire, cynicism that he could get into his writing; one even uses the phrase "Hechtian man." Corliss writes: "It is his crisp, frenetic, sensational prose and dialogue style that elevates his work above that of the dozens of other reporters who streamed west to cover and exploit Hollywood's biggest 'story': the talkie revolution."

Yet when one reads down Hecht's filmography, noting that he had a hand in *Gilda, Spellbound, Wuthering Heights,* one also notes that his was not the only hand. Corliss rightly remarks that any true assessment awaits discovery of which movies Hecht substantially wrote and what were the contributions of the men who collaborated with him. "For, just as Hecht is often ignored in discussions of Hawks or Hitchcock," Corliss says, "so are Charles MacArthur, Charles Lederer, and Gene Fowler forgotten on those rare occasions when Hecht's work is seriously appraised."

"I can't help it," the agent in "Concerning a Woman of Sin" frequently tells his clients. "I guess I'm not a judge of movies. I hate 'em too much." Did Ben Hecht, too, hate them? Hard to say. Surely, he hated Hollywood, which he regarded as a combination gold and salt mine. "Anyone with a good memory for clichés and unafraid to write like a child can bat out a superb movie in a few days," he remarked in his autobiography. He nowhere that I know speaks of a love for the movies; and one never gets from him the standard nonsense either about the special glories of the cinematic art or (as we have seen) about the movies as the great art of democracy.

Then why did Hecht, caring so little for the movies or for the money, work so hard at his writing? Ben Hecht had a boredom problem. As he grew older, he maintained, it was boredom that caused him to seek out "the ego disturbances which women can provide"—as pretty a euphemism for skirt-chasing as one is likely to find. Without what he called "the menace of ennui," he said that he would never have written for the theater or the movies. "Work itself, swift, half-mindless and exhausting, a happy drug," was what he required. And as long as he was working, why not make it pay off?

One believes Hecht when he says, in his autobiography, "the money I earned meant almost nothing." Certainly he found efficient ways of ridding himself of it: keeping a staff of servants that included a driver, a trainer, a cook, and, when in Hollywood, an additional kitchen-maid staff of three; toss in alimony, heavy taxes, two homes (one in Nyack, New York, the other in Oceanside, California), and other sideline amusements, and you can understand how in 1954 Hecht could write that for the past twenty-five years he had been "without a bank balance, owning neither stocks nor bonds, always broke, always battling my way out of debt, without money laid up for a rainy day and without even an insurance policy to provide for my family after I die. . . ." Such were the personal finances of the man known to be one of the great money-writers of his day.

But Hecht's career in the movies was simplicity itself next to his relationship with the Jews and with his own Jewishness. Not that he ever had great qualms about being a Jew. For the most part, it seems to have been a matter of indifference to him. His first wife was not Jewish, his second wife was. Formal religion appears to have played hardly any part in his upbringing. His was not the world of Irving Howe's fathers—socialist, labor union, left-wing idealistic—but instead was predominantly small business, or at any rate small-business-minded. In *A Child of the Century,* though he insists that "my family remained like a homeland in my heart," he also insists that "I have never lived 'as a Jew' or even among Jews."

The only one of Hecht's novels that still has the power, if not to enchant, then to disturb, *A Jew in Love,* would be instantly labeled anti-Semitic had it not been written by a Jew. The novel begins: "Jo Boshere (born Abe Nussbaum) was a man of thirty—a dark-skinned little Jew with a vulturous face, a reedy body, and a sense of posture." The descriptions that follow do not become more charitable.

Jo Boshere (the character is said to have been modeled in part on the publisher Horace Liveright, but there must be even more of Ben Hecht in him) is an intellectual and a successful

New York publisher. But above all he is an egotist with a romantic conception of himself and an unappeasable need to dominate others. *A Jew in Love* has to do with Boshere's unrelenting attempts at such domination, particularly over women. Otherwise, it is plotless. One reads on with mild interest and strong disgust about such characters as the Broadway journalist Gabe Solomon (a miniature portrait of George Jessel), whose "talk of women would have abashed a gynecologist." But more interesting than this sort of thing is Jo Boshere's violent rejection of Zionism. Boshere tells his sister that she is a Zionist " 'because you hate Jews, you're ashamed of being a Jew.' " And in the same conversation, he says:

> I know what this Jew Consciousness is, because I once had it. It's the consciousness of not being a normal social human being. Just as the taint of homosexuality gives a man the miserable feeling of not being entirely a man. Once in a while a Jew comes to light whose ego is stronger than his label, who has enough brains, character, genius to lift his soul out of the God damn slimy stranglehold of Jew consciousness.

The attack on Zionism in *A Jew in Love* is notable because roughly ten years later—owing to Adolf Hitler—Hecht would be on his way not only to becoming a Zionist but, as he candidly put it, a "propagandist" for the Irgun, the Jewish organization in Palestine pledged to remove the British from the region—by violence, among other means—and to form a Jewish state on both banks of the Jordan.

Hecht became involved with the Irgun through a column he wrote for the New York daily *PM* on the reluctance of important American Jews to speak out strongly against Hitler. Having been politicized by Hitler for the first time in his life, Hecht was shamed and outraged by this reluctance. He was driven to even greater rage when he learned that Joseph Kennedy, then ambassador to England, had warned the powerful figures in

Hollywood to remain silent on the persecution of the Jews in Europe lest the war against Germany (in which the United States was anyway not yet engaged) come to seem "a Jewish war." To make an elaborate story simple, in response to this column, two members of the Irgun called on Hecht one afternoon to seek his support for their program to save the Jews of Europe by sending them to Palestine.

Although so far as is known Hecht saved no European Jews through his work with the Irgun, and although he did not advance the Irgun cause in any finally lasting way, he nevertheless proved very strong in the line of agitprop. He wrote a series of inflammatory newspaper ads variously attacking the State Department, Franklin Delano Roosevelt, and all the major American Jewish organizations ("Hang and burn, but be quiet, Jews / The world is busy with other news," ran the refrain to one such effort). He also organized a star-laden pageant about the Jews of Europe entitled *We Will Never Die* that filled Madison Square Garden two nights running and then went on to play Washington, Philadelphia, Boston, Chicago, St. Louis, and Los Angeles.

Hecht's actions were not without personal consequences. He turned out to have a knack for making enemies almost as great as his knack for making money—and in not much smaller numbers. Because of his Irgun connection, movies on which he worked were blacklisted throughout the United Kingdom. In Hollywood, never known as the capital of courage, he was now offered only half his former fees for screenplays, and then only if he would agree to work without credit. None of this slowed him down or caused him to reconsider his commitment. The famous cynic had turned into a passionate idealist.

Passionate, but not particularly well-informed. *Perfidy* (1961), Hecht's book about the postwar trial of Rudolf Kastner, the man who on behalf of the Jewish Agency negotiated with Adolf Eichmann for the lives of Hungarian Jews, shows both his strengths and weaknesses as a writer. No need to rehearse the intricate details of the Kastner trial here, but suffice it to say that Hecht, in 1961, used his book on the trial to reassert the Irgun line. This line held that during the war Chaim Weizmann, David Ben-Gurion, Moshe Sharett, and other leaders of the Labor Party in Mandatory Palestine, of which Kastner was a high-ranking member, betrayed the Jews of Europe in order to gain concessions from the British, who at the time wanted no great influx of Jews into Palestine lest it upset relations with the oil-rich Arabs. In defending Kastner after the war, Hecht argues, Israel's government—that is to say, the Labor Party—was in reality defending itself.

It is a devastating charge—that the state of Israel was built on the willingness of its leaders to allow the Jews of Europe to die—and one that Hecht, for all his considerable skill at marshaling evidence and his powers of phrasemaking and caricature, finally cannot make stick. Lucy S. Dawidowicz, the historian, remarked that Hecht, being "neither a historian nor a chronicler," got a great deal askew, and she patiently sorted out his historical confusions, adding that she was disappointed to find that Hecht, "as a novelist and playwright," did not have more compassion for the complex plight of the people he was writing about.

But Ben Hecht was less a novelist and playwright than he was a journalist and a screenwriter, professions that emphasize the sensational and melodramatic over the complexities of history and the troubling mysteries of the human heart. After a life of writing, Ben Hecht was disqualified from writing well about the one subject in the world—perhaps the only subject in the world—he had come really to care about. Talent long misused has a way of wreaking its own revenge.

Still, after one has chopped away at his work there remains something impressive about Ben Hecht. Such was his energy, his appetite for life, his odd courage, his self-awareness even of his own weaknesses, that he seems to require being judged by other than the usual standards. He was himself much more interesting than any character he ever created for the stage, screen, or fiction. Saying this is less a tribute to him as a writer than it is to him as an extraordinary man.

Ben Hecht died of a heart attack in his apartment in Manhattan on April 18, 1964, at the age of seventy-one. At the funeral service eulogies were read by Menachem Begin and Peter Bergson (both formerly of the Irgun), and the actors Luther Adler and George Jessel. It is comforting to recall that, back in the 1920s, when Jessel attempted to collaborate with Hecht on a play, Hecht told his friend Gene Fowler that he never met anyone "so eager to flaunt his stupidity, low-grade human values, and jackass vanities to the world." There is no business like show business.

Hazlitt's Passions

I N *The Birth of the Modern,* his panoramic history of world society between 1815 and 1830, Paul Johnson refers to William Hazlitt as "a truly great writer, perhaps the first truly modern writer in England." Johnson, working an extremely crowded canvas, never gets around to saying just why he thinks Hazlitt is perhaps the first truly modern writer in England. Yet his is an assertion that gains immediate assent; it feels, somehow, right. Among Hazlitt's contemporaries, Coleridge was certainly more wide-ranging, Wordsworth in his particular line deeper, Lamb more winning. But Hazlitt, for a multiplicity of reasons, feels more like our contemporary, which is another way of saying that he seems more modern.

Hazlitt, Our Contemporary—it sounds, I fear, like one of those rather dreary lectures read in a patches-on-the-elbows brown tweed jacket from yellowing paper, in which one attempts to make the case for the relevance of a writer whose work is obviously deader than a Rudy Vallee lyric. I should like to go at things from a different angle, since Hazlitt's writings are for the most part clearly and vibrantly alive, and attempt to show that his modernity, which is very real, does not always honor either him or us.

Hazlitt was an extraordinary writer, yet he was also a writer who had more flaws than the normal man. This might not matter but for the fact that much of what he wrote itself insists on doing away with the distinction between the man and the writer in him. He could be deeply stupid on some subjects and quite close-minded on others. He was awkward, passionate, shy, brilliant, and often foolish, a man of absolute integrity who was probably a genius, the word we fall back upon to explain talent of a power for which we cannot otherwise account. As Hazlitt said apropos of Cobbett, so more pertinently may one say apropos of Hazlitt: "It is easy to describe second-rate talents, because they fall into a class and enlist under a standard: but first-rate powers defy classification or comparison, and can be defined only by themselves."

About William Hazlitt's own talent there cannot be much argument. Paul Johnson notes that Hazlitt "has strong claims to be considered the first British art critic of significance," and Kenneth Clark called him "the best English critic before Ruskin." Thomas McFarland, in his book *Romantic Cruxes* (1988), writes that "he may be the finest pure critic of literature that English culture has brought forth"; and by pure critic Professor McFarland means a critic who does not write out of a moral or cultural program—he cites Matthew Arnold and T. S. Eliot—but rather deals directly with works of literary art. Keats marveled at Hazlitt's unerring "depth of Taste" in all things having to do with art. "We are mighty fine fellows," Robert Louis Stevenson once remarked to William Henley, "but we cannot write like William Hazlitt." P. G. Patmore, describing his friend Hazlitt's mental quickness, wrote: "Hazlitt could perceive and describe 'at sight' the characteristics of anything without any previous study or knowledge whatever, but by a species of intellectual intuition." Hazlitt himself said that he "never worshiped the Echo," by which he meant that he came by his views and opinions absolutely on his own.

William Hazlitt was born in dissent—no minor biographical fact—and died in discouragement. His was a short, disorderly, tumultuous, sad, and finally immensely impressive life. He lived fifty-two years, wrote several books, made many enemies, and died both broke and, it is fair to say, brokenhearted. Perhaps no writer of his quality was attacked so viciously in his lifetime as he, though he must have valued his enemies, at any rate to the extent of never for a moment having wanted them on his side, and he certainly came near giving as good as he got. (Keats held that Hazlitt "is your only good damner, and if ever I am damn'd—damn me if I shouldn't like him to damn me.") Perpetually harried by financial worry, he wrote nearly all his works under pressure and on the run. He produced brilliant criticism under the constraints of journalism; in his familiar essays he produced literature almost by the way, and into the bargain much improved the form by opening it up to more serious subjects. He was tactless, abrasive, dogmatic, obsessive, in many ways quite hopeless, and yet one of the few authentic heroes of literature.

William Hazlitt was born in 1778, the third surviving child of a dissenting minister of the Unitarian church who was never to live in anything approaching comfort. Upon his father's death, Hazlitt referred to him as his anchor, but the Reverend William Hazlitt was an anchor that bobbed about a good bit, going from one inadequate living to another. He had favored the side of America during the Revolutionary War, and this cost him favor and hence tenure at various churches he served. In 1783, he sailed for New England with his family, and after four years and much disappointment and illness discovered that the New World was not the solution either. Hazlitt wrote that he remembered "once hearing a shrewd man say that he would never send a son of his to my father, lest the boy should be so schooled in truth as to be disqualified from getting his living in the world." Hazlitt's father knew, and soon so would his son, that the things he most honored the world cared for but little. "One image," his son wrote, "he had set up in his mind: it was Truth. One idol he had: it was Justice. One aspiration he had: it was Liberty." Hazlitt loved his father, and wrote that "when I think of the thing I am, I know that all I most care to remember in what I have been and done, has come to me through him."

Between the ages of nine and fifteen Hazlitt lived, quite happily, in the market town of Wem, in Shropshire, on the border of Wales, where his father had his modest clerical living. At fifteen, he was sent off to the New College at Hackney, a Unitarian academy, on a scholarship that stipulated he study for the ministry. But before that the great formative event of Hazlitt's youth, and indeed of his life, had taken place: the Revolution in France. He was eleven when it occurred, but it would be at the center of much that he thought and did in the forty-one years left to him. "It seems to me," he later wrote, "as if I had set out in life with the French Revolution, and as if all that had happened before that were but a dream." And all afterwards, perhaps, something of a nightmare. "The light of the Revolution, dabbled though it now was with drops of crimson gore, still circled my head like a glory," he wrote. Hazlitt not only had his politics early fixed by the French Revolution, but early, too, learned the seriousness of politics. In 1791, the Birmingham home of the dissenting minister Joseph Priestely, a friend of Hazlitt's father, was robbed and burned by a mob goaded into action by Priestley's reply in opposition to Edmund Burke's *Reflections on the French Revolution*. In politics, people of that day, as we should say today, played hardball.

By fifteen, then, Hazlitt had a nearly fully formed politics of his own. When the French Revolution went bloody, he blamed it on England's war against France, which he thought whipped up French hatred at the mere thought that the old monarchy, with all its abuses, might be restored. He saw the great, the central, the indispensable problem of his time as that of the need to free mankind from the tyranny of monarchy, which was, in his view, everywhere an obstacle to progress, hope, decency, and truth. His politics having been formed over the problem of liberty—to him in his certitude it was neither a question nor an issue—his friends and enemies followed there-from. On his deathbed, he worried about the Bourbons regaining the throne of France.

The adolescent Hazlitt must have been a bit of a prig, moral-political division, so passionate, so full of politics was he, like those children who have been reading *The Nation* or the *National Review* since the age of eleven and have all the answers at four-teen. In his forties, Hazlitt wrote to his son that it was "my misfortune perhaps to be bred up among Dissenters, who look with too jaundiced an eye at others and set too high a value on their own peculiar pretensions." The youthful Hazlitt was a perfect little red-hot Jacobin. But—a crucial but—he was not that alone. He was a boy whose imagination was fired by Bible stories, whose heart was stirred by *Tom Jones,* whose life was permanently altered at seeing Sarah Siddons play Lady Mac-beth, whose timbers were shivered by reading Schiller's trag-edy *The Robbers*. Even as a boy he was used to reasoning things out on his own. He had considerable powers of reflection, and would go off by himself and think things through. An opinion once taken on he seldom deserted.

What Hazlitt did desert, not long after his entrance at New College, was the notion of following his father into the Uni-tarian ministry. For one thing, the world at large had great allure for him. For another, though Hazlitt would always remain respectful of the religion of his father, he was too set in his own difficult ways ever to hope to find and keep a living as a minister. He must early have sensed the oddity of his own personality. The man who would one day be known as one of the great practitioners of the essay was not, for example, able to write assigned essays in school; writing was already too important for him to expend it upon trivial classroom work.

Hazlitt had a temperament problem, which did not allow him to be other than he was, and an integrity problem, which did not allow him to change himself for anyone. Normally, these might be considered happy problems. But they turned out to be both the making of him and the cause behind much of his difficulty in life. Sensing his faith and his reason in conflict, Hazlitt decided that, if he was not to live with contradiction in his own soul, he would have to forgo a career in the ministry, even if this would cause his father sadness. "You have done everything in your power to make your son a wise and useful man," the head of the New College at Hackney wrote to Hazlitt's father upon William's announcing his not wishing to become a minister, which meant his withdrawal from the school, "and may we not hope that he will be a wise and useful man in some other sphere of life? What that other sphere will be I cannot point out. . . ."

Neither for a good while could Hazlitt. He left school at seventeen. Dissenters were not then allowed admission to Oxford or Cambridge. For a painfully long spell he worked away—with excruciating slowness—on an ambitious essay that set out to prove that men were not inherently selfish. "For many years of my life I did nothing but think," he later wrote. "I had nothing else to do but solve some knotty point, or dip into some abstruse author, or look into the sky, or wander by the pebbled sea-side. . . ." As so often with Hazlitt, who was wont to find the bad in the good and the good in the bad, he also later wrote, referring to these years: "I can write fast enough now. Am I better than I was then? Oh no! One truth discovered, one pang of regret at not being able to express it, is better than all the fluency and flippancy in the world."

He lived with his father or sometimes with his older brother John, a painter of miniatures. Owing to a family connection, he knew William Godwin, author of *Political Justice,* through whom he came to meet Coleridge, one of the decisive influences on his life. Working on his essay, which he titled "On the Disinterestedness of the Human Mind," he wrote to his father to report that he has "ventured to look at high things." He also let his father know that the work proceeded slowly, though he felt he wrote more easily than he once did. Around this time he discovered the prose of Edmund Burke, which he later allowed that he had tried half a dozen times, unsuccessfully, to describe, but which quite simply blew him away. Reading Rousseau, which he also did around this time, made for another Eureka moment in his life. Burke and Rousseau, two altogether contradictory figures, were further influences on Hazlitt.

The essay on the disinterestedness of the human mind, begun in 1796, was eventually published in 1805 under the title *An Essay on the Principles of Human Action*. In between times, Hazlitt set out on a new career, that of portrait painter, which, after his early failures at religion and philosophy, was to prove his third false start. The landscape painter Philipp Hackert once told Goethe, when the poet showed an interest in painting, that "you have talent, but you are incompetent." Something of the reverse was true of Hazlitt, who was competent but, by his own high reckoning, without talent. Stanley Jones, in his excellent biography of Hazlitt, remarks of Hazlitt's painting that in it he "never threw off the paralysis of imitation nor moved forward to the frontiers of originality that he later successfully crossed in his writing." Hazlitt had several commissions to do portraits, but his perfectionism joined to his strong sense of his own inadequacy—Titian, Rembrandt, and above all Raphael were among his models—stood in the way of his completing many of them.

Although Hazlitt failed as a painter, his interest in painting made him all the better as a writer. It not only made him an impressive art critic—he was among the first to recognize the genius in the early paintings of Turner and splendid at describing all that went on in a painting—but it gave something akin to a painterly quality to his prose generally. ("A genuine criticism," he would later write, "should, as I take it, reflect the colours, the light and shade, the soul and body of a work.") Something similar might be said about the ultimate utility of his failure at philosophy. He would describe his own prose as endowed with the thought of a metaphysician and the tact of a painter. Of course, if one succeeds, as Hazlitt later did with his essays, then in retrospect it seems as if even one's starkest failures have contributed to that success.

Not everyone would agree about the degree of Hazlitt's success as an essayist. As a useful corrective to the all but locked-in reputation of Hazlitt as great essayist, one can scarcely do better than to read Leslie Stephen on Hazlitt. In a brilliant criticism in *Hours in a Library,* Stephen says straight away that he thinks Hazlitt not capable of "the highest kind of excellence." He thinks him a man "whose personal and public sentiments [were] so invariably blended in his mind that neither he nor anybody else could have analyzed their composition." He thinks Hazlitt a man wrapped within multiple masks of "cunning egotism," and that it does not in any way redound to his credit that all his life he held to the same views: "A man whose opinions at fifty are his opinions at fourteen has opinions of very little value," he writes. (Hazlitt had claimed that "a person who forgets all the sentiments and principles to which he was most attached at nineteen can have no sentiments ever after worth being attached to.") His politics, moreover, "were simply the expression, in a generalized form, of his intense feeling of personality." He was "no genuine democrat," for no party was good enough for him, and, writes Stephen, "he hates 'both mobs,' or in other words, the great mass of the human race." ("Mankind are a herd of knaves and fools," Hazlitt wrote. "It is necessary to join the crowd, or get out of their way, in order not to be trampled to death by them.") Everything that Leslie Stephen says is dead-on, devastatingly true, but, somehow, it isn't quite the whole truth.

Precocious and yet a slow starter, Hazlitt dabbled and dithered. He spent four months in Paris, copying the great masters in the Louvre. He wrote a grammar, did abridgments, edited and completed the memoirs of Thomas Holcroft, published an attack on Malthus's theory of population, continued to take on commissions for portraits, and functioned as something of an odd-jobs man in the arts. But he didn't really get underway until financial pressure had set in in earnest, and once it had it never left him. Henceforth, writes Catherine Macdonald Maclean, one of Hazlitt's earlier biographers, "never in all his life . . . even on his deathbed, was he to know respite from financial anxiety and literary labour."

It was his marriage, in 1808 (when he was thirty), and the subsequent birth of two sons—one of whom died in infancy—that forced Hazlitt to strap on the harness of more regular employment. As Leslie Stephen rightly put it, Hazlitt, in his thirties, with a wife and son, "at last discovered the great secret of the literary profession, that a clever man can write when he has to write or starve." Not his marriage but the need to support it by steady literary production was the making of William Hazlitt, who, given his dreaminess, his penchant for brooding at great length over subjects, his perfectionism, might have ended an obscure footnote in literary history: a sometimes sullen chap who used from time to time to show up at Charles and Mary Lamb's "Wednesdays" and occasionally explode into passionate utterance over politics.

As for Hazlitt's marriage—it was the first of two—it is part of his history with women, and a grievously sad history that is. William Hazlitt, to put it very gently, had a woman problem and an especial talent for looking to the wrong women to solve it. His friend P. G. Patmore said that he never knew Hazlitt when he wasn't in love; and part of the difficulty here is that he seems never to have been in love with the women he married. "A cynic," wrote Paul Elmer More, "might point a moral from the fact that the only events of Hazlitt's life which were utterly free from the intrusion of passion were his two ventures into matrimony." Hazlitt's taste in women, but not in wives, ran to country girls or chambermaids—"humble beauties," as he referred to them—in any event, to women well below him in intellectual sophistication. Poor, foolish man, he wanted both to idealize women and to make them over; his *Liber Amoris,* which caused such a scandal in its day and seems so pathetic in ours, carries the subtitle *The New Pygmalion.* Much the largest portion of "On the Conduct of Life; or Advice to a School-Boy," Hazlitt's essay in the form of a letter to his son, is about women, and all of it is cautionary, ending with his telling the boy that "Love turned away his face from me." He meant that it did so his life long.

In his diary, Henry Crabb Robinson claimed that "like other gross sensualists, [Hazlitt] had a horror of the society of ladies, especially of smart and handsome and modest young women." A gross sensualist seems off the mark. Any consideration of Hazlitt's tortured relations with women has to go back to what is known as the incident at Keswick. This incident—misadventure? contretemps?—took place in the Lake District in 1803, when Hazlitt was twenty-five and an itinerant portrait painter. Nobody knows precisely what happened, but the best guess is that Hazlitt made advances to a village girl who not only repulsed his advances but set the village toughs on him, so that Hazlitt was fortunate to escape with his life. "The minx made a fool of him," Stanley Jones economically puts it, "and the episode ended in ludicrous catastrophe and ignominious flight."

No further mention need have been made of it, except that Wordsworth, in response to Hazlitt's review of the *Excursion* in later years, loosed the story, with colorful details added, in the long-standing method of going after the character of the critic when you can't bear the criticism. With the Keswick story as ammunition, Wordsworth tried to ruin Hazlitt's friendship with Charles Lamb, Henry Crabb Robinson, and others. More devastatingly, however, it was later used by Hazlitt's quite unscrupulous enemies on *Blackwood's Magazine,* where, in painting him as a brute out of control, the story was used as political propaganda against him. (These same enemies claimed Hazlitt was a drunk and referred, famously in that day, to "pimpled Hazlitt," though Hazlitt was apparently not more than a regular drinker in a hard-drinking age and had a clear complexion.) Wordsworth must have first heard the story of the incident at Keswick from Coleridge, who later claimed that Hazlitt, on the run, came to him, and that he gave him "all the money I had in the world, and the very shoes off my feet to escape over the mountains." That detail about the shoes off his feet makes one wonder what Coleridge might have been smoking the day he retold it.

The relationship between Hazlitt and Coleridge is a story in itself, and one that scholars of romanticism are apparently not yet agreed upon. Thomas McFarland, for example, in *Romantic Cruxes,* thinks the relationship central: he flicks a wet noodle at David Bromwich, who, in his book *Hazlitt: The Mind of a Critic* (1983), seeks to minimize its importance. One thing is clear, and this is that Hazlitt returned again and again to the subject of Coleridge, and in his work would cross a crowded street to spit on his shoes. In his essay "On Depth and Superficiality," for example, Hazlitt refers to Coleridge as "a great but useless thinker." In "On the Prose Style of Poets," he claims Coleridge's prose "swelling and turgid—everlastingly aiming to be greater than his subject; filling his fancy with fumes and vapours in the pangs and throes of miraculous parturition, and bringing forth only *still-births.*" But in his *Lectures on the English Poets,* Hazlitt says that Coleridge is "the only person I ever knew who answered to the idea of a man of genius," adding that "his thoughts did not seem to come with labour and effort; but as if borne on the gusts of genius, and as if the wings of his imagination lifted him from off his feet."

Hazlitt's most impressive portrait of Coleridge appears in his essay—one of his very best—"My First Acquaintance with Poets." This essay was written in 1823, long after the two men, Hazlitt and Coleridge, had complicated their relationship to the point of alienation, and it is a tribute to the generosity in

Hazlitt that he recalls with such large-hearted fidelity how impressed he initially was by Coleridge and how important he once was to him. Hazlitt was not yet twenty, Coleridge twenty-six upon their first meeting, and the occasion was a sermon Coleridge was to deliver at a Unitarian church in Shrewsbury, ten miles' distance from Wem. Hazlitt made the trek on muddy roads in January to hear him, for Coleridge was already a celebrated figure. Coleridge launched into his sermon "like an eagle dallying with the wind." Listening to him. Hazlitt heard "the music of the spheres. Poetry and Philosophy had met together." And in one of those passionate, slit-your-own-gut-open sentences, sometimes telling you rather more than you wish to know, Hazlitt, early in the essay, acknowledges his intellectual debt to Coleridge:

> My soul has indeed remained in its original bondage, dark, obscure, with longings infinite and unsatisfied; my heart, shut up in the prison-house of this rude clay, has never found, nor will it ever find, a heart to speak to; but that my understanding also did not remain dumb and brutish, or at length found a language to express itself, I owe to Coleridge.

In *The Spirit of the Age,* Hazlitt takes the machine gun to Coleridge, leaving an intellectual corpse riddled with holes. The theme of this essay is how Coleridge blew everything by talking away his gifts. "If Mr. Coleridge had not been the most impressive talker of his age, he would probably have been the finest writer; but he lays down his pen to make sure of an auditor, and mortgages the admiration of posterity for the stare of an idler." Hazlitt notes the tangential quality of Coleridge's mind, its dilatoriness and digressiveness. As a prose writer, Coleridge's mind was often the scene of a bloody battlefield in which prolixity battled obscurity to a dead draw. Or, as Hazlitt puts it in a single shot that plunks three balls into the pocket: "If our author's poetry is inferior to his conversation, his prose is utterly abortive." Yet in his *Lectures on the English Poets,* published seven years earlier, Hazlitt notes of Coleridge that "he is the only person from whom I ever learnt anything." He then adds: "There is one thing he could learn from me in return, but *that* he has not."

Hazlitt does not say what that "one thing" is, but a reasonable guess would be that what Coleridge could have learned from him was political constancy. Everything that Hazlitt says about Coleridge is true enough, but behind it, even so, was the feeling of betrayal that he felt against Coleridge and the Lake Poets—Wordsworth and Southey chief among them. To put it in one unkind, very modern word that he himself does not use, Hazlitt thought that they were "sellouts." Hazlitt was above party politics, was not a Whig and certainly not a Tory, but he did think himself a member of the party of liberty ("of all the loose Terms in the world," wrote Edmund Burke, "Liberty is the most indefinite"), and it was this party that the Lake Poets had, in Hazlitt's mind, deserted.

Hazlitt, as Professor Jones remarks, "took public events hard," and none harder than those connected with France and that nation's revolution. It won't do to press the analogy too hard, but in several respects Hazlitt was to the French Revolution what many modern intellectuals—they still even now walk the streets—have been to the Russian Revolution. Unlike these contemporary counterparts, Hazlitt did not attempt to cover up revolutionary bloodshed, though he did sometimes justify it. Where opinions on the French Revolution are divided, Hazlitt is never quite to be trusted. He allows for Wordsworth's originality and power, but you sense him pulling back from a larger appreciation of him because Wordsworth later concluded that there might just have been other dawns when it was perhaps even more blissful to be alive and more heavenly to be young than that of the dawn of the French Revolution. Hazlitt will allow that Southey's "prose-style can scarcely be too much praised," add that "he is steady in his attachments, and is a man in many particulars admirable, and in all respectable," but cannot forbear closing: "his political inconsistency alone excepted." Over the subject of Napoleon, Hazlitt was able to get into a fight with Charles Lamb for Lamb's political indifference, which, given the latter's famous good nature, apparently wasn't an easy thing to do.

William Hazlitt was in that category of persons who, in order to like them, one has *really* to like them. I happen to be in the category of persons who *really* like Hazlitt, but one has to admit that he must have been a very great trial to his friends and a delight to his enemies in the large exposed target he gave them. Geoffrey Keynes, his bibliographer, has remarked that no one who reads Hazlitt remains neutral about him. Virginia Woolf wrote that "no man could read him and maintain a simple and uncompounded idea of him." In "On Depth and Superficiality," Hazlitt wrote of himself:

> I am not, in the ordinary acceptation of the term, a *good-natured man;* that is, many things annoy me besides what interferes with my own ease and interest. I hate a lie; a piece of injustice wounds me to the quick, though nothing but the report of it reach me. Therefore I have made many enemies and few friends; for the public know nothing of well-wishers, and keep a wary eye on those that would reform them.

That is fair enough, even if a bit self-glorifying, but Hazlitt, being Hazlitt, cannot of course let it go at that, and so must close the passage by zinging Coleridge, who "used to complain of my irascibility in this respect, and not without reason. Would that he had possessed a little of my tenaciousness and jealousy of temper; and then, with his eloquence to paint the wrong, and acuteness to detect it, his country and the cause of liberty might not have fallen without a struggle." His loyal friend Lamb said of Hazlitt: "I wish he would not quarrel with the world at the rate he does; but the reconciliation must be effected by himself, and I despair of living to see that day." Nor would he.

But in order to admire Hazlitt you don't even have to like him. His talent, which was doubtless inseparable from his crotchets, his intellectual aggression, his thorny nature, simply commands admiration. "The virtue of his work," wrote Paul Elmer More, "lies not in his analytic criticism, which can be studied apart from his own language, but in the fusion of passion and insight." That is precisely wherein Hazlitt's power lay. In most writing, passion brings opacity and obscurity in its wake; the angrier one becomes the cloudier and more muddled one's thought. With Hazlitt passion in argument seemed to result in even greater penetration. He was easily the greatest polemicist of his own highly polemical age, and perhaps one of the greatest polemicists in all of intellectual history.

Professor Jones makes the useful point that Hazlitt's polemical exchanges were more than mere argument against enemies, and they would be of no interest if they were. ("Nothing," as Cyril Connolly once rightly put it, "ages like hate.") Instead they were a mode of thought that in his hands turned argument into literature. Professor Jones writes:

> All such exchanges are evidence of [Hazlitt's] disinclination to pontificate, of his dislike of the egotistical; his views are commonly defined dramatically, on specific occasions, by opposition to those of others. Ultimately grounded in principle, they are immediately polemical; they manifest his leaning towards the marriage of the general and the particular, of the abstract and the concrete, of the universal and the individual. He saw the clash of argument as a means of escaping from self-communion into the dramatic and so of acceding to universality, a means of liberation from the sterility of the immured self.

The Hazlitt of the fiery polemics, of the impassioned art criticism, of the jaunty writing about the theater, the literary critic, the familiar essayist, and the writer who finally belonged to literature had first to serve his apprenticeship in daily journalism. This he began in 1812, at the age of thirty-four, covering the House of Commons for the *Morning Chronicle,* for which he received his first steady income, four guineas a week. His own obvious talent soon freed him from the gallery of the House of Commons and the tedium of reporting the empty utterances of politicians, and he was set to writing drama criticism, which he did surpassingly well. Presently he was writing on other subjects—art, literature, politics—and his writing began to appear in other papers, including Leigh Hunt's *Examiner* and the *Times.* Fearless, confident, knowing his own views and not much concerned with the views of others, except to topple them, he was among the first critics to recognize and support the genius of Turner in painting, Edmund Kean in acting, Keats in poetry.

Hazlitt's earlier prose was that of a toy philosopher, stiff, slow, awkward, the writing of a student imitating quite well but nonetheless still imitating a metaphysician. But now he realized that if he was to make his way as a journalist, he would have to write as a man writing to men; he sought to achieve what, in his essay "On the Prose Style of Poets," he called the "genuine master-spirit of the prose-writer," which was "the tone of lively sensible conversation." He later told the painter James Northcote that, when he began to write for the newspapers, he "had not till then been in the habit of writing at all, or had been a long time about it; but I perceived that with the necessity, the fluency came. Something I did, *took;* and I was called upon to do a number of things all at once. I was in the middle of the stream, and must sink or swim." He swam, as we now know, not merely well but like an Olympian.

Hazlitt's essays have immense flow. He once compared Edmund Burke's prose to a diamond. "It has always appeared to me that the most perfect prose-style, the most powerful, the most dazzling, the most daring, that which went the nearest to the verge of poetry, and yet never fell over, was Burke's." If Burke's prose was comparable to a diamond, Hazlitt's own prose most closely resembles a cascade, a waterfall, a body of beautiful white water, a rapids. One has to attend closely to all that he says, as one does to every stretch of white water, for crags, tree limbs, and odd debris float past. Surprises are contained in the codas of sentences, as for example in the following from the paragraphs on the poet Tim Moore in *The Spirit of the Age:* "Or modern poetry in its retrograde progress comes at last to be constructed on the principle of the modern opera, where an attempt is made to gratify every sense at every instant, and where the understanding alone is insulted and the heart mocked." Formulations come fast and furious: "the want of passion is but another name for the want of sympathy and imagination"; "mere good-nature (or what passes in the world for such) is often no better than indolent selfishness"; "the principle of life and motion is, after all, the primary condition of genius"; and "there is nothing so tormenting as the affectation of ease and freedom from affection." As for invective, he could serve it up, vast quantities of it, at typhoon intensity. Of William Gifford, he wrote:

> Mr. Gifford was originally bred to some handicraft. He afterwards contrived to learn Latin, and was for some time an usher in a school, till he became a tutor in a nobleman's family. The low-bred, self-taught man, the pedant, and the dependent on the great, contribute to form the Editor of the *Quarterly Review.* He is admirably qualified for this situation, which he has held for some years, by a happy combination of defects, natural and acquired; and in the event of his death it will be difficult to provide him a suitable successor.

"I think what I feel," Hazlitt noted in the preface to his *View of the English Stage;* "I say what I think." Many people say what they think they feel, but to say it just so is the trick. "To write a genuine familiar or truly English style," Hazlitt wrote in "On Familiar Style," "is to write as any one would speak in common conversation, who had a thorough command and choice of words, or who could discourse with ease, force, and perspicuity, setting aside all pedantic and oratorical flourishes." This Hazlitt could do, consummately.

Still, he was better at the sentence than at the paragraph, and better at the paragraph than at the complete composition. Much in Hazlitt is unshapely; many of his essays—even his superior ones—end up in the air, which is to say arbitrarily, unsatisfactorily, badly. In explanation, if not extenuation, of this, it is well to remember that Hazlitt turned out his prose at a fierce rate. At one point he went off to his country cottage at Winterslow where in a month's time he wrote nine full essays. One is inclined to wonder what he might have done had he worked more slowly. But then one is brought up by the recollection of Karl Kraus's withering aphorism about a journalist being someone who, given time, writes worse.

It was a point of pride with Hazlitt, as it ought to be with any writer capable of honestly saying as much, that "I never wrote a line that licked the dust." At the same time, he did not mind kicking a goodly amount of dust over his friends. Hazlitt was eager to write for the *Edinburgh Review,* for example; that magazine paid him well, and its editor, Francis Jeffrey, on more than one occasion proved his friend by bailing him out of financial difficulty and on others did a good bit in his service by cleaning up his prose for publication. But Hazlitt did not see this as in any way debarring him from writing the following in *The Spirit of the Age:*

> The faults of the *Edinburgh Review* arise out of the very consciousness of critical and logical power. In political questions it relies too little on the broad basis of liberty and humanity, enters too much into mere dry formalities, deals too often in *moot-points,* and descends too readily to a sort of special-pleading in

defence of *home* truths and natural feelings. In matters of taste and criticism, its tone is sometimes apt to be supercilious and *cavalier* from its habitual faculty of analysing defects and beauties according to given principles, from its quickness in deciding, from its facility in illustrating its views. In this latter department it has been guilty of some capital oversights.

Which Hazlitt doesn't in the least mind going on to point out and elaborate upon.

For a powerfully intelligent man Hazlitt had a powerfully high quotient of naiveté. He did not so much overrate the truth as he overrated its powers of persuasion. It is so that the truth will set you free, but you ought to know that, enunciated tactlessly enough, it is likely to leave you no shortage of enemies to have to deal with in your freedom. "All the former part of my life I was treated as a cipher," Hazlitt wrote when he began to be well known, "and since I have got into notice, I have been set upon as a wild beast." He was accused of dishonesty, of writing ungrammatically, of being brutish with women. It was his politics, with his take-no-hostages polemical style, that set the wolves on his trail. Professor Jones puts the case well: "The reputation he gained by his criticism was constantly jeopardized by the enmity stirred up by his political writings, and it was owing to these that he was pursued with abuse for the rest of his life, and abandoned to disparagement and neglect after his death."

That Hazlitt was so harassed by enemies makes all the stranger his decision to publish, in 1823, *Liber Amoris*, his account of his dreary love affair with Sarah Walker, one of the daughters of the tailor in whose home he, Hazlitt, took lodgings in London after he and his wife had separated (though not yet divorced). Hazlitt's love affair with Sarah Walker was his midlife *Human Bondage*, played without a clubfoot but, in reading Hazlitt's own pathetic account of it, with something one is inclined to view as close to a clubhead. Sarah Walker was nine-teen, Hazlitt forty-two, when, in 1820, they first met. She brought him his morning tea, and allowed him to caress her before she set out on her other morning rounds. "I cannot describe the weakness of mind to which she has reduced me," he wrote, in a letter that appears in the thinly fictionalized account provided in *Liber Amoris*. But he was wrong; the book does describe, all too clearly, how stupefied he became.

Many are the views of Hazlitt's sad unconsummated love for Sarah Walker. The best face put upon it is perhaps that drawn by Professor Gerald Lahey, the editor of a scholarly edition of *Liber Amoris* (New York University Press, 1980), who sees in it "a parable of the entire Romantic period trying to come to terms with its flawed visionary conception of reality." Yet one wonders if this isn't what the English used to call over-egging the pudding. What Hazlitt seems to have done is vastly over-rate a not very attractive young woman from the workaday lower-middle class. The painter Benjamin Haydon nicely caught Hazlitt's situation: "the girl really excited in him a pure, devoted and intense love. His imagination clothed her with that virtue which her affected modesty induced him to believe in, and he is really in love with an ideal perfection, which has no existence but in his own mind." Hazlitt told the young woman he would divorce his wife for her; and in fact he did, striking the modern literary note in being perhaps the first famous writer to be under the gun for alimony and child support.

Hazlitt seems to have told everybody he saw about his infat-uation with and ill-treatment at the hands of this young woman, including his eleven-year-old son. In fact, she didn't especially treat him ill, unless one is ready to call ill-treatment her refusal to go along with his fantasies about her. She was quite correct, when he asked her to come live with him, to tell him "that it would be no use if I did [for] you would always be hankering after what could never be." She was rightly put off with his talking so much about her not only to friends but to her own family. At one point he went so far as to assign another man the task of attempting to seduce Sarah in order to test her moral standards. (She passed.) In short, Hazlitt made a pest, a jerk, a royal fool of himself.

One thing to make a fool of yourself, another to publish an account of your foolishness, which Hazlitt did in *Liber Amoris.* Why did he do it? Some contend that he needed to do so to burn Sarah Walker out of his system; some that it took great courage for him to do so; some that having done so proved Hazlitt no gentleman, which, when it came to women, it is probably fair to say that he wasn't, having, in this realm, only three settings on his emotional dial: worshipful, vengeful, and indifferent. My own guess is that he probably did so because he was the pure type of the writer, as we have come to know it in our day, who cannot let anything like a serious experience go unwritten about.

Liber Amoris, despite occasional touching passages, does not have any real standing as literature. What is of interest about it is that for its time it marks a new candor in confession—and a very modern candor in its unpleasantness, its lack of interest in redemption, and, one must add, its self-deception. Hazlitt knows that he has made a fool of himself, but blames this alternately on the guile of Sarah Walker, on the overwhelming power of love, on everyone and everything but himself. *Liber Amoris* feels very much a predecessor of the Norman Mailer, Robert Lowell school of sloppy confession without remorse that has had a strong run in recent decades.

Was Hazlitt, in *Liber Amoris,* attempting to emulate Montaigne, whose "inexpressible frankness and sincerity, as well as power" he much admired, Montaigne in whom there "is no attempt at imposition or concealment, no juggling tricks or solemn mouthing, no laboured attempts at proving himself always in the right, and every body else in the wrong"? If so, he made a rum job of it. This most gifted of English essayists, persistent student of human nature though he wished to be, seems to have had little talent for introspection. He was nearly always in battle, always agitated, always angry, a paranoid who made his own real enemies. He was too much the moralizer and too little the moralist. Montaigne looked to himself to understand the world. Hazlitt looked at the world in puzzlement over why it did not understand him. Not quite the same thing.

Yet the pathetic affair with Sarah Walker seems to have increased Hazlitt's strength as a writer. When he published *Characteristics, In the Manner of La Rochefoucauld's Maxims* in 1823, the year after his affair with Sarah Walker, he noted that the only point on which he dared to claim comparison with the French master was that neither of them had a theory to maintain. But, in fact, after the events recounted in *Liber Amoris* Hazlitt's essays took on a greater richness owing to an implicit theory. This had to do with his renewed appreciation of the mixed qualities of motives in life, of the element of irrationality often in even the most mundane of human affairs. In his essay "The Main-Chance," he set out to show how small a part reason plays in life next to parts played by passion and sheer human oddity. In "My First Acquaintance with Poets," he remarks upon the exhaustion of enjoyment and hope as one grows older: "As we taste the pleasures of life, their spirit evaporates, the sense palls; and nothing is left but the phantoms, the lifeless shadows of what *has been*!" Hazlitt suffered but not for nothing.

Although Hazlitt claimed that Sarah Walker was "my life" and that "it is gone from me, and I am grown spectral," he still had expenses to meet, his writing was much in demand by newspapers and magazines, his political passions were undimmed, he had his son's future to think about, he wished to see the Louvre again and Italy for the first time. He even remarried, unsuccessfully, and in the last years of his life set out on a mammoth biography of Napoleon, his hero of heroes, a work of justification which he had hoped would be his own greatest literary monument. (When Napoleon went down at Waterloo, Hazlitt took the defeat personally. "He seemed prostrated in mind and body," Benjamin Haydon wrote, "he walked about unwashed, unshaved, hardly sober by day and always intoxicated by night, literally, without exaggeration, for weeks; until at length, wakening as it were from a stupor, he at once left off all stimulating liquors, and never touched them after.") He wrote the brilliant pieces that make up *The Spirit of the Age* in 1825, but melancholy suffuses his later familiar essays. "I turn back from the world that has deceived me," he wrote in "A Farewell to Essay-Writing," "to nature that has lent it a false beauty, and that keeps up the illusions of the past." In this same essay he remarks upon our indifference to that which is worthy in life, caught up as we are in "the present vexation, the future disappointment."

Hazlitt had a sufficiency of his own present vexations and future disappointments: the many attacks on him (William Gifford's *Quarterly* claimed his essays oozed a trail of "slime and filth"); the sadness of his relations with women; the endless broken friendships; the dismantling of the French Revolution and the defeat of Napoleon—nothing, it must have seemed to him, worked out. All that was left to him was pride in his integrity and the surprising number of his books (when young he "had no suspicion that I should ever become a voluminous writer"). He once said that he took pleasure in life only from paintings, books, and nature. Notably absent from this list is people. Referring to the writer in general but to himself more pertinently, he wrote that "the coldness and jealousy of his friends not unfrequently keep pace with the rancour of his enemies."

Not long before he died—of stomach cancer, in September of 1830—this almost instinctively disputatious man asked only three things of life before he departed it: that he die with someone he loved beside him, that he have some evidence of hope for mankind of the sort that the French Revolution gave him when young, and that he leave "some sterling work" behind him. Only the latter, as we now know, came about. Still this often disagreeable man, whose truculent personality rendered him lonely most of his days, can never be removed from the small but courageous company of those writers who knew not how to lie or to fudge, but could only convey the complicated truths they found in their own troubled hearts.

The Short Happy Life of Robert Louis Stevenson

"TALENT WITHOUT GENIUS isn't much," remarked Valéry, "but genius without talent is nothing whatever." Robert Louis Stevenson had talent in abundance, and he was touched by genius, but how often the two combined in his work remains a question not easily answered. Stevenson (1850–1894) will soon be dead for fully a century, yet his literary reputation is still unsettled. William Lyon Phelps thought that he belonged with Fielding and Scott, Dickens and George Eliot, Meredith and Hardy. Henry James acclaimed him "an exquisite literary talent." Yet George Moore, despite the enduring popularity of *Treasure Island* and *Kidnapped,* said that Stevenson "imagined no human soul, and he invented no story that anyone will remember," while John Jay Chapman accused him of merely aping his literary betters with the result that he was nothing more than "the most extraordinary mimic that has ever appeared in literature." Long moldering in his tomb atop Mount Vaea in Samoa, Stevenson himself may not feel the question of his literary reputation a very pressing one. But to those of us who have a minor mania (if not a full-blown rage) for order, and to whom Robert Louis Stevenson's career and accomplishments have seemed as gray and cloudy as a February afternoon in his native city of Edinburgh, the attempt to place Stevenson has seemed long overdue.

Stevenson's was one of those large, flowing talents of the kind that always seem to leave lots of spillage in the form of unfinished books and finished books that probably ought never to have been begun. (He claimed to have made ten or twelve serious runs at writing a novel before completing his first, *Treasure Island,* at age thirty-one.) I mention the spillage only because Stevenson was working from a cracked glass to begin with, by which I mean that his health was wretched. From early childhood he suffered upper respiratory ailments—even today it is not completely certain that it was tuberculosis—that left him wracked by coughs and ruined by fevers; he grew up bone-thin and slightly bug-eyed, perpetually susceptible to illness, disease, and every physical disaster. In Augustus Saint-Gaudens's memorial medallion of Stevenson, the subject is working, characteristically, in bed, a blanket over his propped up knees, a pad on his lap, a cigarette in hand.

While Stevenson was still alive, Henry James, in an essay in the *Century Magazine,* did not scruple to remark that "it adds immensely to the interest of volumes through which there draws so strong a current of life to know that they are not only the work of an invalid, but have largely been written in bed, in dreary 'health resorts,' in the intervals of sharp attacks." In "Aes Triplex," one of Stevenson's best essays, he said, well knowing whereof he spoke, that the human body, viewed pathologically, is "a mere bag of petards." In the same essay, written when he was twenty-eight, Stevenson wrote that "it is better to lose health like a spendthrift than to waste it like a miser . . . better to live and be done with it, than to die daily in the sickroom." He himself died, after putting in a morning's writing, giving a French lesson to his stepgrandchild, and helping his wife prepare a mayonnaise, in Samoa, of a cerebral hemorrhage, at the age of forty-four.

Stevenson loved life, and with an intensity perhaps granted only to those who are denied full participation in it. He took life not as a struggle but as an adventure. Although he might from time to time complain of one or another of his many maladies "unhorsing" him, he always rode on, viewing himself, in Walt Whitman's phrase, one of "freedom's athletes." A literary man to the tips of his long and emaciated fingers, he nonetheless despised all that he thought deadening in literary culture. He disliked realism of the kind made famous by Zola for its heavy emphasis on technique, and of it wrote: "Those who like death have their innings today with art that is like mahogany and horsehair furniture, solid, true, serious and dead as Caesar." A good part of his enthusiasm for Whitman was owing to the fact that the American poet struck "the brave, vivacious note," building courage in his readers and defeating indifference. Again and again the appetite for life, with its small but regular pleasures, comes through in Stevenson. Let theologians and philosophers argue whether life gives preparation for death or death gives meaning to life; as far as Stevenson was concerned, "a good meal and a bottle of wine is an answer to most standard works upon the question."

How explain this inexorably cheerful view of life on the part of a man whose early years supplied the perfect conditions to breed a prince of grievance and gloom? As a first datum, take the city of Edinburgh. In a brief essay on Edinburgh, the city of his birth and upbringing, Stevenson noted that "the weather is raw and boisterous in winter, shifty and ungenial in summer, and a downright meteorological purgatory in the spring." In Edinburgh, Stevenson adds, "the delicate die early, and I, as a survivor, among bleak winds and plumping rain, have been sometimes tempted to envy them their fate." To grow up in fragile health—and Stevenson's respiratory ailments were discovered when he was but two years old—in a city of tempests, lashing rain, and perpetual damp was an early indication that life's blessings are not evenly distributed at birth.

Stevenson's parents, in their odd differences of temperament, were themselves a mixed blessing. Owing to his mother's poor health—his illness is said to have been inherited from her—he was an only child in a house that sometimes took on the air of a sickroom. He probably also inherited his cheerful disposition from his mother, for she was intrepidly optimistic, to the point of sailing off to the South Seas with her son and his family when she was well along in life. His father offset his mother's jolly optimism with regular plunges into a deep melancholia that biographers tend to chalk up to the grim pessimism found at the heart of Calvinism. An engineer specializing in lighthouses, as his father before him had been, Thomas Stevenson was known for his work in optics as applied to lighthouse illumination. The Stevensons never bothered to patent any of their inventions; holding government appointments, they felt that in good conscience these patents were owed to the nation. But then conscience was ever of concern to Stevenson's father, whose sense of his own unworthiness his son called "morbid." Stevenson loved his father, and remarked upon his droll humor and the charm of his talk. When the small boy Louis, as Stevenson was called, would wake from one of his many nightmares, it was his father who would arrive to soothe him with tales of adventure that he had made up.

In later life Stevenson wrote plaintively to a friend that "the children of lovers are orphans." Certainly his parents loved each other, and his mother's illness—while he was a child she was nearly an invalid—may have diverted attention from himself. One of the chief effects of this was to throw Louis, like many another English or Scottish middle-class child, into the hands of a nurse-nanny; in his case into the hands of a woman named Alison Cunningham. "Cummy," as he called her, was very keen for religion, and kept her highly imaginative charge nicely revved up with fire-and-brimstone stories. "He was from a child an ardent and uncomfortable dreamer," Stevenson wrote of himself in an essay called "A Chapter on Dreams." His troubled dreams about losing salvation often combined with dreams about failure in school, so that in a standard nightmare, "he seemed to himself to stand before the Great White Throne; he was called on, poor little devil, to recite some form of words, on which his destiny depended; his tongue stuck, his memory was blank, hell gaped for him; and he would awake, clinging to the curtain-rod with his knees to his chin."

Yet the picture I seem to be limning of a sickly child with a febrile imagination set aflame by religious fantasies, a boy so crushable that he therefore must easily be crushed, is a distortion. He may have been ill but he wasn't unhappy; his illness merely forced him to live more in his mind than other children, devising games to be played upon the counterpane, inventing stories to pass the secluded days. The future author of *Treasure Island* and *Kidnapped* was already working at his apprenticeship. He had powerful inner resources—and powerful outer ones, too. Boy and man, Robert Louis Stevenson was one tough and willful hombre. So far as one can make out, he never finally did anything in life that he really didn't want to do.

No weakling could have defied his father, as Stevenson did, on the two things in life that were most important to him: religion and work. As he grew older, Stevenson began to feel more acutely the chill of Scottish Calvinism. The deadliness of Edinburgh sabbaths with their pervasive restrictions seemed pointless to him and the emphasis on sin, as construed in his father's home and church, only made sin itself more enticing. As a young man, Stevenson, partly out of a distaste for polite Edinburgh society, began to develop a taste for bohemianism and low life. He ran with his cousin Bob Stevenson, three years his elder, who is said to have taught him, in the words of the editor W. E. Henley, to "think and drink." Out of a mixture of curiosity and desire, he had a go at the brothels of Victorian Edinburgh. With his cousin and a few selected cronies, he hung around the shadier pubs in the city's slummier neighborhoods, where his companions, as he later noted, were "seamen, chimney-sweeps, and thieves." "My circle," he added, "was being continually changed by the action of the police magistrate."

In a fit of foolish candor when he was twenty-two, Stevenson proclaimed to his father that he was agnostic. "You have rendered my whole life a failure," Thomas Stevenson replied. Life at home afterward was dour; Stevenson likened it to "a house in which somebody is awaiting burial." In one of their several arguments about religion, Stevenson's father shot out at him: "A poor end for all my tenderness. I have worked for you and gone out of my way for you and the end of it is that I find you in opposition to the Lord Jesus Christ—I find everything gone." Loving his father, Stevenson did not find this easy to take. (Good old guilt, the gift that never stops giving.) Yet he stood his ground, muting his opinions when not absolutely swallowing them, in later life abiding quietly by his father's religious rules when in his company, so that in time religion no longer stood, boglike, between them.

It was assumed that Stevenson would follow the profession of his grandfather, his father, and his uncles—that of lighthouse engineer. At the University of Edinburgh he studied for a scientific degree. When only twenty he wrote and read a paper entitled "A New Form of Intermittent Light" before the Royal Scottish Society of Arts. Doubtless he could have succeeded well enough as an engineer, yet, as he made plain in his essay "The Education of an Engineer," the work, for all its satisfactions, was not for him: "It takes a man into the open air; it keeps him hanging about harbour-sides, which is the richest form of idling; it carries him to wild islands; it gives him a taste of the genial dangers of the sea; it supplies him with dexterities to exercise; it makes demands upon his ingenuity; it will cure him of any taste (if ever he had one) for the miserable life of cities." All well enough, but "when it has done so, it carries him back and shuts him in an office!" Stevenson briefly describes the drudgeries of the inside-work aspects of engineering—applying "long-sighted eyes to the petty niceties of drawing" and so forth. Yet there is something a bit disingenuous about it all, for long before he had determined to be a writer. When he apprised his father of this, Thomas Stevenson took the decision with calm resignation, asking only that his son now study law so that, should the always precarious trade of literature not provide a steady income, he would have something to fall back upon. (With their use of parental guilt and of law school as a fallback position, these Scottish Calvinists begin to sound more and more like the Jews of nineteenth-century Protestantism.) Stevenson did in fact study law, though less than passionately, and even passed the bar, though he never practiced.

Robert Louis Stevenson went from a childhood of inventing stories in his head to an adolescence of scribbling away at them in earnest. An indifferent student, he served a most serious novitiate in literature. Janet Adam Smith, in her slender volume on Stevenson in the Duckworth Great Lives series, writes of him at university: "His real work, he considered, was to learn how to write. As he walked about Edinburgh and the Pentlands he was always trying to find the right words for what he saw, and jotting them down in a notebook. Whenever he read something that seemed particularly well or neatly said, he sat down and imitated the author." Careful words set out in a confident cadence were his aim, and if he did not instantly achieve it on the page he apparently could unfailingly bring it off in conversation. The wife of an Edinburgh engineering professor described the youthful Stevenson as this boy "who talked as Charles Lamb wrote, this young Heine with the Scottish accent." Sidney Colvin, Professor of Fine Arts at Cambridge, who first met him when Stevenson was twenty-two, has left the following account of the charms of his conversation:

> He would begin no matter how—perhaps with a jest at some absurd adventure of his own, perhaps with the recitation, in his vibrating voice and full of Scotch accent, of some snatch of poetry

that was haunting him, perhaps with a rhapsody of analytic delight over some minute accident of beauty or expressiveness that had struck him in man, woman, child, or external nature. And forthwith the floodgates would be opened, and the talk would stream on in endless, never importunate, flood and variety. A hundred fictitious characters would be invented and launched on their imaginary careers; a hundred ingenious problems of conduct and cases of honor would be set and solved; romantic voyages would be planned and followed out in vision, with a thousand incidents; the possibilities of life and art would be illuminated with searchlights of bewildering range and penetration, sober argument and high poetic eloquence alternating with coruscations of insanely apposite slang . . . and all the while an atmosphere of goodwill diffusing itself from the speaker, a glow of eager benignity and affectionate laughter emanating from his presence, till every one about him seemed to catch something of his gift and inspiration. This sympathetic power of inspiring others was the special and distinguishing note of Stevenson's conversation.

Stevenson's clothes did not attract less attention than his conversation. He dressed out of the let-'er-rip school of haberdashery, partly owing to the fact that his father kept him on a short financial leash. He might wear a red sash round his waist, an odd colorful piece of cloth at his throat, a rumpled velveteen jacket, a shawl across his thin shoulders, some strange piece of headgear. He wore his hair long and none too clean, a thick and somewhat droopy mustache depended from his upper lip, a wispy imperial from his lower. He was five feet ten but his thinness, owing to his endless illnesses, made him seem well above six feet, at least in photographs and paintings. In John Singer Sargent's famous portrait, Stevenson has the elongated look that certain funhouse mirrors give, though all who knew him averred that Sargent's is a fine likeness. I tend to think of him, physically, as a disheveled version of Comte Robert de Montesquieu, Proust's model for Baron de Charlus, dressed out of a Goodwill shop.

This freakishly dressed, splendidly well-spoken young man did not take long to capture the attention and affection of his elders. In London in 1874, when Stevenson was twenty-three, Sidney Colvin put him up for the Savile Club, formed five years earlier and known as the preferred meeting place of the young and brilliant and promising. There his dazzling talk impressed, among others, Edmund Gosse, himself now launched on a literary career (Gosse was five years older than Stevenson). Soon Stevenson's essays and reviews began appearing in the *Fortnightly,* the *Academy,* and Leslie Stephen's *Cornhill,* where for a while his contributions, signed R.L.S., were thought to stand for the Real Leslie Stephen.

Although Stevenson was from the outset an immensely productive writer, he disavowed literary fertility, claiming, "I am constipated in the brains." He appears to have been one of those essentially slothful and disorganized people who turn out a vast quantity of work as part of the general effort to avoid doing that work that they are supposed to be doing in the first place. Some people before they begin writing need near perfect conditions: good health, psychological security, Trappist monastery quiet, two grants, and a gentle climate. Others can write with creditors' knuckles at the door, on choppy seas, while hemorrhaging. Robert Louis Stevenson was of the latter kind. He was a natural writer, not that writing came easily to him—there are, as someone once said, no Mozarts in literature—but in that he loved fashioning phrases, constructing sentences, building paragraphs. "No other business offers a man his daily bread upon such joyful terms," he wrote about writing in "Letter to a Young Gentleman Who Proposes to Embrace the Career of Art," and then he adds:

> I take the author, with whose career I am best acquainted, and it is true he works in a rebellious material, and that the act of writing is cramped and trying both to the eyes and the temper; but remark him in his study, when matter crowds upon him and words are not wanting—in what a continual series of small suc-

cesses time flows by; with what a sense of power as of one moving mountains, he marshals his petty characters; with what
pleasures, both of the ear and eye, he sees his airy structure
growing on the page; and how he labours in a craft to which
the whole material of his life is tributary, and which opens a
door to all his tastes, his loves, his hatreds, and his convictions,
so that what he writes is only what he longed to utter.

No matter how complicated Stevenson's life, in the midst of
the complexity he generally emerges, manuscript in hand,
without complaint. "There should be no honours for the artist," he wrote in the same essay; "he has already, in the practice
of his art, more than his share of the rewards of life; the honours are pre-empted for other trades, less agreeable and perhaps more useful."

As for complications, Stevenson added richly to his own
when, at twenty-six, he fell in love with a woman some ten
years older than he who was already married, with a seventeen-
year-old daughter, an eight-year-old son, and a recently deceased
infant over whom she was still grieving. A more convenient
lover, one might have thought, must have been available; still,
"the blind bowboy," as Stevenson referred to Cupid, had struck.
Fanny Osbourne was an American, Indianapolis-born, small,
dark, game, a bit of bluestocking, even more (in the words of
J. C. Furnas, Stevenson's biographer), an "aesthetic *parvenu*."
Without much in the way of funds, and perhaps even less in
talent, she had come to Europe to study painting. Stevenson
met her at Grez, a village and art colony near Fontainebleau,
where he had gone for his health, she for her painting. To
make a lengthy romance short, once Fanny was able to clear
the decks of her first husband through divorce, she and Stevenson married. He was then twenty-nine, in ill health, and unable
to earn a living even for himself. "And yet when all has been
said," as he wrote in part two of his essay "Virginibus Puer-
isque," "the man who should hold back from marriage is in the

same case with him who runs away from battle." Not quite the way a contemporary marriage counselor might put it, perhaps, but it captures nicely its author's sense of life as an adventure.

Young men who marry women who already have children are the world's supreme optimists. Stevenson is of their class, and perhaps beyond. When he followed Fanny Osbourne across the ocean and thence across the continent to Monterey, California, he had neither health nor the least prospect of wealth. "I am an author," he wrote to a future brother-in-law, "but I am not very likely to make my fortune in that business, where better even than I are glad to get their daily bread." It was quite a bargain: he was acquiring as a wife a woman who had been round the block a time or two and who was scarcely ten years younger than his mother, while she was acquiring, as J. C. Furnas puts it in his excellent biography, "a rickety economic casualty." On Stevenson's side, all were united in their opposition to the marriage. His literary friends in London tried systematically to discourage him; his father in Edinburgh threatened to disinherit him. Stevenson, working away in a furnished room in San Francisco on five or six different economically unpromising literary projects and suffering from malaria and rotting teeth, was not to be dissuaded from his course. One recalls that the elder and wilder of the two Duries brothers in Stevenson's novel *The Master of Ballantrae* flips a coin whenever a fateful decision is required. Stevenson had something of the same willingness to leave his fate to chance. He married Fanny Osbourne in San Francisco on May 19, 1880.

Fourteen years of life were left to Robert Louis Stevenson. These were spent in an atmosphere of domestic chaos that might have driven a less spirited and more serenity-seeking man to slip away on a moonless night to join the Foreign Legion. Until the final move to Samoa in 1890, the Stevensons changed residences—usually for reasons of health or for journalistic opportunity—from California to Scotland to Switzerland to France to England to upper New York State to Honolulu to the South Seas. The cast of characters hauled along on this odyssey included stepchildren and a grandchild, a spendthrift and shiftless stepson-in-law, a somewhat intemperate Skye terrier named Bogue, a cat that could not be housebroken, a French-Swiss maid of the type that used to be known as "a treasure," various Polynesian servants, and at one point a Chinese chef with the hilarious name of Ah Fu. Sciatica, Egyptian ophthalmia, and severe hemorrhages were but a few of the afflictions suffered by the head of this traveling circus; death, which could never have been far from his thoughts during his many bouts of illness, he described as "the wolverine on my shoulders." All this while he plowed and plugged away at a gallimaufry of projects: novels, stories, essays, journalism, finishing more than anyone might think possible, leaving some uncompleted, walking away from others (among the latter, a biography of William Hazlitt, which is a volume in that most portable of libraries: books one would love to have read but for the inconvenient fact that they were never written).

As long as you're up, a contemporary who reads about Stevenson's travail feels like exclaiming, get this man a grant—make it a double MacArthur. In fact, despite his impressive rate of literary production, Stevenson, given the expenses caused by his illnesses and by his familial responsibilities, could not make his nut. He was able to keep afloat only through help from his father, who was at first strongly opposed to his son's marriage but soon enough kicked in for £250 a year, and extra when more was needed. Quarrel though they might, Stevenson must have known that he could always count upon his father, and often did, and his father never failed him.

The book that finally put Robert Louis Stevenson into the black was *Treasure Island,* which began as a lark when Stevenson, amusing himself with his stepson Lloyd's paints, drew a treasure map of an imaginary island. He next constructed a story to go with the map, which he wrote at the rate of a chapter a day and read each night to his family, then living near Braemar in Scotland. Both Stevenson's father and his stepson enjoyed it immensely and added bits of detail that he inserted into the text. The story originally appeared, under a pseudonym, in a boy's magazine called *Young Folks*. "If this doesn't fetch the kids," remarked Stevenson, "why, they have gone rotten since my day." The original title for the story was "The Sea-Cook," after its most interesting character, Long John Silver, who, it will be recalled, served as a cook on the *Hispaniola*, the ship in the novel. In its book form the title was changed to *Treasure Island*, which naturally seems much the superior title. But then, as the small store of publishing wisdom has it, the winning title for a best-selling book is that which happens to have been given to a book that sells extremely well.

Treasure Island was not, as J. C. Furnas recounts, a smashing best-seller, but instead a book that slowly built its audience until it became part of that small shelf of books that every middle-class English-speaking boy is supposed to read. Its early admirers, however, were quite as often adults as children; Gladstone is said to have stayed up through an entire night reading it; the critic Andrew Lang pronounced it, as a romance, beneath only the *Odyssey* and *Tom Sawyer*. Its author originally received (at *Young Folks's* space rates) roughly thirty-four pounds for its serialization and a hundred for its publication in book form. Slowly but inexorably, reprint followed reprint. "In his lifetime," writes James Pope-Hennessey in his 1974 biography of Stevenson, "it was appearing in [editions of] tens of thousands. Louis had his first taste of fame."

With the publication of *Treasure Island* in 1883, just after Stevenson's thirty-third birthday, he began slowly to turn from being a small-public to a large-public writer, from being a "detrimental" (as he put it in his essay "Authors and Publishers") to a successful author. When *The Strange Case of Dr. Jekyll and Mr. Hyde* appeared in 1886, it sold forty thousand copies in its first six months and had three separate dramatizations for the stage. *Kidnapped* (1886), like *Treasure Island,* became a steady earner of royalties. Offers of work for serious fees began arriving from America: $10,000 to write a weekly column for the *New York World,* $3,500 to write a year's worth of monthly essays for *Scribner's Magazine.* "The good fairy," writes J. C. Furnas, "was dipping in with both hands." Stevenson became one of nine members elected annually to the Atheneum Club in London. And he had gained entrance into an even more select club—that of the small circle of intimate friends of Henry James.

The friendship of Henry James and Robert Louis Stevenson was founded on their passionate interest in the art of fiction and their respect for each other as very different practitioners of that art; and it was perpetuated by the love that sturdily grew between them. The friendship began when, in 1884, Stevenson published in *Longman's Magazine* "A Humble Remonstrance" to James's essay "The Art of Fiction," published earlier in the same journal. Stevenson's remonstrance, written with evident and great regard for James, sets out the case for his own kind of fiction, and does so with a subtlety of tact, a measured elegance of style, and a depth of knowledge that Henry James found irresistible. He didn't, in fact, try to resist it, and directly wrote to Stevenson to say that they had more belief in common than he perhaps knew and that "it's a luxury, in this immoral age, to encounter some one who *does* write—who is really acquainted with that lovely art."

In *Henry James and Robert Louis Stevenson: A Record of Friendship and Criticism* (1948), Janet Adam Smith writes: "James and Stevenson clearly loved each other; but they also needed each other." When they met, James was forty-one, Stevenson thirty-four. Yet, as Mrs. Smith goes on to say, both of them "thought more profoundly about their art, and cared more intensely for it, than any of their contemporaries"; both had a strong sense of the sacredness of their craft and of its demands;

and both felt something many notches below awe for the opinion of the public on literary quality, with Stevenson at one point allowing, in a letter to Edmund Gosse, that "there must be something wrong in me, or I would not be popular." As Mrs. Smith rightly remarks, "they certainly were the two most conscious novelists of their time in England."

Although James had met Stevenson earlier, and was not much impressed with his bohemianism, thinking him a bit of a *poseur,* they first became friends in Bournemouth, where Stevenson was on the mend from yet another of his illnesses and James was attending his invalid sister Alice. Intimacy between them appears to have been almost instant. Fanny Stevenson wrote to her mother about James: "I had always been told that he was the type of an Englishman, but, except that he looks like the Prince of Wales, I call him the type of an American. He is gentle, amiable and soothing." Apparently sufficiently so for Stevenson soon to speak and write to him with full candor about his art. After telling James how much pleasure he took from reading *Roderick Hudson,* he was not above recommending that, if a new edition were to be run off, James might go through the text and strike out the words "immense" and "tremendous," which he thought overused. In the same letter, in a postscript, he informed James that "I can't bear *The Portrait of a Lady.*" He cheered James on during the composition of *The Princess Casamassima,* congratulating him on his being able to "do low life," adding that "it was of that nature of touch that I sometimes achingly miss from your former work."

Although of the two men James was aesthetically much the more highly developed, the most he allowed himself by way of criticism of Stevenson's work in their correspondence was to remark that his verses "show your 'cleverness,' but they don't show your genius," and to complain, ever so mutedly, about missing the "*visible,*" "the *personal* painter-touch" in Stevenson's book *The South Seas* and in his novel *Catriona.* James understood Stevenson better than Stevenson understood James, but then James understood him better than any of his other friends of longer standing. He was the only one among them not to oppose Stevenson's final settlement in Samoa, though he was to miss him sorely. James realized that if Stevenson continued to live in Europe, he would have to continue to abide in one or another health spa, or, as Stevenson himself once put it, in the "Land of the Counterpane," where his life approximated that of "a weevil in a biscuit." Writing about Stevenson after his death, James noted that in Samoa "he found, after a wonderful, adventurous quest, the treasure island, the climatic paradise that met, that enhanced his possibilities; and with this discovery was ushered in his completely full and rich period, the time in which . . . his genius and his character most overflowed."

"Unexpurgated heaven" Stevenson called the climate in Samoa, which for him it was since it gave him back his health at forty, or at least more of it than he was able to enjoy in many years. Fanny and he and their complicated family had plenty in the way of details to keep them jumping when Stevenson bought the Vailima estate near the municipality of Apia and set out to build a cluster of houses for his family and servants and a large manse-like structure for family meetings. The Samoans called him Tusitala, which means teller of tales, and his relations with those Samoans he encountered were splendid, chiefly because he never lorded it over them and had an instinctive appreciation for their ways that Franz Boas himself would have found admirable. As he wrote to a friend from Bournemouth who was about to begin missionary work:

> Forget wholly and for ever all small pruderies, and remember that you cannot change ancestral feelings of right and wrong without what is practically soul murder. Barbarous as the customs may seem, always hear them with patience, always judge them with gentleness, always find in them some seed of good; see that you always develop them; remember that all you can do

is to civilize the man in the line of his own civilization, such as
it is.

Sound advice, and Henry Adams, while touring the South
Pacific with his friend the painter John La Farge, might have
done well to have taken it when visiting the Stevensons. Adams
encountered them shortly after they had themselves arrived at
Vailima, and his reaction to them was pure snobbery. The
squalor of the setting hit him first, and then their garb bowled
him over. "Imagine a man so thin and emaciated that he looked
like a bundle of sticks in a bag, with a head and eyes morbidly
intelligent and restless," Adams wrote to his friend Elizabeth
Cameron. "He was costumed in a dirty striped cotton pyjamas,
the baggy legs tucked into coarse knit woolen stockings, one
of which was bright brown in color, the other a purplish dark
tone." When Adams, the past century's least casual American,
could get his mind off those socks, which wasn't easy, he
described Stevenson's nervous manner of talk, "for he cannot
be quiet, but sits down, jumps up, darts off and flies back, at
every sentence he utters, and his eyes and features gleam with
a hectic glow." On another occasion, after admonishing himself that in his correspondence he must stop ridiculing Stevenson, who had been most obliging in arranging letters of
recommendation for him in the South Pacific, Adams describes
him as looking "like an insane stork" and Fanny, whom he had
earlier likened to "a half-breed Mexican," as being as "stalwart
as any other Apache squaw." Snobbery has perhaps never more
completely negated intelligence.

Robert Louis Stevenson did not get his wish of dying a violent death ("to be drowned, to be shot, to be thrown from a
horse—aye, to be hanged"), but at least he evaded, through
cerebral hemorrhage, the death through "slow dissolution" that
he feared most. His funeral was a Cecil B. De Mille production. Forty Samoan tribal chiefs, working through the night,
with knives and axes cut a path up the steep incline of Mount

Vaea, at whose summit he wished to be buried. The following day his body in its coffin was carried up the path on Samoan shoulders to be buried in a grave from which the Pacific Ocean could be viewed thirteen hundred feet below. Fanny Stevenson lived twenty years longer, and died in California, though her daughter buried her ashes in her husband's grave atop Mount Vaea.

What was not buried on Mount Vaea was the legend—or, as it is more often called, the myth—of Robert Louis Stevenson, which began in earnest with Stevenson's death. George Saintsbury called him "the most brilliant and interesting by far" of the English writers of the second half of the nineteenth century. "Vergil of prose," chipped in Richard Le Gallienne. "He was the laureate of the joy of life," wrote a contributor to the *Atheneum*. Arthur Conan Doyle set him alongside Poe and Hawthorne as one of the three great short-story writers. Arthur Quiller-Couch weighed in with: "Put away books and paper and pen. . . . Stevenson is dead, and now there is nobody left to write for." Interest in the facts of Stevenson's life was unending; not since Byron had biographical curiosity about a writer run quite so high. "Within thirty years every living human being whose cat had patronized the same veterinarian as Bogue [the Stevensons' Skye terrier] had published dilute memories of Robert Louis Stevenson," J. C. Furnas writes in his biography. "In short," as Chesterton remarked in his 1927 study of Stevenson, the entire fuss was "overdone; it was too noisy and yet all on one note; above all, it was too incessant and too prolonged."

And yet it could scarcely be resisted. The profusely talented young writer whose flame lights the sky, then gutters, and is snuffed out is a story with repeated and, apparently, endless appeal. It is the story of the god Adonis, young and beautiful and too soon dead. It is the story, in literature, of Keats and Byron and Rupert Brooke and, in America, of F. Scott Fitzgerald and James Agee. The story is generally made more piquant when the young writer leaves behind an unfinished masterpiece, as Fitzgerald left behind *The Last Tycoon* and Agee *A Death in the Family.* Stevenson left behind a novel, said to be a third complete, entitled *Weir of Hermiston,* and it is frustratingly fine. He also left behind a reputation, doubtless much overdone, as a saintly man. "He became the most exquisite English writer of his generation," wrote Edmund Gosse, "yet those who lived close to him are apt to think less of this than of the fact that he was the most unselfish and lovable of human beings." Gosse also wrote: "I ought to remember [Stevenson's] faults, but I protest I can remember none."

After such inflation, it did not take the deflators long to arrive. Sniffing around in Stevenson's private life, literary journalists and scholars tried snouting out various truffles of scandal: love affairs, illegitimate children, bigamy (on Fanny's part) were set upon the table. The critical reaction soon enough set in. George Moore, John Jay Chapman, Thomas Beer wrote that Stevenson was vastly overrated; E. F. Benson, C. E. M. Joad, Frank Swinnerton argued that he was no more than second-rate. For Swinnerton "the extravagant nonsense written and thought about Stevenson since his death" only impaired his literary reputation, making it all the plainer that "with all his writing he took the road of least resistance, the road of limited horizons. . . ." Swinnerton could find no more in Stevenson than "a fragment, a handful of tales and two boys books . . . and the charm of Stevenson's personality." As for charm, Swinnerton added: "Charm as an adjunct is very well; charm as an asset is of less significance." When the deflators depart, they don't leave much.

Not that Stevenson hadn't doubts about his own literary quality—doubts that even the most patent evidence of worldly success could not shake. This evidence came in the form of a large and steady sale of his books, admiring letters from famous as well as younger writers that made plain his world fame, and plans on the part of his English and American publishers to bring out a collected, twenty-volume Edinburgh Edition of his writings—this last rather impressive for a man still in his early forties. Yet he continued to think of himself as merely the "author of a vast quantity of little books." He told his stepson Lloyd that "what genius I had was for hard work," and, in a letter to Sidney Colvin, remarked, "I cannot take myself seriously as an artist; the limitations are so obvious."

Are they? A final judgment about Robert Louis Stevenson's quality is not so easily made. Given all that he had to overcome to achieve what he did, there is simply no setting aside his life—as Henry James rightly noted after Stevenson's death, it had been his fortune to become, like Samuel Johnson, a "Figure." In *Treasure Island* and (to a lesser extent) *Kidnapped,* he produced two authentic children's classics; and in *The Strange Case of Dr. Jekyll and Mr. Hyde,* with its central insight into the duality of human personality, he placed a psychological metaphor permanently into the language in a story that continues to interest new generations of intelligent readers, while keeping academics happily whittling away at their workbenches. Stevenson was the literary equivalent of the decathlon athlete: competing in ten different difficult events yet holding world records in none. He wrote essays, novels, children's verse, political journalism, boys' books, poetry, plays, short stories, mysteries, and memoirs—almost all of it interesting, some of it touching greatness, yet very little wholly, shimmeringly splendid and powerful in the way one requires of the highest art.

Along with his extraordinary variousness, there is the problem of Stevenson's style. Often, when complimented on a piece of work, he would attribute what success he had achieved in it to this or that "trick" of style. He worked very hard on his prose. It is not going too far to say that he was a brilliant stylist; it is going altogether too far, however, to say that he had his own style. He had instead *styles*. When Stevenson set out to tell a story, he searched for the best style in which to tell it. Sometimes, as in *The Master of Ballantrae* and in *Treasure Island,* he would switch styles by switching narrators in mid-book and then switch back again. Sometimes he would appropriate another writer's style—as he did, without happy effect, George Meredith's in his, Stevenson's, novel *Prince Otto.* Even his essays, familiar, personal, and marvelously good though many of them are, do not have a distinctive and unified style; they, too, lack an original feel and could have been written by several other Victorian men of letters.

The music critic Ernest Newman used to maintain that all important composers, when studied carefully, leave fingerprints that reveal what he called the "physiology of their style," which was itself the basis for their psychology. Anyone who reads large amounts of a particular writer comes in time to discover similar literary fingerprints—sentences or passages that one greets by recognizing that this is the author in his most essential self, pure Jane Austen or Tolstoy or Dickens or George Eliot or Conrad or James or Chekhov or Kafka; it could only have been written by him or her and by no one else. Stevenson's books are filled with wondrous passages, rhythmic and ringing and resonant with penetrating observation and felicitous sentiment—and yet they are not characteristically his but beautiful writing merely. A writer who took great pains with prose style, he finally left no fingerprints of his own.

Henry James, who wrote about Stevenson with the sympathy of a good-hearted friend, remarked in an essay of 1887 that "each of his books is an independent effort—a window opened to a different view." James noted Stevenson's love of style, and, in a fine touch of merry malice, late in his essay wrote that Stevenson's "ideal of the delightful work of fiction would be the adventures of Monte Cristo related by the author of *Richard Feverel.*" But if James found no characteristic style in Stevenson, he did find a characteristic note, which was the love of life and especially of life lived by the young. "The part of life that he cares for most is youth, and the direct expression of the love of youth is the beginning and end of his message. . . . In a word, he is an artist accomplished even to sophistication, whose constant theme is the unsophisticated."

Toward the close of his essay, James remarks on the quarrel in *Kidnapped* between the novel's two heroes, David Balfour and Alan Breck, a quarrel that comes about, it will be recalled, almost as much through fatigue as through anything else. James found an impressively deep psychological truth in this brief scene, finding in it "a real stroke of genius, [that has in it] the very logic and rhythm of life—a quarrel which we feel to be inevitable, though it is about nothing, or almost nothing, and which springs from exasperated nerves and the simple shock of temperaments." It was in search of such artistic touches that James read, and he has taught others of us to be on the lookout for them. James ends his essay by saying that such a fine touch is Stevenson's pledge of future artistry of the highest and finest caliber.

Yet Stevenson, finally, was less interested in such touches than in getting the swords out again, moving the action along, telling his story without too much fuss and bother. G. K. Chesterton, who (like James) wanted to have a high opinion of Stevenson and who wrote about him in the wake of Stevenson's detractors, noted that Stevenson was altogether too economical in his storytelling, and felt that he would have profited by availing himself of more Victorian capaciousness: "It is exactly because Balfour or Ballantrae only do what they are meant to do, and do it so swiftly and well, that we have a vague feeling that we do not know them as we know more loitering, more rambling or more sprawling characters." Stevenson's problem, I understand Chesterton to be saying, is that he too carefully observed what he, Chesterton, called "the niceties of technical literature," by which he meant that Stevenson was too much the professional writer and did not let himself go in the direction of Whitman, the great Victorian novelists, Henry James, and all true artists—the direction, that is to say, of one's own artistic instincts and idiosyncrasies.

Stevenson had the talent to write stories like "The Beach of Falesá" and "The Suicide Club" that are almost as good as anything in Conrad and Kipling, and essays like "The Lantern-Bearers" and "Aes Triplex" that are almost as good as anything in Hazlitt and Lamb, but not quite the genius to be absolutely himself on the page. Had he possessed that genius, he might have surpassed them all. If literature, as Van Wyck Brooks once defined it, is a great man writing, the best place to discover the great man who was Robert Louis Stevenson is in his letters. There one can depend upon finding adversity met by unrelenting cheerfulness, misfortune by undiminished courage. ("Literally no man has more completely lived out life than I have done," he wrote in the last year of his life to his friend Charles Baxter. "And still it's good fun.") It is a magnificent human performance, and puts one in mind of a sentence in Stevenson's youthful essay on John Knox, in which he compares the difficulty of Knox's early life to the serenity of his later life. "One would take the first forty years gladly," Stevenson wrote at twenty-four, "if one could be sure of the last thirty." The man who wrote that sentence had forty-four years in all, and within them, against formidable obstacles, achieved a very great deal. With another thirty years to live, what might he have done? That, alas, is another of those questions too sad to pursue.

Chamfort, Artist of Truth

A DMIRERS of the form known as the aphorism have always been few and aphorists of the first class, naturally enough, many fewer. The aphorism is an acquired taste; it provides something substantial, tangy, yet more than a touch sour, rather like the best Greek olives. Aphorisms are generalizations of universal, or nearly universal, significance, written out of one's experience, or more likely disenchantment with one's experience. If proverbs tend to tell us that we shouldn't expect people to be better than they are, aphorisms are more likely to tell us just how bad they can be. "We all have strength enough," writes La Rochefoucauld, nicely striking the characteristic note of the aphorist, "to endure the troubles of others."

Those among us who take pleasure in aphorisms do not, then, come to them for cheering up. They can of course be immensely amusing, which the best among them generally are, and this, to be sure, can provide its own sort of cheer. But the bone truth is that aphorisms, while they need not be bitter, are usually better for being so. The closest synonym to an aphorism is a maxim, and sometimes the two words are used interchangeably, though the notion of advice that clings to the word "maxim" does not cling to the aphorism, which has tended to seem freer to observe the pretentious, ridiculous, paradoxical, and (sometimes though not very often) surprisingly majestic quality of human conduct.

The aphorist is by nature, if not always by birth, aristocratic. He is a man who does not bother to argue or to explain; he asserts, and, if he has got it right, his assertion is sufficient unto the day. Implicit in the brevity of the aphorist's assertions is an impatience with logical proof. He also operates at a high level of generality. "Great thoughts are always general," wrote Dr. Johnson, "and consist in positions not limited by exceptions, and in descriptions not descending to minuteness." When the aphorist stylishly remarks upon the conduct of human behavior—and without style, that preservative of literature, the aphorist has no hope of his works living beyond the time it takes to write them—he assumes that readers as worldly as he will recognize instantly that what he says is true. If not, too bad, and, come to think of it, not too surprising, either. One doesn't, after all, expect the butterfly being pinned to the velvet cloth to appreciate the elegance of the lepidopterist's efforts.

Universal though the truth of the aphorism attempts to be, it is very far from impersonal. On the contrary, the true aphorist leaves the stamp of himself, through his style, on each of his aphorisms. Scarcely could it be otherwise, for the literary act that is the aphorism is one in which the author sets out to tell you precisely what he thinks. Usually what he thinks is opposed to the conventional opinion on most subjects. In asserting his own truths, the aphorist separates himself from the platitudes and received wisdom on every subject that he touches. Nietzsche, who was himself partial to the form of the aphorism, once noted that every idea has its autobiography. So, one might add, does every aphorism. "The artist doesn't see things as they are, but as he is," an anonymous aphorism runs, and it applies nicely to that artist in the briefest of all prose forms, the aphorist. His intention, like that of all artists, is to convince us that the way he sees things is the way they truly are.

   Not long ago, as the editor of an intellectual quarterly, I
received a batch of aphorisms from a man of whom I had never
heard before, but whom I took to be in his forties. He had
sent these aphorisms to me for publication. They were not at
all bad, his aphorisms, and I found myself writing to tell him
that I would indeed publish them if only his name were Winston Churchill or Charles de Gaulle, but I could not do so as
long as his name was what it was—it was, such is the heavy
irony life dispenses, Smith—nor, I quickly added, would I be
able to publish them if they were written by someone named
Joseph Epstein.
   My logic here—if logic be the right word—is that the
aphorism has become so old-fashioned a form that, in order to
have one's aphorisms published, one really ought to be well
known to begin with. It was no longer possible, I felt, simply
to have thought long and written with high style and concision
about general subjects, and expect to find someone willing to
publish one's lucubrations. To publish fewer than a fairly large
body of someone's aphorisms, or at least those of someone
who is not otherwise known to the world, seemed to me a bit
beside the point. The point here is that the composition of
powerful aphorisms implies a life behind them of the most
varied and interesting experience. If one wants to publish
aphorisms today, it is best, as a precondition, to become very
famous before doing so.
   The honor roll of the great aphorists requires only a very
small scroll. The fingers of both hands can almost include all
those who can make some claim to have a place in world literature. Let me count their names: La Rochefoucauld, La Bruyère, Vauvenargues, Pascal, Joubert, Rivarol; switching from
French to Teutonic culture now, let us add G. C. Lichtenberg,
Schopenhauer, Nietzsche, Karl Kraus; and a lone Romanian,
a contemporary named E. M. Cioran. William Hazlitt wrote
aphorisms, jolly dark ones too—"The youth is better than the
old age of friendship" and "I believe in the theoretical benev-

olence and the practical malignity of man"—but not enough of them are superior. Emerson is often included among the ranks of the great aphorists, but, to my taste, he is too vatic, not to say uplifting, and I am prepared to say boring. But then Emerson did not, strictly speaking, write aphorisms but instead in an aphoristic style, which allows anthologists to pluck discrete aphorisms from the often heavy pudding of his prose.

My list of aphorists shows the form to have been taken up overwhelmingly by Frenchmen. A certain amount of sense inheres in this fact of literary history. If vengeance, as the Italians say, is a dish best served cold, for the French disgust is best served cool and with disdain, and cool disdain is perhaps the key note for the aphorist. When Germans express disgust—as in Schopenhauer or Nietzsche—it tends, like so many things German, to be rather overdone. Apparently neither the English nor the Americans have felt disgust with sufficient intensity to produce a strong line of aphorists, which is a testament either to their societies or to the naiveté of their writers.

I have delayed including the name Chamfort (1740–1794) among the great aphorists until now because his place among them is not an altogether understandable one. "A passionate man," an aphorism of Stendhal's has it, "is never witty." Yet Chamfort, one of the great aphorists of his own or any other age, gives the lie to this particular aphorism. Few men have been wittier, and perhaps none more passionate, if one measure of passion be sustained agitated feelings. ("Few have any idea," Chamfort wrote, "how much wit it takes never to be ridiculous.") Even for an aphorist, Chamfort could be very dark. In his biography of Chamfort, Claude Arnaud quotes the Abbé Morellet on his frequent conversations with this extraordinary man:

There were two features to his conversation. It always touched on people and never on things, and it was constantly misanthropic and excessively denigrating. The turns of phrase with which he demonstrated his hatred for humanity in general as well as his specific aversions were captivating in their originality . . . but I left Auteuil hundreds of times with a heavy soul—after mornings of listening to him recount anecdote after anecdote for two hours, inventing epigram after epigram with indefatigable ease—as though I were leaving the scene of an execution.

Yet Chamfort has always had his admirers, and they have made up a most impressive literary cast. Tell me who admires you, Sainte-Beuve somewhere says, and I shall tell you who you are. Schopenhauer much admired Chamfort and Nietzsche did so even more. Stendhal read him with appreciation. Everything Chamfort wrote, said Cocteau, that connoisseur of tomorrow, "seems as if it were written yesterday." Camus thought him *un écrivain classique* and felt it possible to speak of him without paradox as a novelist. Closer to our own day the poet W. S. Merwin has translated a generous selection of Chamfort's aphorisms, characters, and anecdotes under the title *Products of the Perfected Civilization*. E. M. Cioran has spoken of the impulses of gratitude that he feels toward Chamfort—and Job.

Yet Chamfort's remains considerably less than a household name. Even among people who know and care about literature, he is not always known; or if his name is known, what he stands for is a bit blurred. Part of the problem is that Chamfort was both a political figure—though a minor and for the most part behind-the-scenes one—and a writer, and that much of what he wrote in the earlier phases of his career—plays, pamphlets, criticism, poetry—today isn't quite negligible. Adding to the complication is that his career is parted by that most tumultuous of events of the eighteenth century, or perhaps of modern history itself, the French Revolution, and so one must consider, in effect, not one but three Chamforts: the careerist of the ancien régime, the flamingly enthusiastic revolutionist, and the dispossessed and disenchanted figure on whom the revolution turned.

What anyone with the least biographical interest wants to know about an aphorist he admires is whether he had more wit than character—or, to put the case more positively, whether his character was commensurate with his wit. This question must often have occurred to Chamfort himself. This exquisite writer—with all the strengths and weaknesses that the adjective implies—was a misfit: in some ways a misfit by fortune, in some ways by nature, and in more important ways a self-made misfit. Chamfort was a man who made and unmade himself, not once but several times in the course of his life.

The first and crucially significant fact about Chamfort is that he wasn't born Chamfort—a name he took up later in life— but was born out of wedlock, to an aristocratic mother and an obscure cleric, in 1740, in Clermont-Ferrand, whence also derived Pascal. The child was, in effect, farmed out to the family of a grocer and his wife, who had lost a child of their own born on the same day as he. He was raised by this family under the name Sébastien Roch Nicolas. The boy learned who his true mother was when he was seven or eight. This knowledge established him for life in his ambiguous, highly charged relation with the aristocracy of the ancien régime, and with an early appreciation of how far people will go to maintain appearances. It left the young boy with a sense of himself as a victim, but a victim always with a high opinion of himself. He grew up, consequently, with great ambition and an ample grudge. Mediating between the two—between his aspirations and his anger—became the story not alone of his career but of his life.

"Careers open to the talents" was scarcely the motto of the ancien régime, but talent of a certain kind, combined with ambition, could, with luck, find its way. Chamfort, clearly, did. He was a brilliant student, and won various medals in competitions open to students across France. He was adept at languages, ancient and modern, and the clerical principal of the school in Paris at which he was educated thought he might make an excellent priest. According to Claude Arnaud, Chamfort (still young Nicolas) quickly disabused the principal of that notion. "I'll never be a priest," he informed him. "I'm too fond of sleep, philosophy, women, honor and real fame; and not fond enough of quarrels, hypocrisy, honors, and money." Arnaud also tells us that Chamfort even then considered himself a genius; and later in life he would write that "geniuses belong to no family, no century, no nation—they have neither ancestors nor descendants."

Few things so improve the appearance as a good opinion of oneself. But in this realm Chamfort stood in little need of improvement. As a young man, he was devastatingly handsome and very well turned out. A woman with whom he slept reported: "You think he's only Adonis, yet he's Hercules"—a remark every young man would like on his calling card. As with many a delicious remark in that day, it got around, accruing to the young Chamfort's reputation for charm and—how to put it?—dexterity. In an age of artifice, he created himself with careful attention to detail: changed his name while leaving the truth about his birth a mystery; dropped two years off his age to create the impression that he was even more precocious than he was; acquired the knack of gaining the patronage of the most important personages of the time; "and mastered the art," as Arnaud puts, of "knowing exactly when to go too far."

In short, the young Chamfort was turning into a man of precisely the kind the mature Chamfort would despise. Do we have a case here, in Chamfort's ability easily to insinuate himself into the most select segments of society, of the well-known Groucho Complex, which holds that there can be no point in joining any club whose standards are so low that they are willing to accept oneself as a member? Only in part, I think, for to

get Chamfort right one has to add the elements of a heightened critical sensibility that led into something akin to self-
hatred at the sign of his willingness to abase himself before his
putative superiors.

Chamfort quickly enough grasped, then mastered, the artificiality of Parisian life. Sainte-Beuve says of the young Joseph
Joubert, a near contemporary of Chamfort's, "he lived there
[in Paris] as one lived then: he chatted." So did Chamfort—
brilliantly. He also wrote a rather callow play, *La Jeune indienne*,
that received the approval of Voltaire. D'Alembert extended
him his patronage. He corresponded with Rousseau, the one
writer among the great French prose writers of the age—and
the age was clearly one for prose, not poetry—whose work he
seems unstintingly to have admired. He understood that literary talent meant entree into the highest society, yet he also
sensed, as Arnaud puts it, that "high society appears to respect
those who appear to hold it in contempt." Contempt Chamfort did not have to feign, especially for aristocrats, whose pre-
tenses to superiority he despised.

Along with literary talent, the art of seduction had its utility
in the Paris of Chamfort's day. Laclos, author of *Les Liaisons
dangereuses,* was born only a year later than Chamfort. It is
perhaps well to recall that Chamfort wrote the aphorism around
which Laclos might be said to have constructed his novel: "Love,
such as it exists in high society, is merely the exchange of whims
and the contact of skins." He himself knew no shortage of
women who were ready to transact precisely this exchange,
among them the actress Mlle. Giurmand, who was famous for
the perfection of her bosom and who did her makeup each day
before the portrait that Fragonard had painted of her.

Chamfort often used his amatory powers to revenge himself
on aristocrats for what he felt were social slights. His own
beauty, as Arnaud nicely puts it, "was one injustice that Chamfort bore lightly." But then, at the age of twenty-five, he was
struck by one of fate's mysterious darts and in a single shot his

own good looks and his health were gone. A still unknown disease hit him—some allege it was venereal—affecting his nerves, his complexion, his chest, his bladder, his eyes, leaving him unable to read or to walk, and turning him over to the horror of eighteenth-century medical treatment. His elegant appearance, his youthful air, were destroyed. He took to his rooms. His onward and upward progress ceased. His already advanced misanthropy had found its autobiographical *raison d'être.*

Those who have written about Chamfort differ on the question of the origin of his dark views: some say they are owed to the socially demeaning facts of his birth, some to this devastating illness, some to a superior lucidity let loose in a rotten age. About the darkness of these views there can be no controversy. After the unexplained attack of his illness, he steeled himself. Removed from the sex wars—in which, as he would later write, "the heart must break or turn to bronze"—he devoted himself more earnestly to literature. But try as he might, he was unable to kill entirely the aspirations that seemed inseparable from his character. Chamfort remained a man who desired everything and detested himself for his own desires. His was a case, perhaps not all that uncommon, of eating your cake and hating it, too.

To be sure, there are tableaux of Chamfort that soften the view of him as the always angry young man, in a state of perpetual perturbation, the persistent good hater. In the pages of Arnaud's biography, we discover Chamfort stroking Mme Helvetius's angora cats, who were fed on a strict diet of chicken breasts; meeting Benjamin Franklin, who himself had an idea or two on the art of seduction; actually in love for a brief time with Marthe Buffon, a woman older than he who died only six months after their relationship had got underway in earnest and of whom a contemporary said that Chamfort had loved her "as ardently as a mistress, as tenderly as a mother." A not uncommon sight in the rarefied circles in which he traveled was that of Chamfort holding forth, talking brilliantly, captivating everyone. One witness to his talk, who for a long stretch saw him daily, said that he never repeated himself, another that he made people laugh and think simultaneously.

These scenes of the gentle life are counterposed against the almost endless internecine literary squabbles for which the time was famous, a time of impressive ingratitude, relentless jealousy, and devastating put-downs. (Of Jean-François de La Harpe, a rival and exceedingly rivalrous man of letters, Chamfort said that he frequently "hid his vices behind his faults"—a very crisp little two-cushion shot.) Chamfort took a good thumping from critics for his second play, *Mustapha et Zéangir*. Owing to this thorough shellacking, Chamfort acquired paranoia, the disease of the intellectuals, of serious dimensions. Given the general disputatiousness, not to say backstabbing, of intellectual life in the ancien régime, and the non-metaphorical backstabbing in the revolution that followed hard upon it, his paranoia would serve Chamfort well. So would it serve his aphorisms, which he began writing around this time—roughly 1777, when he was thirty-seven—for it was in these aphorisms that he first dropped the dry and artificial style of neoclassicism in which all his public writing had been composed and now wrote as he spoke, lucidly, beautifully, devastatingly.

Chamfort qualifies as a genius, even though it is a bit difficult to say what, precisely, his occupation was. Continually—one is almost ready to say continuously—attracted and repelled by the rewards of society, he fairly regularly ducked in and out of it, but in 1780, when he was forty, he resolved no longer to write for the public. (The following year, 1781, he was finally elected to the Académie Française, to which he had been seeking membership for many years.) But now he planned to rusticate himself. He was a man who could live well enough on his despair, bemoaning the fate of the literary man in his time, contemptuous of the class whose approval he also sought—

that, along with the various government pensions he had accrued, made life, however dark, endurable.

Arnaud remarks that Chamfort was "born at the wrong time." He tells us that he and Laclos perhaps shared "the intuition that their half-century would be remembered less for its literature than for its mores and fashions, ideas and conversation." Chamfort himself noted, in one of his aphorisms: "Reading through the memoirs and literary monuments of the century of Louis XIV, one finds even in the bad company of the age something that is missing in the good of our own." The period tossed up odd talents such as Rétif de la Bretonne and Chamfort himself; today the only writer of the period who is still considered of central importance is Rousseau, and perhaps one could add Diderot. Yet Chamfort's life was not so much divided as cleaved by that event of singular significance, the French Revolution—an event that simultaneously shortened his life and lent him part of the significance he has today. Without the intercession of the French Revolution, Chamfort would have been remembered, if at all, as an elegant fop with an impressive control of language, another literary man on the make, a Julien Sorel who missed the guillotine.

There are times in intellectual history when politics sweeps the boards. During such times politics absorbs, becomes, finally is everything. All talent turns to politics, and art, literature, music, family life, and everything else is secondary, if not altogether beside the point; or so at least they seem to those who live during such times. The years leading up to, through, and immediately after the French Revolution were such a time. Chamfort, despite his claims to wish to live outside society, was quite as swept up as any intellectual of his day in the events of the French Revolution. He might, in his aphorisms, mock society as "nothing but the contentions of a thousand clashing petty interests, an eternal conflict of all the vanities that cross each other, strike against each other, are wounded and humiliated by each other," but when the action of the revolution began Chamfort was there, a player very close to its center. Nietzsche, in *The Gay Science,* remarks: "That a man who understood men and the crowd as well as Chamfort, nevertheless joined the crowd and did not stay aside in philosophical renunciation and resistance, I can explain it to myself only in this way: He had one instinct that was even stronger than his wisdom and had never been satisfied—hatred of all nobility by blood."

As late as 1784, Chamfort accepted the post of principal secretary to Mme Elizabeth, the sister of Louis XVI, which didn't stop him from writing, in collaboration with Mirabeau, *Consideration of the Society or Order of Cincinnati,* a Rousseauistic pamphlet making a strong case against nobility. ("He is," said Mirabeau of Chamfort, "the flint I need for my musket.") He had earlier joined a number of younger political intellectuals, known as the Bellechasse group, of whom Talleyrand would go on to become the most famous member. Chamfort wrote one of the first arguments for republican government during the ancien régime. Later, along with Mirabeau and Talleyrand, he joined the Club of Thirty, which prepared the ground for the first democratically run election ever held in France. As Arnaud says, "Chamfort was born too early—or too late—to produce a major literary work, but he had arrived just at the right time to change the world."

Chamfort's deep antipathy to the nobility is not difficult to trace. It had its beginnings in his own disgraced birth, and came to its maturity with Chamfort himself, who needed the approval of the nobility for any advancement he wished to make. This antipathy to the nobility plays throughout Chamfort's aphorisms. He took what Montaigne said of nobility, "Since we cannot achieve it let us avenge ourselves by speaking ill of it," and remarked that it would be better rewritten as "I detest that nobility which made me avoid what I loved, or could have loved." Behind much of the rancor in the aphorisms lie the sad twists that Chamfort felt he had to undergo in his own personality before those who were above him in rank but, as he well knew, in nothing else. A man without money or a title, he averred, was more estranged than "a Frenchman in Peking or Macao or a Lapp in Senegal." "To acquire fortune and distinction in spite of the disadvantage of having no ancestors, and to do it in the midst of that crowd who received everything at birth, is like winning, or stale-mating a game of chess after giving one's adversary a rook, or castle. . . . One can manage without a castle, but not without the queen."

The French Revolution was thought to give everyone back the queen through beheading the real queen and her husband, Louis XVI. Chamfort exalted in the revolution, at least for a time. His resentment, his Rousseau-like idealism, his quite genuine feeling for the underdog, all got a good workout in the first years of the revolution. "Society is made up of two great classes," Chamfort wrote, in one of his most famous aphorisms, "those who have more dinners than appetite, and those who have more appetite than dinners." Now at last he didn't have to hide the side on which his own true feeling lay. Arnaud reports that "he was a happy revolutionary . . . [hewing] a middle path between intrigue and uprightness, pragmatism and utopia." Where once he claimed a noble ancestry, now he vaunted his lowly upbringing. He stripped away all the luxuries from his personal life. He justified the early days of the Terror. Heads on pikes, the creaking inexorable wheels of the tumbril, the persistent snap of the "national razor" didn't cause him to flinch. "These days you have to be cruel out of humaneness," he said. He was himself asked to be director of the Bibliothèque Nationale. He demurred, but later agreed to accept a co-directorship.

As Chamfort's generation was replaced by the generation of Danton and Robespierre, with Marat overlapping both, the second Terror began in horrendous earnest. Chamfort's own position became precarious under this reign of lawyers turned revolutionists. He was twice arrested, first after being accused of advocating criminal behavior by a spy who wanted his job at the Bibliothèque Nationale and who claimed to hear him approve of the assassination of Marat by Charlotte Corday, the granddaughter of Corneille; and the second time for putatively refusing to dissociate himself from Charlotte Corday and thus, in the mad logic of the revolution, proving his accuser correct.

Upon this second arrest, Chamfort was sent to the prison known as Madelonnettes, where, Arnaud reports, meat went untouched because it was rumored to have come from the bodies of victims of the guillotine. What wasn't rumor was the filth and stench of this, the beastliest jail in Paris. Chamfort was made to spend two nights in Madelonnettes, among rats real and metaphorical. His brief sojourn in this prison was a jolt to more than his, Chamfort's, metabolism; he, who felt he had sacrificed so much for the revolution, now could not but know that he was likely soon to be sacrificed to it himself. He vowed, come what may, never to return to Madelonnettes.

Revolutions, like many varieties of slug, ingest their own kind, and so eventually did the French Revolution swallow Chamfort, one of its most ardent early provocateurs, ideologues, and supporters. When told that the theater in Paris was being poorly attended, he remarked that "tragedy no longer has the same effect once it roams the streets." And so when it was announced to Chamfort, who after his stay at the Madelonnettes was under house arrest, that he would have to return to prison, he quietly finished his simple dinner of soup and coffee, retired to his bedroom, and proceeded hideously to butcher himself.

With a mis-aimed pistol shot Chamfort first blew out his right eye; he then attempted to cut his throat; and finally he slashed himself about the arms and legs. In all he inflicted twenty-two wounds upon himself without completing the job. He would later claim that Seneca, a richer man, had servants to help him and so was able to make a tidier job of his own suicide. Chamfort would live five or so months longer, but inept treatment of his wounds—in closing them up, the attending physician neglected to leave drainage slits—brought about his death on April 13, 1794. "When a man lies dying, he does not die from his disease alone," wrote Péguy. "He dies from his whole life."

No one would have known about Chamfort's aphorisms but for their having been discovered and saved by his faithful friend Ginguené, who eventually brought them to the public under Chamfort's own ironically intended title *Products of the Perfected Civilization*. The irony, heavy-handedly bitter, is that Chamfort found civilization, both under the monarchy and under the revolution, as far as possible from perfected. "Prejudice, vanity, scheming," wrote Chamfort, "these are what govern the world," and he goes on to report that "he whose only principles of conduct are reason, truth, and sensibility has nothing in common with society," concluding that "it is within himself that he must seek out and find virtually all his happiness."

Here we have the *donnée* for nearly all aphorists. Ah, if only man had the simple good sense to be content in solitude. Pascal said it first: "All the misfortunes of men derive from one single thing, which is their inability to sit quietly in a room." La Bruyère chimes in with: "In France, it takes much firmness of spirit and a great breadth of understanding to do without offices and positions, and be willing to stay at home and do nothing." Chamfort, too, maintains that "the world hardens most men's hearts," and giving oneself up to several days of society leaves one troubled and sad, and the only advantage of having been out in the world is "the pleasure it lends to retirement." Elsewhere he says that the ability to say "no" and "the ability to live to oneself are the only two ways of preserving one's liberty and one's character." The problem, for Chamfort and for the others, was managing to stay home, out of the tumult, in repose, quietly, thinking.

"That of all days is the most completely wasted in which one did not once laugh," wrote Chamfort. Yet, one's sense is, he was more likely to have been the cause of laughter in others, with his lacerating wit, than in himself, who was often the object of his own witty lacerations. Traditionally, aphorists come on cooly elegant in their disdain, but Chamfort, as Sainte-Beuve remarked, "scorched the paper" on which he wrote. He is almost always the angry aphorist. He claims no wisdom, unlike La Rochefoucauld or La Bruyère or Vauvenargues. They used scalpels, he a broadax; they took lessons from life, he remained furious about it; they aimed for the most heightened objectivity, he could never slip his passion; they wrote as if from outside life looking in, he wrote as if fully caught in life's whirlpool. "Living," he wrote, "is an ailment which is relieved every sixteen hours by sleep. Death is the cure."

The history of literature could be written around the subject of writers finding their true forms. Sometimes the forms are there waiting, and sometimes they have almost to be invented. Although he came to it late in his life, the aphorism was perfect for Chamfort, though he himself never had the time to make more perfect his own aphorisms. W. G. Moore, in *La Rochefoucauld: His Mind and Art,* has recounted the social context in which La Rochefoucauld, who is the father of the form, created his own aphorisms. They began in a game, played among the circle of Mme de Sable, where social observations were set out and then honed to their greatest possible pungency and brevity, in the attempt to turn them into epigrams. La Rochefoucauld's manuscripts show how he would often begin with a full paragraph and then, slowly, thoughtfully, clip and prune and boil a thought down to its quintessence. Final approval in many instances awaited the word of Mme de Sable. In this purifying process, where economy was so highly valued, abstraction naturally emerged prominent. Who knows out of how much in the way of discussion, writing, and editing La Rochefoucauld's "The head is always fooled by the heart" was born?

None of this is meant to imply that La Rochefoucauld's elegant, economical aphorisms were made by method alone. They were made, above all, by experience. La Rochefoucauld lived in what the Chinese, in their famous curse, called "interesting times"—that is, a time in which men had plenty of latitude to show their more disgraceful side—in those civil wars in France during the minority of Louis XIV known as the Fronde; and he lived long enough to have been disappointed by life, which used perhaps to take a bit longer than it does now. Chamfort, too, lived in "interesting times"; he also lived long enough to be disappointed in love and by ambition. Add to this the rancor that, as a bastard, was part of his birthright and you have the classical profile of the natural aphorist.

Georges Poulet has written that Chamfort is only of interest from the time that he began to write his aphorisms. "Before that there had undoubtedly been other versions of Chamfort: an ambitious hack, a dandy, a passionate lover." All of these, of course, were grist for the mill, which ground exceedingly fine, of the aphorist. "Love," wrote Chamfort, "has not permitted its secret to be revealed; man knows it only on the condition of not being able to divulge it, and he loses the memory of it the moment his passion ceases, for that secret is nothing other than love itself." As Poulet rightly notes, the man Chamfort constantly executes in his aphorisms "is indeed Chamfort himself." The bitter lessons learned by that unhappy young man went into the stiletto-like sentences of the mature writer. "A philosopher," he wrote, "must start by experiencing the happiness of the dead."

A good part of what impresses the modern reader with Chamfort is not only his essential loneliness but his own lucid sense of how precisely alone in the world he was. "Preserve, if you can, the interests that attach you to society, but cultivate the feelings that separate you from it," he wrote. Yet the feelings that separated Chamfort from society, from his fellow man, from nearly everyone, seemed to come naturally enough to him. He is one of those loners in literature, in the line of Baudelaire, Dostoevsky, Schopenhauer, Nietzsche, Camus. The reason each of these writers was essentially alone is that each was intent on discovering an ethic that would comport with the prominent fact of evil in man and in nature, each was contemptuous of intellectual mediocrity and philosophical sham, and each permitted no easy optimism or belief in the rehabilitation of man through progress in history. "What is a philosopher?" asked Chamfort. "He is a man who opposes Nature to Law, reason to custom, his conscience to public opinion, and his judgment to error."

Chamfort was a moralist who distrusted even his fellow moralists. The argument has been made that even the relatively rough form of some of Chamfort's aphorisms is based on the almost systematic hatred in Chamfort of systematic thinking. Professor Eve Katz has written that Chamfort's aphorisms "do not, like La Rochefoucauld's, for example, rest on the assumption that one can enclose an entire philosophy in one or two sentences. They do not lay claim to certainty. They do not presuppose that there are limits to ideas and that one can give them definitive expression." She quotes, in support of her argument, another of Chamfort's aphorisms:

> In order to view things correctly, one must give words the opposite sense to the one the world gives them. Misanthrope, for instance, means philanthrope; bad Frenchman means good citizen, which implies certain monstrous abuses; philosopher means "a simple man, who knows that two and two make four, etc."

Perhaps the best way—which is also to say, the best reason—to read Chamfort today is for his honesty. For honesty, if it cuts deeply enough, is itself a variant of truth, and discrete touches of penetrating honesty may have to do until a more elaborate or systematic version of truth is available to those of us of an even mildly skeptical nature. The Chamfort who gives pleasure of a lighter kind is the Chamfort who wrote

> It is commonly believed that the art of pleasing is a great means of achieving wealth; knowing how to be bored is an art which succeeds still better. The talent for acquiring wealth, like the one for succeeding with women, can be reduced practically to that.

It is the Chamfort of the quick and deadly definition—"Love: agreeable folly," "Ambition: serious imbecility," or "Celebrity: the advantage of being known by those who do not know you"—whom one finds so companionable, however oddly the word "companionable" may seem to fit this dark and lonely writer. Yet it was Chamfort who remarked that "in certain friendships one enjoys the happiness of the passions and the approbation of reason as well," which constitutes a quite respectable blurb for the intellectual profit his own writing brings.

In his aphorisms, Chamfort is a writer dedicated to acting with honesty, living with limitations, and striving always for truth. "Enjoy and give pleasure, without doing harm to yourself or to anyone else—that, I think, is the whole of morality," he wrote. His own was a life far from filled with enjoyment, and in the end he did the ultimate harm to himself, yet today, roughly two hundred years after he wrote it, Chamfort's encapsulated prescription for morality rings true, and the ring of truth is the only serious criterion for judging an aphorism. Coming from the man who wrote that "pleasure may be based on illusion, but happiness rests on truth," this is in itself a small but impressive and, yes, finally happy tribute to Chamfort the aphorist, the artist of truth.

Selling Henry James

T HE JUDGES have spoken, and I am declared a clear
winner. "Don't worry, Mom," as victors by knock-
out used to say on the old Gillette Friday-night-
fight broadcasts, "I'll be home early." The judges in this instance
are the students in a Henry James course I taught for the first
time to undergraduates at Northwestern University, and their
judgments come in the form of student evaluations. I have just
been presented with a packet of these evaluations. To switch
from boxing to poker, read 'em and leap, which my heart did,
at least briefly, in appreciation for finding my own pedagogical
efforts so warmly received. Allow me to quote from a few of
these evaluations, partly to give some rough notion of what
students who study literature are up against these days and
partly out of sheer pathetic vanity:

- Excellent. Perhaps the best course I've taken in college.
- It was refreshing to look at the work [of Henry James] as
  just *good* literature, and not to have to worry about Marxist,
  capitalist, feminist interpretations.
- Each class period was among the shortest 110 minutes of
  my week. Interesting. Stimulating. Controversial.
- It was refreshing to talk about what an author was actually
  saying, rather than what he wasn't saying or didn't know he

was saying. This class was one of the high points of my four years at Northwestern—I'm glad I had it during my final quarter.
• Top-notch—the champagne of academic experience.

That last item reminds me that Mumm's the word—or perhaps ought to have been about such obviously inflated praise. But then I am so pleased that this course seems to have gone over with its audience that perhaps I am a bit out of control. I set out to teach it, I must confess, with some trepidation. I say "with some trepidation," but it occurs to me that I have done most of my teaching with some trepidation, though I have been told that such nervousness as I might feel doesn't show. Something else that doesn't show, at least so long as one is teaching other than foreign languages in the humanities, is one's effectiveness. How much of what one is saying is getting through to students? How much thinking of a subtle or textured kind can one expect to be absorbed by students between the ages of eighteen and twenty-two who, if memory serves, have a few other things on their minds?

Confidence in these matters is for fools. Five or six years ago, a colleague, not normally given to bragging, told me that something quite magical had been happening to his teaching. He didn't quite know how to explain it, but suddenly it all seemed to be coming together for him. In class he would find himself making startling connections, things flowed as never before, fascinating, possibly even original insights that had not hitherto occurred to him seemed to be there when he needed them.

That same afternoon I ran into one of the most impressive of the then-current batch of undergraduate literature students. She was quick at acquiring foreign languages; was writing a senior paper on Rilke for Erich Heller; had been earnest enough to sit through an entire course of mine, for no credit, on the sociology of literature, for which she did all the reading and contributed brilliantly to classroom discussion. In a casual, merely making-conversation way, I asked her how her quarter was going. "All right," she said, "but for Professor X.'s class [the colleague mentioned in the above paragraph]. He's so dry, so dogmatic, so clearly talking to himself." Whoops. I took—and continue to take—the moral of that story to be, Never say you are teaching well.

I was not about to say that I do, but I do say that I especially wanted to teach Henry James well. As a graduate student in a different class once said to me of another student who was floundering and about whose fate she was worried, so I now say about Henry James: "I love him, you see." James seems to me the most artistically intelligent, the most subtle, finally the greatest American writer. No other American writer has given me so much pleasure nor, I believe, taught me so much about literature and life. I wanted ardently to get my appreciation for James across. I wanted converts, not to my precise views, but to at least a rough recognition of Henry James's immense achievement.

Before this could be done, I suspected, there was the need to scrape free the barnacles of cliché that have clung to the vessel of James's reputation. The cliché that he was a very great snob—"an effete snob," into the bargain, in Theodore Roosevelt's phrase—must be chipped away. So, too, the notion that Henry James's subject was an impossibly rarefied one, that he wrote almost exclusively about people who could really never have existed: unanchored in work, nationally rootless, without financial concern, detached in nearly every way, sheer engines of pure and apparently inexhaustible cerebration. Although Henry James was an immitigably highbrow writer—some would say the first American modernist writer, given his tireless interest in the formal properties of his art—he also happens to have been an extraordinary comedian, in my opinion one of the fun-

niest writers going. The cliché of Henry James as a great square
stiffo, the ultimate stuffed shirt, this, too, had to be quickly
swept away.

Were my students even aware of these clichés? Difficult to
know. But then it is a bit difficult to know what, exactly, is
taught to undergraduates nowadays. In the course descriptions
that go out each quarter, which I admit to reading in good
part for the unconscious humor I find in them, one often
encounters offerings promising the latest theory-a-go-go written in the most rococo gibberish. But then there are also standard survey courses and teachers who haven't gone in for the
nouvelle intellectual diet. My guess is that an undergraduate
majoring in English at Northwestern today is likely to have
been taught a single work by James—*Washington Square,* perhaps, or *Portrait of a Lady,* just possibly "Turn of the Screw."

I recalled my own introduction to Henry James as an undergraduate at the University of Chicago in the middle 1950s. It
came when I was twenty years old in a course in the modern
novel taught by Morton Dauwen Zabel. The novel was *The
Spoils of Poynton,* a book of 1897, when James had already begun
to write in his late—which is to say, more complex and circum-
ambulating—style; and its subject, that of the passing on of a
lovingly gathered collection of antique furniture, doubtless must
have seemed rarefied in the extreme to a Midwestern boy to
whom the entire notion of "antique" held not the least interest. How much of the novel I could be said to have compre-
hended I cannot say. Yet I came away with respect for it, which
was in part owing to the respect I had for the respect in which
my teacher held it. I did at least grasp that Henry James was
serious stuff, and that if I were one day to consider myself a
serious literary man I should have to return to him.

It's probably a bad idea to ask how much anyone gets out of
a book. ("None of us," writes Ned Rorem, "can ever know
how even our closest friends hear music.") The question is

especially complicated when applied to the young. I think of myself at nineteen reading Proust. What was going through my mind? Probably chiefly delight at the notion of myself reading Proust. When young, one does a great deal of reading that, if one is going to be among that small portion of people who go on to take books seriously, will have to be done again. As an earnest student of mine once put it shortly before his graduation, "God, I wish I had a chance to do a second draft on my education." Some of us have been lucky enough to be able to arrange our lives spending the rest of our days putting draft after draft on our education.

Yet a teacher of the young must not dwell on the question of what, even roughly, his students derive from the books he teaches them. My own assumption is that they, or at least the best among them, do not get much less than I do; and I have always tried to teach to the best in the class. To do less would be to lapse into condescension of a kind that would be defeating. This doesn't mean that I don't stop to explain and discuss fundamental matters—how symbolism works, what constitutes style—but I do assume that my students read for the same reasons that I do: aesthetic pleasure and spiritual profit.

Not that this need preclude a certain quiet cozening on this teacher's part. In teaching Henry James I viewed myself as a salesman. Like a salesman, I saw no point in making it any more difficult than necessary for a customer to say Yes. No point, in my view, in throwing anyone in at the deep end of the pool. Not that Henry James's pool has a shallow end; he adored, he positively wallowed in complexity, and toward the end of his life he told his niece that he wished he could find a more elaborate way to pronounce his own name. But some Jamesian works are a good deal less daunting than others, and I planned to begin with these, working my way through and up to the more complicated. Here is my reading list in the sequential order that students would be asked to read James:

1. "The Art of Fiction"
2. "The Figure in the Carpet"
3. "The Aspern Papers"
4. *Washington Square*
5. "Daisy Miller"
6. "The Pupil"
7. *The Europeans*
8. "The Turn of the Screw"
9. *The Princess Casamassima*
10. *The Ambassadors* (to be read for the final exam)

Class enrollment was set at thirty students. I wanted the course to be built around discussion of works, for I thought that straight lecturing would be deadly. Something like forty-seven students registered for it, but I closed out enrollment at thirty-six. What their motives—beyond course credit—were in taking the course I do not know. Most were upperclassmen, four were graduate students; the student who wrote far and away the most brilliant examination in the course turned out to be a sophomore.

First day of class, right out of the chute, the sales pitch began. After setting out the ground rules—examinations, papers, grades, attendance—I announced what I took to be the point of the course. This was to establish in their minds an appreciation for the work of one of the most subtle of American writers, an understanding of what constitutes an exemplary career in literature, and, somehow, through all this, I hoped they would take away something that, in ways that could not be predicted, would alter, however slightly, their ways of thinking about life and make them a little bit smarter.

I next touched briefly on a question that, fifteen or twenty years ago, would simply never have arisen—that of "how" we shall read Henry James. "I suppose my answer to this question," I said, "is, 'As intelligently as possible.' I do not myself read him as a Marxist, a Freudian, a Deconstructionist, a Poststructuralist; I don't read him to discover that he might be 'elitist,' or 'pro-capitalist,' or 'anti-feminist,' or anything of the sort. One of the interesting things about Henry James is that he makes all these ways of reading seem rather beside the point. I read him for the pleasure of his language, for his wit, for his meaning, which, if I may say so, is not always that easily caught. A critic named Philip Rahv [surely no one in the class, graduate students included, is likely to have encountered that name], who once remarked that James was a secular New Englander, interested in the same moral questions that his fellow New Englanders had been interested in, once formulated James's way of coming at these questions thus: For Henry James 'any failure of discrimination is sin, whereas virtue is a compound of intelligence, moral delicacy, and the sense of the past.' "

Raising the sales pitch slightly, I began, in a brief lecture on Henry James's life, by calling him a genius. A genius, though, I emphasized, of a particular kind. Henry James's genius was not of the natural kind but came about as the result of fortunate circumstances—chief among them being born into the James family—and the most careful self-cultivation. And I quoted James himself, in *The Tragic Muse,* on the nature of genius in the arts: "Genius is only the art of getting your experience fast, of stealing it, as it were. . . ." It is also, of course, the ability to make the most of this experience, to have the energy and determination to make that experience count and to make it tell in works of art. I also quoted James on another character in the same novel: "Life, for him [one Mr. Carteret], was a purely practical function, not a question of phrasing." To which I added that they, my students, ought to know right off that for Henry James not entirely but in good part life was a matter of phrasing—the right phrasing. I'm fairly sure no one in the room quite knew what I meant.

The second session of class I brought in a photograph of Henry James in his early sixties, my only visual (non-audio) aid. In this photograph, which I acquired some years ago from the Smith College Archives, James wears pince-nez and is without his beard. I asked the students to take a minute or so with the photograph so that they might recall that the man they would be reading all quarter really was of flesh and blood, however god-like at times he may seem. I also suggested that the more penetrating among them might just discover, behind what at first glance seems a most formidable late-nineteenth-century countenance, a slight but very sly humor lurking.

Together the class and I worked our way through the essay James titled "The Art of Fiction." He wrote it in 1884, when he was forty-one, well launched on his career but far from having attained the heights he would soon reach. The essay is too rich to summarize here, but it is about what James calls the "artistic idea" and the variety of possibilities that novels provide—which "are as various as the temperament of man, and [are] successful as they reveal a particular mind, different from the others"—and all that the glorious form of the novel, then attaining its preeminence as a literary form, was capable of achieving in the hands of serious practitioners. Best as I remember it, the discussion was not exhilarating—it is generally easier to teach imaginative than critical works—but earnest, and at least nothing flat-out stupid was said. I also handed out Xerox copies of a sheet of quotations. The most impressive of these, from James's essay on Turgenev, I read aloud, prefacing it by saying that James himself, in the same essay, remarks that when we read a writer of real power we want to know what he thinks about the world. This quotation, I think, comes as close as any single passage from James that I know to answering that question.

> Life *is*, in fact, a battle. On this point optimists and pessimists agree. Evil is insolent and strong; beauty enchanting but rare; goodness very apt to be weak; folly very apt to be defiant; wickedness to carry the day; imbeciles to be in very great places,

people of sense in small, and mankind generally, unhappy. But the world as it stands is no illusion, no phantasm, no evil dream of a night; we wake up to it again for ever and ever; we can neither forget it nor deny it nor dispense with it. We can welcome experience as it comes, and give it what it demands, in exchange for something which it is idle to pause to call much or little so long as it contributes to swell the volume of consciousness. In this there is mingled pain and delight, but over the mysterious mixture there hovers a visible rule, that bids us learn to will and seek to understand.

I closed that second class, our first working session, by quoting James yet again: "In every novel the work is divided between the writer and the reader; but the writer makes the reader very much as he makes his characters . . . the reader would be doing his share of the task; the grand point is to get him to make it." Would James be able to turn this trick with these students? Remains, as political journalists hedging their bets say, to be seen.

"Taught what seemed to me a decent class yesterday," my journal for March 30, 1990, reads. "Some bright and earnest kids in the room, I think." The fact is that, over the years, I have had little to complain about in my students at Northwestern. There have been the usual contingent of the mediocre; a vastly smaller contingent of the genuinely hopeless; but always I have come upon a small number of superior students who are capable of passion and intelligence about art and other artifacts of the mind. Northwestern does not do all that well in the snobbery sweepstakes that I think undergraduate education in the United States has become; in rankings that appear in newspapers or news magazines from time to time, it is usually listed in some such slightly dreary position as fourteenth or eighteenth best school in the country. Who knows what this means—and who cares? But what I do know is that, in order to get into Northwestern, which asks high grades and SAT scores, these students have had to have acquired the habits of achievement—which is to say, they do the work. Ask them to read a novel by next Thursday, and generally almost all will have done so; and those few who have not will feel damned guilty about it. I, for one, am glad they do feel guilty.

Originally, the James course was to meet from nine to ten-thirty, but then I thought perhaps Henry James at nine in the morning might be pushing it, and so I changed the time to ten-thirty to twelve. The room we met in was on the fourth floor of an old Charles Addams–like building called University Hall, which had good light and for some reason thirty or so extra chairs, all metal and plastic, many of which seemed to be massed up at the front of the room, giving the joint the feel of an abandoned warehouse once owned by a Scandinavian furniture company. Within a week or so, I learned the names of the students, whom as always I addressed as Mr. and Miss, and had my initial hunches about their differing intellectual quality. A graduate student named Pataky, who spoke ardently and well, could be depended upon to come in anywhere from five to ten minutes late. Soon it began to feel like that strange academic social unit—a class.

I generally began each session by gassing away for twenty or so minutes on a general subject, such as the distinctions between highbrow, middlebrow, and lowbrow art, the meaning and use of irony as a literary method, the relation between morality and the novel, the best short formulation of which, in my opinion, remains that of R. P. Blackmur: "Novels do not supply us with morals, but they show us with what morals have to do." Sometimes I would use my twenty or so minutes to talk about a more strictly Jamesian subject: James's friendship with Edith Wharton; the history of his reputation; his working methods, including the switch from handwriting his novels to dictating the later books to a typist. But the greatest portion of time in class was given to discussion of Henry James's stories and novels.

Henry James is nothing if not discussable. He never comes

straight out to tell you what to think, though those of us who have lived long with his fiction have a pretty good notion of his partialities. He had a positive horror of generalization. When T. S. Eliot famously said that Henry James had "a mind so fine no idea could violate it," he did not mean that James couldn't understand or handle general ideas, but instead that his mind was too finely textured ever to be dominated by an idea and that he carried on his own aesthetic operation at a level well above the ideational. "It is the business of literature," wrote Desmond MacCarthy, "to make ideas out of facts." James was content to work with the facts alone—the lush, languorous, lovely facts—and let his readers discover in his writing such ideas as they deemed useful, so that many a Henry James story or novel, ending in renunciation or death, leaves a reader to work out the true meaning of what he has read on his own. Some people hate this challenge; others among us feel that this is precisely how sophisticated commerce between a novelist and his audience ought to be carried on. Naturally, I hoped my students would develop the respect for Henry James and the aesthetic patience required to join the latter camp.

Certainly, the very first story in the course, "The Figure in the Carpet," called for aesthetic patience in the extreme. It is a story about a search for the deep and underlying meaning of a writer's work. "My little point," the writer in question calls it, then enlarges upon his meaning:

> "By my little point I mean—what shall I call it?—the particular thing I've written my books most *for*. Isn't there for every writer a particular thing of that sort, the thing that most makes him apply himself, the thing without the effort to achieve which he wouldn't write at all, the very passion of his passion, the part of the business in which, for him, the flame of art burns most intensely? Well, it's *that!*"

Readers of James's splendid story will recall that, although most of it is about trying to discover what that little point, the figure in the writer's carpet, really is, we never finally find out. We can only surmise, which is far from everyone's idea of how a story ought satisfactorily to end. What is more, it is very difficult to be human and not draw parallels with the writer in the story and its author and wonder what the figure might be in Henry James's own carpet. At least I hoped it was difficult. I put this story first on our reading list because I wanted students to begin thinking of James's general intention, the passion of his passion, the part of the business in which, for him, the flame burned most intensely.

I teach by what is very loosely called the Socratic method, though I am much better dressed and epically less intelligent than the man after whom it is named. Chiefly, I interrogate, sometimes pressing fairly hard, asking four, five, six questions of the same student, yet stopping, I trust, well short of the general tone of the Gestapo. I ask a question, then call on those students who raise their hands. If no one raises his or her hand, I call on someone anyhow. I try quietly to convey that it is a mistake to come to one of my classes unprepared. Nothing wrong with injecting a small element of fear in education. I know fear contributed greatly to my own.

Building gradually in complexity and in length, the course next took up "The Aspern Papers," a *nouvelle*, "the beautiful and blest *nouvelle*," James called it. He was much enamored of the form, for it allowed him to undertake serious psychological examination while practicing what he termed "exquisite economy in composition." I hadn't read "The Aspern Papers" in more than twenty years and on rereading this "other story about Venice" it struck me as even better than I remembered it: more subtle, more powerful, more beautiful. I attempted to teach it around a general issue—that of the correctness of digging into the past of the personal lives of famous people to make them public in the name of scholarship, biographical interest, art, or what have you. I did not neglect to mention, by way of introduction, how lively this issue remained in our own day (the Mencken *Diary* had just been published against Mencken's own wishes with serious consequences for the author's reputation), and I brought up the fact that Henry James himself had at one point burned forty years of his own correspondence, lest it fall into the hands of a "publishing scoundrel" like the narrator of "The Aspern Papers."

A number of other ways of approaching the work were available, not least among them as a study into the nature of an *idée fixe,* or, as F. W. Dupee puts it in his book on James, as a book about the "power [of the past] to bargain with the present." But I could have lingered as well on the sheer beauty of James's rendering of his story, fondling details, highlighting descriptions, noting the scores of delicate phrasings. When James speaks of Juliana Bordereau, the aged lover of the dead poet Jeffrey Aspern, he remarks that, as an American, she had first come to Europe before "photography and other conveniences [had] annihilated surprise." Forgive a bit of gushing, but that phrase "annihilated surprise" seems to me worth the entire price of the ticket. I pointed this out in class; I mentioned other lovely Jamesian touches. But when teaching the work of genuinely elegant prose writers I have always felt that I have never done this element in their work sufficient justice. If poetry is what is left out of translation, it is the fine and artful details that tend to depart in teaching.

The student response to "The Aspern Papers" seemed to me generous in its appreciation. I felt that there was a strong sense in the room of the quality of the work that we had just read and of the superiority of the artistic intelligence that had produced it. Meanwhile, personalities began to emerge, and they were not uninteresting. Of a class of thirty-six students, twelve or so were fairly impressive talkers, and three or four were capable of saying things of the kind that kept the old professor on his own wobbly toes. The class, in other words, had begun to take on character, and it was not a displeasing one. "Students in my Henry James course seem filled with goodwill," I note in my journal for April 7. "Don't know if my Henry James sell is working, but thus far no one is walking out."

Washington Square, the next book in the course, is a novel that James chose not to include in the New York Edition of his works, *The Novels and Tales of Henry James,* which he prepared for publication between 1905 and 1909. Around the time the Edition began to appear, James wrote to the novelist Robert Herrick that "by the mere fact of leaving out certain things (I have tried to read over *Washington Square* and I *can't,* and I fear it must go!) I exercise a control, a discrimination, I treat certain portions of my work as unhappy accidents." Not a good decision, in my view, for this slender novel, written when James was thirty-seven, continues to stir the mind and agitate the heart of an attentive reader. Dealing with one of the great Jamesian themes—the immorality of an attempt by one human being to dominate the spirit of another, or to use another as a means to his or her own ends—the novel also provides a potent argument against theoretical modes of thinking in its attack on the figure of Dr. Austin Sloper, the successful physician who kills the love and respect in which he was held by his own daughter by treating her as essentially a pawn in a chess game of his own theoretical imagining. Scientific by training, the doctor is a man used to dividing people into classes and types, and, as he avers at one point in the novel, nineteen times out of twenty he is right. The problem is that the twentieth case can be decisive—it can be, this twentieth case, your own daughter. Implicit in this I read James's criticism of scientific—and in our day, social-scientific and psychoanalytic—thought. "Never say you know the last word about any human heart," James wrote, and it ought to stand as the permanent motto for those, great writers and all readers alike, who take their instruction from literature seriously.

In class, discussion of *Washington Square* revolved around the question of how Henry James had taken a relatively small

cast of what looked to be fairly stock characters—an ugly duck-
ling daughter, a busybody aunt, a severe father, a handsome
fortune hunter—and made them vivid and serious and
immensely interesting. I recall the talk about this question being
of good quality. I raised the question, too, of how James was
able to transform his heroine, Catherine Sloper, the ugly duck-
ling daughter, from a rather dreary, misbegotten young woman
to a formidable, quite admirable woman of resolute character.
I mentioned a formulation of Desmond MacCarthy's in this
connection, which runs, if I have it correctly, that in the novels
and stories of Henry James only the good are beautiful and
there is no shortcut to being good. All that it generally takes
to qualify as good in James is consistent kindness, heightened
awareness, scrupulosity of behavior, and just possibly an act of
renunciation that at the time it is made is likely to seem the
moral equivalent of amputation. Yet in James it always, in the
elaborate working out of his plots, seems persuasive.

I was putting in a good deal of time in class preparations,
and I found I was enjoying myself greatly, looking forward to
entering class and feeling a slight drop in emotional temperature after each session was over. This was owing in part to the
students, but even more, I believe, to Henry James. A few
months before the course had begun, I read some of James's
novels that I had not read before (*Watch and Ward, Confidence, The Reverberator, The Tragic Muse*) and reread others
that over the years had become blurry in memory (*Roderick
Hudson, The American, The Bostonians*). I also read the one-
volume abridgment of Leon Edel's original—and, in my opinion, triumphant—five-volume biography of Henry James. I read
some of James's art criticism and reread some of his travel pieces.
I read a fair amount of the vast body of criticism of James; and
in so doing was reminded how the revival of James's reputation in the 1920s and 1930s, consequent upon the creation in
the university of American literature as a respectable academic
subject, happily paralleled the emergence of a brilliant group

of critics, including T. S. Eliot, Yvor Winters, Lionel Trilling, Philip Rahv, F. W. Dupee, Joseph Warren Beach, William Troy, Edmund Wilson, and Jacques Barzun, all of whom much admired James and wrote interestingly on him. For four or five months, then, I had been living on an almost exclusively Henry James literary diet and felt myself flourishing on it.

Odd but I have found that I can write with enthusiasm about things I dislike—anger, after all, can be an inspiration—but I can only teach with delight what I love. Part of the reason for this may be that, with undergraduate life so brief, it seems pointless to me to waste any portion of it asking students to read and think about third- and fourth-rate things. One can scarcely hope to acquaint them, in the span of four years, with more than a soupçon of the ample quantity of the first-rate available in art and thought. Besides, I have my own selfish motives for teaching. Apart from doing one's job—teaching the *Kinder* properly—I need to feel some sense of intellectual progress while doing so, usually in the way of feeling I am getting a bit smarter myself, and possibly learning a thing or two about writing. Teaching Henry James allows one to think one is progressing in both ways.

Not that all was euphoria. "Daisy Miller," which I taught to introduce James's international theme—or, as he called it, "the Americano-European legend"—presented a few bumps in the road. ("Daisy Miller" was the story that gave James his initial jolt of fame: the character of the American girl loose on the Continent established a type, as F. Scott Fitzgerald was later to do for the flapper; and James was asked to provide stories of the same kind for other magazines, which, being Henry James, of course he didn't.) One of the difficulties the story provided was that many of James's little jokes about the vulgarity of the Miller family sailed blithely over the heads of students for whom vulgarity isn't currently a vivid category. A small business early in the story, for example, has Daisy's younger and thoroughly spoiled brother announce the names of the

members of his family each with his or her middle initial: Annie
P. Miller, Ezra B. Miller, Randolph C. Miller. The use of the
middle initial is a wholly American phenomenon, and James
brings it in merely to show the comic combination of American naiveté and pomposity. Explaining this admittedly minor
point, I distinctly felt a collective fish eye upon me, as if the
entire class were asking itself, "Why is this man bothering to
tell us this?"

But the problem went deeper. It felt somewhat strange to
explain to a roomful of students who, so far as I knew, had
been going at it with their boy and girl friends since high school
that there was something quite scandalous about a young
American woman going about Rome unchaperoned but otherwise quite innocently with a lower-middle-class Italian. In
"Daisy Miller" Henry James wrote a comedy of manners, a
rather dazzling one at that, but when manners change radi-
cally, as they have in our time, other comedies are played. Or
so I felt up there in front of the class explaining what exactly it
was that Daisy did to scandalize the American colony in Rome
in the last third of the nineteenth century.

Things picked up with "The Pupil," one of James's mid-
dling-long stories, written when he was forty-seven and very
much at the top of his game. It is a pure Jamesian tale, fascinating in and for itself. It tells the story of a young man who
hires on as a tutor to a sickly boy of vastly precocious sensibility and intelligence who is being brought up by a family of
failed social climbers who are monstrously unreliable. The tutor
quickly senses how extraordinary the boy is, and rather more
slowly discovers how shabby is the family. Meanwhile, the two
of them, tutor and pupil, in moments of shared fantasy, talk
about how fine it would be if they could one day escape the
family and live together on their own.

At the close of the story precisely that opportunity arises,
and the tutor, vacillating ever so slightly, is caught doing so by
the boy, which causes his already weakened heart to fail. It is a

story that demands the utmost attention, particularly at the very end, lest the tutor's vacillation be missed. Many students did miss it, and a good discussion followed upon the subject of whether a young boy would have been so delicately attuned as to be able to pick it up. "Why," said one of the best students in the class, who didn't really think so young a boy could pick up so subtle a hint as James provides, "in order to do so, he'd had to be a little Henry James." (As the odious radio performer Art Linkletter used to say, "Don't kids say the darndest things?")

Not long after this I ventured a quotation about "The Pupil" from F. W. Dupee: "A kind of fraternal-homosexual affection unites the boy and the tutor in 'The Pupil.' " Anything to it? I asked. I myself didn't think there was, though I did not just then say so. But suddenly the discussion in the room was once again enlivened; the class, in fact, divided. A few students came forth to say they felt that homosexuality was the key to the story. Another student said that he hadn't really thought of it before, but now that it had come up he discovered a few passages—one of which he read out to the class—that sounded rather homosexier than he had at first realized. On and on it went, unresolved as the bell rang to end the class. In the hall, Miss Jennie Davidson, who has been in another of my classes, remarked dryly that perhaps there ought to be a statute of limitations on discovering homosexuality in literature. No dope, Miss Davidson. At the next class session I simply announced that, for my money, the element of homosexuality in the story, if indeed it could be said to exist, was quite beside the point. But then, I added, you must realize that a critic's work is never done. How many students in the class picked up the irony of that last comment I am not prepared to say. I felt, though, that I owed it to them not to explain it.

It was in "The Pupil," too, that that miserable old hag Auntie Semitism staggered into the room. In a line toward the middle of the story James notes of the boy's family: "They were good-natured, yes—as good-natured as Jews at the doors of clothing shops! But was that the model one wanted one's family to follow?" Several were the Jewish students in the class. The teacher's last name is Epstein. What was to be done? I offered a brief sermonette—the question had come up near the end of a class—saying that I wished Henry James's work was entirely clear of this sort of blotch, but it wasn't. In this he did not, as he did in so many other ways, rise above his time and social class. I then went on to say that it might assuage people much disturbed by this to know that, in the Dreyfus Affair, James was absolutely on the correct side, applauding Emile Zola's *J'accuse* and deploring the anti-Semitism of such long-time French friends as Paul Bourget, which quite sickened him.

When I asked how many in the class had ever heard of the Dreyfus Affair, none had. Everyone who teaches has stories about what shockingly obvious knowledge the current generation of undergraduates doesn't have. For my part, I must report that I no longer get much worked up by this sort of thing. If I knew anything about the Dreyfus Affair as an undergraduate, it couldn't have been much. Such historical material as most of us possess we come to through our special interests or by simple accident. Thus I know a fair amount about the Russian Revolution but not a single fact about the administration of President James Polk. Perhaps the one serious difference between my students and me at their age is that, I suspect, I was more embarrassed about my ignorance than they, and I may still be.

More significant is what the lack of experience owing entirely to being young does to one as a reader. This came up when we read *The Europeans,* another novel James claimed not to think much of but which impressed me (and F. R. Leavis, among others). In this slender novel, in which the international subject runs the other way round, with two immensely Europeanized Americans visiting their New England cousins, the conduct of the characters and the nature of the situation into which James has inserted them, calls for a reasonably strong flow of generalization on the author's part. "It must be admitted . . . that nothing exceeds the license occasionally taken by the imagination of very rigid people" is a mild example. But the generalization that incited the most strenuous comment was that which reads: "a woman looks the prettier for having unfolded her wrongs or sufferings." What about it, I asked, is this true? Do women look prettier under such conditions?

The young women in the room with conventional—and none were rabid—feminist views felt not. They were generally committed to denying that there are any serious differences between men and women, which may or may not be sound social policy but is certainly tough on literature, which is in good part the historical record of these very differences. Others, male and female, who thought of themselves as operating solely on reason, said that they just didn't see how this generalization could hold up. A few students—all of them women—said, yes, that it seemed to them true, at least when they recalled women they knew who recounted genuine sufferings to them. (Mere kvetching, I insisted, didn't count.) I said that I thought James's generalization true, too, though my word on this point didn't come anywhere near carrying the day.

I asked what checks there were on generalizations, and when no one came forth with any, I said that I could myself think of only two: reason and experience. The interesting problem, I noted, was that experience, as Pascal and other powerful thinkers have testified, frequently outrages reason. I cited an instance from an Anthony Powell novel. In the novel the narrator remarks of another character that he was very quick at picking up speaking knowledge of foreign languages and that, like every other man whom the narrator knew who had this skill, this man, too, was fundamentally untrustworthy. "Crazy," I said to the class, "quite nuts, right?" Much shaking of heads in agreement. "Very well, then, what am I supposed to do if the only four men I have known who are similarly quick at picking up speaking knowledge of foreign languages are also, yep, fundamentally untrustworthy?" No advice was offered.

As for the hard sell, I thought it going very nicely indeed when, the week that we read "The Turn of the Screw," the class overwhelmingly rejected Edmund Wilson's theory that everything the governess saw and felt during the course of the story was imagined, the result of neurotic sexual repression. The theory was rejected, moreover, on the interesting grounds that, in the class's view, it made the story itself less interesting; that it somehow degraded James's artistic intention; and that, finally, Henry James being Henry James, his intentions ought to be assumed to be of the highest. (Philip Rahv, writing about "The Turn of the Screw," similarly remarked: "So far as intention goes, we should keep in mind that in James we are always justified in assuming the maximum." Don't grown-ups say the darnedest things?)

I also sensed, in our discussion of "The Turn of the Screw," a patience with James's ambiguity. Perhaps it had come with all else that we had earlier read of James, but there seemed to be an understanding that for Henry James ambiguity, along with irony and penetrating observation, had its own rich artistic uses. "The Turn of the Screw" is the ultimate tale of ambiguity; it is built upon ambiguity. Edmund Wilson was not wrong when he said that in it "almost everything from beginning to end can be read equally in either of two senses." The story's devastating ending, in which the governess, hitherto entirely a force for good, contributes to the child Miles's death, is itself a paradigm of the ambiguity in the human soul, where good and evil often cohabit. But without the students' respect for James's intentions and understanding of his use of ambiguity, I don't think we could have worked our way through this great *tour de force* of James's with anything like the appreciative reading that emerged.

"May 23, 1990. Taught first flat Henry James class yesterday. Too few students finished reading the 591-page *Princess
Casamassima,* the little dears. Too late in the quarter to yell at
them." In fact, I was angrier than this journal entry reveals;
lest there be any doubt, "little dears" is pure euphemism. The
academic quarter was drawing to a close; papers were due in
other courses; examinations in other courses would soon have
to be taken. Let us not speak of love lives, emotional crises,
and simple lassitude, complications not unknown to phylum
studentia. Still, with the greed of every selfish teacher, I wanted
these students to save their very best for me, which, up till
now, I think the majority of them had done.

I also wanted to make good use of *The Princess Casamassima*
to help nail down my quarter-long hard sell. In many ways it
is among my favorite of Henry James's novels. James never
availed himself of a larger canvas. Not only is the book filled
with rich and beautiful things, but in it James puts to rout
almost all the arguments that have been used to make him seem
a less complete writer than he really is. The dark third chapter
of the novel, with its terrifying tour through Millbank Prison
for women, is as good as anything Dickens ever did in the
same line and worthy of the great Russians. The cast of characters in the novel ranges through the entire English class system. James's depiction of working-class characters is beautifully
brought off, and without a trace of snobbery. "I take no interest in the people," says Mme Grandoni, a secondary yet important character in the novel, "I don't understand them and I
know nothing about them. An honorable nature, of any class,
I always respect; but I won't pretend to a passion for the ignorant masses, for I have it not." *The Princess Casamassima* is, in
fact, a philippic in novel form against political snobbery and
shows its dread consequences in the world. It is also the ultimate defense of the literary mode of thought, as opposed to
the political or social-scientific, and sets out, with no ambiguity this time round, the forces that, for the literary imagination,

rule the world. As another character in *The Princess Casamas-sima* puts it:

> The figures on the chessboard were still the passions and jeal-ousies and superstitions and stupidities of man, and thus posi-tioned with regard to each other at any given moment could be of interest only to the grim invisible fates who played the game—who sat, through the ages, bow-backed over the table.

Well, perhaps no salesman can expect utter satisfaction. Bet-ter to close the deal and move on to the next customer. I think that with perhaps a third of these students I got across what it meant for Henry James to be "the historian of fine con-sciences" that Joseph Conrad called him. Maybe, too, at the end of our nine weeks together reading this one writer, several of these students would depart with a glimmer of what James himself meant when he said, "It is art that *makes* life, makes interest, makes importance, for our consideration and appli-cation of these things, and I know of no substitute whatever for the force and beauty of its process." At the end of the course, they wrote those generous student evaluations. The two sets of examinations they wrote for me were strong, with an occa-sional James-like formulation popping up in them. "James's endings," wrote one student, "seem often to be the twist of the knife rather than the actual stab." "In this story, as in so much of James," wrote another, "the victories are small, and often so much more valuable because of it."

What sticks? Will there be a residue? What remains? Will any of these students eventually join the narrator of James's story "The Next Time," who remarks of the select band of readers devoted to high literary culture, "We're a numerous band, partakers of the same repose, who sit together in the shade of the tree, by the plash of the fountain, with the glare of the desert round us and no great vice that I know of but the habit perhaps of estimating people a little too much by what

they think of a certain style"? These are questions the answer
to which a teacher of Henry James wishes to but cannot know.
Still, the prospect of having possibly put two or three more
Jamesians in the world, from the standpoint of a high-pres-
sure, hard-sell literary salesman, makes all those mornings talking one's head off seem, just possibly, worth it.

Joseph Alsop and the WASP Ascendancy

A T VARIOUS MOMENTS in his long career as a journalist in Washington, Joseph Wright Alsop must have thought to liken himself to Henry Adams. But even if he did not, on the dust jacket of his posthumously published memoirs, *"I've Seen the Best of It,"* which in late-life illness he produced with the help of the journalist Adam Platt, his publishers do it for him. Perhaps the temptation could not be resisted. Both Adams and Alsop were set by birth above the ruck of grubby politics, and yet at the same time both were endlessly fascinated by them. In fact, Alsop was neither so intelligent nor so wellborn as Adams—he "of ancient presidential race," as Henry James jokingly called him—with neither so deep nor so thoroughly soured a mind. Yet, during certain historical moments, Joseph Alsop, even though assigned by his profession to the sidelines, had had his innings.

By birth Alsop was a member of what remained of the patrician tradition in American public life—a tradition, to be sure, already much diminished and attenuated by the time he came to it in his adulthood in the early 1930s. No more argument need be made for this attenuation than that Alsop was a workaday journalist and columnist who wrote for a living and who at the end of his life claimed to have knocked out close to a thousand words a day since beginning in 1932 as a newspaper reporter. For journalism, by its nature, speaks to descent in the social scale, at least for the wellborn. One can be a patrician and one can be a journalist, but when the two words are placed together—thus: patrician journalist—they seem to want to resist juxtaposition, perhaps out of fear of forming an oxymoron.

Henry Adams was himself for a spell—between 1868 and 1873—a political journalist, but a journalist in the service of reform, publishing articles on the civil service, the gold conspiracy, and other matters of public policy and finance. Yet all this was distanced and quite grand, entailing nothing so dreary or sweaty as earning money or sucking up to powerful politicians. Joseph Alsop, by contrast, was truly what used to be called "working press." He began writing feature articles for the old *New York Herald-Tribune,* of sacred memory, and before long went on to become one of that paper's main men in Washington and subsequently an important American columnist.

Yet even Alsop's initiation into journalism—downward mobility though it may have represented—was made possible by his social connections. In *"I've Seen the Best of It,"* Alsop recounts how, around the time of his graduation from Harvard, his family met over the problem of "what to do with Joe." His father concluded that Joe had no head for business. Law school was mentioned, but as an undergraduate Joe had had a quiet and not altogether enviable reputation as a fairly industrious drinking man at the Porcellian Club (the best, socially, that Harvard had to offer), and it was feared that three years at Harvard Law might turn him from a heavy social into a permanently serious drinker. But since Joe wrote fluent letters to his grandmother, the family, following her lead, decided to get in touch with "nice Helen Reid," whose husband Ogden then owned the *Herald-Tribune.* No sooner said than done.

This was at a time, the early 1930s, when not many university graduates worked as reporters on newspapers; and as for people of Joseph Alsop's social class, what they chiefly had to do with newspapers was to keep their names out of them or, sometimes, own them. What, precisely, was Alsop's social class? "I am," he says of himself, "by way of being a very minor member of the ever-diminishing group of survivors of the WASP ascendancy." Those capital letters, of course, stand for White Anglo-Saxon Protestant, but behind them stands a good deal more: a concatenation of genealogies, social relationships, financial arrangements, and institutional affiliations which, in their interconnections, and in their preponderant spirit of taking care of one's own, could make city hall in Chicago under the late Mayor Daley look like the agora in fifth-century Athens.

Alsop's father had, along with family money, a seven-hundred-acre farm in Connecticut, near the town of Avon, south of Hartford. But Joe Alsop's true sociopolitical clout came from his mother, whose own mother was a younger sister of Theodore Roosevelt. Two of his mother's first cousins, then, were Eleanor Roosevelt, the wife (as I suppose one must now add for the benefit of the young) of Franklin Delano Roosevelt, and Alice Roosevelt Longworth, the closest Washington has ever come to having a powerful social hostess whose wit had real bite. When, for example, Alsop made the mistake of telling his cousin Alice that Wendell Willkie's Republican support in the 1940 presidential election came from the grass roots, she replied, "Yes, from the grass roots of ten thousand country clubs."

Alsop, in his memoirs, never gainsays the importance of his birth. He allows that his has been "a very lucky" life, and that a substantial part of his good luck came through being (again) "a minor member of this now-vanishing group, the WASP ascendancy." The truth is that Alsop was one of those men who, through energy and ambition, would have succeeded in spite of being born with every advantage. At the same time, those advantages were quite real; they formed not only Alsop's character but his expectations, and the way they bore on his career forms much the most impressive material in his memoirs.

The Slavicist Roman Jakobson, in attempting to dissuade Harvard from hiring Vladimir Nabokov for its Russian department, remarked that Nabokov's distinction as a writer did not necessarily fit him for teaching. "Are we next to hire an elephant to be professor of zoology?" Jakobson asked. The answer, one would have thought, would be yes, if the elephant really knows his subject. Joseph Alsop, though himself a WASP in high standing, turns out to be an excellent WASPographer. He is very good on WASP linguistics (always prefer the older name or word for the thing named); WASP haberdashery (London for suits and shoes); furniture (it was a certain kind of beeswax that gave WASP homes their distinctive smell); cookery (fresh and lots of it, always prepared by hired help); ways of handling money ("Money was the true preoccupation. Money was the source of the ascendancy's authority"); snobberies (even the youthful Eleanor Roosevelt, he alleges, was not above anti-Semitism); and prejudices (against modern art, learning, and bookishness generally: Endicott Peabody, the headmaster of Groton, promised Alsop's mother that he would do his best to knock the boy's precocious reading habit out of him).

To the manor born, Alsop is by social manners never bored; and he fills in all the fine little distinctions and discriminations by which the exclusionary subculture of his upbringing lived and finally died. He has a good sense of that culture's strengths (decisiveness, and a willingness to devote oneself selflessly to the country and to institutions generally) and weaknesses (a narrowness of outlook that often kills sympathy). He avers, rightly I suspect, that, without the collapse of WASP culture—whose onset he dates to the Depression, which "totally demoralized most of its members"—ethnic groups would still be excluded from many major institutions in the United States today. At the same time, without sentimentalizing WASP culture, Alsop was entirely comfortable in it. In his last years, dying of lung cancer, he claimed that his idea of heaven was still to be well dressed at an outdoor New England wedding. Joseph Alsop, it must be understood, was a snob: true, a snob who thoroughly understood snobbery and quite properly deplored its destructive results, but for all that still a snob. To take up Roman Jakobson's trope, knowing zoology does not cause the elephant to lose its trunk and large ears.

If social rank has its privileges, the privileged, when drawing too heavily on their social account, can themselves come off as pretty rank. So must Alsop have seemed in the city room of the *Herald-Tribune,* where, as he says, Stanley Walker, the paper's managing editor, referred to him as "a perfect example of Republican inbreeding." In recounting his early days on the paper, Alsop tells of standing on a picket line for Heywood Broun's American Newspaper Guild on a cold winter's night got up in a heavy (and no doubt expensive) raccoon coat. He tends to represent himself, during those newspaper days in New York, as something of a charming upper-class anomaly, and the only thing in dispute in the description is the word "charming." Richard Kluger, in *The Paper* (1986), a history of the *Herald-Tribune,* tells rather a different story. His account features an overdressed, rich, fat boy—Alsop, who was short, in those days weighed in at well over two hundred pounds—who read Proust at his desk, peremptorily called "Boy" when he needed a pencil or anything else, and was said not to bother cashing his paychecks. Outside of the office he lived hand-somely, keeping in his charge a Japanese houseboy named Buto whose wife served as his cook. All this would probably have been insuperable had Alsop not been good at his job—which he was. He wrote easily, he was not in the least daunted in interrogating important people—by his social lights, they were not all that important—and he turned in excellent copy.

Alsop's big break came when he was sent to do feature pieces about the Lindbergh kidnapping case. He acquitted himself well and this led, in 1935, to a transfer to the paper's Washington bureau. In the 1930s the WASP spirit still prevailed in Washington, and so the city was a perfect assignment. His cousin Eleanor was then First Lady, and his social connections among the Ivy League brain-trusters whom cousin Franklin had brought to the White House did not hurt, either.

Snobbery in Washington takes funny forms. In that Southern town, birth and breeding are all very well, and it is surely nicer to have them than not; intelligence comes in handy, too; but nothing is so nice or so handy as crude old-fashioned power. Power it is that makes people in Washington vibrate and the city hum.

Alsop tells, for example, that at his own dinner parties he used to stick with the old English upper-class custom of men and women separating for half an hour of talk after the last course had been cleared, until Katharine Graham, the publisher of the *Washington Post,* told him that, unless he knocked this little ritual off, she would cease to dine in his house. Alsop reports that since her friendship meant a great deal to him, he did indeed knock it off. But one wonders what he would have done if someone with less power than the publisher of the *Washington Post* had cornered him on the subject. (Averell Harriman, Alsop reports, "insisted on this [same] ritual until the day he died.")

From the outset, Alsop fitted in nicely in Washington, owing not least to his connections. "You know, Alsop," Arthur Krock, then chief of the *New York Times* Washington bureau, told him, "the first thing you have to realize is that in Washington newspapermen have no place at table." But then no other newspaperman could claim a relative in the White House or another relative who was as strong an ally as Alice Roosevelt Longworth. "Besides a few columnists," he reports in his memoirs, "I was the only reporter I can recall who frequented Dining-Out Washington." Dining-Out Washington included such social matriarchs as Mrs. Longworth, Mrs. William Eustis, Mrs. Dwight Davis, and Mr. and Mrs. Robert Bliss, whose Dunbarton Oaks home is today a famous center of Byzantine studies.

In his depiction of Dining-Out Washington, Alsop is a good deal less like Henry Adams than like the Duc de Saint-Simon, that fastidious chronicler of magnificence and petty social distinctions at the court of the Sun King. Describing the food at Mrs. Longworth's table, Alsop reminds one of the little Duc on Louis XIV's gargantuan dinners. Whether dilating on the delights of terrapin eggs floating in rich sauces, the four-day soak of Virginia hams in the tubs of guest bathrooms where the water was changed twice daily, or the picking and preparation of the tenderest young vegetables for parties of forty or more, Alsop, whose weight went up from 215 to 245 pounds in his early years covering Washington, takes, one senses, more than a literary interest in his subject:

> To these basics were added delicacies: shad in season, not boned but so slowly cooked in a sealed container that the bones melted, giving it ten times the taste of the flannel-like fish we get today; shad roe in mountains; soft-shell crabs; oyster crabs, which are tiny parasite crabs that inhabit oysters and have the tastes of both animals, not exactly in mountains because they were too expensive, but as a recurrent prize dish; in the autumn, turkey broilers (meaning specially fed, very young turkeys that were literally small enough to split and broil), reed birds, the pride of Southern houses; all sorts of game as well as guinea hen; then, too, there were the game birds one sees no more like plovers and wild turkey; and there was, above all, terrapin in season.

Throughout these memoirs Alsop shows, as Henry James once remarked apropos of Henry Adams, "a surviving capacity to be very well taken care of." One takes away from the book mental snapshots of a man being trundled about in rickshaws, always keen for and ever critical of his vittles, with many houseboys to see after his personal needs, interested in clothes, enjoying his booze, with cases of superior champagne laid in the basements of splendid houses. The one sensual element left out is the sexual, which in memoirs not otherwise notable for their discretion, is conspicuous by its absence.

On the question of writing about one's sex life, I have always been greatly impressed by a brief passage near the end of J. R. Ackerley's memoir *My Father and Myself.* There Ackerley, after recounting his travails as a cruising homosexual with a taste for what used to be called "rough trade" that led him into all sorts of ghastly scrapes, tells how acquiring a dog, an Alsatian bitch hound, provided him with what he felt he had all along been seeking in the young men he used to pick up. This, Ackerley claims, was what "I had never found in my sexual life, constant, single-hearted, incorruptible, uncritical devotion." And then, after setting all this out, he remarks, "One of my friends, puzzled by the sudden change in my ways, asked me whether I had sexual intercourse with her [the dog]." The answer, it turns out, is no, but, given the nature of Ackerley's book, the question is not an inappropriate one. The moral for writers, I take this passage to imply, is that they must answer all questions that their work raises, not to mention some that silence itself can raise.

Alsop speaks not at all about the sexual side of his life, except to announce that, at the age of fifty, he proposed marriage to Susan Mary Patten, the widow of a recently deceased school friend.

I wrote her from the [1960 Democratic] convention in Los Angeles, proposing that she form a new partnership—with me, headquartered in Washington. She came to the capital shortly after the inauguration [of John F. Kennedy] to make her decision, and, fortunately for me, it was a favorable one.

In her own memoirs, Susan Mary Alsop does not say much about her marriage to Joseph Alsop, except to note that he was a good stepfather, taking pains to teach Latin to her two children from her earlier marriage. What we have here, from all appearances, is a marriage of convenience, which twelve years later, in 1972, suddenly became inconvenient. "Susan Mary and I loved each other very much," he writes, "but irritated one another far too often for a really successful partnership."

Alsop's bachelor state had certain advantages. It gave him fluidity, both social and professional, and in his career the two were almost always combined. He flourished professionally in Washington, where his first job was to cover the Senate. There were no blow-dryers in senatorial washrooms in those days; extreme idiosyncrasy was still abundant among such senators as Joseph T. Robinson of Arkansas, Carter Glass of Virginia, and Charles McNary of Oregon. Congressional staffs, which Alsop regards as "certainly the greatest and most pernicious organizational change that has overtaken the American government in my lifetime," had not yet come to their current position of dominance. Security was not a worry of daily life, and one could dine at the homes of the powerful without discovering large men with walkie-talkies hiding in the bushes. For that matter, one could walk up to the White House without having to give one's Social Security number at the gate.

This was during the years 1936–37, which Alsop claims were, in Washington, "a paradise for political reporters." He was in his middle twenties and seemed to go from strength to strength. Along with giving satisfaction to his employers on the *Herald-Tribune,* he and Turner Catledge, the *New York Times* man, teamed up to write regular articles on the Washington political scene for the *Saturday Evening Post,* which had an enormous readership and conferred something close to national celebrity on its writers. While still in his twenties, Alsop was offered, at three times his current salary, a syndicated column which he wrote with Robert Kintner, then the *Herald-Tribune*'s man at the Treasury Department and later chairman of the National Broadcasting Corporation.

Alsop tried to base his columns on reporting as well as on opinion. He was a legwork man. Early in his Washington career he devised three reportorial rules from which, he claims, he did not often deviate:

> One was always do your best to learn your subject so that you don't ask foolish questions; two, always do your best to avoid wasting time during an interview, even when your line of questioning follows a tortuous and difficult trail; and, third, no matter how big a bastard you have to talk business with, never be rude unless the bastard is rude first.

Still, rules, principles, and legwork aside, Alsop owed some of his success to his connections. Even though, as he writes, "I was never on intimate terms with my distant relative [FDR] in the White House," he had ties through family or school with such high-level public servants as James Forrestal, Robert Lovett, Dean Acheson, and Archibald MacLeish—and if not with them, then with their wives. "All the men I have named—and usually their wives—had fun in one another's houses, and I am proud to say they came often to my house. All sorts of matters were discussed that, as a newspaper man, I should not normally have heard." But he did—and, owing to social connections, always would.

Although his mother was a staunch Republican, much interested in Connecticut politics, Alsop became a Democrat during the New Deal. He admired FDR without particularly liking him. He faulted him on style, the president's personal manner having a false, glad-hander ring to Alsop, though he would eventually rate him, along with Washington and Lincoln, as one of our three greatest Presidents. He had a much greater regard for Henry L. Stimson, who had been Herbert Hoover's secretary of state and would be FDR's secretary of war, and whom he describes thus:

> In matters of style, the white-whiskered, straight-backed Stimson was as impossibly grand a figure as there was in Washington; and in matters of substance, he was as great a public servant as this country has ever seen. I held the great statesman in awe, and on the few impersonal occasions when we did meet, I could manage little more than a muted and respectful greeting.

With American entry into World War II in 1941, Alsop gave up his column to enlist in the armed forces. Through an elaborate string of events and snafus, he eventually served the better part of four years in China with General Chennault's American Volunteer Group, more popularly known as the Flying Tigers. He served Chennault as, in his words, an "aide and chief odd-jobs man." He was captured by the Japanese and, with other people then thought to constitute a hostile population, was interned for seven months in Hong Kong, during which time he read and, under instruction, learned four thousand Chinese characters, three thousand of which he could write.

Alsop had a knack for turning the war into his oyster. Service in the Far East finds him, for example, being carried about in a wicker chair toted by four men. In Rangoon, he employs a "bearer" to look after his personal needs. He reads Toynbee in a hammock on an airplane. "Perhaps it is a major failing," he writes, "but throughout my long life I have always sought out people who, for either love or, more usually, for money, will care for my daily needs." In Chungking, for six dollars a day, he finds quite elegant digs, which include "three excellent but far too copious meals, . . . a ration of Chungking gin, the services of a valet, and the privilege of having guests whenever I pleased."

Even in China, social life for Alsop did not feel much differ-

ent from Washington. The socially ubiquitous Diana and Duff
Cooper—he was Churchill's Minister for Far Eastern Affairs—
show up. (Alsop, in his Duc de Saint-Simon mode, explains
that Lady Diana slept with her eyes open; owing to too many
face-lifts, she was unable to close them.) When they meet, Alsop
is warmly greeted by General Douglas MacArthur, who "knew
I was a formerly prominent member of the press and vaguely
connected to the Roosevelts." When he dines at the Chiang
Kai-sheks, the feeling is not unlike the Roosevelt White House:

> It had the same fantastic mixture of people, the same slightly
> suspicious food, the same curious atmosphere of graciousness
> mingled with constraint, even the same earnest, devoted, and
> slightly bossy female followers of the lady of the house to hand
> out the food and shepherd the customers.

Even in the midst of the terrors and complications of war,
there is time for gossip, as when the wife of the British ambassador to China, Lady Violet Seymour, asks Alsop if the president still "sees" her friend Lucy Mercer.

Always the insider, Alsop, as a member of General Chennault's staff, was called in to brief President Roosevelt about
the complicated situation in China, where General Joseph Stilwell despised and wished to eliminate Chiang Kai-shek, whom
he referred to as "a grasping, bigoted, ungrateful little rattle-
snake." As the man assigned to advise Chennault on political
and logistical matters, Alsop felt that Stilwell's hostility to Chiang
was a grave mistake, in every way, and, exerting what pressure
he could, he simultaneously reassured the generalissimo and
his family that things would be settled in their favor and worked
to remove Stilwell from his post in China. By his own account,
he made a modest contribution toward achieving both goals,
and there is no reason to disbelieve him. "My years in China,"
he writes, "were the only ones of my professional life in which

I ceased to be a commentator from the sidelines and became a minor actor in the historical process itself."

After the war Alsop returned to newspaper work, now join-ing with his younger brother Stewart in writing a thrice-weekly column under the rubric "Matter of Fact." In this new part-nership, Joe tended to do much of the traveling, for he had a personal rule forbidding him to write about any country he had not visited, while Stewart, who had a wife and children, looked after the store in Washington. The column would even-tually be syndicated in 137 newspapers. Richard Kluger con-tends that it owed its success to being "rooted in hard reporting."

Alsop allows that he and his brother had "developed a rep-utation for mild public pessimism." In fact, the Cassandra-ish impulses of the Brothers Alsop—Joe speaks of "a flair for calamities"—earned them the nicknames Doom and Gloom, and when they really got going (on such issues as nuclear armaments) they could make Chicken Little look like Dale Carnegie. When the brothers split up professionally in 1958—Stewart, who needed money for his large family, was offered a full-time job writing for the *Saturday Evening Post*—and Joe continued to write the column alone, *Time* magazine remarked that "the eloquent voice of Joe Alsop, amplified by syndica-tion, ha[s] dedicated itself to the cause of scaring tranquil humanity into its wits."

Joseph Alsop's politics were what must now be called cold-war liberal. He refers to himself in his memoirs as "a lifelong Democrat," though this was true only with qualifications. He was not, for example, an Adlai Stevenson man, being put off by Stevenson's habit of always bringing Abraham Lincoln into the conversation—a sign, or so Alsop felt, that he was in need of a psychiatrist; and then when, in his acceptance speech to the Democratic convention in 1952, Stevenson put himself in the place of Jesus—"Let this cup pass from me"—Alsop felt the time had come to punt:

The more I saw of Stevenson, the more I thought of the world he came from: the cultivated, old-fashioned, only-WASP-family-in-town world where cast-iron deer adorned every front lawn and ladies in white lace dresses and lingerie hats took tea and finger sandwiches under the elms. American upper-class genteel was the note, and I had long ago concluded that one could not be a serious politician and be genteel.

Alsop's political and social circles in the postwar years were one and the same. Charles Bohlen, Averell Harriman, Dean Acheson, Robert Lovett, John McCloy, and George Kennan were among its main members. "These were civil servants of a type that is no longer found," Alsop writes. He is not without criticism of these men, averring that Harriman was "one of the most self-absorbed and coldly ambitious men I have ever seen in government" and that Kennan's elitist views made him "more wrong than anyone else and more right than anyone else." Still, here was modern WASPdom at its most impressive. As Alsop observes:

> Although schooled in the great law offices and banking houses of Manhattan and more often than not Republican by inclination, these men tended to be both nonpartisan and, it sometimes seemed to me, almost excessively nonideological. Entering government from a sense of duty, they stayed on for a variety of reasons: for patriotism, for power, but mostly because, in the very long run, they could find no parallel outlet for their considerable talents in the private world.

Alsop speaks of enjoying "the postwar time perhaps more than any other in my professional life." During this period, he covered the war in Korea, where A. J. Liebling likened him to "a rich man's Ernie Pyle" and where, in his first direct experience of a shooting war, he claims to have conquered the cowardice under fire that all men fear. But what must have pleased him even more about this whole period was that he could number himself among those who were never cowed by Joseph McCarthy. The senator, in fact, accused both Joe and his brother Stewart of being Communists, impeccable though their anti-Communist credentials were. But Alsop consistently wrote against him anyway, even going so far to out-McCarthy McCarthy by discussing, in print, the allegedly non-Euclidian sexual relationship between the senator and his two chief aides, Roy Cohn and David Schine.

Although it was not true of all among them—John Foster Dulles was a notable exception—for the most part men of WASP background in public life stood up to McCarthyism rather well. One thinks of Dean Acheson and Henry Luce as well as Joseph Alsop. McCarthy, to them, was a buffoon and a boor, and, they soon enough recognized, a damned dangerous one. As for his accusations that some among them were betraying the United States, so secure were they in thinking of it as their country that their only response was outrage. WASPishness does—or at least did—have its privileges, not all of them snobbish.

This same sense that it is our country and damn worth fighting for may have been behind Alsop's position during the Vietnam war. He was a hawk all the way as, earlier, he had been about the Bay of Pigs operation, deploring only its ineptitude. National self-interest, and patriotism, too, were in no serious way problematic for WASPs of Alsop's generation. But his generation was also being shuffled off the stage:

> Increasingly, it seemed to me, the tragic defeats of this country—whether abroad in Vietnam or at home, as in the case of Richard Nixon's Watergate scandal—were greeted with unseemly crowing among members of my old trade [journalism]. This crowing made me feel isolated and suddenly out of fashion.

The Vietnam war was perhaps Alsop's most troubled time. He never, in print or in any other public way, criticized the

American military in Vietnam, and for this he took a beating, politically and socially. Washington *bien pensants* did what they could to humiliate him. Art Buchwald, in a now-forgotten play, *Sheep on the Runway*, lampooned Alsop in the figure of a pompous and overheated newspaperman. Adam Platt quotes John Kenneth Galbraith calling Joseph Alsop a "leading non-combatant casualty of Vietnam" and adding, "From a much-feared columnist, warrior, and prophet he has become a figure of fun." (In his memoirs, Alsop attempts to pay Galbraith back by recalling how John F. Kennedy used to read "aloud with comic emphasis," at small dinner parties at the White House, long letters of advice sent by Galbraith from his post as ambassador to India.) His views on Vietnam put Alsop out of fashion in social Washington, and this, for a man social to the bone, could not but have hurt. Still, he stuck to his views.

The fall had to have been all the more staggering for coming just after Alsop had climbed what even he must have construed as the Mount Everest of Washington social life. I refer to the Kennedy years, during which Alsop rode very high. "I found a political favorite in John F. Kennedy," he writes, and in 1960 many people felt he was overstepping the bounds of journalism in his partiality, for in some quarters he was thought to be "an informed member of the Kennedy pre-convention team." Although some in the Kennedy camp tended to distrust him, the Brothers K., John and Bobby,

> often asked my advice, not because they thought it was worth having, but because John Kennedy particularly had a strong respect for what may be called "WASP Establishment opinion." I think he used me as litmus paper with which to test WASP reaction to his ideas and initiatives.

If this is really why Kennedy consulted him, the return payment was all that Alsop could want. He and his wife were regularly invited to the White House, and, better yet, John and

Jacqueline Kennedy frequently came to Alsop's house for dinner. ("Let us be vulgar and have some fun," says a character in "Pandora," a Henry James story set in Washington, "let us invite the President.") Still better, on the night of his inauguration, the new president ended his evening by dropping in at Alsop's Georgetown home. As Alsop recounts all this in his memoirs, in gushing detail, one can almost hear the pounding in his snobbish heart.

What I suspect John F. Kennedy got out of it, apart from the pleasure of Alsop's company, was a strong WASP connection. Old Joseph Kennedy, a roughneck and a freebooter, an Irishman and a Catholic, had had it made plain to him on more than one occasion by people in positions of social power that there were some things money could not buy. But what money could not buy, truly big-time power of the kind that came with the presidency could—and did. Part of the public's attraction to John F. Kennedy, it is not going too far to say, was that he had the suavity and self-assurance of the WASP without having to carry the burden of prejudice and dreary narrow-mindedness that was also part of the WASP tradition and heritage. John F. Kennedy, in other words, could live and act like a WASP without having to be one. And the regular company of Joseph Alsop would assure him that, socially, he had succeeded where his father had not.

When John F. Kennedy was killed in Dallas, his death struck Alsop more forcibly, he says, than that of his own father. The Kennedy years in Washington were the last in which he felt "a really young man." "Nothing would ever be the same in my life again," he writes, "or, it hardly needs saying, in the life of the country." (In my view, it needs more than saying, it needs critical examination; but let that pass.) After the Kennedy presidency, life, as Alsop relives it in his memoirs, was all downhill, and not long after he brings *"I've Seen the Best of It"* to a quick close.

In 1974, when his brother Stewart died after losing a brave

bout with cancer, Alsop retired as a journalist. To help pave the way for his retirement he sold off some of the art he had begun collecting in China during World War II. He still had fifteen years to live after quitting journalism. He put in a great deal of time on a thick volume titled *The Rare Art Traditions,* which is full of loose learning and interesting information but lacks the authority that only a life spent with so rich a subject confers. His appetite for the good party—stimulating company, exquisite food, superior wine—never diminished, despite the fact that he was now playing the old familiar WASP role of the back number. (Clifton Webb did it best in the movies.) It is as a back number that he writes:

> The truth is, I could no longer understand what was happening in America, perhaps because I had finally become an old man, frozen in the viewpoints of the past. The pleasures the young indulged in during the 1960s seemed to me strikingly unpleasurable. The work of the younger artists struck me as thoroughly ridiculous or boring or, more often, both. And the chatter of the newly fashionable writers and so-called intellectuals began to drive me mad.

When Alsop was told that he had lung cancer—he was a full-court cigarette smoker, putting away as many as ninety-five a day—he chose not to put himself through the tortures of oncological therapy. Instead he determined to live out the days left to him, as his brother had done many years before, in the hope of being able to enjoy them. He died in 1989, less than two months short of his eightieth birthday.

What Joseph Alsop's very readable memoirs, with their alternating interest in major events and minor gossip, make plain is that to be a journalist is, in the nature of the job, eventually to fall out of favor, fashion, and even phase with one's countrymen. Insider though Alsop always was, this much can be said for him: he had the integrity to write only what he believed, or at least believed was good for the United States. He wrote hundreds of thousands, perhaps millions, of words of opinion on endless political problems, questions, issues, and in the end one has to wonder—as he must often have done in his last years—what it all came to. The answer, alas, is not very much. But then the journalist's unwritten contract is to be allowed to feel the excitement of having a small hand in current affairs with no greater risk than being proved wrong, in exchange for which he is guaranteed that everything he says will, before long, be quite forgotten.

Still, all things considered, Alsop had a pretty good roll of the dice, a first-class seat all the way. If he lived to see his own social class go off in a collective loss of confidence, at least it was not in a tumbril. Joseph Alsop would himself have made an excellent secondary character in a novel not by Henry James or even by Somerset Maugham but, such was the falling-off in the character and interest of the class which formed and conditioned his every idea and thought, by John P. Marquand. It is a novel one can already imagine moldering, dusty and forgotten, on some back shelf.

Mencken on Trial

> *Reading what is printed about myself, I am made to*
> *realize how little a man makes himself understood by*
> *his writings.*
>
> —H. L. MENCKEN

WAS H. L. Mencken an anti-Semite? With the publication in 1989 of Mencken's *Diary*, the question began to seem a rhetorical one, its answer so obvious that it appeared to call for another question in reply. Was H. L. Mencken an anti-Semite? Is the Pope Catholic? Do accordion players fancy gaudy rings? Do grizzly bears neglect to use dental floss?

For years there has been muffled talk, and some of it not so muffled, about Mencken and the Jews. The first, the most direct, the least sparing came from Charles Angoff, who was an assistant editor on Mencken's famous magazine, the *American Mercury,* and later its managing editor. In 1956, the year of Mencken's death, Angoff, who was himself Jewish, published *H. L. Mencken: A Portrait from Memory*. A chapter of nine pages in this book is given over to "The Jews," and its author's chief charge reads:

> Mencken's "anti-Semitism" could be sensed better than described in words, because it was so deep-seated and so furtive and so

obscured by professions of loyalty to the principles of civil lib-
erties and to what he would call "the canons of civilized living."
His anti-Semitism, in other words, was of the same kind as the
anti-Semitism of Richard Strauss and Knut Hamsun and Arnold
Toynbee and former President Abbott Lawrence Lowell of
Harvard.

Other expressions of disquiet have been heard. Some time
ago a Jewish newspaper in Baltimore, the city where Mencken
was born and where he lived his entire life, ran a longish piece
recording a number of less than respectful if not downright
anti-Semitic-sounding remarks attributed to Mencken. In Carl
Bode's *Mencken* (1969), which remains the most ample biography, anti-Semitism does not arise as a serious issue. But in a
book of 1978, *Mencken: A Study of His Thought,* by Charles A.
Fecher, there appears a troubling footnote about a manila
envelope of notes stowed away in the Mencken Room of the
Enoch Pratt Free Library in Baltimore. According to Fecher,
if this material were ever to become public, it could give rise
to "the accusation, which [Mencken] had to face a number of
times while he was living, that he was anti-Semitic." But Fecher
then concludes:

> Actually, and in spite of these notes, I think it safe to say that
> he was not, but anyone seeking to defend him from the charge
> would admittedly have his hands full if the prosecution were
> permitted to introduce the folder in evidence.

The interesting twist here is that Fecher, whose 1978 book
about Mencken is almost wholly admiring, has himself now,
in effect, become the prosecutor. The venue of the trial is *The
Diary of H. L. Mencken,* of which Fecher is the editor. His
prosecution is neither enthusiastic nor relentless but instead
disillusioned and regretful. But it is, make no mistake, emphatic.
In his introduction, after noting Mencken's strong antipathy

to radio and to the journalism current in America during his later years, Fecher writes that "much more important, and infinitely less comprehensible, are his attitudes toward the war that was raging during much of this time, toward Franklin D. Roosevelt, toward black people, and most especially toward Jews." Two pages later he reminds his readers that he had earlier sought to defend Mencken from the charge of anti-Semitism; but that was before he had seen Mencken's diary. "Today," he writes, "I would be much less ready to take such a stand. Let it be said at once, clearly and unequivocally: Mencken was an anti-Semite." Qualifications follow, but no plea for special dispensation: ". . . the ugly strain runs through these pages almost like a leitmotif, and it would have been intellectually and editorially dishonest to try to excise it and pretend it was not there."

The trial has been played fairly prominently in the press. Charles A. Fecher's own comments, along with a selection of items from the *Diary*, aroused sufficient interest to put the story of Mencken's alleged prejudice against Jews, as well as blacks, on the front pages of a number of major newspapers. The *New York Times* op-ed page, on December 13, 1989, ran two pieces on the Mencken *Diary:* one by Russell Baker, who grew up a few blocks from Mencken's Hollins Street house and who now explained that "in that setting, southwest Baltimore in the 1930s and 1940s, we were all racists and anti-Semites, and much more that now seems just as unsavory"; and a second by a journalist named Gwinn Owens, whose father comes in for some rough treatment in the *Diary* and who suggested that this book "reveals a man who was shockingly anti-Semitic and racist, to the point where his stature as a giant of American letters may be in danger."

In a review in the daily *New York Times,* Herbert Mitgang, allowing that the offending content makes up only a small part of the *Diary* ("perhaps 1 or 2 percent"), asserted that "of course, even a few drops of midnight poison are enough to damage

Mencken's reputation seriously." In the *Washington Post*, Doris Grumbach, under the title "Mencken: Just Plain Anti-Semitism," closed her generally hostile review by attacking anyone who might choose to defend the book or Mencken as possessing "an anti-Semitic sensibility." Meanwhile, in Sioux Falls, South Dakota, a newspaper publisher who is a member of the Oglala tribe announced that because of "the racist and sexist remarks Mencken made in his diary," he wished to return the H. L. Mencken Writing Award he had won four years earlier.

As someone who has written in an admiring way about H. L. Mencken, I took none of this as particularly good news. I am well beyond the age of expecting unblemished behavior from writers, artists, or musicians, and I am no longer even sure that I agree with George Orwell that "one has the right to expect ordinary decency even of a poet." But about H. L. Mencken, despite all his youthful bravura claims of rowdiness, there has always seemed to me something not just essentially bourgeois but upstanding. Anti-Semitism, whatever else it is, is not upstanding.

One in what might be a small chain of keys to understanding H. L. Mencken has to do with the vast discrepancies between his public pronouncements and his private behavior. Not an uncommon phenomenon, this, especially among intellectuals and artists; in practice, it usually reveals itself through statements of the highest moral tone behind which one regularly finds behavior selfish and squalid. With Mencken, however, something like the reverse obtains. He railed against the asininity of marriage, and then, at fifty, married and lived happily with a woman who he knew was very ill and who died five years later. Against the clergy he fired away every chance he got, but he took time to help a nun with her Ph.D. dissertation on James Huneker and dined frequently with a Methodist bishop nearly all of whose views he had mocked in print. He made himself out a heavy boozer ("with a liver far beyond pills or prayer"), yet, though he imbibed his share, he regulated his drinking, never let it interfere with the prodigious amount of work he turned out, and in the end, as Churchill said of his own drinking, got more out of alcohol than alcohol got out of him. And of the Jews? Alistair Cooke once said, with only slight exaggeration, that *all* of Mencken's best friends were Jews.

Mencken wrote of Beethoven: "He is a great tragic poet, and like all great tragic poets, he is obsessed by a sense of the inscrutable meaninglessness of life." Mencken was not so much obsessed by as convinced of the inscrutable meaninglessness of life. He believed that no one knew why sin and suffering were sent into the world, what motives lay behind natural laws, why man had his present form, or who created the universe. Any-one who claimed to know the answer to any of these questions he took for a con artist. Mencken was, if a philosophical term be wanted, a laughing pessimist, who held that although we may live in the dark, this need not prevent our laughing in the dark. The laughter came, for him, from the spectacle of what he called "abounding quackeries"; a quack was anyone who claimed to penetrate the meaning of life. He felt it important to learn to laugh lest one slide down the chute of melancholy.

Mencken truly, even hugely, enjoyed the spectacle that life presents, and so long as he did, the enjoyment shone magically through his writing. Some years ago I was asked to give the annual H. L. Mencken Lecture at the Enoch Pratt Free Library in Baltimore. (There is something like a patriotic feeling about Mencken in Baltimore; the lecture takes place on what is offi-cially designated as Mencken Day.) In preparation for this lec-ture, over a five- or six-week period, I read through a number of Mencken's books. I read them early in the morning and I noted an odd thing, which was that, so pleasing was the pros-pect, I nearly bounded out of bed to do so. Mencken used to make fun of what he called "uplifters," but reading him seemed to uplift me greatly. And not me alone. At dinner after the lecture, I sat next to an amiable Baltimore businessman of no

literary pretensions whatsoever, who happened to be the current president of the Mencken Society. "What do you get out
of reading H. L. Mencken?" I recall asking him. "That's easy,"
he said. "He makes me happy."

The spectacle that Mencken's own performance provided was
itself mightily impressive. The best account I know of it was
written by Walter Lippmann, who in 1926 called Mencken
"the most powerful personal influence on this whole generation of educated people," and who described him at the top of
his game:

> His humor is so full of animal well-being that he acts upon his
> public like an elixir. The wounds he inflicts heal quickly. His
> blows have the clean brutality of a natural phenomenon. They
> are directed by a warm and violent but an unusually healthy
> mind which is not divided, as most minds are, by envy and fear
> and ambition and anxiety. When you can explain the heighten-
> ing effect of a spirited horse, of a swift athlete, of a dancer really
> in control of his own body, when you can explain why watching
> them you feel more alive yourself, you can explain the quality of
> his influence.

Mencken achieved these effects through an alchemical distilla-
tion of superior craft, delicious wit, and utter courageousness
of opinion. The first can be acquired; the second is a gift; the
third may no longer have a place in American life.

Some while ago I had lunch with a man who wanted to
produce a one-man show, on the model of Hal Holbrook's
Mark Twain Tonight, to be called *Mencken Alive!* A nice title, I
thought, and when I asked how he had come upon it he replied
that he still occasionally heard people say, when they were confronted with some fresh hypocrisy or novel piece of nonsense,
if only Mencken were alive today to write about this. But in
fact one wonders if Mencken would flourish among us today.

Too many subjects might be out of bounds to him. Nearly forty years after his death in 1956, he might be surprised to discover that there is rather less freedom of speech than when he was alive—freedom of the kind on which he absolutely depended.

One large area now out of bounds is the ethnic subject. To it a single unwavering rule applies: If you can't say anything nice about an ethnic group, shut up. Since there is much that is not nice to say, all such talk has therefore become a form of oral *samizdat*. One speaks among friends but one almost never writes about the ethnic subject, or remarks upon it in any public way. Given the tumult that the posthumous publication of Mencken's *Diary* has caused, perhaps one ought to say it is safest not even to remark upon it in private, to oneself.

As one who keeps a journal and has a decided taste for the ethnic subject, I cannot help wondering if I ought not clean up my own private thoughts a bit. In recent months I can think of at least two damaging entries in this line. The first runs: "Read thin (intellectually thin) book on gossip by two insane-looking Jewish sociologists in preparation for my *American Scholar* essay." And then there is this item: "Amusing conversation over the telephone with the novelist McG. Much Irish charm, Boston accent thrown in at no extra cost. Felt I wanted to bring a drink to the phone." Of course I am Jewish, and I am married to a woman whose father was Irish, which may get me off the hook here, though with the thought police coming into even greater control, possibly not. But then I am reminded that McG. (as I am calling him here) told me a story about a Jewish woman, an editor in New York, who in a book review wrote the following: "With the exception of Oscar Wilde, the Irish have never been known for their sexual prowess." The sentence so ticked him off that McG. wrote to the woman, whom he knew, wondering if it would not also be true to say that "The Jews, too, are not especially known for their sexual prowess, with the exception of Leopold and Loeb." She never spoke to him again.

Generally the Irish, in my experience, do not exhibit too great a touchiness about ethnic jokes or even slurs. In this same conversation, when the subject of newspapers happened to come up, I mentioned that nowadays I turn directly to the obituaries. "Ah," McG. sighed, "the obituaries. We Irish refer to them as the sporting pages." I had not heard that before. If I had known him a bit better perhaps I would have asked McG. if he knew the definition of an Irish homosexual, which turns out to be an Irishman who prefers women to alcohol. I came across that in Ned Rorem's *Nantucket Diary*. It is a joke that reminds one that homosexuals might just as well be an ethnic group, since they have developed the requisite touchiness, many among them speak of themselves as if they were a single unified body, and no one is permitted to say anything critical about homosexuality in public. (I recall a reference in one of H. L. Mencken's essays of the 1920s to a moralizing minister caught in a YMCA with a boy having "non-Euclidean sex"; try that out in public today.)

I used to tell a story, which took place in my twenties, about the time I answered an ad in the *New York Times* for a house rental in Babylon, Long Island. The owner, a Mr. Mitropoulos, turned out to be almost a stage-comedy Greek: florid, barrel-chested, thick wavy white hair beginning about an inch and a half above his eyebrows. As soon as I sat down next to him in the front seat of his 1959 Lincoln, we shook hands, he looked me in the eye, and in a thick Greek accent he asked me if I was Jewish; after I allowed that I was, he said:

"Mr. Epstein, before we begin our business dealings you should know it takes six Syrians, four Turks, and two Jews to cheat a Greek."

I didn't, by the way, rent the house. I do occasionally tell the story, though not to everyone. I am one of those touchy

Jews myself, generally on the lookout for insult, a veritable truffle dog of anti-Semitism. Reading, I espy the word *Jew* a few paragraphs ahead on the page, my mental radar begins to twirl and twitter, knives come unsheathed, torpedoes click into firing position. My response has been bred in the bone, not only from millennia of history but from growing up in the city of Chicago, where Jews were a small but prominent minority and where what one was—the phrase "ethnic affiliation" had not yet come into being—was no trivial datum. Next to the stereotyped image of the Jews, that of the Irish was almost a pleasure: a charming boozer is much to be preferred to a cunning, conniving, under-the-table man, and this is putting the stereotype most politely.

Anti-Semitism has always constituted xenophobia to the highest power—and then some. It has been irresistible to fools throughout history, and not to fools alone. Among serious literary men, Dostoevsky, G. K. Chesterton, Ezra Pound, T. S. Eliot, D. H. Lawrence went for it. What, one is now forced to ask, about H. L. Mencken?

At stake is the reputation of a writer until now taken to be this country's greatest journalist, one of our most important literary critics, and an original comic talent of the highest order. If H. L. Mencken was an anti-Semite, all that is not merely diminished but perhaps, in the current atmosphere, wiped out. The reputation of an artist of the first magnitude can perhaps withstand the charge of anti-Semitism. (". . . We spent the weekend at Eastbourne, visiting some friends called Schiff— very nice Jews," wrote T. S. Eliot in 1920 to his mother.) But for a writer like Mencken, whose work deals directly in assertion and strong opinion, filled with craft but without the mediation of art, the charge of anti-Semitism or any other genuinely vicious prejudice constitutes a devastating blow against him. Those of a major poet's works that are not directly marred by anti-Semitism remain beautiful. But all of Mencken's views are suddenly in deepest doubt. It would be a sadness and a serious injustice to get him wrong on this matter.

The particular charges against Mencken as they have emerged in the reviews and stories about his *Diary* are that he was a racist as well as an anti-Semite, that he was disregarding of Hitler, and that he was more than a little nuts on the subject of Franklin Delano Roosevelt. Based on a reading of the *Diary* alone, a case can be made for some of these charges. Alas for quick and simple judgments, there is more than the *Diary* to be dealt with in Mencken's vast literary production—at one point in the *Diary* he estimates that he has written more than ten million words. For example, the last column that Mencken wrote for the *Baltimore Sun* on January 1, 1939 (before resigning in disagreement over its position on Roosevelt and World War II) was titled "The Problem of the Refugees" and was a plea to save the Jews of Central Europe from Hitler. It could not have been more correct. The following passages ought to be kept in mind alongside the charges of anti-Semitism against their author:

> Either we are willing to give refuge to the German Jews, or we are not willing. If the former, then here is one vote for bringing them in by the first available ships, and staking them sufficiently to set them on their feet. That is the only way we can really help them, and that is the only way we can avoid going down into history as hypocrites almost as grotesque as the English.
>
> The initiative should be taken by the so-called Christians who are now so free with weasel words of comfort and flattery, and so curiously stingy with practical aid. In particular, it should be taken by the political mountebanks who fill the air with hollow denunciations of Hitler, and yet never lift a hand to help an actual Jew.

These are, of course, public utterances, brave and bold ones. What Mencken wrote in his *Diary* are private utterances, which are very different, as he knew quite as well as anyone, and perhaps better than most of those who have written about the *Diary*. It is far from clear that Mencken wanted his *Diary* published; it strikes me as clearer than not that he preferred that it never be published. When he deposited it with his other papers at the Enoch Pratt Library, Charles A. Fecher reports, he affixed a label instructing that it was "not to be put at the disposal of readers until twenty-five years after my death, and is then to be open only to students engaged in critical or historical investigation, approved after proper inquiry by the Chief Librarian." At the Pratt Library, the board of trustees decided otherwise. The material seemed to them too interesting and too valuable to be kept exclusively for the perusal of a few stray scholars, and so they sought the legal opinion of the attorney general of the State of Maryland, who in 1985 ruled that "the Library has a legal right to publish the diaries." It now begins to look as if the trustees did Mencken, or at least his reputation, a bad turn. They fed a man known for his candor into the maw of an age wishing to be known for its false spirit of caring.

The circumstances under which Mencken kept his diary are worth underscoring. For one thing, he did not begin it until he was fifty years old, in 1930. The final entry is dated November 15, 1948, eight days before the stroke from which he would recover to live until January 1956, but with the cruel trick of brain damage that rendered him, most word-minded of men, unable either to read or write.

Mencken's *Diary* entries are written neither in the staccato, telegraphic mode of many diarists nor in the often rather gaudy comic style of Mencken's journalism. They are stylistically straightforward and absolutely correct. (Mencken seems never to have written an ungainly sentence.) He typed out many of the entries; some are quite long. Fecher reports that this published version of the *Diary* constitutes roughly a third of the whole. As editor, he made his selections with the intention of giving a rounded sense of Mencken's life during the eighteen years chronicled, and my sense is that he has succeeded. I assume, too, that the amount of allegedly objectionable material Fecher chose to include is roughly representative of the whole, and that there is some material of the same nature in the unpublished portions.

The years during which Mencken kept his diary were for him dark ones—years of loss and defeat. At the beginning of the *Diary,* Mencken has been married only three months; he is still editor of the *American Mercury;* the Depression is under way. He will lose, first, his wife, the anniversary of whose death he often notes. ("Sara will be dead ten years tomorrow. It seems a long, long while, yet she still remains living to me, and seldom a waking hour passes that I do not think of her.") He will lose his popularity among the young, whom the Depression will drive into a left-wing radicalism that he—enemy of puritanism, of the genteel tradition, of mainstream American politicians—thought no more than another form of utopian quackery. He will watch Franklin Delano Roosevelt and the New Deal, neither of which he could abide, go from strength to strength with the electorate. With the onset of World War II, and his decision no longer to write for the *Baltimore Sun* papers, he will lose his platform as a regular commentator on current events. Friends will die; the talents of other friends will dissipate. Possessed, like any true hypochondriac, of vast knowledge of his own health, he sees life as a race between his sclerotic arteries and his bum heart. He is a man approaching the end of his life alone, and feeling greatly out of synch with those around him; he does not find the world, every day and in every way, getting better and better. Quite the reverse.

If the *Diary* is dark, even at times gloomy, it is by no means uninteresting. Not the least interesting thing about it is that while Mencken was writing its often bleak entries he was also writing the three autobiographical volumes—*Happy Days*

(1940), *Newspaper Days* (1941), and *Heathen Days* (1943)—
that are so filled with the love of life, its oddity, comedy, and
richness, and that have given his readers so much pleasure. Of
course, in the autobiographies he was writing about the past.
It was only the present that put him off, with its insipidity, its
intellectual conformity, its politics. Writing in the *Diary* about
his father, a businessman who worked diligently until his death
at forty-four and during that time earned enough to keep his
family in comfort and saved enough to maintain it indefinitely
afterward, Mencken notes: "If he were alive today he would
be a member of that class of reactionaries which is execrated
by all right-thinking Americans."

Demoralization over the spirit of the age was not, however,
permitted to get in the way of productivity. "Looking back
over a life of hard work," he writes in 1945, "I find that my
only regret is that I didn't work harder." When he has bouts
of bad health, his principal complaint is that he cannot sit as
long at his desk as when healthy. Between the ages of sixty and
sixty-five, despite a number of illnesses, he will produce no
fewer than five books, including a thick supplement to his
monumental *The American Language.* His correspondence is
never less than heavy, and some days he receives and answers
as many as twenty-five or thirty letters, "mainly from persons
I don't know." Even though he no longer writes for the paper,
nearly every working day he goes to the offices of the *Baltimore
Sun,* where he continues to be paid to attend business meetings and serve as a consultant. He works on future books, some
of which he eventually has to abandon. In 1943 he estimates
that he has written 65,000 words in his diary alone, "the
equivalent," he records graphomaniacally, "of a good-sized
book." He takes it as a matter of pride that he will probably
leave as complete a record of his life and times as any writer
who has ever lived.

The portrait of Mencken that emerges as one works one's
way through the eighteen years covered by the *Diary* is that of

a man who is not only out of it but rather takes pride in being out of it. He does not drive a car. He thinks radio is aimed at imbeciles; and television, which he glimpses in the late 1940s, he is sure will be even worse. Newspapers increasingly cater to morons, not least among them the *Sun* papers in Baltimore, which "degenerate rapidly to the estate of third-rate provincial journals" and which may one day be remembered "largely and perhaps even mainly because I worked for them." (True enough, as it turns out.) The firm of Alfred A. Knopf, whose author he has long been and on whose board of directors he sits, begins to publish trashy books—specifically, in 1944, a book of prayers for soldiers and sailors. Everywhere he looks he sees institutions in decay. Even the quality of beer has dropped off badly. "The decent pleasures of life have diminished enormously in my time," he writes in his sixty-sixth year.

Some of this might be put down to growing older. But more appears to be going on, for the bitterness of many of the entries in the *Diary* is real and cuts deep. Nothing literary about it, either, like the aristocratic crankiness of the older Henry Adams, or the late-life cut-rate Hobbesianism of Edmund Wilson. A streak of such darkness, an air of hopelessness, always ran in Mencken. As early as 1927, when he was forty-seven, in an essay titled "On Suicide," he wrote:

> . . . I am conscious of no vast, overwhelming and unattainable desires. I want nothing that I can't get. But it remains my conclusion, at the gate of senility, that the whole thing is a grandiose futility, and not even amusing. The end is always a vanity, and usually a sordid one, without any noble touch of the pathetic. . . .

Later, in the *Diary,* one finds him writing, "Nine-tenths of the people who call me by telephone I don't want to talk to, and three-fourths of the people I have to take to lunch I don't want to see." Although he is inevitably the best of family men—

PERTINENT PLAYERS

236

visiting relatives, ready to pick up the tab for the nursing-home bills of a mildly senile uncle—he records that "my brother August and I, sitting by the fire in the evening, often congratulate ourselves on the fact that we have no children, and that there is only one child in our whole immediate family." The future he envisions as endless wars in which "the boys stand a good chance of being butchered in their young manhood, and boys and girls together face a world that will be enormously more uncomfortable than the one my generation has known."

Easily the bleakest entry in the published *Diary* concerns the death of one Lillie Fortenbaugh, Mencken's neighbor for fifty years. "She was," he writes, "a complete moron and led a life of utter vacuity." He describes her days, devoted to window shopping, going to movies, listening to speeches on the radio and the "yowling of so-called news commentators." "The lives of such poor simpletons always fascinate me," he writes:

> So far as I know, Lillie never did anything in all her years that was worth doing, or said anything worth hearing. . . . It is hard to think of a more placid life, and she apparently enjoyed it, but it is likewise hard to think of one more hollow. It was as insignificant, almost, as the life of her dog.

Rough stuff, but then during these years Mencken's nerves must have been rubbed raw by what he judged to be the horrendous state of the world and by the fact that for more than twelve years he had to live under the presidency of the man he despised more than any other in American politics and whom he more than once described as having "the Christian Science smile." Roosevelt-haters have always been abundant, but Mencken was among the most strenuous. Various reasons have been adduced for the strength of his antipathy. One has it that he never forgave Roosevelt for one-upping him decisively at the 1934 Gridiron dinner for journalists in Washington. At that dinner, Roosevelt, following Mencken, who had delivered a humorous and rather mild attack on the New Deal, read a powerful polemic against journalism that turned out to be taken from a scathing piece of Mencken's own, titled "Journalism in America." It left the audience in shock. Mencken does not mention this in his diary, but according to Fecher he swore to "get even."

Yet Mencken would have had ample reason to hate Roosevelt without requiring personal animus as a goad. He held, to begin with, that "all government, in its essence, is a conspiracy against the superior man," and so it followed that the less there was of government, the better all round. The notion that professional social workers like Harry Hopkins or the Brain Trust gathered together by Roosevelt knew what was best for the country Mencken found appalling. ("Of such sort," he wrote in 1935 in the *Baltimore Sun,* "are the young wizards who now sweat to save the plain people from the degradations of capitalism, which is to say, from the degradations of working hard, saving their money, and paying their way.") His distrust of politicians generally was very great, and in a lecture at Columbia, "The Politician," he remarked that what got them elected was "simply their power to impress and enchant the intellectually underprivileged." Roosevelt, to his mind, gave all this an extra spin. "He was the first American to penetrate to the real depths of vulgar stupidity," Mencken wrote in his diary the day after the president's death. "He never made the mistake of overestimating the intelligence of the American mob. He was its unparalleled professor."

And on top of it all, Roosevelt was the president who led the United States into World War II. To Mencken this must have brought back the nightmarish quality of his own experience during World War I, and Roosevelt must in some ways have reminded him of Woodrow Wilson, who had "all the peculiar illusions and delusions that belong to a pedagogue gone *meshugga.*" Early in World War I, before America came in on the side of the British, Mencken had written pro-German pieces for the *Sun;* these drove readers wild and caused grave problems for his editors, whose line was pro-British.

Anti-German feeling in the United States seems to have been greater during World War I than that provoked by the monstrousness of the Nazis during World War II. "I will be very interested to hear from you how St. Louis is taking the affair . . ." T. S. Eliot wrote to his mother in 1917. "I can imagine the mob breaking the windows at Faust's Restaurant, and sacking the Anheuser-Busch, and Mr. Busch giving a million dollars toward national defense." During World War I, the German language was outlawed from many public schools, Beethoven was regularly eliminated from concert programs, sauerkraut was renamed Liberty Cabbage. Around this time, I have read, Germans and Jews in the United States who had *stein* in their last names began pronouncing it *steen,* in the hope of de-Germanizing themselves.

In this atmosphere Mencken became *persona non grata* as a journalist, and was in effect blacklisted from almost all newspapers and magazines. He put his energy into writing books. But he never forgot the overheated American reaction to World War I, and this must have conditioned his own highly skeptical reaction to our entry into World War II. The hysteria induced by war, the clamp it put on criticism, the spirit of propaganda it fostered, all made him extremely edgy. His complaint against the *Sun,* which plays throughout the *Diary* during the war years, is that in reporting the war it had let its critical guard drop and was reduced to the role of cheerleader.

To suggest, however, that Mencken was pro-Hitler, as some critics of the *Diary* have done, is calumny. Fecher does not go this far, though he does cite the paucity of references to Hitler in the diary with (one senses) eyebrows raised. Yet a diary is not a current-events course, and in fact very few entries in Mencken's *Diary* touch on the news. Mencken had a good eye for tyranny. As early as 1919 he knew that the Russian Revolution was a cheat; and in 1922 he wrote, "Communism, as the example of Russia shows, is not a fountain that gushes peace, justice, and plenty, but a sewer in which they are drowned." But partly because of his experience in World War I, and partly because of his abiding suspicion of the British, he tended at first to underplay the danger of Hitler and the Nazis. In 1936 he wrote to Theodore Dreiser, "My belief is that the Jews in this country are diligently preparing for themselves the damnedest anti-Semitic movement ever heard of. . . . Hitler has driven them all crazy." About the potential of Hitler, he could not have been more wrong.

But about Hitler himself Mencken was unequivocal. In 1939 he wrote to the Yale sociologist A. G. Keller: "I dislike all of Hitler's ideas save one, and that is the idea that England should keep out of Central Europe. When it set up Czechoslovakia and Poland it made another war inevitable." To another correspondent he wrote that he was "entirely out of sympathy with the method used by Hitler to handle the Jewish question," and that he was not unaware that "intolerable brutalities have been practiced." When the Friends of Germany, a group sympathetic to the Nazis, offered Mencken an honorary membership, he declined instanter, replying that the Nazi politicians, owing to their "extraordinary imbecility," had "destroyed at one stroke a work of rehabilitation [between Germans and Americans] that has been going on since the war, and they have made it quite impossible to set up any rational defense of their course."

In this same letter Mencken likened Hitler's speeches to those of "an imperial wizard of the Ku Klux Klan"—and this brings up the question of Mencken's own views of blacks. Fecher does not actually use the word "racist" to describe those views, but he does say that nothing could "erase a deeply ingrained conviction [on Mencken's part] that black people were by their very nature inferior to white." Fecher quotes Mencken referring to his housemaid as belonging "to the Afro-American race, and show[ing] many of its psychological stigmata"; and Fecher adds, Mencken "considers it unnecessary to go on and explain what these 'stigmata' are." In fact, in this particular instance Mencken makes it perfectly plain that he is referring to the woman's superstitiousness, for she does not want to touch a house key recently in the possession of another woman who had worked for the Menckens and who had just died. Apparently, under contemporary thought control it is impermissible to suggest that an uneducated black woman of a certain time and certain place might have been superstitious (*kayn ayin horeh*). If you can't say anything nice . . .

The most odious of racial epithets comes up once in the *Diary,* in a nonracial context, when Mencken uses the phrase "nigger in the woodpile." But Mencken was highly democratic in his mockery of all ethnic groups: Scots, Irish, Greeks, his own "Krauts" (to use a phrase he did not shy away from, either). About blacks specifically the *Diary* contains a number of items that, quite apart from their truth quotient, have been ruled out as unsayable today. For example, bemoaning the general decay of the neighborhoods surrounding his Hollins Street house, Mencken writes:

> Unhappily, the low-class blacks who formed part of the wartime immigration show no sign of returning home. They find life in Baltimore much pleasanter than it was in their native wilds, and when hard times come again they will all go on the dole. The city jail is already full of them, and four or five are in the death house.

Like all interesting writers, Mencken went in for risky generalizations, to which, when possible, he preferred to give a comic twist: "Why is it as surprising to find an unassuming and intelligent fellow among [actors] as to find a Greek without fleas" is a fair example. But what saves him is that he always judges individuals above groups and races. In the *Diary,* he notes his attempts to get the journalist George S. Schuyler, a black man, a job on a newspaper or magazine, but without success. "When I compare him to any of the dunderheads now roaring on the *Sun*," he writes, "I am sharply conscious of his enormous superiority. He is not only much more intelligent than they are; he is vastly more honest." Earlier, he recounts a visit to the house in Baltimore in which he was born and which is now in a neighborhood "that has been given over to Negroes for many years, and has steadily deteriorated" (unsayable). The block opposite has been condemned for a federal project of some kind. Meanwhile, he discovers a black man, working with a white plasterer, rehabilitating the house he, Mencken, was born in. He seemed, Mencken writes, "a very intelligent and decent fellow," adding that "in even the worst slums there are plenty of such men." But between the government project and his neighbors, he is being gouged, squeezed, sandbagged. "He is one of the forgotten men who always suffer when schemes of uplift are afoot."

As for those of "the Hebrew extraction," as my black sergeant in basic training used to refer to Jews, here the terrain gets rather more tricky. In the published *Diary* Mencken offers no generalizations on the subject. But if someone he writes about is Jewish, he usually (but not always) mentions it. George Boas, a philosophy teacher at Johns Hopkins, is "a brisk, clever Jew," and his wife is "a French Jewess" who, though polite, "finds it hard to conceal her distrust of me as a German." In an entry Fecher does not print but which he quotes in his introduction, we are told that Mencken refers to two well-known Baltimore businessmen as "dreadful kikes." But he sometimes lets opportunities escape that no true anti-Semite would: he mentions, for example, a professional deadbeat in Baltimore named Jerome P. Fleishman, but says nothing about his being Jewish, although his name would certainly suggest it. On the other hand, the sales manager at Knopf, whose idea it was to print the trashy prayer book mentioned earlier, is named Bernard Smith, of whom Mencken comments: "What his name was before he changed it I do not know. He, too, is a Jew, and moreover, a jackass." It is possible Mencken is criticizing the man not only for his publishing practice but for his falsity in trying to hide his identity by changing his name.

Then there is the entry about the last Jew in the Maryland Club, which seems to have gotten into all the newspaper stories in which Mencken has been proclaimed an anti-Semite. Mencken was himself a member of the Maryland Club, and here he merely recounts the brief history of Jews in the club as told to him by the club's secretary, whom he has met on the street. These seem to have been two in number: one, a man from out of town named Winter who it turns out changed his name from Winternitz and who nobody knew was Jewish until he brought his very Jewish-looking father as a guest for dinner; and the other a man named Jacob Ulman, who was married to a great-granddaughter of Thomas Jefferson and had little to do with other Jews in Baltimore. The secretary tells Mencken that after the death of Jacob Ulman the board of governors decided there would be no more Jews in the club. Mencken closes the entry with this deadpan sentence: "There is no other Jew in Baltimore who seems suitable."

What, really, is being said here? Since Mencken was quite without conventional snobbery, and since many of his friends in Baltimore were Jews, it hardly seems likely that he actually believed no Jew in Baltimore was good enough to be a member of the Maryland Club (the increasing expensiveness of which he complains about in a later entry). Is it possible he means no Jew in Baltimore is sufficiently fraudulent to divest himself of all his Jewishness and Jewish connections in order to become a member of the club—that no Jew is enough of a stuffed shirt to qualify? It is, I think, quite possible.

A "shrewd Jew" is how Mencken refers to Morris Fishbein, editor in the 1940s of the *Journal of the American Medical Association,* but he ends by saying, "and I am inclined to believe that his services to American medicine have been extremely valuable." Leonard Weinberg, a successful Baltimore attorney who came up through night school, "now represents a great many of the richer Jewish firms in Baltimore. . . . Rather curiously for a lawyer of rich employees, he has maintained a level head, and on occasion has actually represented unions. He is a highly intelligent fellow, and his observations are always sharp and sound." Mencken describes Lawrence Spivak, later known as the founder and producer of the radio and television show *Meet the Press,* as "a young Harvard Jew," then goes on to praise him as "energetic and intelligent" and to remark that "since he became business manager of the *American Mercury* he has increased the advertising revenues, and shown his capacity in other directions."

Once in the *Diary* Mencken substitutes the word "Jews" for Hollywood, and another time he refers to "the Jews of Hollywood"—as in "The Jews of Hollywood have certainly not given [Dreiser] much money"—yet in the 1930s and 1940s, that was not an inaccurate sociological description. He remarks of Charles Angoff that "like most of the other young Jewish intellectuals (but unlike Lawrence Spivak), Angoff inclines to Communism. . . ." And he adds: "Angoff is an excellent managing editor, but his writings remain unimpressive, and his politics are mainly silly." That is certainly a correct appraisal of Angoff's talent as a writer; everything about his Mencken book feels wrong and sounds false—and the general sense that the book conveys is that of a man working off a deep grudge against his subject.

What about the connection Mencken draws between "most of the other young Jewish intellectuals" and Communism? The line was written in 1934, and Jews, especially in New York City, were in fact going in for sectarian Communism in disproportionate numbers. In the *Diary,* Mencken plays on this quite frequently. After a lecture, confronted by hostile questions, he notes that most of the radicals questioning him are Jewish. The unionists causing trouble at the firm of Alfred A. Knopf are also noted as Jewish. Of *PM*, the radical New York newspaper of the 1940s, Mencken writes: "It is simply a Yiddish paper printed in English." Does all this constitute anti-Semitism? Or have we once again hit upon another of those unspeakable subjects?

Would a serious anti-Semite note, disapprovingly, the anti-Semitism of others? Mencken does, when in the *Diary* he remarks that Dreiser "broke out into an anti-Semitic tirade" against his publisher (Horace Liveright), or that Gerald L. K. Smith "is preparing to get aboard the great anti-Semitic movement now rolling in New York [in 1937]." Mencken also reports Samuel Eliot Morison, the Harvard historian, telling him in 1942 that his students, in Mencken's words, "were mainly Jews, and that few of them showed any capacity."

But more decisive—perhaps most decisive—is the fact that, though greatly opposed to the conduct of World War II, and though detesting Franklin Delano Roosevelt, not once does Mencken blame American entry into the war on the Jews or Jewish pressure groups or on Jewish dealings *sub rosa*. For any sort of earnest anti-Semite, especially one in as generally dark and depressed a state as Mencken was during these years, one would think the temptation to accuse the Jews would have been irresistible. Mencken, at least in those portions of the diary Fecher has chosen to print, resists—completely.

And so, as one runs through the thirty or so references to Jews in the 463 pages of the published *Diary*, one is somewhat surprised, after the newspaper stories, to discover what the fuss has been about. If it is about adjectives, anyone who looks beyond them—beyond what I call the newspaper level of truth—will be disappointed. Mencken, as Lawrence Spivak recently told the writer Sheldon Richman, "talked about Jews the way Jews talked about Jews." Which, one is inclined to add, may be part of the problem.

But let us call this little inquisition to a close. To reverse

Charles A. Fecher, let it be said at once, clearly and unequivocally: Mencken may have been tactless, he may have been foolhardy enough to think that a man could write what he pleased in his private diary, he may have been singularly unprescient in failing to realize that what he wrote sixty years ago would be read by an age as happy in its virtue and self-righteousness as our own. But H. L. Mencken was no anti-Semite, no enemy of the Jews. For that, he would have had to be, as in a very different context he called Woodrow Wilson, and as he himself obviously was not, *meshugga.*

The Reputation
of George Orwell

NEARLY A DECADE after the heavily over-Orwelled if otherwise unfateful year of 1984, and more than forty years since his death in 1950, one still feels that nothing like a clear picture of the precise quality of George Orwell has emerged. Fame—a great, billowy, international cloud of fame—has got in the way. Ozone-like layers of controversy, chiefly having to do with conversative and left-wing claimants to Orwell's political legacy, have further obscured the atmosphere. The highly uneven nature of Orwell's writing has sent up yet more in the way of mist. Q. D. Leavis, for example, who early praised Orwell's essays and criticism, asked that he write no more fiction. Then there is Orwell's life, which from one standpoint appears so seamless, an unblemished sheet of uninterrupted goodness, and then from another makes him appear a cold and rather tasteless fish indeed. This is the Orwell whose first wife felt that her husband's work came before her and, in fact, before everything else in life, and who died during an operation for an illness—presumably cancer—that he, busy fellow, scarcely knew about.

Fame of the kind enjoyed by performing artists, politicians, and other public figures is rarely available to writers and creative artists generally. Whenever he was in danger of thinking himself famous, Virgil Thomson used to say, he had only to go out into the world to disabuse himself of the notion. Soon after the burial of Balzac, a writer always keenly interested in fame, the bookkeepers at the Père-Lachaise Cemetery sent their bill for services to the family of "M. Balsaque." Surely there must be a lesson here somewhere.

George Orwell's fame—which has been largely a posthumous phenomenon—has been not only extraordinary but across the board: popular, academic, intellectual. What put Orwell on, in fact all over, the map were his two international bestsellers, *Animal Farm* (1945) and *Nineteen Eighty-four* (1949). These books have been translated into more than thirty languages and have by now sold scores of millions of copies. In the English-speaking world, they are nearly unavoidable; for some years now students generally encounter *Animal Farm* in junior high school or its equivalent and *Nineteen Eighty-four* in secondary school and are frequently asked to read an Orwell essay or two in university composition courses: "A Hanging" (1931) or "Shooting an Elephant" (1936), perhaps, or "Politics and the English Language" or "Why I Write" (both 1946). Among schoolchildren nowadays, the name George Orwell may be better known than William Shakespeare.

Unfortunately for Danielle Steel and Euclid, it is neither number of books sold nor number of children forced to read an author that confers upon him true literary fame. Instead it is the currency of his ideas that matters. Here Orwell has scored, and scored heavily. "Orwellian" has clearly left "Kafkaesque," "Chekhovian," and other literary eponyms far behind. Partly, of course, this is owing to recent decades having been—if you will allow the expression—highly Orwellian. But partly it has to do with the stark clarity of Orwell's ideas, or at least the chief ideas of *Animal Farm* and *Nineteen Eighty-four*. So much is this less so in Orwell's other writings—his essays and nonfictional books—despite the lucidity of each discrete work, that the question of whether Orwell was finally a man of the left or not will probably never be entirely settled.

Between the "finer-grain" and the "broader-outline" writers, Orwell was surely among the latter—among, that is, those writers whose work can be reduced to its essential ideas, as the work of Henry James, Marcel Proust, and George Santayana cannot. So much have the ideas extracted from Orwell's writing been in the air that one needs scarcely to have read him to have a strong notion of what these ideas are. Just as one need not have read through Marx to be aware of the class struggle and economic determinism, or have read much of Freud to know about the Oedipus complex and the importance of dreams, slips, and early sexuality, so one does not really have to have turned a page of Orwell to know that "some pigs are more equal than others," that "Power is Knowledge," and that Big Brother (that creep) is watching you.

In personal testimony to this fact, I can report that, toward the end of 1984, the year of the great Orwell glut, I was asked to add to the slag heap by giving a little talk on *Nineteen Eighty-four*, which I glumly agreed to do. It was only when I sat down to prepare this talk that I realized that I had never read *Nineteen Eighty-four*. I had seen the American movie version, with the impressively sweaty-faced Edmund O'Brien playing Winston Smith; I had for years heard bandied about— no doubt bandied about myself—such terms as "newspeak" and "doublethink"; I had read a number of essays on the novel; but as for actually having read the novel itself, nope, I couldn't rightly say I that I had. When I did get around to reading it, I found it rather disappointing; like most of Orwell's fiction, it was thin on detail and the working-out of the plot seemed unconvincing. As a dystopian novel, I thought it less prescient than Aldous Huxley's *Brave New World* (1932); as a specifically Cold War novel, it couldn't lay a glove on Arthur Koestler's masterpiece, *Darkness at Noon* (1940). But the more interesting point is that, such has been the fame of *Nineteen Eighty-four*, one not only can come to believe one has read the novel when one hasn't but, more amazing still, such has been the spread of the novel through the general culture, it may well be that one doesn't really have to have read the novel at all, so long as one doesn't agree to go about giving talks on it.

Not only has Orwell's fame spread wide and cut deep, but there has become, somehow, something sacrosanct about him and his works. This, too, is a posthumous phenomenon. While he lived, Orwell had more than the normal allotment of enemies. Chief among them were political intellectuals, and in the 1930s, when Orwell came to literary maturity, to be intellectual was by definition to be political. One of Orwell's specialties was attacking intellectuals, and especially catching them out at disseminating left-wing cant, upon which he, Orwell, loved to stomp. ("All left-wing parties in the highly industrialized countries are at bottom a sham," he wrote in his essay "Rudyard Kipling" (1942), "because they make it their business to fight against something which they do not really wish to destroy.") Orwell was much better at influencing people than at making friends, at least when alive. Now the situation appears nearly to be reversed. Excepting only the most artery-hardened Marxists, everyone is Orwell's friend nowadays. Devotion to Orwell has become no laughing matter. Or so I conclude from the fact that, after all these years, no one so far as I know has published a parody of Orwell—an easy enough job, one would think, given the many strongly characteristic tics and turns of Orwell's readily recognized prose style, with its aggressively commonsensical spin. It is easy to imagine what Orwell might have thought of the Orwell phenomenon:

> As I write, this room is rapidly filling up with the stench of smelly little orthodoxies, and they are all about me. Every neo-con, lib-lab, beard-bearing student-humping academic, every *Nation* reader, language snob, think-tank barnacle, priest, admiral, Harvard child-psychologist, CEO is aware that I am high on the list of entirely O.K. writers. "Orwell" has become one of

those magic words, like "Art"; say it and everything is fine. You have only to quote me and your case is made. The grandchildren of people who fifty or sixty years ago would have been pleased to wipe their boots on me are now forced to read me in paperback. It's no use pretending that the sheer power of my writing has brought this about, or that such a diversity of admirers have all come round to my general views. The last man you want to trust is the man whom everyone thinks is admirable. "Saints," I once wrote, "should always be judged guilty until they are proven innocent." The same holds true for writers, except that, as any writer worth his salt will tell you, no good writer is ever innocent.

In one of those complex, less-than-straightforward letters of rejection that publisher's editors frequently find themselves writing to authors, T. S. Eliot, after rejecting *Animal Farm* on behalf of the firm of Faber & Faber, wrote to Orwell that he regretted the rejection and that "I have a regard for your work, because it is good writing of fundamental integrity." My guess is that Orwell would have had no difficulty accepting that as a fair description of the quality of his writing. It strikes me as dead on target: "good writing of fundamental integrity." Nowhere did Orwell suggest that he thought himself a writer for the ages, a universal genius, a figure of the kind that, posthumously and through the vagaries of circumstance, he has become: translated into all languages, required reading for schoolchildren, quoted approvingly by natural enemies.

How intricate and never quite arbitrary a thing is reputation in literature! In one instance it can be aided immensely by early death (James Agee), in another by longevity (Robert Penn Warren). Unpopular politics have crushed a writer's reputation (Wyndham Lewis), while careful radicalism can elevate another writer's reputation (Robert Lowell). Some writers appear to have gained as greatly by withdrawing from the scene (Thomas Pynchon) as others have by clever self-promotion (Truman Capote). Reading the obituaries for Mary McCarthy, one of the more famous serious writers of our day, I had the thought that Miss McCarthy's fame had always depended upon her being alive to reinforce it. Her early rise in reputation depended in part on her youthful good looks, no matter how clever she was as a critic. In the fiction of her early and middle years, she sustained her reputation by her continuing ability to outrage through gossip and scandal. In her later years, a doyenne now, it was her being outraged that people tended to be concerned about, for she could be enormously disapproving and had ample supplies of anger for those of whom she disapproved. But now that Mary McCarthy is dead, good looks, outrageousness, disapproval, anger—all count for nothing. Only the work remains—much of it in her case, as has been said before, destructive and marred by a falsely moral snobbery— and since this gives so little in the way of pleasure or instruction, it is likely soon to dissipate, then disappear.

Mary McCarthy was among those who attacked Orwell. In 1969, she thought that he left no generative political ideas, that his concept of decency was badly in need of definition, that he was conservative by temperament and thus almost instinctively opposed to fashion, change, and innovation—that, finally and in 1969 devastatingly, he probably would have been on the wrong side in Vietnam. Others have written against Orwell: Anthony West attempted to diminish him by psychoanalyzing him; Kingsley Martin claimed that in *Animal Farm* he had lost faith not merely in the Soviet Union but in mankind; D. A. N. Jones felt that he unfairly blackened the picture against left-wing intellectuals and was father of the bashing of feminists, pacifists, homosexuals, and other left-minded groups that Jones views as part of the political distraction and irrelevance of the current day. Firing away with howitzers, Uzis, and squirt guns, Raymond Williams, Conor Cruise O'Brien, and Terry Eagleton have all, in their turn and in their different times, taken their shots at him. Still others have spat upon, bepissed, and whacked away at the statue of Orwell, but without in any serious way staining it, let alone tipping it over.

No critic of high standing has ever claimed that George Orwell was a first-rate novelist, though John Wain, Kingsley Amis, Philip Larkin, and other distinguished writers have written approvingly of his novels. Orwell did not write enough literary criticism to qualify, strictly speaking, as a literary critic. When he did write about writers—as he did about Dickens, Kipling, Tolstoy, Henry Miller—his impetus was generally extra-literary. A number of his familiar and personal essays are immensely impressive, but the quantity of these essays is not great. As with every journalist who works on weekly and fortnightly deadlines—as Orwell did on the *Tribune* and the London *Observer*—some weeks he was much better than others, and on many of those other weeks he could be pretty thin. He was splendid as a critic of popular culture—was something even of a pioneer in this field—but he could also come near ruining his work here through the intrusion of his own often rather coarse politics. After his admirably lucid account of the widely read sub-literature known as boys' weeklies, and a measured analysis of their social import, Orwell could not refrain from remarking that the stories in the boys' weeklies lead their readers to believe "that there is nothing wrong with laissez-faire capitalism"; and he ended his essay, most disappointingly, by suggesting that, given the significant impression that youthful reading tends to leave for life, it is surely time to develop left-wing stories for the boys' weekly market.

Orwell died, of tuberculosis, in 1950 at the much-too-early age of forty-six. In a relatively brief writing career, he produced a vast amount of work. Except toward the end of his life, when the royalties from *Animal Farm* began to arrive, he produced what he did under considerable financial strain. His wretched health increased the strain. Although Orwell much admired craft, and more than once wrote of the importance of the aesthetic element in his own writing, the circumstances under which he worked were always arduous and scarcely allowed for Flaubertian meticulousness. If not altogether by choice, he was much less the artist than the professional writer. He was also, as he came to learn, chiefly a political writer. "When I sit down to write a book, I do not say to myself, 'I am going to produce a work of art.' I write it because there is some lie that I want to expose, some fact to which I want to draw attention, and my initial concern is to get a hearing." Cyril Connolly later seconded this point, remarking that Orwell was "a political animal" who "reduced everything to politics. . . . He could not blow his nose without moralising on conditions in the handkerchief industry."

"Good prose," Orwell famously wrote, "is like a window pane," and the absence of artful window dressing in his own prose has been part of Orwell's attraction for many readers. He commanded a prose style that strongly implied truth-telling ought to take precedence over art. In some of his work— one thinks of the chapter on the role of the POUM in *Homage to Catalonia* (1938) that he acknowledges may ruin his book but must nevertheless be included to set the record straight— this seemed to set Orwell *above* art, which, from a certain point of view, isn't a bad place to be.

Not, however, in the opinion of everyone. Conor Cruise O'Brien, reviewing the four-volume *Collected Essays, Journalism and Letters of George Orwell* when it appeared in 1968, interestingly noted that "plain language has a tendency to become extreme—which is why the other kind of language is generally preferred—and thus a laudable peculiarity of style made Orwell seem more extreme than he was." It has also made arriving at anything like a consensus about his true literary quality difficult. No agreement exists, for example, about which of Orwell's books is his best. Some profess admiration for *Homage to Catalonia;* some say the first, others the second half of *The Road to Wigan Pier* (1937) represents his best work. Mary McCarthy called *Down and Out in Paris and London* (1933)

Orwell's "masterpiece"; Cyril Connolly felt the same book was not more than "agreeable journalism" done much better by Henry Miller. Most sophisticated readers, when asked where the best of Orwell is to be found, reply, the essays; but even here consensus never quite arrives. Edmund Wilson, while admiring Orwell generally, thought that in his literary essays he had "the habit of taking complex personalities too much at their face value, of not getting inside them enough." Newton Arvin thought Orwell, as an essayist, "an excellent writer on certain sorts of subjects," but not up to writing on figures of the high cultural complexity of Yeats. Evelyn Waugh noted of Orwell: "He has an unusually high moral sense and respect for justice and truth, but he seems never to have been touched by a conception of religious thought and life." Apart from showing how discrepant opinions about Orwell can be, these views show how apt other writers were to read into Orwell, or discover missing from him, those qualities they thought most important in their own work. What was the quality in George Orwell that made other writers read him as if he were a Rorschach test? And might not this quality, too, be connected in some central way to the unflagging prominence of Orwell's reputation?

To get at the complex nature of Orwell's reputation, clearly something like a book-length study is required, or so at least Professor John Rodden, who teaches rhetoric at the University of Virginia and who has written such a book, must have felt. *The Politics of Literary Reputation,* which carries the subtitle *The Making and Claiming of "St. George" Orwell,* is a vast production. The book is easily double the length of any single book its subject ever wrote, and carries behind it, in a giant academic caboose, more than twelve hundred footnotes, most of them discursive. Professor Rodden has to have read nearly everything ever written about or connected with or even loosely tangential to George Orwell, popular and academic, English, American, and European. The small-type index feels like the telephone directory of a small town. It is an exhaustive study.

Professor Rodden writes well enough, in a style that combines intellectual journalism with a heavy though not deadly admixture of academic locutions. There is little about his book, like so much current academic criticism, that bears the unmarked but unmistakable legend TO THE TRADE ONLY. And yet there is something about *The Politics of Literary Reputation* that makes it the near reverse, in the cant phrase, of "a good read." It is instead a rough and rambling "read." Less like a "read" at all, it feels like a long career, in which all one's movement is lateral. Professor Rodden views Orwell from every possible angle—as Rebel, as Prophet, as Common Man, as Saint—but somehow the portrait that emerges from all these angle shots comes out less rounded than blurred. Pace and progress seem to play no part in the argument. The struggle to get in everything is paramount. Rodden seems perpetually to be reconstructing "four phases of Orwell's reputation in postwar Germany," or demarcating his "three *Tribune* 'lives' between 1937–47," or noting that this or that critic's "history of reception" of Orwell's work can be divided into four or five parts. Near the close, Rodden refers to his book as "this project," and project is how the reader—including the entirely interested reader—comes to view it, too. An exhaustive study, as I say.

Yet, for all Professor Rodden's labors, one feels that the job has not been done—that is, if the job has been to account for why a writer of George Orwell's particular quality has loomed as large as he has in the contemporary world. We get a great deal of background on the issues, questions, and problems connected with Orwell's career. We learn much about what he meant to his contemporaries, the generation immediately following them, and to the left-wing intellectuals of the current day. We are filled in on the dispute over the ultimate character of Orwell's politics and hence over the matter of his political legacy. Professor Rodden takes positions, is not shy about announcing his own politics ("left-of-center white male of working-class origins, a post–Vatican II Catholic liberal"), or fearful of speculating upon why one critic found Orwell attractive and another finds him repulsive. Rodden glues literally hundreds of small mosaics to the wall, but, somehow, a picture refuses to cohere. What one is left with are data, a vaster collection of facts about the career of a single writer than has perhaps ever before been gathered in a single place. But data, however interesting, remain data.

What is missing, I believe, is a stronger element of literary criticism than the author of *The Politics of Literary Reputation* chooses to provide. The choice was a deliberate one—"This book," writes Professor Rodden, "aims chiefly to describe the making and claiming of a reputation, rather than to argue a specific case for its upward or downward revaluation"—but it is not clear that the two activities, criticism and description, are so easily separable. Insofar as one of the tasks of criticism is to establish the quality of a writer with a view toward placing him among his contemporaries and predecessors, the reputation of any serious writer is almost always best understood from the perspective of criticism. Another of the tasks of criticism—one of the major ones, surely—is to confer just reputation. An unjust literary reputation, as ought by now to be well known, can be as easily built on a writer's defects as on his strengths (see, not merely passim, the last thirty or so years of American novelists). In the case of Orwell, one wonders if the question of how he arrived at his extraordinary reputation isn't bound up with the answer to the literary critical question of what kind of writer he was, strengths, defects, ambiguities, and all.

George Orwell has become a hero of culture. Other literary men have been heroes of culture over the past century, Henry James, James Joyce, T. S. Eliot among them. But these men derived their status from their art, for which they made heroic sacrifices and on which they left a permanent impress. But

Orwell is extraordinary among heroes of culture in not being exclusively an artist, or even, strictly speaking, a figure whose most strenuous efforts were invested in high culture. One might even say that Orwell's status derives in good part from his very artlessness. Max Beerbohm once declared that "to be interesting, a man must be complex and elusive," citing the examples of Byron, Disraeli, and Rossetti as among the most interesting men in nineteenth-century England. But Orwell's power, much of his interest to us, comes from the reverse qualities: his simplicity and straightforwardness, at least as these are exhibited in the character he projected in his most powerful writing.

From the standpoint of reputation, character has always been Orwell's strongest asset. It was imputed to him early and continued to be conferred on him posthumously. "I was a stage rebel," wrote Cyril Connolly, who went to St. Cyprian's and then Eton with him, "Orwell a true one," adding: "The remarkable thing about Orwell was that alone among the boys he was an intellectual and not a parrot for he thought for himself." The imputation of strong character would heighten over the years. When Lionel Trilling came to write about Orwell, in an introduction to a 1952 edition of *Homage to Catalonia,* character had turned into virtue. Trilling allowed that Orwell was "not a genius," but emphasized that Orwell's virtue comprised "not merely moral goodness, but also fortitude and strength in goodness." That he was not a genius made him, in Trilling's view, all the more important, "for he communicates to us the sense that what he has done any one of us could do." (In Trilling's essay there follows a paragraph of extraordinary qualification that begins, "Or could do if we but made up our mind to it," which suggests most of us cannot; and here one senses how Lionel Trilling, that academic Demosthenes, his mouth filled not with pebbles but perpetual qualifications and hesitations, must have achingly envied Orwell's plainspokenness and readiness to act on his views.) From boy of character to man of virtue, Orwell was next (though not in strict chronological order) transmuted into "the wintry conscience of a generation," in V. S. Pritchett's obituary article in the *New Statesman* of January 28, 1950, "a kind of saint," a "Don Quixote" whose "conscience could be allayed only by taking upon itself the pain, the misery, the dinginess and the pathetic but hard vulgarities of a stale and hopeless period." One would like to think that George Orwell, reading all this, would have been mildly amused.

Yet these have been the terms in which, for the vast most part, Orwell has been judged. As Professor Rodden puts it, "If we see Pritchett's obituary [which also appeared in a somewhat different version in the *New York Times Book Review*] as one of those reception moments to which readers have repeatedly returned—like Trilling's introduction to *Homage to Catalonia* and Connolly's characterization of Orwell in *Enemies of Promise* (1938)—it offers further insight into the reputation process." Cyril Connolly, Lionel Trilling, and V. S. Pritchett make for a pretty fair triumvirate of testimonials, representing English and American literary criticism at its best from its aesthetic through its morally serious strain. Yet can the terms for judging Orwell that they have set down be sustained in our day?

I do not myself think that they quite can be. I say this with no great glee, for Orwell has been one of a small number of modern writers from whom my own way of viewing the world derives. Although one is trained, in judging literature, to ignore the life of a writer and concentrate on the work, anyone with any normal human feeling is always secretly delighted to learn that a writer he admires is also a man or woman he can respect. Part of the attractiveness of Orwell has of course been the respect that the integrity of his life invites. No finality in biography is available, and it may yet turn up that Orwell perpetuated some hideously caddish acts. But just now it does seem that a good part of the reason for the reverence in which he is held is the stupidity-ridden, disgrace-laden, generally shameful history of intellectual life of the past half century or so, against which

Orwell's relative normality, common sense, and decency stand out.

At the same time, it ought not to stand in the way of a clear judgment of Orwell's work. Orwell was himself much concerned about what it is that makes for survival in literature and about the changing nature of literary reputation. In "Inside the Whale" (1940) he took up the change that had swept over the remains—that is to say, the poems—of A. E. Housman, who had been an important figure in his own generation when Orwell was young but seemed less so later. With typical good sense, he writes: "There is no need to under-rate him now because he was over-rated a few years ago." I don't mean to imply that Orwell, too, was overrated; he said things crucial to his day, and in so saying helped form not only the terms of the discussion but the history of that day and became one its central writers. Rereading Orwell in our day, one's admiration for his insight and intellectual courage do not lessen. Quite the reverse; much that he wrote then seems no less pertinent now, and not as prophesy but as simple truth. Yet much in Orwell can also seem thin, or oddly skewed, inadequate, or simply wrong. George Orwell has reached that privileged position of high reputation where his weaknesses can be openly dealt with because his strengths are no longer in serious dispute. The time, surely, has come for a fuller portrait.

It will not, for example, any longer do to consider George Orwell principally as a cold-war writer. He was partly that, of course; one of the best and most important, possibly the primary anti-totalitarian writer of the late 1930s and 1940s, a time of great denial of the murderousness of left-wing totalitarianism. Orwell was a strong and straightaway anti-Communist. It was an honorable and lonely position, and one which a man who earned a small living by his writings paid for by being denied entry into many magazines. The significance of this strain in Orwell cannot be gainsaid; nor is it quite time, at least in the gardens of the Third World, to shuck it all off as once pertinent but no longer. But Orwell's anti-Communism grew not alone out of his historical experience—with his self-acclaimed talent for facing unpleasant facts—but also out of his exposure to intellectuals under political pressure. He repeatedly said that "the intellectuals are more totalitarian in outlook than the common people." He said it in dozens of different ways, and none of them tactful. "The truth is, of course," he wrote in "Raffles and Miss Blandish" (1944), "that the countless English intellectuals who kiss the arse of Stalin are not different from the minority who give their allegiance to Hitler or Mussolini."

Although Orwell described himself in *The Road to Wigan Pier* as "a semi-intellectual," he was among modern writers the fiercest anti-intellectual going. Perhaps he was just enough of an intellectual—bookish, someone interested in the play of ideas—to have understood and despised the type. Having gone to Eton but not on to university, Orwell was nicely positioned to feel no inferiority toward the general class of English intellectuals and yet not quite feel himself of that class, either. To become an intellectual was, for Orwell, to become deeply out of it, hypocritical, stupid, inhumanly corrupted, spiritually bankrupt. Here is a small bouquet of Orwell's prime remarks about intellectuals:

> They take their cookery from Paris and their opinions from Moscow. —*The Lion and the Unicorn* (1941)
>
> It is only the "educated" man, especially the literary man, who knows how to be a bigot. —*The Road to Wigan Pier*
>
> One has to belong to the intelligentsia to believe things like that [that America had entered World War II to prevent an English revolution]; no ordinary man could be so stupid. —"Notes on Nationalism" (1945)
>
> [The leftish politics] of the English intellectual is the patriotism of the deracinated. —"Inside the Whale"

England is perhaps the only great nation whose intellectuals are ashamed of their country. —*The Lion and the Unicorn*

Orwell wasn't much cheerier on the subject of what one might think of as intellectual auxiliaries. "A humanitarian is always a hypocrite," he wrote, "and Kipling's understanding of this is perhaps the central secret of his power to create telling phrases." Of Ezra Pound in particular, but of the conduct of artists generally, he noted: "One has the right to expect ordinary decency even of a poet." And of course his devastating shot at the grotesque unreality of those who flocked to contemporary socialism, which appears in the second half of *The Road to Wigan Pier,* once read can scarcely be forgot: "The fact is that Socialism, *in the form in which it is now presented,* appeals chiefly to unsatisfactory or even inhuman types." Details not withheld: "One sometimes gets the impression that the mere words 'Socialism' and 'Communism' draw towards them with magnetic force every fruit juice drinker, nudist, sandal-wearer, sex-maniac, Quaker, 'Nature Cure' quack, pacifist and feminist in England." It gets worse, wilder, and, if you happen to be sitting on the right side of the aisle, even funnier.

Having declared intellectuals poison—and "the modern English literary world, at any rate the highbrow section of it, a sort of poisonous jungle where only weeds can flourish"—Orwell was thrown back on the figure he frequently referred to in his writing as "the common man." Sometimes this "common man" is assumed to be of the working class, a man who, quite rightly in Orwell's view, is entirely uninterested in the philosophical side of Marxism, with its "pea-and-thimble trick with those three mysterious entities, thesis, antithesis, and synthesis." Sometimes he is the "ordinary man," who "may not flinch from a dictatorship of the proletariat, if you offer it tactfully; [but] offer him a dictatorship of the prigs, and he gets ready to fight." People of "very different type can be described as the common man," Orwell wrote in his essay on Dickens.

But what marks this common man above all for Orwell is "a native decency," a distaste for abstraction, and an appreciation of the small pleasures and surface delights of life. When Orwell writes that "the common man is still living in the mental world of Dickens, but nearly every modern intellectual has gone over to some or other form of totalitarianism," he means that the common man retains a bred-in-the-bone respect for loyalty and kindness, courage and freedom, a hatred of unfairness and oppression, and a love for life in its everyday quality that the intellectual has bred out of himself. Mary McCarthy, it will be recalled, felt Orwell's concept of decency needed refining, but then she was herself almost the perfect type of intellectual and wasn't, in Orwell's view, likely to have understood it in any case.

Orwell understood it and tried by his best lights to live it. After his youthful years in the British imperial police in Burma, after his days of deliberately going down and out, he tried to live like the common man, at least in the outward appurtenances of his life. Bernard Crick's biography of Orwell, the most complete we now have, recounts several of the details of Orwell's almost aggressive anti-bohemianism. On the other hand, he was blocked off from living in an easy middle-class way not only by his meager earnings as a free-lance writer but even more by his strong antipathy to the bourgeois life from which he had come. ("To have a horror of the bourgeois," said Jules Renard, "is bourgeois.") The result was that Orwell and his wife Eileen tended to muddle along somewhat grimly between working- and lower-middle-class living arrangements, with Orwell affecting proletarian habits. He smoked shag cigarettes, slurped his tea out of the saucer, cared not at all about clothes. In the last years of his life, with the royalties that were beginning to come in from *Animal Farm,* he bought a farm in Jura, in the Scottish Hebrides, where, with his sister and adopted son under his roof, he attempted to live the life of the hardscrabble farmer. As best he could, Orwell attempted, to use the French phrase he himself would doubtless have abjured, to live *dans le vrai*.

He attempted to write, too, *dans le vrai*, and one of his working assumptions, though so far as I know he never put it straightout, was that the truth of life has been distorted by much literature. As a literary critic, he was best as a revisionist—revising the received opinions about other writers that felt wrong to him. Allowing for Kipling's worst thoughts, he goes on to make the points that "Kipling deals in thoughts which are both vulgar and permanent," that "few people who have criticized England from the inside have said bitterer things about her than this gutter patriot," that he wrote "with responsibility" and knew that "men can only be highly civilized while other men, inevitably less civilized, are there to guard and feed them." (W. H. Auden, in his political phase during the 1930s, Orwell called "a sort of gutless Kipling.") He de-Marxified Dickens, showing how little interested in politics Dickens was, and asserted that "he was popular chiefly because he was able to express in comic, simplified and therefore memorable form that native decency of the common man." Brilliantly, he notes: "The outstanding, unmistakable mark of Dickens's writing is the *unnecessary detail*." In what is Orwell's best literary essay, "Lear, Tolstoy and the Fool" (1947)—an essay that anticipates and is superior to Isaiah Berlin's *The Hedgehog and the Fox*— he sides against Tolstoy, whose "main aim, in his later years, was to narrow the range of human consciousness," and with Shakespeare, who "loved the surface of the earth and the process of life . . . [and whose] main hold on us is through language."

George Orwell was half an artist. This was not sufficient to make him a memorable novelist, but it did put him in the class of the best English essayists, all of whom have also been, in their various ways, half artists. Serious visual art and music never come in for mention in Orwell; he is dead to the artistic significance of religion, toward which he was generally—and in the case of Roman Catholics particularly—antagonistic. But about literary art he was passionate: "So long as I remain alive and well I shall continue to feel strongly about prose style, to love the surface of the earth [the same phrase he uses in connection with Shakespeare], and to take a pleasure in solid objects and scraps of useless information." In another time, he might have been able to give way to this side of himself. But not in that in which he lived. In his own time politics was unavoidable, and he saw his job as reconciling "my ingrained likes and dislikes with the essentially public, non-individual activities that this age forces on all of us." As for his own ambition, about this he is entirely clear: "What I have wanted to do throughout the past ten years," he remarked in "Why I Write," "is to make political writing into an art."

How successful was Orwell at turning political writing into an art? Very, is one's unhesitating first response. A tradition of sorts was there. Burke, Paine, Cobden, Hazlitt, Macaulay had each produced political writing that—sometimes in flashes, sometimes in sustained patches—remains powerful, beautiful, greatly moving. In this tradition, political writing that aspired to art tended to go for the searing and the soaring, flame-throwers followed by French horns. Part of Orwell's distinction as a political writer is that he departed from this tradition by playing it flat and playing it straight. He described the indecency of shooting a Fascist when the man is running while trying to hold up his trousers; he described the loathsomeness of tripe on a coal miner's table; always and everywhere he described smells and filth, discomfort and disgust, and made plain that in war and in poverty "physical details always outweigh everything else." When he took on a political subject, Orwell regularly warned against his bias, he struggled on the page before the reader to be as honest as possible within that bias; and his interest in any political event or issue had nothing to do with his establishing his own superiority to it. This was, in political writing, revolutionary, and, since Orwell's death in 1950, it remains without parallel.

Yet the limitations built into making political writing an art, and thus giving it a chance for survival, are considerable. For one, political writing is called into being by events and issues, and events and issues are in the fullness of time settled, dissolved, simply forgotten. Of the writing about them, only the rhetoric remains, trailing the stale odor of once-strong opinion. For another, in politics, unlike in art, it is important that one be correct, or at the very minimum not altogether wrong. In "Politics vs. Literature" (1947), his essay on Swift, whom he called "one of the writers I admire with the least reserve," Orwell asks: "What is the relationship between agreement with a writer's opinions, and enjoyment of his work?" Orwell doesn't quite get around to answering this question, so let me answer it for him by saying that, in politics, where agreement exists it is usually immensely improved.

As for Orwell's own politics, a subject of much contention, it can be said that all interpretations are equal, but some are more equal than others. In "Why I Write" he set them out in a single sentence: "Every line of serious work that I have written since 1936 [since, that is, his experience of international betrayal in the Spanish Civil War] has been written, directly or indirectly, *against* totalitarianism and *for* democratic Socialism, as I understand it." That sounds plain enough, but a twist is added: the progressive party of Orwell's time so revolted him— as, he notes, Swift was revolted by the progressive party of his own—that Orwell's most penetrating and original writing is about the detachment from political reality of left-wing intellectuals and its serious consequences in a world where horror, suffering, and organized murder are real enough. Yet throughout his work there is a persistent rattling against the evils of "the utter rottenness of private capitalism"—for leftists of Orwell's generation capitalism was a way station directly on the road to fascism—clichéd references to the filthy rich ("The lady in the Rolls-Royce car is now more damaging to morale than a fleet of Göring's bombing-planes," he wrote in *The Lion and the Unicorn*), false assertions ("Laissez-faire capitalism is dead"), and much else that one could pop into print in next week's issue of *The Nation* without anyone noticing.

On his deathbed, apropos of Evelyn Waugh, in his journal Orwell wrote: "One cannot really be a Catholic and grown up." In *Homage to Catalonia,* he wrote: "When I see an actual flesh-and-blood worker in conflict with his natural enemy, the policeman, I do not have to ask which side I am on." (The man could be a rapist, George; better ask.) Israel was for him just another variant of nationalism, and he despised national-ism in all its forms. "The opinion that art should have nothing to do with politics is itself a political attitude," he wrote, in a sentence that not only illustrates Conor Cruise O'Brien's remark that "plain language has a tendency to become extreme" but has caused great mischief by being interpreted to mean that, at bottom, everything in the world is political in any case, so let 'er rip. Orwell was wrong about many things, and about some things not merely wrong but crudely, callowly wrong.

But on many important things Orwell was right. He was right to trust his instincts over his political opinions whenever the two clashed. He was right in recognizing that the major political question of his time was how best to confront totali-tarianism and all its deceptions; and right again to do so head on, with all his art and all his heart and the vast quantity of courage at his command. He was right in his impatience with intellectual cant, and percipient in early underscoring the con-nection between totalitarian habits of thought and the corrup-tion of language. Orwell was scarcely a genius, nor even, in any striking way, an original thinker. What he was was honest and what he had was unshakable integrity, and these qualities, working their magic, lent his writing great force and made him a figure crucial for his time and left him a model for our own.

However high George Orwell's reputation may have risen, no matter how low it may one day fall, all this is finally part of the history of publicity. What matters is that through moral effort he made himself into a good writer. That is permanent, not subject to fluctuation, can never be taken away.

Robert Hutchins, the Sad Story of the Boy Wonder

B Y THE TIME I first met Robert Maynard Hutchins, in 1966, he was sixty-seven years old and, I now realize, intellectually quite dead. He carried around, however, a splendid corpse. "Presence" was the word then often applied to Hutchins. When he walked into a room—even a large, high-ceilinged, noisy room—everyone noticed; any room he sat in, he seemed to dominate. He was tall (nearly six feet three), naturally slender, and had what used to be called a fine bearing. He wore clothes well, without seeming to care much about them. (In 1949, the American Tailors Guild, citing his "learned look," voted him third on its list of best-dressed men.) His hair was full and wavy and white; the bones in his face were strong but refined. When I knew him, the feature that seemed primary was his mouth: it smiled rarely, and then usually wryly, and laughed almost never—a mouth that was a touch prim and slightly disapproving.

I was twenty-nine and very much in awe of Robert Hutchins, who had left the chancellorship of the University of Chicago in 1950, or five years before I came there as a student. But I always felt that the aspects of the university I most appreciated were owing to Hutchins's twenty-one-year tenure as its head. When I was a student at Chicago, Hutchins was a name that could put an end to friendly parties or enliven dull ones—

no one, on the subject of Robert Hutchins, was neutral. There were those who felt that his were years of divisiveness, distraction, and general decay. Lawrence A. Kimpton, who succeeded him as chancellor, remarked that nothing Hutchins did at the university "had any degree of permanence, except for the financial headaches, the neighborhood deterioration, and the faculty embitterment." But then there were such men as Edward Levi, himself later president of the university, who not merely admired but loved Robert Hutchins for his high-mindedness and for his courage in acting always in consonance with his ideals.

The context for my meeting Hutchins was that I had recently been hired as a senior editor at Encyclopaedia Britannica, Inc., where he was chairman of the board of editors. Hutchins's connection with Britannica was a lengthy one, beginning back in the 1940s, when General Robert E. Wood of Sears, Roebuck transferred the Britannica Corporation to William Benton, Hutchins's classmate at Yale, in a complicated arrangement that paid out a handsome royalty to the University of Chicago. For a time Benton, who had made an early fortune in advertising (the Benton & Bowles agency was his and his fellow Yalie Chester Bowles's), worked for Hutchins at the university as a vice president for public relations; but Hutchins would work for Benton for much longer, and eventually become his stipendiary. Neither greedy nor even greatly money-minded, Hutchins, accustomed as a young man to going first-class, lived as if perfectly unaware that any other class was possible. "If you have to look at the meter," was one of his well-known sayings, "don't take cabs." Past the age of twenty-five he probably never paid for a cab out of his own pocket.

Neither of us paid for lunch that day, which was at the Tavern Club, a block or so south of the Britannica offices across the Chicago River on Michigan Avenue. Seven or eight Britannica editors were at that lunch, with Mortimer J. Adler at the head of the table as our ostensible host. I was seated to

Hutchins's left. Everyone tried to steer the conversation around toward him, almost as if we felt under an obligation not to let Robert Hutchins grow any more bored than he already appeared to be, though it was clear there was little any of us could do to prevent it. At one point he leaned toward me and, remarking that he understood I had gone to the University of Chicago, asked, "Have they brought football back yet?" I assumed he was joking. "Not the last I heard," I said, and asked if he had much occasion to visit the university. "Never," he said, with the kind of finality with which a man might answer a question about whether he still saw an old mistress or ex-wife. I recall wanting to break in to tell him that attending the university had been the crucial intellectual event of my life, but then he did not seem the sort of man to whom one blurted out such avowals. After lunch, waiting for the elevator, he stood posture perfect in a charcoal gray suit, red vest, and black knit tie, raincoat draped over one arm, a cigarette in hand, looking like a more handsome version of the actor Conrad Nagel, a man with only the simulacra of responsibilities whose real life, or so it seemed to me, was essentially finished.

Jobs that other men should have felt pleased to have achieved at the culmination of their careers, Robert Hutchins had as a young man—by current reckoning, as hardly more than a boy. In 1927, at the age of twenty-eight, he was appointed dean of the Yale Law School; in 1929, at the age of thirty, he was made president of the University of Chicago. To be considered promising is one thing; to have one's promise so quickly acknowledged and rewarded, quite something else again. Robert Hutchins's youthful promise seems not in any way to have daunted him. He appears to have reacted much as did the young Otto von Bismarck, who, upon being entrusted with a very delicate diplomatic mission in his early twenties, is supposed to have declared: "What is being asked of me is clear. Whether I have the talent and understanding sufficient to accomplish the task is God's affair."

How it came about that Hutchins was offered such jobs so early has long been something of a mystery, at least to me. That mystery has now been cleared up by a full-scale biography, *Unseasonable Truths: A Life of Robert Maynard Hutchins* by Harry S. Ashmore, a friend and, in his last few decades, close colleague of Hutchins. Ashmore's biography sets out to be definitive, which, factually, it probably comes close to being. It is, however, something less than that psychologically. As befits the portrait of one friend by another, Ashmore has told the truth but not the whole truth. He does not probe into areas where his subject might be vulnerable, he tends to eschew motive when dubious behavior calls for interpretation, he everywhere gives his subject the benefit of the doubt, and he operates on the assumption that Robert Hutchins was a great man, instead of merely a greatly interesting one.

Unseasonable Truths is also somewhat skewed by the fact that Ashmore first came to know Hutchins after his glory days were done. The editor of the *Arkansas Gazette,* for which he helped win a Pulitzer Prize during the Little Rock desegregation crisis, Ashmore was first impressed into the Hutchins crew as a board member of the Fund for the Republic, of which Hutchins was president, in 1954. He went on to work at the Encyclopaedia Britannica and at the Center for the Study of Democratic Institutions (where, for a time, he was also president). Ashmore, then, knew Hutchins during the period in his life when he, Hutchins, was learning the bitter lesson that the world would be recalcitrant to all his efforts to reshape it. Ashmore tends to see these as years of noble experiment, bold engagement, impressive idealism. He does not allow that to an outsider they might seem one vast stretch of misbegotten ideas, high self-delusion, ridiculous waste, and immitigable sadness.

Certainly, it did not begin that way. It began as if Robert Hutchins were assembling America's perfect résumé, one that would perhaps culminate in a final entry of Chief Justice of the Supreme Court, or possibly President of the United States.

Hutchins never made the vulgar and silly error of starting at the bottom or even at the middle. He was wellborn, as these things are reckoned by genealogy, with family members on both sides going back to settlement in New England in the late 1600s. Like many among his notable contemporaries— E. E. Cummings, Henry Luce, and Norman Thomas come to mind—Robert Hutchins was the son of a minister. Reverend William Hutchins was a Presbyterian with a congregation in Brooklyn when Robert was born. Reverend Hutchins later became a professor at Oberlin Theological Seminary in Ohio and, after that, president of Berea College in Kentucky. The Hutchinses were a family in which puritan notions of public service and academic achievement were much-honored traditions.

Hutchins was himself always an excellent student, but, one gathers, of the quick-study kind: quick to grasp, quick to execute, quick to move on. Apparently he was naturally gifted at things of the mind; he was good at acquiring foreign languages, and in later life wrote a clear, impressively concise, confident prose. Even fellow students who did not like him— an element of arrogance, or at any rate of seeming arrogance, put many people off Hutchins all his life—had to respect him because he was so obviously intelligent. Both at Oberlin College, where he began his undergraduate education, and at Yale, where in 1919 he picked it up again in his junior year after serving with the U.S. Ambulance Service assigned to the Italian army toward the close of World War I, Hutchins breezed by. Highly intelligent, supremely self-confident, "collar-ad handsome" (in Harry Ashmore's phrase), Hutchins, despite having rather less money than many of his classmates, nonetheless was a great success at Yale.

Certainly Yale posed no academic problem for Hutchins, unless it was boredom. But then boredom was one of the perennial Hutchins problems. The ambulance corps in Italy had presented vast stretches of boredom, undergraduate study at Yale meant boredom, much of the work of a university president would spell boredom, and boredom after his years at Chicago seemed to cling to him like a bad case of dandruff. Like dandruff, Hutchins's boredom was palpable during those meetings I sat in with him at Encyclopaedia Britannica in Chicago. I recall one in particular in which Mortimer J. Adler, speaking with the stammer caused by a racing mind, set out eleven arguments in favor of a policy for which he desired Hutchins's consent. Hutchins stared down into the bowl of his Dunhill pipe until Adler had finished, then removed the pipe from his teeth, announced, "I do not consider that an adequate statement of the alternatives," replaced the pipe, and mentally floated off to God knows where.

Boredom with undergraduate study caused Hutchins in his senior year to leave Yale College and enroll in the law school. Law was the one thing that did not bore him, or so for a while it appeared. It was at law school, he would later maintain, that his education, at the age of twenty-one, finally began. "It is sad but true," he subsequently wrote, "that the only place in an American university where the student is taught to read, write, and speak is the law school." Although he left Yale Law to teach at a private school for a year, when he returned—as a student holding down a full-time job as secretary of the Yale Corporation—he finished top of his class and second on the state bar examination. As the law school's most brilliant graduate, he was offered a job on the faculty, which, in 1925 at the age of twenty-six, he accepted.

Four years earlier Hutchins had married a tall, striking young woman of his own social and economic position—long on genealogical lines, short on cash—named Maude Phelps McVeigh. She was of artistic temperament, a sculptor and later a novelist good enough to be published by New Directions in her day but no longer, I can testify, very readable in ours. They were a dazzling couple, Bob and Maude, something out of F. Scott Fitzgerald; unfortunately, out of *Tender Is the Night*

more than any other novel, for Maude Hutchins was to undergo
nervous breakdowns and to bring her husband much domestic
grief and not a little public embarrassment, at one point obliging him to vacate the capacious president's house at the University of Chicago and hide out in various downtown hotels
while running the university's affairs from an office in the Loop.
Like T. S. Eliot, who also encountered long periods of misery
with his first wife, Hutchins, after a difficult divorce, perhaps
seeking stability, married his secretary. But then misery in marriage is not something that tends to be factored in when a
man's classmates vote him, as his at Yale voted Hutchins, "most
likely to succeed."

Hutchins might more accurately have been voted "most
quickly to succeed." At the Yale Law School he took only two
years to rise from instructor to associate professor. He taught
evidence, and soon became a strong critic of established views
of the subject. He was one of those professors, Felix Frank-
furter of Harvard most prominent among them, who pro-
tested the handling of evidence at the trial of Sacco and Vanzetti.
When the then dean of the school left to take up a judgeship
on the U.S. Court of Appeals, and the faculty could not decide
on either of the two leading candidates for his replacement,
Hutchins emerged as a compromise candidate. More pertinently, he was supported for the job by the president of Yale,
James Rowland Angell, who not only admired his earlier work
as secretary of the Yale Corporation but, as a former academic
psychologist, agreed with Hutchins on the need to bring the
findings of contemporary social science into the study of law.

Hutchins was appointed full professor and for two short
terms was called acting dean, after which the "acting" was
dropped from the title. In the event, he turned out to be an
excellent dean. He broke the logjam of retrograde tradition
which had kept the law school from being first-rate. He altered
the curriculum so that a principled understanding of the law
along with a mechanical one was taught. He opened enroll-

ment policy, so that family pedigree was no longer the primary consideration for acceptance. He enlarged the faculty, making a number of interesting appointments, among them Jews. In a very short while he had begun to transform a dull institution into an impressively lively one, and in doing so he found himself, as Harry Ashmore writes, "accorded a place in the very front rank of American educators."

As at the Yale Law School, so at the University of Chicago; Hutchins at the outset was not in the running when Max Mason retired from the presidency of the university to become president of the Rockefeller Foundation. The university's search committee came up with a list of no fewer than fifty-six names, and that of Robert Hutchins was not on it. But once again a split among factions made it possible for him eventually to be offered the job. One faction on the faculty was worried lest a new president turn Chicago, which was from its beginnings a great research university with an emphasis on graduate study, into something more collegiate, on the model of Princeton or Yale. Others wanted undergraduate study to be given more attention. Still others felt that Chicago was beginning to lose its experimental air and so wanted someone who could restore the school's intellectual excitement. Given so many cross-purposes, interlaced with such elevated aspirations, many candidates were soon weeded out.

At this point Robert Hutchins, younger than many assistant professors on the Chicago faculty, began to be seriously considered. In some quarters his youthfulness worked against him. President Angell of Yale, the same man who had supported Hutchins for the law-school deanship, wrote to say that he was still five or ten years shy of the maturity required for the presidency of a major university, arguing that he had no acquaintance with general educational problems and tended to be intolerant of people who disagreed with him. On the other side, Hutchins's youth was his great selling point. A powerful

trustee named Edwin Embree, president of the Julius Rosen-
wald Fund, expressed concern lest the university settle into solid
respectable mediocrity, and registered the opinion that Hutchins possessed precisely the "youth, imagination, and courage"
Chicago needed to lead it back to its great days under William
Rainey Harper. After all, Harper had himself been only thirty-
five when, with large injections of Rockefeller money, he became
the first president of the University of Chicago in 1891. In a
final series of interviews with trustees and senior faculty,
Hutchins, with his charm, forthrightness, and suave confidence, must have blown away any further possible objections
to his candidacy. In April 1929 he was offered the job. The
career of "the boy wonder" of American higher education had
begun in earnest.

A little jump in standard of living went along with the new
job. The Hutchinses now had five live-in servants, among them
a butler, a cook, maids, and a nurse for their young daughter,
not to mention a gardener and a chauffeur. The presidential
mansion was refurbished for them, with a sculpture studio
especially built for Maude. Handsome allowances for travel and
entertainment made it unnecessary for Hutchins to go very
deep into his annual salary of $25,000. The Hutchinses sum-
mered with the John D. Rockefeller, Jrs., in Seal Harbor; during the regular university year they were courted by such trustees
as Harold Swift, the heir to the meat-packing fortune, who
loved the university, and by the rich of Chicago who had cultural pretensions. In recounting these details, Harry Ashmore
paraphrases Robert Hutchins's quip about resembling the man
who had no desire to be a millionaire, merely to live like one.
Like many a good joke, this one was at bottom serious. Hutchins seems never to have cared greatly about money; but prosperity, as they will tell you at your local racetrack, takes little
getting used to, and henceforth Hutchins never lived other
than as well as possible.

In its standard version, the myth of Robert Hutchins at Chicago has it that a young and idealistic president in fairly short order turned a respectable but rather staid university into a toweringly great institution. He was able to achieve this in large part through the personal magnetism of the visionary, for Hutchins was nothing if not a man with a steady vision of the course higher education ought to take in the modern world. Hutchins was also the last of the strong university presidents, in the line and tradition of Charles W. Eliot of Harvard, Daniel Coit Gilman of Johns Hopkins, Nicholas Murray Butler of Columbia, an educational innovator, reformer, leader. He made enemies, to be sure, but he also changed the character of higher education, not only at his own institution but nationally, with results that continue to reverberate into our own time. Such, as I say, is the standard version of the myth.

In fact, when Hutchins arrived at Chicago in the autumn of 1929, the school, though it lacked the social cachet of Harvard, Yale, or Princeton, was probably, department by department, the most intellectually impressive university in the United States. It had been first-class right from the outset, an achievement owing to two factors. The first was William Rainey Harper, a shrewd judge of scholarly talent with a clear sense of what he wanted—namely, a research institution centered on graduate study and modeled on the German university. The second was the money of John D. Rockefeller, Sr., who backed Harper all the way and provided a model of selfless munificence. The combination of Harper's energy and imagination and Rockefeller's money built a great university faster than it had ever been done before or is likely ever to be done again.

Harper was said to have been a brilliant teacher, and in his original plan for the university he did not scant undergraduate instruction. After his death in 1907, however, the teaching of undergraduates received less and less attention. When Hutchins arrived, he apparently decided it was here that he could

best make his own impress. But there was this decisive difference between Harper and Hutchins: the former was a scholar
who knew that the soul of a great university is in scholarship,
while the latter was at best someone for whom the world of
scholarship was, if not alien, then certainly foreign territory.

There is a story Harry Ashmore does not mention about the
young Bob Hutchins. While a junior professor at Yale, he was
in contention for a Rockefeller Foundation fellowship that
would allow him to undertake two years of independent study
wherever and with whomever he wished. When Hutchins
learned he was to be made dean of the Yale Law School, he
removed his name as a potential candidate for this fellowship.
Years later, Hutchins told the historian Abraham Flexner that
if he had accepted the fellowship he would never have been
made president of the University of Chicago. "Maybe not,"
Flexner is said to have replied, "but you would have been prepared to be."

"The Young Rush In" is the title Mortimer J. Adler gives to
the chapter in his autobiography in which he recounts Robert
Hutchins's and his own first year at Chicago. Adler was three
years younger than Hutchins; they first met when Hutchins
was at Yale, and shortly after accepting the presidency of Chicago Hutchins was able to arrange a three-year contract for
Adler as associate professor of philosophy. Straightaway the
two men became identified as speaking with one voice. We are
talking here about a very odd couple indeed. No Don Quixote
ever had a less practical Sancho Panza at his side than Robert
Hutchins had in Mortimer Adler. By his own admission, Adler
was even less experienced in academic politics than Hutchins
and (in Adler's words) "equally, if not more, impetuous and
impatient."

The relationship of Hutchins and Adler was a peculiar and
fateful one, and through various joint projects—among them,
Encyclopaedia Britannica and The Great Books of the Western
World—would last the rest of Hutchins's life. Adler was not a

mentor but rather more like an intellectual coach or trainer. He was better educated than Hutchins, and an even quicker study. Socially and in every other way, however, Hutchins was the dominant and superior figure. On the several occasions when I saw the two men together—they were then both in their sixties—the deference all went one way. Adler treated Hutchins with reverence, Hutchins, it seemed to me, treated Adler with an ever so slightly amused condescension. (Hutchins's only true confidant was Thornton Wilder, the novelist and playwright, his classmate at Oberlin and later at Yale, whose background—Protestant, ministerial, intellectual, and puritanical—was similar to his own.) But Hutchins and Adler's earlier years together must have been more in the nature of an intellectual, if not a spiritual, partnership.

In their first year at Chicago, Hutchins and Adler were like two Quiz Kids run amok. Earlier, Hutchins had confessed to Adler that, before becoming president of a major university, he had never given much thought to the subject of education. Adler allowed that he hadn't, either. Yet each young man, in his own self-assured way, felt that no subject could elude his own extraordinary ratiocinative powers. Together they nicely illustrated the limitations of having a powerful IQ with nothing in the way of subtlety, experience, or humility to go along with it.

Right off Adler made plain his contempt for the pragmatic, Deweyan tendency of the university's philosophy department, and for the intellectual quality of the senior men who staffed it, and word of this quickly got back to them. Adler next wrote a series of memoranda on what he took to be the fallacious assumptions of the social sciences—then as now, *la spécialité de la maison* at the University of Chicago—and formulated his findings in an address before the local Social Science Research Council. The first sentence Adleresquely ran: "Current research programs in the social sciences are misdirected and methodologically ill-advised because of erroneous conceptions of the nature of science which comprise the 'raw empiricism' characteristic of contemporary social science." At lunch at the faculty club with a number of members of the physics department, Adler remarked that electrons, if Niels Bohr was correct, acted just as angels did, if Thomas Aquinas was correct. ("Should auld Aquinas be forgot" was a favorite Hutchins pun.) This, as you might imagine, put him in solid with the scientists at the university. And the winter quarter wasn't even over.

Before it was, three members of the philosophy department had threatened to resign over an attempt by Hutchins to get three youngish men of Adler's choosing evaluated along with the candidates being offered jobs by the department itself. Hutchins eventually had to back down, and he found himself saddled with legislation that henceforth restricted his hand in making faculty appointments. He also had to stand by while his friend Adler was bounced out of the philosophy department, with nothing for it but for Hutchins to make him an associate professor in the law school.

Hutchins's own cavalier style did not help smooth the way. Although he was quite good at raising funds, he used to keep a sign in his desk, brought out to be displayed among friends, that read, "We Launder Dirty Money." A sign atop his desk read, "Don't tell the president what he already knows." Lengthy memoranda from faculty or administrators would frequently meet with replies of a single sentence or even a single word. (Harry Ashmore quotes a colleague, Giuseppe Borgese, amusingly complaining that Hutchins's terse style refused to recognize the "voluptuous role of the paragraph.") Certain jobs, and one might think university presidencies among them, call for the abandonment of irony, but Hutchins refused to abandon his, and his quips and cutting remarks tended to get around. Laird Bell, one of the lawyers representing the university in the famous Walgreen case in the middle 1930s, when the university was charged with subversive teaching, is supposed to have said to Hutchins on their way into a hearing, "I'll give the university a hundred dollars for every wisecrack you don't make."

Such behavior set the stage for one of the great, prolonged pseudo-events in the intellectual history of the University of Chicago: what has since come to be known as the Chicago Fight. This broke out in earnest in 1934 when Hutchins delivered an address, entitled "The New Atlantis," arguing that contemporary higher education, however scientific its pretensions, was at its core anti-intellectual. Driven by the need to acquire ever new facts, such education was entirely devoid of general propositions which might subsume and lend order to those facts. Worse yet, Hutchins reported:

> There are no principles. The world is a flux of events. We cannot hope to understand it. All we can do is to watch it. This is the conclusion of the leading anti-intellectuals of our time, William James and John Dewey.

The Chicago Fight has been variously described as a battle between facts and ideas, between Deweyan empiricism and Aristotelian-Thomist metaphysics, between sheer belligerence and utter benightedness. For nearly half a decade it kept the university in a state of high agitation. After Hutchins's speech, Adler jumped in with a number of lectures of his own; and a Mortimer J. Adler lecture could get things to the stage of rancor faster than two divorce lawyers. Debates were held, editorials written, friendships broken. Lined up against Hutchins and Adler and their followers were a number of key figures in social science, among them Louis Wirth, Harry Gideonse, and the brilliant economist Frank Knight. Many wild things were said on both sides, and Hutchins was never to get quite free of the taint of Thomism while he remained at Chicago. But what made the whole thing a pseudo-event, as Edward Shils, who was on the scene, has pointed out, was that it had scarcely any effect on the true life of the university. While Hutchins and

Adler were arguing away against the emptiness of science and social science that proceeded without metaphysical underpinnings, precisely those two spheres of intellectual activity went on adding to the already great prestige of the University of Chicago, and continue to do so even to this day.

Insofar as Hutchins's antagonism toward academic specialization, his insistence on the formulation of the principles underlying knowledge, and his distaste for the "pastlessness" of empirical science and social science helped to shape actual education at Chicago, they did so in his reform of the undergraduate College. Hutchins always felt that these reforms did not go far enough, and in fact his ideas, such as they were, were later put into purer form at St. John's College in Annapolis. But what Hutchins achieved at Chicago was impressively radical for its day.

Many aspects of Hutchins's reforms were of administrative interest only; and some were almost immediately abandoned by his successor, Lawrence Kimpton. Notable among them was the decision to allow bright high-school students to enter the College at the end of their sophomore year, thus beginning their higher education at roughly fifteen. This particular innovation opened the way for A. J. Liebling, in *The Second City,* to remark that "the University of Chicago's undergraduate college acts as the greatest magnet for neurotic juveniles since the Children's Crusade, with Robert Maynard Hutchins . . . playing the role of Stephen the Shepherd Boy in the revival."

At the heart of undergraduate reform at Chicago was what we should today call a core curriculum. The College offered a number of survey courses with such boring titles as Humanities I, II, & III, Social Sciences I, II, & III, Natural Sciences I, II, & III, and so forth, with very few variations. No textbooks were used in any of these courses, only original material: Thucydides and Condorcet, and Freud, not accounts of Thucydides, Condorcet, and Freud written by professors at Southern Methodist University.

As for the quality of the education, it varied, as elsewhere, from teacher to teacher. I myself, when I entered the College five years after Robert Hutchins had left, found the reading and the general atmosphere much more impressive than anything that went on in the classrooms. As for the atmosphere, "Every queer and unusual student who disliked athletics and the normal outlets of young people was attracted to Hutchins's College," Lawrence Kimpton would later say. That is a bit strong, but, true enough, one's fellow students were a touch exotic. Certainly there was no type that the university produced as there was once a Princeton man or a Bennington girl. What they had in common was a certain breadth of intellectual ambition behind which lay, I believe, the figure of Robert Hutchins. His persistent putting-down of vocationalism in education and, by implication, his disdain for professionalism—some of which is set out in his book, *The Higher Learning in America*—found its most receptive audience among the undergraduates at his own university.

For all that Hutchins was wrong or even irrelevant about so much that was important in education, there was nonetheless a grandeur about him, and it was not a false grandeur, or something that could be chalked up, as we tend to do nowadays, to style or "image." His was bound by inner integrity. Hutchins was, for one thing, intellectually courageous, with nothing of the public-relations man about him; he almost always said what he thought and was prepared to take the fire for having done so. He was politically courageous, too, as witness his unflappable conduct during the Walgreen affair; he was sound on academic freedom, and protected those of his faculty whose political opinions rendered them vulnerable to outside pressure from congressional committees or anyone else. Nothing about Robert Hutchins was small, nothing mean or meaching. He was clearly cut out for great things.

Why, one wonders, did he not achieve them? If Robert

Hutchins's spirit lingered over the University of Chicago long after he left it, his flesh longed to depart much earlier than it did. Hutchins himself used to say that ten years was just about the outer limit for someone to hold on to a university presidency, which would have made his own departure date 1940. But even before that date arrived, Hutchins, after his various intramural battles with Chicago faculty, was considering other jobs. Mortimer Adler had advised him to pack it in and take on the presidency of St. John's in Annapolis. But much larger, lusher fish were sighted. According to Harry Ashmore, Hutchins was offered the presidency of the New York Stock Exchange but turned it down. Harold Ickes, FDR's secretary of the interior, approached him not long afterward about the chairmanship of the National Recovery Administration, though this particular deal fell through. Hutchins later rejected the chairmanships of the Securities and Exchange Commission and the Federal Communications Commission, even though Roosevelt himself suggested that taking such jobs might place him among the candidates for the vice-presidential nomination on the 1940 Democratic ticket.

The job Robert Hutchins apparently truly wanted was a seat on the Supreme Court. But when the first of two such seats became available, it went to Hugo Black; the second went to Hutchins's longtime friend William O. Douglas. Roosevelt, evidently, never felt fully confident that Hutchins was, in the phrase of a political insider whom Ashmore quotes, "on 'our side.'" So the only job Hutchins really wanted and actually lobbied for, the one job he felt he could have rested content in, was simply not available to him.

In the time left him at Chicago, Hutchins still had lots of fireworks to shoot off, flares to send up, grenades to lob. To go from smaller to larger explosions, Hutchins arranged to drop football, and took Chicago out of the Big Ten: "Football has the same relation to education," he famously said, "that bullfighting has to agriculture." As the United States headed toward World War II, Hutchins found himself increasingly sympathetic to the isolationist position, though as a liberal he could never be an America Firster. Irony of ironies, it was to be the University of Chicago, led by this self-declared isolationist, that supplied the resources and facilities to Enrico Fermi, Leo Szilard, Harold Urey, and the other high-powered scientists who worked on what was then known as the Metallurgy Project but what all now know would eventually lead to the development of the atomic bomb. By the time the war was over, Harry Ashmore reports, Chicago "had handled a greater volume of military projects than any other single institution." What, one wonders, if Hutchins had been frankly in favor of the war?

With the end of the war, university life must have seemed even duller to Hutchins. He had the idea of forming the Committee on Social Thought, which, for better *and* worse, may be said to have been the origin of so-called interdisciplinary studies in higher education; it was also an excellent resort for extraordinary people who did not seem to fit comfortably in conventional academic niches. When called in on any important appointment—especially from among the German refugee scholars sent into exile by Hitler—his instincts tended to be sure and correct. He remained a powerful raiser of funds; he was always good with the rich, though not above making witticisms about them behind their backs. "The rich," he used to say, "have one thing in common: a short attention span. When you have that kind of money you don't have to listen."

As Hutchins came near his twentieth anniversary as president of Chicago, his own work must have bored him blue. He had turned, as he told Mortimer Adler, from an educational administrator to an educational philosopher. His speeches, usually short, never sweet, generally laced with irony, began to be increasingly laden with those pronunciamentos of the snore-inducing kind in which, in our own day, university presidents have come to specialize: education for democracy, education for leisure, education for freedom. There is something particularly hopeless about such subjects, and Hutchins was too clever a man not to recognize it. A man so intellectually ruthless with everyone else could not have been easy on himself.

Hutchins was a notably efficient worker. He rose early, dealt tersely with his correspondence, speed-read his way through memoranda, proposals, and other university business documents, kept to a strict schedule with his daily round of meetings and interviews. He was said to have been able to compose and memorize a speech for perfect delivery in three or four hours. Harry Ashmore recounts a great many such details, but it is a failing of his biography that he tells us very little of Robert Hutchins's intellectual life. What books did he not speed but merely read? In what direction did his taste run in things of the mind? Did he like novels? (He wrote some faintly amusing light verse.) Did he read history? Did he read at all? When at one point the Committee on Social Thought, at the inspiration of the Chicago editor and publisher Henry Regnery, brought out a magazine entitled *Measure,* Hutchins served as chairman of its editorial board. Regnery recalls a meeting of the board at which manuscripts were passed out to board members, and someone handed Hutchins an essay on the law. "Why are you giving this to me?" Regnery remembers Hutchins saying. "I no longer know anything about the law. I don't know anything about anything."

When in 1950 Hutchins was offered the key associate directorship of the Ford Foundation, responsible for activities having to do with education and world peace, he took it without much hesitation, resigning officially from Chicago at the close of the 1951 spring term. In those days as in ours, apart from a career in the U.S. Senate or as a state governor, where else could a former president of a major university go but into a job at one of the richer foundations? The comforts are roughly the same, the aggravation is less, and the air of unreality likely to be even greater. Irving Kristol once told a young man about to take a foundation job that he would never eat another bad lunch and that no one would ever again tell him the truth. Hutchins made much the same point shortly after joining the Ford Foundation. "It's a nice job," he said. "You meet such interested people."

For the last twenty-six years of his life, Robert Hutchins lived chiefly in that world. Harry Ashmore devotes more than half his book to these years—to the skirmishes, power struggles, and shifting alignments within the institutions in which Hutchins worked—but in anything resembling solid achievement it all came to damnably little.

In time, Hutchins's job with the Ford Foundation turned into the presidency of the Ford-underwritten Fund for the Republic ("a wholly disowned subsidiary of the Ford Foundation," as he once described it); and then the Fund for the Republic gave way to the Center for the Study of Democratic Institutions in Santa Barbara, California. Dwight Macdonald, in *The Ford Foundation: The Men and the Millions,* passes along the remark of an unnamed observer that Hutchins, with Ford money, was now trying to buy what, as president of the University of Chicago, he couldn't himself sell—namely, his old ideas about education.

It turned out that he couldn't buy them, either. Nor did he have much better luck with some of the other ideas he had acquired: the idea of world government, with its apparent need for endless drafts of a world constitution; the idea of the so-called dialogue, stressing the importance of intellectual collaboration; and, as an offshoot of the latter, the great splashy international conferences, such as the Pacem in Terris affairs and others that he organized in Florence, at Wingspread, in Rome; and more of the same, sad, thin stuff—all of it talk talk talk, and so little of it good talk.

Liberal-left though the general drift of Hutchins's thought tended to be, he was for the most part disdainful of the political movements of the middle and late sixties. The emotionalism of the counterculture and its crude Marxism, Harry Ashmore reports, put him off; the general coarseness of it all could not have helped. Not that he couldn't match the New Left at the level of the inflammatory, uninformed generalization, as in the following item: "All we can say of American education is that it's a colossal housing project designed to keep people out of worse places until they can go to work." But then Robert Hutchins's radicalism, as Ashmore wisely notes, was not, like that of the sixties young, rooted in fantasies of alienation; he had not given up on America and its institutions.

Nobody, however, was really listening to Hutchins during these years, except the stray millionaire he was able to get to pick up the tab for one of his conferences or to meet the expenses for the chat and buffet and salaries at the Center in Santa Barbara. He was never able to attract truly serious people permanently to the Center; despite everything the place offered in the way of luxury and the little it asked in the way of work, it must have resembled nothing so much as an endless talk show to which no one was tuned in. Hutchins had to settle for second- and third-rate academics and such occasional intellectual celebrity freaks as Alex Comfort (author of *The Joy of Sex*) and Bishop James Pike (who claimed to have been in touch with his dead son). He was loyal to all these people. One of the main patterns of his life was his persistent and enduring loyalty—to, as it seems to me, the wrong people. He died in 1977 worrying about what would become of the Center that in the end he knew was a flop. "Well," he wrote to his friend Thornton Wilder a few years before his death, "it was a great idea." But it was not even a good idea, not for a minute.

In the lives of the great, every turn, each unexpected twist, seems in retrospect the exactly right one. Accidents, setbacks, illnesses, unhappiness, family tragedy—all seem to conduce to the production of the masterworks, the grand discoveries, the saving of the nation. In the lives of the almost great who fail, the reverse seems to obtain. Every break, piece of good fortune, natural advantage conduces to the series of sad botches that end in ultimate failure. It was to Thornton Wilder that Hutchins wrote: "I was right to leave [the University of Chicago]; but I went to the wrong place [the Ford Foundation]." But any other place, one feels on reviewing his life, would have been the wrong place, every turn probably a mistake.

Had Hutchins been less quick, less handsome, less lucky in his early years, might he not, given his natural superiority, have done something genuinely, breathtakingly extraordinary? Perhaps; perhaps not. Poor Hutchins. His life was of a kind to set one to composing apothegms about the sad fate of those whom the gods, with their well-known taste for irony, too heavily favor when young.

My Debt to
Isaac Bashevis Singer

I MET the late Isaac Bashevis Singer only once, briefly but unforgettably, in 1963. It was in Manhattan, at the apartment of one of his early translators. He was then fifty-nine, no kid, but only just coming into his own in a serious way as a writer now frequently published in English. I had read everything of his I could find. I admired him without qualification—thought him the possessor of a powerful artistic talent, a man touched by magic and greatly blessed and to be revered. Captivating on the page, he was not disappointing in person.

Twelve or fourteen people were in the apartment that evening—literary intellectuals, academics, editors. Singer did most of the talking, not in any unpleasant or pushing way but instead by general agreement. He was obviously more distinguished than anyone else in the room, had lived a more interesting life, had more to report. He told, as no doubt he would subsequently retell hundreds of times, about the mildly comic situation of being, then in his late fifties, still the youngest regular contributor to the Yiddish-language *Jewish Daily Forward;* he talked a bit about Jewish intellectual and literary life in Warsaw; I recall his saying that he had translated Thomas Mann's *The Magic Mountain* into Yiddish. He reported that he did not read the *New York Times* but instead preferred the *Daily News,* which, with its extensive coverage of murders, kidnappings, rapes, divorces, and scandals, was so much richer fare for a novelist. All this was set out in a calm, slightly creaking voice, heavily accented, without any show of unseemly pleasure at being the center of attention.

One of the things Singer happened to mention that evening was the loss of his parakeet. A rather birdlike man himself—the once little boy with blue eyes and red earlocks described in his memoirs was now bald, without eyebrows, slightly beaky, and somewhat avian in his physical delicacy—he was quite mad for birds. With his penchant for the mystical and the pantheistic, he thought birds were possessed of some obvious if undefined spiritual qualities. I forget the name of his lost parakeet; it was endearing rather than grand or comical; it might have been something like Farfele.

In any case, the morning after that evening my wife happened to find a parakeet in a park near our apartment. I called Singer, who grew quite excited. "My darling Farfele has two dots over its beak. Does dis boid?" The telephone balanced between my head and shoulder, my wife nearby holding the parakeet gently in her hand, I checked it for dots over the beak. None. "Farfele has a bright yellow spot at the tip of his right wing. Does maybe your boid have such a spot?" No such spot. Great writers put you in their world, and here I was, in my own kitchen, suddenly become a character in an Isaac Bashevis Singer story. We went through another few checkpoints, when we both concluded that the parakeet my wife had found was not the dear and esteemed Farfele, he should only live and be well. I remember being disappointed that this was not Singer's bird, for it would have been a fine way for me to repay him, however partially, for all that I felt I owed him.

One of the things I owed him was—and remains—the important debt of helping to put me in touch with my own almost entirely lost historical past. My guess is that many of his readers were in the same condition as I, and that this was at least part of the profit we all derived from him and part, too, of the explanation for his popularity among American Jewish readers. What this condition might be called is Jewish historical blackout. I know I was not alone in suffering it. Brought up in a non-observing but nonetheless proudly Jewish home in Chicago, I was sent to Hebrew school, where I was instructed in the pronunciation of Hebrew letters and vowels and in the meaning of a few words, and from which I was freed at my bar mitzvah. Later I took pride in the formation of the state of Israel. Athletes, actors, writers who happened to be Jewish always had special pull with me. I enjoyed an uncomplicated, happy Jewish chauvinism.

Yet I knew very little about Judaism and even less about my own background as a Jew. And by my own background I mean my own family's relatively recent history in Eastern Europe. My father's father was very serious about his Judaism, and about his Jewishness, too, having been an early Zionist and, I am told, one of the important figures in Hebrew education in Montreal. He spoke very little English, and on the four or five occasions we were together—the last when I was eighteen—we were hardly able to communicate at all, which is one of the great regrets of my life. I should have liked to have learned not only more about him but about our family history in Bialystok, whence he came to settle first briefly in St. Paul, Minnesota, and then finally in Montreal.

Because I was never really able to cross the barrier of our different languages to speak with my grandfather, I never learned about his (and hence my own) forebears, and so my own personal family history stops, dead and very incomplete, with him. (My other grandparents had died either before I was born or in my infancy.) My mother and my father, both the children of immigrants, were unable to tell me anything about their parents' parents. In bustling, crowded lives, hungry for success and assimilation, neither apparently ever bothered to ask. I have found that a vast preponderance of my Jewish friends and acquaintances, at least those of East European ancestry, are in the same condition of ignorance. To be so oddly pastless has always seemed extraordinary to me, especially for Jews, curious, talkative, endlessly self-analyzing people that they tend to be.

Through fiction, Isaac Bashevis Singer—and I. J. (Israel Joshua) Singer, his older brother, who was also a novelist— filled in some of the gaps in my ignorance in a way that reading history and scholarship was never quite able to do. The brothers Singer made the world of East European Jewry come alive for me like no one else; their portrayals of life among Jews in backwater shtetls and in cities like Warsaw, Lublin, and Lodz had a vividness that surpassed—not that there needs to be a competition about this—anyone else I had read. Isaac Bashevis Singer wrote about Warsaw the way Theodore Dreiser wrote about Chicago. When you read him you felt you had been there, walked the city's streets, "come into possession of it," as Henry James might have said. And what one came into possession of was a world much richer than one had hitherto imagined.

If part of Isaac Bashevis Singer's success derived from his putting many of his readers in touch with a past that had hitherto been closed off to them, perhaps a larger part was owing to his sheer powers of storytelling. In interviews, lectures, public statements, Singer insisted over and over that writers must, on some level, give their readers pleasure. For him this pleasure was to be had through narrative. In his Nobel Lecture in Stockholm, after reading a paragraph in Yiddish about how the honor bestowed upon him was also a recognition of the Yiddish language in which he wrote, Singer said:

> The storyteller and poet of our time, as in any other time, must be an entertainer of the spirit in the full sense of the word, not just a preacher of social or political ideals. There is no paradise for bored readers and no excuse for tedious literature that does

not intrigue the reader, uplift his spirit, give him the joy and escape that true art always grants.

Singer not only wrote entertainingly but did so for a wider audience than most serious writers any longer even hope for. The distinction between high or sophisticated and popular art was wiped out in his work. He won the acclaim of critics and the devotion of true though not necessarily university-educated readers. Many years ago a cousin of mine, a very intelligent woman then in her early forties, who had never gone to college and who had no particular literary interests, mentioned that she and her husband were off for a week-long holiday in Bermuda and asked if I had anything in the apartment that she might take to read on the beach. Much that was in my personal library—poetry, criticism, history, philosophy—seemed inappropriate. What I eventually offered her was Isaac Bashevis Singer's novel *The Slave*. She loved it. "A marvelous book," she reported to me upon her return. "By the way, this Singer, in what century did he live?"

Embedded in that question, I thought, was a fine compliment—a compliment with a touch of unconscious critical wisdom behind it. For not the least attraction of Singer's fiction is its timelessness. He could write about the Upper West Side of Manhattan in its current state of sad decay and ring just the right note of contemporaneity; he could also drop back a lengthy fifty or seventy years, as in *The Family Moskat*, or a full century, as in *The Manor*, or three full centuries, as in *Satan in Goray*. He could write outside time, as in his famous story "Gimpel the Fool," which has the feel of a tale passed down from generation to generation in the manner of pure folk art. No modern writer in any literature that I know is so adept at setting his stories anywhere he wishes in time. This ability sets much of Singer's writing finally beyond time, which is of course where everyone who thinks himself an artist wishes to be.

The timeless quality in Singer's work comes from his having grown up in something very near a time warp. Singer was born in 1904, in the village of Leoncin, in the province of Warsaw, the second of four surviving children of parents with long lines of rabbis on both sides: his father claimed an ancestor who was a disciple of the eighteenth-century founder of Hasidism, the Baal Shem Tov. Singer's father was himself a man of impressive piety (as readers of *In My Father's Court* know), superior in his learning, and a bit aloof from the world, a Jew who wore the clothes and practiced the customs of the Hasid and who as a boy and young man had wished to live with the kind of purity that would allow him to become saintly and enable him to perform miracles. In *Love and Exile,* one of his autobiographical works, Singer describes his father as "good-natured, full of faith in almost all people. His only desire was to have time and strength to serve God and study His Torah."

Singer's mother was a very different story. The daughter of the rabbi of Bilgoray, she is said (in Paul Kresh's *Isaac Bashevis Singer: The Magician of West 86th Street*) to have taught herself to read Hebrew and to have known the Bible "almost by heart." She was sharp, doubting, penetrating: worldly where her husband tended to be otherworldly, pessimistic where he tended to be optimistic, arguing with God where he tried only to understand Him. Of his mother Singer wrote that

> she suffered not only her own afflictions but also those of mankind. I could see in her eyes great compassion when she read in the Yiddish newspaper about those who were run over, robbed, raped, beaten. Every news item made her wince in resentment against the Creator who could see all this misery and remain silent.

"In our house," Singer noted, "the coming of the Messiah was taken most literally." Not, however, by everybody. Not by his sister Hinde Esther, thirteen years older than Singer, and especially not by his brother Israel Joshua, his elder by eleven years. Like many others of his generation, Israel Joshua had been won from their father's ways by the Haskalah, or Jewish Enlightenment. Extreme piety and contempt for that piety existed side by side not only among the Jews of Warsaw but in the Singer home itself. So did superstition and rationality. After a brief stint as a rabbi in Leoncin, for example, Singer's father was hired to run a yeshiva in the town of Radzymin, where he was also to serve as an assistant to the rabbi, whose specialty was making barren women fertile through the use of magical charms.

Around this time, I. J. Singer had already begun to read forbidden books—and, in the Singer household, anything that was not the Bible or a commentary on the Bible was forbidden. It was I. J. Singer, swept up by the Haskalah, who reacted most strongly to what he took to be the medieval world of his father and the Hasidim. In his memoir of his boyhood in the shtetls of Poland, *Of a World That Is No More,* a memoir that is a useful counter to any temptation to sentimentalize the life of ultra-Orthodox Jews in that setting, I. J. Singer emphasizes the superstition, coarseness, and sheer difficulty of shtetl life.

Isaac Bashevis Singer never needed to be the rebel that his brother was, though of course he, too, would eventually leave the ways in which he was raised. Outwardly at least he was milder than his brother, less angry, more open to experience. And experience, living where and when he did, came at him with a great roaring whoosh. Within the Singer household and without, tumult was a staple of daily life. The house in Krochmalna Street in Warsaw where the Singers lived was also where Rabbi Singer conducted his *beth din,* which, as Singer has described it, "was a kind of blend of court of law, synagogue, house of study, and, if you will, psychoanalyst's office where people of troubled spirits could come to unburden themselves." As for Krochmalna Street, it "was full of people, and they all seemed to be screaming." The Jewish section of Warsaw, he remarks in *The Family Moskat,* "was like a bit of Baghdad transplanted into the Western world."

When Singer was thirteen years old, Warsaw was more than 40 percent Jewish. Krochmalna Street teemed with the color and multifariousness of Jewish life, which included rabbis and thieves, artisans and con men, peddlers and prostitutes, hawkers of fruit, vegetables, and radical ideas, fanatics religious and secular. What a lovely enticing prospect for a future novelist to view from the balcony of his parents' apartment! Yet Singer, when young, could only consider it from a distance. As the apparently autobiographical narrator of his novel *Shosha* puts it, "From the time I can first remember, I heard him [his rabbi father] repeat the phrase, 'It is forbidden.' Everything I wanted to do was a transgression."

Less rich but no less rewarding to the future novelist were Singer's trips, with his mother and younger brother Moishe, to his mother's family in the then Austrian-occupied town of Bilgoray on the Polish-Austrian border. There, during World War I, they stayed for fully four years, and there Singer saw Jewish life as it had been lived for centuries. The day was clocked by ritual and prayer. Modernity was for the most part locked out; as Singer noted, "the common people were even more devout than the scholars." Although pockets of the Enlightenment existed, such as at the home of Todros, the hunchbacked watchmaker whom Singer later used as a character in *The Family Moskat,* "on Yom Kippur eve," as Singer wrote in *In My Father's Court,* "the whole town wept." Here Singer was able to witness aspects of Jewish life that had not changed for centuries. "In this world of old Jewishness," Singer wrote, "I found a treasure trove."

Life, it seems, conspires to supply great artists with the material they require. But what is impressive about Singer is how early he knew what kind of writer he wanted to be. He quickly determined that the literature of political and social concern, a vein that his already famous brother had been working, was not for him. He knew straightaway that the delimitations of modernism in literature—with its difficulties, its determination not to worry about any audience but that of fellow artists, its concentration on the problems of art quite as much as if not more than those presented by life—were not for him. "One Kafka in a century," he would later say, "is enough." If Singer was in any way aesthetically radical, it was in the sensuality of his stories and in the use he made in his fiction of the celestial and nether worlds of the occult, the world of spirits.

Although Singer attempted briefly to write his stories in Hebrew, nothing he did in that language pleased him. Neither, at first, did his writing in Yiddish. But it was not long before he hit his stride and his prose caught its correct and confident cadence. He published his first stories, in Warsaw journals, in his early twenties. After he emigrated to America in 1935, Singer stopped writing fiction for a period of five years or so, in despair about both the future of Yiddish and his own then-uprooted life. But once he resumed, he never looked back, and his flow of work—novels, stories, autobiographies, children's tales—ceased only with his death.

Paul Kresh, in his biography of Singer, quotes a Yiddish journalist, Samuel L. Shneiderman, who worked on the same Warsaw journal, *Literary Pages,* with the young Isaac Bashevis Singer and who recalled his early mastery:

> His style—ah that style. From the beginning it was the envy of other Yiddish writers. His mastery of transition, for example— how gracefully he glides from description to dialogue, from the ambience of a place to the action happening there. What a storyteller! The literary world of Warsaw saw it right away—the richness of the language, the imaginative blending of the absolutely real and the totally fantastic—all absolutely new in Yiddish writing.

There are no Mozarts in literature, no true child prodigies, but Singer was apparently as much a natural as a writer can hope to be. As an artist he seems to have come into the world fully formed, so good at his craft so young, so able to vary his style from realistic family chronicle to novels and stories nearly surreal in their dalliance with mysticism to fiction strongly folkloric in its feeling. One does not have the sense of development in Singer's work. He started strong and stayed strong, except for a tailing off toward the end, when his fiction began to lose its imaginative energy and turned very dark. It is much to the point that so knowledgeable a critic as Ruth R. Wisse considers *Satan in Goray,* Singer's first novel, also his greatest.

Singer's work, though not all of the same quality, is bound together by his central concerns, which are at their heart religious. Other modern writers may talk in their fiction about man's soul and his relation to God, but they cannot keep their minds on the subject the way that Singer did throughout an entire career. He could never stop thinking of it. It is what his books, however sexy, charming, or strange they may separately be, are always and finally about.

Yet what exactly do Singer's many novels and stories mean? "I find myself full of faith and full of doubt," he once said. A lifelong student of Spinoza, Kant, and Schopenhauer, a ceaseless reader in the literature of the occult, more than a browser in the wisdom literature of Judaism, Singer always possessed the literary appetite of the quester after ultimate meanings. Did he, it seems fair to ask, find any?

It is easy to ignore this question because Singer's stories and novels provide so many subsidiary rewards. He re-created— or, perhaps better, re-imagined—a world, that of East European Jewry, razed by the monstrousness of history; and the death of that world, as many have commented, seems to make Singer's re-creation of it all the more potent in its magic. Within it, he found an almost endless number of stories to tell, stories of piety and impiety, tradition and the flouting of tradition, stories of derring-do, comedy, sadness, horror, and love—always and endlessly love.

Over and over again Singer insisted that at the heart of all good novels is a love story. "All stories," he said, "are love stories." And all Singer's love stories dealt with sex, for he was a writer who gave ample credit to sex as a drive, a source of human pleasure and trouble, and (most useful for a teller of tales) complication. Some of Singer's more old-fashioned readers used to complain about the sex in his fiction, but most of this sex, it must be stressed, is described with fine economy. Singer is never pornographic but instead powerfully suggestive. In *Scum*, his last, also very sex-ridden, novel, how this works is nicely on display early in the book when Singer notes merely about his forty-seven-year-old hero, Max Barabander: "What he could do with women no one, except the women involved, would believe." La Rochefoucauld said that a filthy mind never sleeps, and here, surely, is a sentence for it to consider in the late night hours.

Over the years critics have argued a fair amount about which are Singer's greatest strengths and which his greatest weaknesses. Many are ready to jettison his two ample family-chronicle novels, *The Family Moskat* and *The Manor*. Neither of these books, it is true, is nearly so well-shaped or powerful as I. J. Singer's *The Brothers Ashkenazi*, a great novel at whose center is perhaps the most extraordinary villain in all of literature, the entire country, no less, of Poland, which, I. J. Singer concludes, deserves all that it has suffered because of its horrendous treatment of the Jews. True enough, Isaac Bashevis Singer did not have his brother's powers of construction, and *The Family Moskat* and *The Manor* are sometimes cumbersome, often creaky—both were written, as were all of Singer's novels with the exception of *Satan in Goray*, for serialization in the *Jewish Daily Forward*. But both nevertheless contain magnificent things: characters, cityscapes, the sense of a destiny spun out of control, the feeling of life becoming unmoored without the anchor of tradition.

Others think Singer at his best in the midlength novel—in such books as *The Slave, The Magician of Lublin,* or *Enemies: A Love Story*. Singer himself claimed to prefer the short story over all other forms, since in the short story "a writer can reach for perfection—more than in a novel." Though there seems to be no critical unanimity on which are Singer's best novels, there is general agreement on which are his best stories. A collection of the latter would include "Gimpel the Fool," "The Gentleman from Cracow," "Yentl the Yeshiva Boy," "Taibele and Her Demon," "The Little Shoemakers," "The Spinoza of Market Street," and perhaps "The Slaughterer" and "A Friend of Kafka." Few of these stories, it is worth noting, have directly to do with the spirits from the nether world that are sometimes a strong element in his fiction.

Many readers identify Singer with, and they think the less of him for, those novels and stories where this element, what Dan Jacobson once nicely termed "the brimstone area," prevails. By the brimstone area, Jacobson means those supernatural elements—dybbuks, demons, imps, on occasion the devil himself—that usually are evoked by Singer to symbolize the power of evil. An admirer of Singer though he is, Jacobson makes easily the best criticism of this element in Singer's fiction. He argues that

> readers who do not share his predispositions are entitled to find that the "symbolization" to which he refers is sometimes too easily brought about, too lovingly and lengthily dwelt upon, insufficiently used or explained in any subsequent action, and insufficiently distinguished from other symbols of the same kind in many other stories.

Did Singer truly believe in such spirits? He often claimed that he did. At the same time, knowing how the world regards such beliefs, he was not above making fun of them, as when he told his biographer that demons were unlikely to flourish in Israel: "They like overcast skies, old houses. I have looked for demons in the Jewish state, but I have found very few." Elsewhere he said that he would pay half a year's income actually to see a ghost. Yet Singer, a man who distrusted and did not often use metaphors, was quite ready to avail himself of these most extravagant of all metaphors, creatures whom few but the mad have ever seen. He must have been agnostic yet hopeful on the subject. More important, he felt them useful to his fiction. "In a way demons express the human subconscious," he told an interviewer. "But to me the demons also symbolize a life without any faith altogether."

What Singer did believe in, without any question, was God. But to believe in God is not to claim to understand Him. Critics for whom the question of God is not, so to say, a lively one attribute Singer's power to other factors, from modernist technique to the glory of his storytelling. Still others hold that behind and beyond all the talk of God there is something else in Singer's work that makes it appeal to the modern reader, suffused as that work is, as one critic has it, "with the prevailing contemporary sense of isolation, disintegration, alienation, and dread." But what makes both the technique and the storytelling possible, why Singer is able to seem at once modern and traditional, is his interest in the endless question of what God has in mind, both for us and for the universe.

The persistent attention to this question gives Singer his right to be considered a major artist. Dan Jacobson touches on this point, in a somewhat skeptical way, when considering the absence of "place" in Yiddish writers:

Theirs is the literature of a people without power (and all its accompanying evils and guilts), without the possession of land, without statehood or political organization, without the freedom to pursue a wide variety of occupations—the literature of a society that was in many immensely important respects maimed and deprived.

All this is quite true and to the point. Yet if your subject is the ways of God toward man, as it indubitably was Isaac Bashevis Singer's, then the Jews of Eastern Europe, for all the reasons Jacobson mentions, are unquestionably your people. After a history of almost unremitting disenfranchisement and persecution, punctuated by pogroms and ending cataclysmically with Nazism, the Jews, above all people, have earned the right to ask certain fundamental questions of God.

Many people in Singer's stories and novels do ask. Asking itself, however, comes near to constituting a transgression. Asa Heshel Bannet, the central character in *The Family Moskat,* is a freethinker who, it turns out, is not very free after all. This same Asa Heshel, toward the end of the novel, reflects bitterly of God: "He creates easily and destroys easily. He has his own laboratory." All Singer's characters have free will—"without free will what is the difference between the throne of glory and the depths of the nether world?" asks a rabbi in the same novel. (Singer himself, during the question-and-answer sessions of his many lectures and readings, used to reply to the question of whether he himself believed in free will by answering: "Of course I believe in free will. What choice have I?") Of Asa Heshel, his first wife observes: "He was one of those who must serve God or die. He had forsaken God, and because of this he was dead—a living body with a dead soul." The simple if devastating point of *The Family Moskat* is that, without God, all of the novel's characters are dead souls, walking corpses. The unforgettable last line of the novel, delivered by a subsidiary character, himself a freethinker, as he awaits the entry of the Nazis into Warsaw, is: "Death is the Messiah. That's the real truth."

Free will, in an Isaac Bashevis Singer novel, usually comes

down to little more than the freedom to choose God's way—or to perish. Modern thought will avail a man nothing. As Rabbi Dan Katzenellenbogen tells his grandson Asa Heshel apropos of modern thinking, "The sum and substance of it is that any sin is permitted. That is the root of the matter." Men—and less often women—in Singer's novels and stories are tossed about by their doubts, dreams, desires. Singer's characters suffer from Pascalian restlessness; they cannot sit, alone, quietly in a room for even an hour. "The main thing," says Max Barabander in *Scum*, "was not to remain passive." Singer himself once said: "We run away from boredom into wickedness, and there is almost nothing in between." Well, there is one thing in between—subjects for the novelist.

Singer made nearly limitless use of the material that issues from this spiritual restlessness. As he told an interviewer in the *Saturday Review* as long ago as 1968:

> To me, in my work, the religious question and the eternal question—why do we live, why do we exist?—are identical. I am not completely a religious writer, but neither am I secular. In my writing religion is always there—even when I write sexy.

To another interviewer he said:

> The supernatural is always in my writing and somehow I always wanted to say to the reader that even though life looks to us chaotic, it is not as chaotic as we think. There is a scheme and design behind it.

What was the scheme, which the design? Singer was never certain enough to say. In *The Penitent,* the narrator is told by the chief character whose story is at the center of the novel: "If you took one step farther, you'd become a full-fledged Jew." To which he adds: "You also know all the good traits of the real Jew." To this the narrator, clearly speaking for Singer, answers: "That's not enough either. For this you must have faith that everything stated in the holy books was given to Moses on Mount Sinai. Unfortunately, I don't have this faith." One can only conjecture in so profound a realm, but my own guess is that Singer wanted this full faith, wanted it ardently, and never found it.

He looked for God, in whom he believed, everywhere. God is in the details, a famous remark has it, and so He lurks in many passages in Singer's novels and stories. In a passage late in *The Family Moskat,* a spy is hung from a tree. "His bare feet dangled above the ditch. A butterfly danced about the fur shako." Birds and cats go about their business in Singer's pages as stars twinkle and the moon cleaves its way through clouds, and the heavens remain eternally the same as people struggle to get through their lives, writhe in their sleep under the burden of their small—though not small to them—worries. There must be a plan behind all this. As Singer writes in *The Penitent,* echoing an old philosophical staple:

If someone found a watch on an island and said it had been made by itself or that it developed through evolution, he would be considered a lunatic. But according to modern science, the universe evolved all on its own. Is the universe less complicated than a watch?

Because Singer was always interested in the larger design, he was for the most part dismissive, even contemptuous, of politics, especially utopian left-wing politics. In one of his stories, "Guests on a Winter Night," he remarks that, of anarchists and radical students, his mother told him, "these sinful creatures had lost both their world and the world to come." Abram Shapiro, the licentious, contradictory, and finally most winning character in *The Family Moskat,* when asked his opinion of who is to blame for the crisis of the Jews in Poland with Hitler at the borders, replies:

Human nature. You can call a man capitalist, Bolshevik, Jew, *goy*, Tartar, Turk, anything you want, but the real truth is that man is a stinker. If you beat him, he yells. And if the other fellow is beaten, then he develops a theory. Maybe it'll be better in the next world.

As for this world, Singer, from the outset, has always seemed to favor the modest, the traditional, the pious among his characters. Men and women who have accepted life in the full harshness of its terms, who go about their business, their prayers, their unquestioning routines—these Singer admires above all. "It's these little nobodies who for two thousand years have carried all of Jewry on their backs," says Asa Heshel in *The Family Moskat*, "as well as all of Christendom. It is they who have always turned the other cheek." Where things go wrong for characters in a Singer story or novel is precisely at the point where they desert the faith and ways of their fathers, be it in the shtetl of Frampol, in Warsaw, in New York, Israel, or Buenos Aires. That way lies Gehenna.

That way, too, lies some superior fiction. Singer unlooses his magicians, his yeshiva boys rattled by enlightened ideas, his women swept away by vanity, and the games begin. Almost always they are sex games. Because the possibility of redemption must be present in his fiction, Singer works best with philanderers. Breaking the seventh commandment makes for better fiction anyway than breaking the sixth: redemption from murder seems distinctly less convincing than redemption from adultery. Besides, adultery, as in the bad old joke about incest, is a game the entire family can play. It is perhaps the most human of sins. As a writer, Singer played a great many variations upon it. Only toward the close did the game begin to run down.

A dark vein had always run through Singer's writing ("man is a stinker," etc.). But for the better part of his career he was best thought of as a tragicomedian. Comedy is possible even on the road to perdition, and Singer was adept at wringing high-spirited laughter from his depictions of characters as various as Gimpel the Fool and Yasha Mazur, his magician from Lublin. But in his later years the laughter was not even hollow; in fact, it was not there. Singer claimed not to be interested in preaching or sending messages, but reading the flat stories in *The Death of Methuselah* (1988) one could conclude only that its author's view of human beings ended with the observation that men are animals and women whores—case closed. In his last published novel, *Scum,* the redemption of Max Barabander is not even considered. "Oh, Mama, I'm sinking into filth up to my neck," he cries toward the close of the novel. Singer just lets him go under.

How account for this? What could have happened to make Singer, in his last years, so dark—and, one must add, so much less interesting—a writer? For the last twenty years of his life, the world treated him as a great man, showering every sort of pleasing attention upon him, ending with the Nobel Prize, which he won in 1978. He had money, critical acclaim, adoring readers, longevity, every reason to feel a sense of impressive achievement. Yet however playful he may have been at lectures, or with interviewers, or among friends, his late work reveals a writer who found people more disgusting than interesting. Why had his skies become so clouded? Critics used to complain that Singer often had problems with his endings: there is a problem with the ending of his own career.

The inclement Isaac Bashevis Singer is nowhere more evident than in *The Penitent,* a brief novel of 1983. That book, which tells the story of Joseph Shapiro, turns out to be an unrelieved philippic against modernity. Modern culture, Joseph Shapiro claims, is good for breeding only "cynics and whores." Modern philosophy, he avers, has a single theme: "We don't know anything and we cannot know anything." Newspapers pay "tribute to every idolatry and spit at the truth." Crime is on the loose and it is the job of lawyers to see that criminals go free. Animals, God's creatures, are slaughtered in the most hideous ways; when it comes to animals, says Joseph, "every man is a Nazi." The sum total of psychoanalysis is always "that someone else was guilty." And Jews, at least Jews without faith, are no better than anyone else. "Every few months they find a new idol, a new illusion, a new vogue, a new madness. They revere all kinds of murderers, whores, false prophets, clowns. They go wild over every little scribbler, every ham actor, every harlot." But enough.

In an author's note at the end of this novel, Singer makes plain that it was not possible for him to share Joseph Shapiro's belief in "a final escape from the human dilemma, a permanent rescue for all time" where Joseph finds it: in a "return to Jewishness, and not merely to some modern arbitrary Jewishness, but to the Jewishness of my grandfathers and great-grandfathers." But it is plain enough that Singer did share much of his character's unrelenting diagnosis of the hideousness of modern life. At one point in this novel, recounting a relapse into sin after his pledge to return to purity, Joseph says to the narrator, "That's how it is with adultery, with theft, with murder, with a craze for honors or for revenge. There is always a letdown. I don't have to tell *you* about that."

Did life let Singer down in some fundamental way that turned him so against it at the close? He insisted that one could be religious and rebellious simultaneously, believing in God and arguing with Him at the same time: "Those who dedicate their lives to serving God have often dared to question His justice, and to rebel against His seeming neutrality in man's struggle between good and evil."

In the end, it was the prevalence of evil that Singer found overwhelming. He was too good—which is to say, too honest—a writer to report things other than precisely as he found them. Why this dark and troubled truth, coming from a powerful writer at the end of his career, should make for not very interesting art is another question.

What is not in question is that Singer's stories and novels figure to have as long a life as those of any other writer of the past fifty years. He was one of the last living links with the Jewish past in Poland. He wrote in a language that had been given up for dead almost from the time he began to use it and into which he pumped impressive new life. That he survived, endured, triumphed, is as astonishing, even miraculous, a story as any he himself could have written.

Desmond MacCarthy's Familiar Criticism

Poor Desmond MacCarthy—so gifted, so charming, so full of promise—never quite came off. To be considered promising when young is at best a mixed blessing. Edith Wharton claimed that, as a young woman of her day, one of her greatest benefits was in never having been considered promising at all: it gave her time to develop in her own way and outside the pressure of expectation. Desmond MacCarthy never lived outside that pressure, and applied a good bit of it on himself. His aim, the assumption others made about him, was that he would one day create some masterpiece of literature—perhaps a richly complex novel or a key work of imperishable criticism—that would both make his mark and redeem his promise. He never did it; never, in fact, even came close.

Desmond MacCarthy stands in what is by now almost a tradition in England of literary flops. Just before him there was J. C. Squire, his predecessor as literary editor of the *New States-man,* and following him were Cyril Connolly and Kenneth Tynan. Each in his day came down from Oxbridge laden with talent and marked for early success. Each knew what was expected of him. MacCarthy and Connolly came near to making a success of failure. Connolly even wrote books about his inability to write books. (In one of his doggerel poems, Edmund

Wilson wrote: "Cyril Connolly / Behaves rather fonnily: / Whether folks are at peace or fighting, / He complains that it keeps him from writing.") "We are admirably successful failures," Desmond MacCarthy wrote to J. C. Squire before the Second World War, when both were coming to the end of their careers.

About success there seems something inevitable, easily explained after the fact, and often a touch boring. In autobiography, surely, interest begins to flag once success arrives. Failure, where it is not grinding and dreary (as in life, admittedly, it all too often is), provides a speculative mind richer material, especially where all the ingredients for success were in place to begin with. Where failure is owing to early death of the kind that has a strong element of self-destruction in it—as, notably, in the American instances of F. Scott Fitzgerald and James Agee—interest is practically guaranteed. But even without the heightened drama lent by early death, the failure of the truly talented suggests questions that speak directly to the mysteries of fate and destiny. Which was the road not taken? How might things have worked out otherwise? Was it all written in the stars, as the astrologers insist, or in the DNA, where the geneticists find it, or in the first years of life, where the Freudians think they have discovered it? I have no wish to disparage success (I have been planning a small success of my own for some years now), yet it is well to remember that it takes a certain not easily defined talent to record an interesting failure.

Desmond MacCarthy was born in 1877, "half-Irish," as John Gross has written, "quarter-German, quarter-French, wholly Etonian." He was an only child, which may have been part of the problem. His mother, who was twenty-one years younger than her husband, was a garrulous woman, romantic and of high pretension, the daughter of a German aristocrat who had failed to make good on his aspiration to achieve fame as a writer and philosopher. She was long-lived and devoted to her son in a not always felicitous way, encouraging him to ascend the heights at the same time that she regularly cut the emotional ground out from under him. His father, a man of the steady habits befitting the bank manager that he was, noted the absence of similar steadiness in Desmond. When the boy was seventeen and still at Eton, he wrote: "You have the disadvantage of being an only child, and it may be that you have the germ of a slight mental weakness, as I have noticed that you still have the nursery habit of dropping things anywhere without thinking of the trouble you are giving."

In *Clever Hearts,* their biography of Desmond MacCarthy and his wife Molly, Hugh and Mirabel Cecil write that both Desmond's parents invested great hope in their son. "Their conviction that they had a remarkable child lay at the root of his own belief that he would one day be a great man—a politician, a sage, a doctor of genius—which later developed into the belief that he could write a great novel." What we have here, as no therapist I have known or have heard about has ever said, is perhaps a case of too much love in the home.

Desmond MacCarthy was able to command as well a great deal of love outside the home. His were not among those typically nightmarish school days that have by now become one of the standard clichés of English writers who came of age late in the nineteenth and early in the twentieth centuries. He was no sickly E. M. Forster—of whose novels he would later hold a low opinion—a child of quivering sensitivity crushed by normally brutish boys of eleven and twelve. Nor were his school days at all like those of George Orwell, who found school to consist chiefly of snobbery and bullying and who took school for life and so lived at odds with society forever after.

No, Desmond's school days—and henceforth I shall refer to him as "Desmond," for intimacy was his keynote as a writer— no, Desmond's school days were almost uniformly pleasant. At Eton, as at the preparatory school he attended between the ages of seven and eleven, he was good at games, efficient enough at his studies, quick to make friends, and withal an immensely attractive boy and young man. "It was at Cambridge that I acquired such faculties as I have possessed of making the most of life," he later wrote in a paper for the Memoir Club, "and at Eton the worldly experience which may be a blessing or a snare." Very early in his life, one's guess is, Desmond, as he wrote of his friend Roger Fry, came to believe "in the wisdom of being happy."

Desmond began his career at Trinity College, Cambridge, in 1894. This was well beyond the time of religious crisis among English undergraduates and just before the time of pervasive homosexuality among the aesthetically cultivated, which, the Cecils say, set in with the advent of Lytton Strachey, whose undergraduate career began in 1899. Desmond slipped into Cambridge life as into a warm and welcoming pool; his congenial nature, good looks, intellectual quickness and curiosity all combined to assure him a place in the best circles of undergraduate life. This, in Cambridge, inevitably meant the Apostles, that select and secret society election to which was said to depend upon the possession of the intellectual graces and good character. Desmond was offered membership in 1896.

At Cambridge Desmond read history and looked into everything else that struck his fancy. He was invited to attend the weekly symposium of the classicist and political philosopher Goldsworthy Lowes Dickinson. The later-to-be successful historian George Trevelyan and his brother Robert, the later-to-be failed poet, were among his closest friends. The philosopher G. E. Moore, who was three years older than Desmond, was another close friend. Moore's stringent intellectual standards and his doctrine of moral purity, as exemplified through honesty in personal relations, aesthetic emotions, and the pursuit of truth, were to become a continuous if mixed influence upon him. The chief literary influences on Desmond at this time were

Henry James, George Meredith, and Thomas Hardy; add to these Samuel Butler, whom he had met through his father when still a boy.

At Cambridge, too, Desmond got his first whiff of intellectual bohemianism. He acquired it through invitation to the Sunday evening salon of Oscar Browning, a don famous in his day, whose penchant for titled undergraduates and interest in the education of the poor demonstrate yet again that snobbery and sentimentality can live snugly together in a capacious breast. But then everywhere he went doors opened for Desmond, who now began to add to his other attributes a justified reputation as a charming talker and courteous listener. Desmond, as an old friend once described him, was "a man who traveled first class through life on a third-class ticket."

Desmond's father had it in mind for his son to read for the law. After his father's death this notion was dropped, and there was talk of his taking an examination for a clerkship in the House of Lords, which figured to open up the prospect of a career in public life. Around this time Desmond also planned a second degree, this one in philosophy, with G. E. Moore as his tutor. But the examination for the clerkship was never taken, and the degree in philosophy dropped, when Desmond decided that he wanted to be a writer. He made this decision while traveling in Europe, where he discovered a talent for idleness and a taste for the spectatorial. His mother, who bombarded him with letters throughout his life, began to doubt his perseverance and wrote him in the following all-too-prophetic terms:

> I do not think you have genius. I think you have *grt* feeling & understanding of the powers & greatness & genius in others, which is clever and delicious & will make yr life always interesting & delightful even in *yr most* despondent moments, but I do not think you have any creative power nor have you endurance enough to be a *grt* man. All those things show very early in

people. Talent is always *there*—it does not grow suddenly—it grows rapidly but from the instant the child is born. You are in matter of thinking and appreciation rather above the average & that tempts you and others, those who love you, to be led to think at *first* you are much more clever than you are.

Desmond's reply is itself most interesting:

I think what you say about my literary power is quite true. I have neither the facility [n]or the energy to make a good easy living by writing. I should be further handicapped by fastidiousness—not one of the necessary qualities of a successful journalist. I know I sometimes write well, but with regard to real talent, I am, I expect, even more doubtful than you.

Desmond was then only twenty-one. He began to plan his novel. He set out in the meanwhile to widen his literary acquaintance, both in reading and among personages. He often visited Samuel Butler, met with Wilfrid Blunt and Leslie Stephen, and first encountered Henry James, whom he much admired, in 1901. He was living in London with his mother; owing to poor investments, the money his father had left was much diminished, forcing everyone to live on a fairly short leash. Desmond, though, was never one to recognize leashes of any length, and spent lavishly on cigars, clothes, and cabs.

Between 1899 and 1903—between, that is, the ages of twenty-two and twenty-six—Desmond attempted to get his great novel off the ground. That he had little success oughtn't to surprise. Few impressive novels of large scope have been written by writers in their twenties; it is well to recall that Joseph Conrad published his first novel at thirty-nine. But all the while that Desmond thought he was writing a novel, he was in reality training to become a critic. In the collection of essays published in 1931 under the title *Portraits,* he wrote to the book's dedicatee, himself at the age of twenty-two, the following note:

Some day, when you came upon a hushed space in life, away from journalism, away from the hubbub of personal emotions, I know you fully intended to listen to yourself; and discovering what you thought about the world to project it into a work of art—a play, a novel, a biography. But confess, you were too careless to prepare that preliminary silence, and too indolent to concentrate. Meanwhile how delightful you found it to imbibe literature at your leisure! And so you read and read. I must say I was grateful to you afterwards, for as a critic I should have run dry long ago if you had not been so lazy.

Nietzsche says that "a married philosopher belongs *in comedy*" but marriage and children for a writer of grand ambition can sometimes be tragic. Desmond had begun writing reviews before his marriage, but his marriage, in 1906, to Molly Warre-Cornish and the birth of children in fairly quick succession—three children in four years—pretty much locked him into journalism for life. Molly MacCarthy's was a most interesting family, and she was herself an impressive person. Her father was vice-provost and librarian of Eton; her Aunt Anny was Thackeray's daughter; and her mother, Blanche, the spiritual head of the household, used to say: "In all disagreeable circumstances remember three things which I always say to myself: 'I am an Englishwoman; I was born in wedlock; I am on dry land.' " Molly, under the name Mary MacCarthy, wrote a charming little volume about her family titled *A Nineteenth Century Childhood* and novels that met with commercial success and kind words from Virginia Woolf. In *A Nineteenth Century Childhood* Molly wrote of Desmond: "He seems to have unlimited time, and though he strolls through life as if it were a vast exhibition, at any booth of which he can tarry as long as it pleases his fancy, he never appears in the least demoralized by leisure; though there are grave headshakings over his 'career.' Everyone may be concerned about him, but he quietly goes his own way."

Molly, when writing that passage, knew considerably less than the half of it. *Clever Hearts,* the Cecils' biography, is in good part the story of the MacCarthys' marriage, and a sorely sad story it is. Most of the sadness in the marriage, in the Cecils' persuasive version, was owing to Desmond. Although the marriage was at the outset felt to be a great love match—Henry James attended the wedding, at which Donald Tovey played Brahms, Schumann, and Beethoven, and G. E. Moore was best man—it wasn't long before troubles of a Bloomsburyish kind set in. Bertrand Russell, who seems to have tried his luck with every attractive woman he ever met, put his moves on Molly, who found him laughable; at any rate the Cecils report that she could not keep a straight face. Desmond kept a very straight face during the love affairs into which he entered, which were always crushing to his wife. When in later years Clive Bell, another persistent Bloomsbury seducer, set his sights on Molly, who was a most attractive woman, she, agreeing to give in, caused Desmond great sorrow. The much vaunted Blooms-bury emphasis on truth and freedom in personal relations, in the sexual realm, only makes sense, if at all, when the people involved do not really love each other. Molly and Desmond did love each other, and so, played under Bloomsbury rules, marital life, or at least much of it, turned out to be hell.

Apostolic succession in Desmond's day led from Cambridge to Bloomsbury. Of the ten men who were members of what Leonard Woolf called "Old Bloomsbury," only three—Clive Bell, Adrian Stephen, and Duncan Grant—were not Apostles, and the others overlapped while at Cambridge. All were in one way or another under the sway of G. E. Moore and his *Principia Ethica,* which gave them what John Maynard Keynes called "a religion." Bloomsbury has by now, through being overwritten about by academics, become Boresbury, and so perhaps the time has come to sheer away the snobbery that has always been at the center of interest in it and see it for the often dreary, just as often comical, spectacle it provided.

The shabby and milquetoasty E. M. Forster; the etiolated Lytton Strachey, looking for all the world as if he had walked out of an Aubrey Beardsley drawing; the lubricious Clive Bell, always on the make; the suave Maynard Keynes, informing governments that they need not worry about balancing budgets while himself shoring up a fortune in the stock market; the Stephen sisters, living lives that will no doubt one day be portrayed on the screen by the Redgrave girls; and off a bit to the side, that strange creature, fit by physique for an aviary, Lady Ottoline Morrell (Lady Omega Muddle, as Lytton Strachey called her)—they were quite a collection of human types, these Bloomsberries.

And Desmond MacCarthy was not the least exotic among them. As he grew older, Desmond grew seedier, so that Virginia Woolf, in her diary in 1928, could describe him as "like a man who has sat up all night in a third class railway carriage. His fingers are stained yellow with cigarettes. One tooth in the lower jaw is missing. His hair is dank. His eye more than ever dubious. He has a hole in his blue sock." Yet Virginia Woolf would also say that she wasn't sure but that Desmond hadn't "the nicest nature of any of us—the nature one would have chosen for one's own." She spoke, too, of hoping one day to make up a short book of his table talk, "which shall appear as a proof to the younger generation that Desmond was the most gifted of us all. But why did he never do anything? they will ask."

There was no shortage of witnesses to attest to Desmond's charm. Lady Ottoline Morrell thought him "full of human kindness and generosity." Leonard Woolf, not a man given to effusions, called Desmond "perhaps the most charming man I have known." The flow of his conversation was famous, and a legendary story attesting to it has to do with his performance one evening, at the studio of Duncan Grant, where it was Desmond's turn to read a prepared paper to the Memoir Club. He proceeded to read an immensely fluent little memoir, from an attaché case that was open on his lap, when the attaché case fell to the floor and, as E. M. Forster recounted after Desmond's death, it was discovered that the case was quite empty. Without a hem, without a haw, Desmond was beautifully making it all up as he went along.

That little anecdote is interesting on more than one count. It reveals not only Desmond's talent as a talker, but his propensity for procrastination. Great as the former was, the latter may have been even greater. He was famous among his friends, and infamous among editors and printers, for his unreliability. Socially as well as editorially, he could be depended upon to be late, or not to show up at all. Frances Partridge, in her diary, referred to "MacCarthyism" as a combination of "the utmost charm and the utmost lack of consideration." Not easy on poor Molly, this little tic of her husband's. He left her with other worries into the bargain: over his long absences in London, over getting his work done, over money. In 1912, when Desmond was thirty-five, Molly wrote to him: "You will turn me into a morose, nagging, peevish, lonely woman—disillusioned & disappointed—and our children will wonder *why* you can't give them a better time, as other Fathers do who have made careers, or have honours, if not wealth, and will think of you as a lazy old man." She closed: "Don't be too angry at my outburst—I love you always but am utterly unstrung by care & loss of faith in you. Send some hope."

Desmond was himself running out of hope. After various odd and short-lived editorial jobs, he was free-lancing, which is no job for the unpunctual and temperamentally unsteady. Feeling the need to find regular work, he wrote to Lady Ottoline: "To accomplish such a thing will be the extinguisher to smouldering ambitions, but anything is better than smouldering without breaking into flame. I have smouldered now for fourteen years—a long time to smoulder, too long to smoulder." The following year, 1913, he signed on as a drama critic at the *New Statesman,* probably at the recommendation of George

Bernard Shaw. But steady work did not put out the coals of ambition. Throughout Desmond's career ambitious projects would be taken up and never quite gotten underway: a play and then a book about John Donne, a book about Byron, another about Tolstoy. And then there was the novel, always the damn novel. Lytton Strachey once read the first chapter of the novel and found it "not very inspiring."

What, really, went wrong? Why couldn't this most talented of men produce anything that seemed worthy of his gifts? It would be convenient to say that there are the pleasures of life and the pleasures of work, and Desmond, given a choice, invariably chose the former. But in fact he was full of guilt, recriminations, a sense of waste. Doubtless he found much delight—and doubtless, too, gave even more—chatting away amongst the rich and smart, but at an evening's end there was his own melancholy to face. Once, comparing himself to Bertrand Russell, Desmond noted: "You see my despondencies come from not feeling up to life, his from not feeling life up to him." Another time quoting Coleridge's son Hartley, who wrote of having "lost the race I never ran," Desmond remarked, "That will do very nicely for my own epitaph and I knew it would rather early."

In *Beginning Again*, the third volume of his autobiography, Leonard Woolf discusses at some length Desmond's sad failure to live up to his promise. Woolf eschews the notion that Desmond talked away his talent, saying that 1.) it "is probably true to say that 'his special gift of conversation' was a cause of his not writing novels, and 2.) his not writing novels was a cause of his special gift of conversation." Woolf thought it went deeper than that, however. He recalled that Desmond had once told him he thought he suffered from a disease: "the moment he knew that he ought to do something, no matter what that something was, he felt absolutely unable to do it and would do anything else in order to prevent himself from doing it."

Desmond once asked Woolf to lock him in a room until he had completed his work on an introduction to the posthumous novel of his friend A. F. Wedgwood. Woolf did, letting Desmond out only to trot off to buy cigarettes, but he doubts that the job finally got done even under conditions of voluntary incarceration.

Leonard Woolf thought, too, that Desmond operated under yet another pressure, and this was that of high perfectionism. This, Woolf felt, was probably instilled in him by G. E. Moore, or what he earlier calls "Moorism," which set the stakes of artistic creation very high indeed. Desmond's own standards in this line were themselves quite lofty. As he demonstrated time and again as a critic, when it came to literature, he knew what the real thing looked like and he knew quite a bit about how it was done, too. He just couldn't do it himself. It was the story of his life, and a very unhappy story it is.

Yet another, perhaps stranger, factor has to be weighed in considering Desmond's inability to produce the great work everyone expected of him: he was too adept at enjoying life to have much need for the compensations that go with the production of art. In a lovely memoiristic essay he wrote about Henry James, Desmond tells about James, resting with coffee at the close of a party of which he, James, had clearly been the life, noting the rest of the party going off onto the verandah, and James remarking to him, "What a charming picture they make, the women there with their embroidery, the . . ." Desmond noted the immense detachment in James's voice as he said this, and it caused him to blurt out, "I can't bear to look at life like that. I want to be in everything. Perhaps that is why I cannot *write,* it makes me feel absolutely alone." At this James leaned forward, grasped Desmond's arm excitedly, and said, "Yes, it is solitude. If it runs after you and catches you, well and good. But for heaven's sake don't run after *it.* It is absolute solitude." Desmond's confession may seem that of a weakling, but it has honesty in it, and lacerating self-awareness, given that he stood in no greater awe of anyone than the genuine artist. Yet the sad truth remained that he liked life too much to give up its quotidian enjoyments for the delayed and very high-risk gratifications required by the most serious art.

Desmond had no recourse but to fall back onto journalism, which Leonard Woolf called "the opiate of the artist" and which for Cyril Connolly was one of "the enemies of promise." Put in these terms, journalism sounds like a low and miserable condition to which no one should fall. Although Desmond referred to himself as a literary journalist, knowing full well that the term had less prestige than that of artist or critic, it is well to remember on how high a level his own literary journalism was pitched. Written chiefly in the form of drama or book reviews, and occasionally as essays for literary journals—much of it done on the run and under the pressure of frantic, threatening deadlines—it is surprising how much of it today not only remains readable but continues to give pleasure and insight, qualities most writers today would settle for and all too few are able to provide.

How did Desmond do it? It will not quite do to state the obvious: he did it through intelligence, charm, and skill, even though he had all three in large supply. Desmond also had a very keen sense of what he was about. Toward the close of a brilliant essay on Prime Minister Herbert Asquith, he wrote:

> Yes, it is difficult for a critic not to believe sometimes that his own mind and his own feelings are more interesting to the reader than his subject, and on occasion it may even be true; but certainly if that is his constant persuasion he can be no critic—an essayist perhaps, but not a critic.

Desmond MacCarthy was an essayist, but one who for the most part required a play or book—some event or artifact of culture—to set him going. He was, moreover, a familiar essayist, in the sense that his tone is entirely, deliciously conversational. Desmond was himself not only a great talker, as all who knew him attested, but both a lover and a connoisseur of good talk. Certainly, he had heard more than his share of the best talk of his time. Of Asquith, Desmond writes that "many men's writing is the spoken word on paper, merely titivated conversation. But he actually spoke the language of the pen." Of the distinguished Liberal statesman Sir William Harcourt, he recalls his having had "the gift of effective assertion"; of Gladstone, that he wrote "spoken sentences, not written ones, composed with a pen by a man imagining himself in the act of writing." And on Henry James he was best of all:

> The spell he exercised by his style was exercised in his conversation. Phrases of abstruse exaggerated drollery or of the last intellectual elegance flowered in it profusely. At first you might feel rather conscience-striken for having set in motion, perhaps by a casual question, such tremendous mental machinery. It seemed really too bad to have put him to such trouble, made him work and weigh his words like that. . . . There was something at once so painstaking, serious and majestical in the procedure of his mind that you shrank from diverting it, and thus the whole of your little precious time with him might be wasted. This often happened in my case during our fifteen years' acquaintance, and I still regret those bungled opportunities.

Desmond's own conversation, by all accounts, was less idiosyncratic, less pyrotechnical. His was the gift neither of epigram nor of repartee. Max Beerbohm, soon after Desmond's death in 1952, recalled the "endearing intimacy" of his voice and said that his talk was essentially "chamber music," for he was very good at bringing other people into the conversation. "He was also," Beerbohm said, "a great user of that attractive, that beguiling phrase 'And tell me.' " Beerbohm concludes that "writing was always to him a task and rather a terror. And that is perhaps the reason why he wrote so splendidly. He had always to do his best." Desmond's best, when he hit it, which was fairly often, was splendid.

One has only to read Desmond MacCarthy on such writers as Joseph Conrad, Henry James, or Marcel Proust to know one is in the company of a man for whom literature is essential to life. He wrote brilliantly on almost all writers that he took up, though never definitively. He seems not to have been interested in the last word; only in having his say. He was less authoritative in tone than authentic in interest, more the connoisseur than the critic. A Desmond MacCarthy essay of any length is likely to include a digression or two ("I distrust the delicacy of the delicate," he writes in his essay on Proust), a bit of autobiography ("I was companionable without exciting envy," he writes about his relationship with Wilfrid Blunt), a statement of bias ("As a rule I find myself in agreement with orthodox opinion upon great writers and tend to feel uneasy when I am not," he notes. "But with [Samuel] Richardson I differ jubilantly"), and if one knows a bit about his life one can read Desmond's own predicament into his judgments upon others ("No man was ever more acutely conscious of himself than Boswell, and therefore more powerfully aware of being a bundle of confused and contradictory impulses. His will was naturally weak . . . and he longed passionately to pull himself together").

What Desmond MacCarthy finally wrote is what I should call familiar criticism. Edmund Wilson once remarked that the "implied position of the people who know about literature (as is also the case in every other art) is simply that they know what they know, and that they are determined to impose their opinions by main force of eloquence or assertion on the people who do not know." In Desmond MacCarthy's criticism, force, main or otherwise, simply isn't brought to bear. In his criticism one reads a man who also knows what he knows but doesn't seem to want to impose anything on anyone. He prefers instead to talk about it, almost as if in a pleasant social

setting. Much of what he has to report is by way of appreciation, but appreciation need not preclude penetration. On Joseph
Conrad, Desmond wrote:

> Many passages express directly what his stories exhibit imagi-
> natively: a judgment which is passionately ethical and a concep-
> tion of nature as indifferent to human values. In a universe,
> beautiful in an inscrutable way, but without justice and honour,
> it is man's glory to have put justice and honour. . . . There is no
> occasion for despair, for in defeat man also is great, and the
> spectacle of the struggle is sublime to the contemplating mind.
> Conrad then has no "message." He has . . . a philosophy of life,
> but it is not the kind which drives a man to win converts. . . . I
> think it was because he had seen so many things in human nature
> and the world that he did not wish to be forgotten or to forget,
> that Conrad, to our great gain, became a writer.

An interest in human nature was at the heart of Desmond's
own passion for literature. He thought human nature far and
away the subject of greatest fascination, and literature provided the best insights into it. The words "human nature" show
up repeatedly in his criticism, and in a discourse entitled "Notes
on The Novel" he wrote: "Goethe, Sainte-Beuve, Baudelaire,
Arnold—if you examine what they have written . . . you will
be surprised to find how much of their criticism is discourse
upon human nature and upon good and evil." Desmond
believed, with Vernon Lee, whom he quoted upon the subject,
that " 'tis his human superiority, not, believe me, his literary
talent" that makes a great writer. He loved literature, and knew
it in its intricacies, but never took it altogether as an end in
itself. As he wrote in "Notes on the Novel":

> In a work of literary art these questions [What do I really care
> about? What Art? God? Men? Myself?], and a hundred more,
> find an answer, though they are not necessarily asked in it. But
> on the pertinacity with which the artist has put them to himself

depend the clearness and depth of his vision; and if he can only reach down to what he has really felt himself, that vision will carry with it an imposing authority for others, possess also a kind of unity which, though philosophically it is no pledge of truth, is nevertheless capable of giving much greater satisfaction to the mind than piecemeal observation of separate truths ever can.

I hope I haven't defanged Desmond MacCarthy, made him seem a critic without any true bite. Geoffrey Grigson took this general line when he wrote about "the Desmond MacCarthy streak in English letters," by which he meant, roughly, bland appreciation. Desmond could be quite tough. As a drama critic, he could kill an entire genre in a single phrase, or at least he has for me in one instance by referring to "the enforced joy of musical comedy." He referred to the misogyny at the heart of Strindberg as "the torments of a hen-pecked Bluebeard." He was death on *Ulysses*, which he thought the creation "of a frightened enslaved mind. Much of it is cold, nasty, small and overserious." He early set himself not to be among those blackmailed by the avant-garde. "The threat is a potent one," he wrote. "All dissidents or doubtfuls are warned that if they are not duly respectful towards the new enormities, they will find themselves numbered among the philistines who, in the past, derided and rejected 'the unknown beauty.' "

Desmond found himself temperamentally at odds with much in modern writing. It was the modern note of self-dramatization that put him off. "I see no reason to suppose that good works of art may not be produced by those whose conflicts and 'efforts toward freedom' are over at the time of writing." Nietzsche's writings were similarly spoiled for him "by being obviously cathartic." His complaint about much modern poetry, from T. S. Eliot on, is that it was taken away from common readers and placed, firmly and forever, in the hands of academics and professionals. "The root of my distrust of the modern movement is that by implication and example it dethrones poetry from the place it has held in the common life of man." Too much of the art of his time reminded him "that art is so superficial, life so profound."

It was the connections between art and life that were most important to him. "It is extremely doubtful whether the aim of the novel is to make an aesthetic appeal," he wrote apropos of Trollope. "Passages in it may do so; but it aims also at satisfying our curiosity about life and engaging our sympathies quite as much as at satisfying the aesthetic sense." More than once he made plain that for him "a work of art whatever its theme must somehow, somewhere, suggest the desirability of life."

Desmond allowed that every writer is in good part the product of the spirit of the time in which he comes into maturity, and that in this regard he was of the time before the First World War. He felt that in the twentieth century fiction was coming to seem more like biography and biography like fiction. ("A biographer," he wrote, "is an artist who is on oath, and anyone who knows anything about artists, knows that this is almost a contradiction in terms.") As he grew older, he worried less about consistency of taste. "Surely we are all gifted with a happy natural inconsistency of taste," he wrote in response to F. R. Leavis's attempts to exclude so much of oddity and interest in literary creation. For Desmond "the important thing is to respond to greatness when we meet it, and to deplore incessantly its absence does not increase our power of response." Neither a law-giver nor a disciple-maker, Desmond MacCarthy was essentially a commonsensical critic.

What made him an uncommon critic, in my view, was his style, his imagination, his impressive understanding of how literature worked, which he knew if not quite from the inside then at least as someone who sorely wanted inside. Desmond knew, as Logan Pearsall Smith said, that style was the "preservative of literature"; and also, if the truth be known, of criticism. His own style was fluent and mellifluous, approximating his talk. (Cyril Connolly spoke of the "wonderful flute of his conversation.") His was a style that worked toward the aphoristic, and often achieved it. "Society changes quickly; the soul hardly at all; it is that which makes [Ibsen's] work permanent." Apropos of the artistic temperament, he wrote: "To achieve self-portraiture a man must be self-complacent and detached." He could also bring off the aphoristic style in longer passages:

> Figures of literature and history live in the thoughts of men on the condition that they change their aspect. Humanity is only interested in past ages and dead authors in so far as it can attribute to them its own passions and thoughts. That they are to go on doing so—seeing now this, now that, in them—is the sign and proof of an immortal creation.

Although Desmond himself wrote so well, he never forgot the limitations of style, or where in literature it simply did not much matter. Goethe, he wrote, "is too interested in truth to be afraid of being dull." Balzac's "work seems to show that the art of writing well is of subordinate importance in novel writing." Desmond thought stream of consciousness misbegotten as a method of accurately recording "a streamy-dreamy state of semi-consciousness," and referred to its use in *Ulysses* as "a tiresome method of conveying the sensation of a snooze." Yet he knew, as he said in connection with Joyce, that "all literary methods are legitimate which succeed."

As a man of extremely wide reading—for all his reputed laziness, Desmond seems to have read a vast quantity of literature—he was marvelously adept at literary comparison, and was able to toss off comparisons that make one happily reconsider writers in their light. "Gibbon, it has been said," he wrote in a brief review of a slight volume about Herbert Spencer, "wrote about himself in the same tone as he wrote about the Roman Empire. Herbert Spencer wrote about himself in exactly the same tone as he wrote about the Universe." When Desmond writes that D. H. Lawrence was the novelist equivalent of Carlyle, or Aldous Huxley the Anatole France of his day, or that "there is a great deal of Byron in Hamlet, or, if you like, of Hamlet in Byron," one comes away with a new handle on all these writers, figures, characters. He was equally good at finding exactly the right quotations to bring out qualities in a writer one hadn't quite noticed before. What Desmond MacCarthy did when he was at the top of his game as a critic was to revivify, to give a new life to, every author he wrote about. One cannot ask much more from criticism.

Desmond's criticism has a winning commonsensicality that is rare in criticism practiced at a high level. As a drama critic, for example, he knew better than to step into the Big Muddy of Shakespeare criticism. He knew that "it is a region of controversy which it is hardly worth while only to visit; you must settle down in it to learn anything—and if you do, you are apt to go mad." Put off by the excessive in art, he wrote of Victor Hugo, Wagner, and Swinburne: "There is a too-muchness about them all." When Swinburne in a poem addresses a cat ("May not you rejoice as I, . . ."), Desmond writes: "Now the public though crass is not such an ass as to put to a cat such a question as that." What finally made Desmond's commonsensicality so winning is that it never descended, as a too strict application of common sense is apt to do in the arts, to philistinism.

Good as Desmond could be at criticism, it is far from clear whether he ever settled into the role of critic. "I am an acute and balanced critic," he wrote to Oliver Esher, who was trying to secure a knighthood for him, "who sometimes writes uncommonly well, but one who has been compelled by the exigencies of earning a living with his pen to express what he has to say about literature and drama as a reviewer and weekly critic of plays." He knew, I think, the value of criticism when done well, and could write: "The creative writer must know his own mind; the critic must also know the minds of other people. He must be able to harmonise personal sensibility with an exposition of case-made law; tradition is also evidence." When Desmond writes about other critics, it is difficult not to read autobiography into his sentences. Apropos of the critic Walter Raleigh, a man of small but elegant output, he wrote: "He was a book-minded man who loved life better than books." And Desmond closes his essay on Raleigh, who was also a famous talker, with this statement: His talk "was a fountain of intellectual high spirits tossing and glittering, playful and surprising. Those refreshed by it found it hard to regret that in him the artist had died into the Improvisatore."

I once asked Sir William Haley, who knew Desmond when he, Haley, was director-general of the BBC and with whom he was a neighbor in the Thames-side village of Hampton, his view of Desmond MacCarthy. Sir William replied:

> Much has been made of the fact that he never wrote a major work. His seven volumes are all collections of short pieces. He was—to borrow one of W. H. Hudson's titles—"A Traveller in Little Things." So was his talk. He never embarked on a sustained major subject. No one expected he would. It was not in his nature. But his character studies, critiques, reviews, general essays were the essence of the way he lived and wrote. . . . He was easygoing. He rarely used his pen in anger. His "Portraits" are of human beings, not of intellectual conceptions. He communicated mostly pleasure and appreciation. So did his talk. I never knew him angry or heard him denounce anybody. Yet his "little things" contain some memorable riches.

Writing about Renan, Desmond accused him of painting in his heroes those traits which he most loved in himself, and he remarked upon this that it showed a sign of "incomplete self-awareness; and self-awareness is a quality which, in a critical as opposed to a creative mind, is of primary importance." Poor

Desmond was never for long able to shake his awareness of the disparity between his aspirations and his achievements. Late in life he said that "renown is a cold hard empty thing compared with the warm admiration of friends in youth and those who have tasted the one are apt to show early a sage's indifference to reputation." One's guess is that he cared less about the world's disappointment in him than in his disappointment in himself.

In *Beginning Again,* Leonard Woolf recounts the last evening he spent with Desmond before his death. He, Desmond, was suffering from asthma, and Woolf had run to fetch a cab for him.

> When I put him into the taxi, he looked, not like an affable hawk [Affable Hawk was a pen name Desmond used for his column in the *New Statesman*] or even a disheveled fledgling, but like a battered, shattered, dying rook. . . . I left Desmond sitting in the taxi, affectionate, dejected, unheroic, because so obviously broken and beaten by asthma and by life; but brave in not complaining and not pretending and in still, when he could, making his joke and his phrase.

Does anything more surely presage a sad old age than great expectations when young? Or is the lesson here instead that only a fool thinks he can have literature and life, too? It might have pleased Desmond MacCarthy to know that, nearly forty years after his death, much of the criticism he wrote under the torture of such self-inflicted pressure not only holds up but yields delight and increases understanding—it might, but I doubt if it would have been enough.

Carl Sandburg,
"the People's Poet"

The Poet is a heroic figure belonging to all ages; whom all ages possess, when once he is produced, whom the newest age as the oldest may produce—and will produce, always when Nature pleases. Let Nature send a Hero-soul; in no age is it other than possible that he may be shaped into a Poet.

—Thomas Carlyle

Passages like my epigraph probably go a long way toward suggesting that Carlyle was more than a little nuts. Who, in our day, would search among poets for a hero? With only a few exceptions, poets in our time have found a home in the university, where they are rather dim figures, permitted to work at their craft, not so much an ornament to the culture as something closer to a parasite upon it, living from grant to grant, workshop to workshop, involved in an intense relationship with the Self, that all-consuming locust of our age, which chomps up all before it. Such, usually without rhyme and often without reason, has increasingly become the obscure habitat and vocation of the poet at the end of the twentieth century.

To find an American poet who received public adulation worthy of the kind of heroism described by Carlyle, one must go as far back as 1878. The poet born in that year was not T. S. Eliot, for some a hero of culture, or Robert Frost, who late in life had an unusually wide public following, but Carl Sandburg, a poet not so much forgotten as scarcely any longer read. Whether Sandburg was truly a poet is itself nowadays in doubt. That in his day he enjoyed the fame accorded to a hero is not.

Carl Sandburg is the only American poet ever asked to address Congress, a date he was able to fit into his crowded schedule in 1959. He also appeared on the *Ed Sullivan Show,* the *Texaco Hour* (with Milton Berle), the early *Today Show* (with Dave Garroway), and *See It Now,* where he was interviewed by Edward R. Murrow. Sandburg once wrote a poem to which, on television, Gene Kelly danced. The house in which he was born was preserved as a memorial to him while he was still alive, and inside its front door hung—no doubt hangs still—a tribute from Stephen Vincent Benét; in part, ungrammatically, it reads: "A great American, we have just reason to be proud that he has lived and written in our time."

Perhaps no poet—or literary man generally—was more gaudily praised in his lifetime than Carl Sandburg. About the first volume of Sandburg's autobiography the playwright Robert Sherwood observed that it was the greatest work of its kind ever written by an American, "not forgetting Benjamin Franklin, nor Henry Adams, nor showing them disrespect." In a book about Sandburg, Harry Golden (of *Only in America* fame) noted: "It is not exaggerated to say you would learn more about the industrialization of America reading Sandburg's poems than you would learn about Elizabeth's England reading Shakespeare's plays." The British novelist and political journalist Rebecca West compared him to Robert Burns as "a national poet." The American socialist leader Eugene V. Debs said that he was "one of the very few really great poets of our day, and the future will know him to the remotest generation." Many years later the television commentator Eric Sevareid remarked:

"I want to say that Carl is the strongest and most enduring force in American letters today." Taken all in all, not a bad little set of blurbs.

Sandburg also enjoyed the kind of fame in his lifetime which, among American writers, perhaps only Mark Twain and Ernest Hemingway had in theirs, and Sandburg's was probably greater. Like theirs, his was not a coterie fame, or fame limited to a university readership. For many years Sandburg was perhaps the most frequently read living writer in American high schools. He was often called "the People's Poet." *Playboy* once paid him $3,600 for six poems and a parable. ("It was fun," Sandburg is said to have remarked, "to be read by the most gustatory audience of readers in America, all of them definitely opposed to artificial insemination.") He also got large fees for poetry published in the *Woman's Home Companion, Collier's,* the *Saturday Evening Post,* and even *Fortune.* Hollywood, which had earlier paid him more than $100,000 to write a novel from which it hoped to make a movie—the project did not work out—hired him once more to work on the screenplay for Fulton Oursler's *The Greatest Story Ever Told.* Sandburg's reputation was large enough for Westbrook Pegler, the New York columnist, to attack him on a number of occasions, usually referring to him as "the proletarian millionaire." For a poet, this was big-time stuff—fame on the show-biz standard.

Sandburg seemed to sustain his reputation, however, only as long as he lived. Once he died (in 1967) it went down faster than the *Hindenburg.* Today, put the name Sandburg on one of E. D. Hirsch's cultural-literacy tests and, my guess is, the response it would elicit would overwhelmingly be "Second baseman, Chicago Cubs." Of course in his last years there were already signs of his future loss of popularity, one of them being that he did not even make Dwight Macdonald's 1960 anthology of parodies—he, poet of the most parodiable of all modern poetic styles. Perhaps a parody of Carl Sandburg would have been considered too easy, which, as I shall try to demonstrate, it certainly is:

> Hot bitcher for the Gnarled,
> Fool Shaker, Shackler of Feet,
> Flayer with Male Toads and the Nation's
>   Fright Hondler;
> Horny, Busty, Stalling,
> City of the Low Rollers.

Sandburg himself was not altogether ignorant of the vicissitudes of reputation. "Fame is a figment of a pigment," he once wrote. "It comes and goes. It changes with every generation. There never were two fames alike. One fame is precious and luminous; another is a bubble of a bauble." And so it was with his fame: the poet in whose honor a day was declared in North Carolina, who received the Albert Einstein Award from Yeshiva University, who had schools and real-estate developments named for him in Chicago, who was given God knows how many honorary degrees from Harvard on down, who won two Pulitzer Prizes (one for the first volumes of his biography of Abraham Lincoln in 1940 and one for his *Collected Poems* in 1951), who was actually regarded as a possible Republican presidential candidate to run in 1940 against Franklin D. Roosevelt, then seeking his third term—the reputation of this same poet is today in a condition he himself called "complete fadeout," with, I should guess, very little chance of revival.

How did Carl Sandburg achieve, sustain, and lose fame so completely? His case presents a fascinating chapter in the history of reputation.

On the subject of Sandburg's ascent, we now have a detailed account in *Carl Sandburg,* by Penelope Niven. The book is very much in the contemporary mode of epic biography—epic in this context meaning nearly endless. If in architecture less can be more, in biography more not infrequently turns out to be less. Miss Niven's book, the result of years of work in a vast Sandburg archive, is another case in point.

Hesketh Pearson, the English biographer, once wrote that "the majority of reliable biographies are unreadable, and the majority of readable biographies are unreliable." I cannot call Miss Niven's biography unreadable, since I seem to have read it; nor am I prepared to say that it is unreliable, since an enormous amount of research has clearly gone into its making. The insurmountable problem with the book is that it is altogether too uncritical of, and insufficiently distanced from, its subject. Miss Niven is all panting admiration for Sandburg, and everything about and connected with him. She is to Carl Sandburg as Carl Sandburg was to Abraham Lincoln. But Sandburg, it will surprise no one to learn, was no Lincoln.

Miss Niven's unstinting admiration leads her to take Sandburg at his own high self-valuation, which further leads her to assume that everything about his life is important, which in its turn leads to an unseemly quantity of gushing on her part. "His poems," she writes, "read in chronology and context, are a man's autobiography, a nation's autobiography." Miss Niven goes on and on about Sandburg's "fiery oratory," his "biting news columns," his "orator's ear for cadence and dramatic effect which led him closer to discovery of his inner, poetic voice." It is all more than a bit of a muchness.

The one thing to be said for biographies on the gargantuan scale is that they do supply an impressive pile of facts out of which a more critical reader may derive his own, often quite discrepant picture of the subject. Such at any rate is my debt to Miss Niven, and I hope I shall be forgiven for putting her diligence to my own very different purposes.

Carl Sandburg was a child of the same Midwest with which his name would be associated throughout his adult life, and remains associated to this day. He was born in Galesburg, Illi-

nois, to immigrant parents, Swedes, in less than easy circumstances. His father was a blacksmith's helper on the Chicago,
Burlington & Quincy Railroad; his mother had been a hotel
maid. He was his parents' second child, the first son of seven
children, two of whom died of diphtheria in the winter of 1892.
His was not an easy youth, being brought up in Galesburg, a
town in which the local chapter of the Women's Christian
Temperance Movement was prominent, and in a household
dominated by a stern father whose unrelieved dourness could
have landed him a walk-on part in an Ingmar Bergman movie.

The Sandburgs lived close to the bone. Buying a house in
Galesburg, August Sandburg had entered into a bad mort-
gage, and his ill luck was compounded by the panic of 1893.
There was not enough money for Carl to go to high school.
Instead he was needed to work—he had a newspaper route,
later delivered milk for a dairy—to bring in money for the
household. He continued his reading with the help of his older
sister, who was permitted to finish high school in the hope that
she would become a teacher, as she eventually did. In an attempt
to Americanize his name, Sandburg called himself Charlie. When
he later decided to write poetry, his father is supposed to have
asked, "Iss dere any money in diss poetry business, Sholly?" It
turned out that, properly worked, there was quite a bit.

Sandburg first saw Chicago, traveling on his father's railroad
pass, when he was eighteen. It blew him away. It also set him
on the road. Not long after, he rode the rails to Kansas, where,
as a hobo, he worked the wheat fields. (The distinction among
tramps, hobos, and bums was that tramps wandered but did
not work, hobos wandered and worked, and bums neither
wandered nor worked.) From his days among tramps and hobos,
Sandburg acquired the rudiments of his lifelong socialism, which
was of the turn-of-the-century, peculiarly American strain, more
populist and sentimental than Communist. This period also
gave him his first inkling that he might one day be a writer.
Coincidentally, it was during these same years, the 1890s, that

Jack London, too, lived as a tramp, extracting much material for his novels and stories. As a training for writers, traveling about the country on the cheap was no bad form of education, better, surely, than graduate school.

Sandburg would eventually go to college, back in Galesburg, but first he joined up for, though he did not fight in, the Spanish-American War, a conflict that produced more casualties from disease than from battle. As a veteran, he could attend Lombard College tuition-free, which he did while working at the Galesburg fire department. His family had meanwhile come up in the world, thanks chiefly to his father's having bought another house, this one large enough to rent out portions to tenants. Charlie—he had not yet returned to the name Carl—was a great figure in college: a serious student, a basketball star, a member of the debating society, editor of the school paper. He had fallen under the influence of a mildly polymathic professor named Philip Green Wright, who was himself, Miss Niven reports, something of a William Morris socialist. Sandburg had also begun reading Charles Lamb, William James, John Ruskin; he discovered Walt Whitman, with whom he would later often be compared and compare himself. He was put up for but did not pass the examinations to West Point; had he been accepted, he would have been in the same class there as Douglas MacArthur.

Midwestern culture in the days of Sandburg's youth and early manhood was largely an oratorical culture, the culture of the Chautauqua movement and of the visiting lecturer. William Jennings Bryan, a powerful speaker, was one of young Sandburg's early political heroes. Elbert Hubbard, advertising man, publisher, vaudeville performer, spellbinding lecturer, and author of the immensely best-selling pamphlet *A Message to García*, was another great figure for Sandburg. Politics and culture, being so closely connected with oratory, were both intertwined with salesmanship. In his own day, Sandburg did a bit of it all: he sold stereoscopic machines, he told Swedish jokes on the stage, he worked in an advertising agency, he gave lectures for fees. During a period when he was selling stereoscopic machines, hawking his poems, and trying to set up lectures, he called himself a "hustler." My sense is that, in good part, a hustler he always remained—and a quite brilliant hustler, too.

Was it Cromwell of whom it was said that he was "wily for the public good"? One might say of Sandburg, in something of the reverse spirit, that he was an idealist who was always in business for himself. When in his early twenties he became an organizer for the Socialist Party in Wisconsin—he was allowed to keep, as wages, the dues of the new members he brought into the party—he viewed his work as in part an excellent way to perfect his performance as a lecturer. Miss Niven prints a 1906 photograph that Sandburg sent out to prospective customers for his lectures: it is very carefully posed to make him seem dark and dramatic. He was always his own best publicity agent. He did a set lecture on Walt Whitman as a brother to the great prophets and teachers, an American dreamer, interested in human betterment. One generally does well to beware those who are always exalting dreamers; they are themselves usually awake at all times to the main chance.

As a young man, Sandburg bounced around a good bit in the Socialist Party, not only organizing but writing and editing for the socialist press. It was through this work that, at party headquarters in Milwaukee, he met Lillian Steichen, who was to be his wife. Later Sandburg, in a bit of (unconscious?) egotism, said of their meeting that he had been looking for "the kind of woman I would be if I were a woman." She had gone to the nascent University of Chicago, she was on a health-food diet, and when they married she agreed to wear a wedding ring only as a "concession to bourgeois morals" and to "satisfy the prejudices of the proletariat." They asked the minister to omit the word "obey" from their vows. She called him Carl, he called her Paula: they were a proto-hippie couple, and if Birkenstock sandals had been invented, they would no doubt have worn them.

Paula Sandburg laid the flattery on her husband with a fork-lift. It was she who first noted that the socialist movement would "need its Poet," she who first called him "the People's Poet." She once wrote to him: "You are a *Man*! You are all the separate intensities of Shelley— . . . Walt Whitman—Marx—Wagner—the Vikings—Christ—Buddha—Lincoln—Heine—Browning—You are all these separate and different intensities. But *harmonized*!" She kept this stuff up his life long. Harry Golden, in his panegyrical book on Sandburg, tells of the woman tourist who impulsively kissed the eighty-year-old poet and to whom Paula said: "That's all right, he belongs to the world."

Paula Steichen was the sister of Edward Steichen, one of the key figures of modern photography, and in him Sandburg might be said to have gotten the brother-in-law he deserved. Each man seemed to go at things at a Himalayan level of generality. Sandburg's favorite book of his own poems is entitled *The People, Yes,* and Steichen's most famous book of photographs (to which Sandburg supplied the text), a worldwide bestseller in its day, is entitled *The Family of Man.* Sandburg wrote a book about Steichen, Steichen frequently (and in rather pompous poses) photographed Sandburg. Each seemed to be regularly calling the other a genius. "He throws a long shadow and ranks close to Ben Franklin and Leonardo da Vinci when it comes to versatility," said Sandburg of Steichen. "On the day that God made Carl," Steichen said at a dinner marking Sandburg's seventy-fifth birthday, "He didn't do anything else that day but sit around and feel good." As Sandburg lived on a fairly steady diet of exaggerated praise of this kind, it is small wonder that he was extremely touchy about criticism.

But to return to Sandburg's youth: while moving from job to job—he turned out advertising copy for a Milwaukee department store, served as secretary to the socialist mayor of

Milwaukee, lectured for the Wisconsin Anti-Tuberculosis Association, did journalism for newspapers and business and trade magazines in Chicago—he also wrote poems. He was a free-verse man—one of those fellows, as Robert Frost famously put it, who prefer to play tennis without a net—and his poems met with uneven success when he sent them around to editors. Sandburg's great breakthrough came in 1914, when Harriet Monroe accepted nine poems for *Poetry: A Magazine of Verse;* she ran them as the lead item in her March 1914 issue under the rubric "Chicago Poems."

Acceptance at *Poetry* was the making of Sandburg. It not only put him in the company of William Butler Yeats, Robert Frost, D. H. Lawrence, Hart Crane, and Edward Arlington Robinson, all of whom published in *Poetry* that year, but gave him a new status as an artist, both in the world and in his own eyes. Culture was the key that unlocked many doors in Chicago. Better yet, his poems represented avant-garde culture: they were criticized in genteel quarters for what was thought to be their brutality. Sandburg, suddenly, became the eponymous leader of something that would be known as "the hog butcher school of poetry." A better debut could not have been imagined.

That Sandburg was now seen—and, through *Poetry,* authenticated—as an artist gave him special cachet even in the hard-boiled world of Chicago journalism. He was fortunate in having landed a job on the *Chicago Daily News,* where he had been recommended to the managing editor, an extraordinary man named Henry Justin Smith, by Ben Hecht, the novelist and short-story writer who was himself then working at the paper. Sandburg "is a man who can write poetry like Whitman," Hecht told the editor. In our day this might get you fired from the *New York Times,* but Henry Justin Smith, according to Hecht, "saw the paper as a daily novel written by a school of 'Balzacs,' but we were missing a poet." Sandburg was not only hired but treated with the highest regard.

A job on the *Daily News* also put Sandburg smack-dab in the middle of what became known as the Chicago Renaissance, that gathering of writers, journalists, and artists which enjoyed a brief efflorescence during the second decade of the century, when H. L. Mencken called Chicago "the literary capital of the United States." More lunching than writing got done, as Ben Hecht noted in his autobiography, and there was much in the way of hijinks at local clubs and restaurants. But Sandburg's reputation benefited from the general *réclame* of the putative literary renaissance in Chicago. His poem "Chicago," which set clichés about the city in stone for future decades, came as close to an anthem as the Chicago Renaissance ever had.

Sandburg was by this time a family man, commuting from and to his suburban home. He and Paula had three daughters. The eldest suffered from epilepsy; the second had been slightly brain-damaged by an automobile accident; the third, Helga, who became a novelist, would later rebel against her father. Sandburg would claim, with justice, that he needed a good deal of money to take care of his first two daughters, who never left the household and who would have to be looked after all their lives. He turned out to be a powerful money earner, not least through lecturing and poetry readings. In time, he added folk-singing to his performances.

Meanwhile, Sandburg's literary reputation continued to grow. He was regularly praised as a poet whose work was vital, brash, "vivid" (as Louis Untermeyer put it in a review in the *Masses*) "with the health of vulgarity." Mencken approved him. Important novelists such as Theodore Dreiser and Sinclair Lewis were also lined up in Sandburg's camp. In time, the photographer Alfred Stieglitz, the painter Georgia O'Keeffe, and the architect Frank Lloyd Wright would weigh in with praise. He was invited to write poems to order for Thanksgiving and for Christmas—and accepted. He was making the transition from writer to performer.

Miss Niven says that Sandburg found "his subject in poetry at last, and through this burning subject, his voice"; she also tells us that "Sandburg was growing toward a poetry as unorthodox and independent as his politics." Perhaps this is the place to say that Sandburg's poetry was not very unorthodox, and his politics not all that independent. Both were essentially sentimental. In his politics, Sandburg was for the People: the little man, the worker, the downtrodden, the ground-down. He was never a Communist, nor was he, like so many American socialists, against American entry into World War I or II. Honorable enough; but when his sentimental political views got into his poetry—and they were the very subject of his poetry—problems inevitably resulted.

In his poetry, as in his politics, he did not have a mind that much liked to go into things. He was always satisfied to stop at the middle distance. "He works in a large, loose medium," the poet Conrad Aiken once wrote, "inextricably mixing the vivid with the false." Sandburg had no real appetite for complexity. He never went very deep—no deeper, really, than the folk songs he sang and eventually anthologized in a best-selling collection he called *The American Songbag*. When his book-length poem *The People, Yes* came out in 1936, Robert Frost objected: "Sandburg is wrong, I say: The People, *Yes,* and *No!*"

Sandburg's reputation, then, did not grow anywhere near so steadily among serious poets and critics as it did in popular circles. Ezra Pound, the Diaghilev of the modern movement in poetry, invited Sandburg to contribute to an anthology, but also said he was not "sure whether your 'Chicago' wouldn't hit harder if it began six lines later and ended five lines sooner." Still, he granted Sandburg his place. Among other American poets, although Archibald MacLeish continued to think well of Sandburg's verse, Frost once remarked that Sandburg's was the only poetry he knew that figured to gain by translation. When the New Criticism came into prominence in the 1940s, Sandburg's prestige dropped further. His rolling rhythms and his garrulity could not hold up under the sort of intense scrutiny practiced by the New Critics.

Read today, Sandburg's poems reveal a dismal sameness. They exhibit mastery over a faded slang, the idiom of a day now done; rhythmically, they still have richness of a kind, which allows them to roll on and on, but with a feeling of uniform thinness. Gertrude Stein once said of the novelist Glenway Wescott that his writing has "a certain syrup but it does not pour"; Sandburg's poetry pours and pours but has hardly any syrup whatsoever. "O prairie mother, I am one of your boys," runs a line in *Cornhuskers*. Clichés run through his verse like calories through cheesecake: see, for instance, "White Ash," a poem about a lonely hooker with a heart of gold. The note of political optimism goes off, gong-like, in several poems: "Man will yet win / Brother may yet line up with brother." Reading Sandburg's poems, one begins better to understand what Valéry meant when he said that "the optimist is always a bad writer."

Reviewing Sandburg's *Collected Poems* in the September 1951 issue of *Poetry*, William Carlos Williams wrote: "In this massive book covering a period of close to forty years the poems show no development in the thought, in the technical handling of the material, in the knowledge of the forms, the art of treating the line." Williams said of "Chicago" that Sandburg's "first brilliantly successful poem should have been his last." And he closed: "*The Collected Poems* make a dune-like mass; no matter where you dig into them it is sand."

By the time Williams wrote that review, Sandburg was well out of—well above—the poetry wars. He had long before then acquired the status of a national treasure. (His editor, upon the publication of *The People, Yes*, told him that the people "damned near owe you a national holiday.") He was, most famously, the author of a huge biography of Lincoln, a work which had proved an enormous commercial success. "The poets have always understood Lincoln," wrote the historian Henry Steele Commager, "from Whitman to Emerson to Lindsay and Benét, and it is fitting that from the pen of a poet has come the greatest of all Lincoln biographies. One of the great biographies of our literature."

Sandburg's monumental portrait of Lincoln—it runs to more than 4,500 pages and eventually appeared in six volumes— was, from the standpoint of his reputation, a beautiful stroke. The great prairie poet writing the life of the great prairie politician—it was a match made, if not in heaven, then in a publicity office. There were, to be sure, critics. According to Edmund Wilson, in reading it "there are moments when one is tempted to feel that the cruelest thing that has happened to Lincoln since he was shot by Booth has been to fall into the hands of Carl Sandburg." But the effect of the biography on Sandburg's career was to connect him with Lincoln in a way that made him seem not only the repository of all Lincolnesque wisdom but the keeper of the Lincoln flame and chief representative of the tradition of our greatest American. As Sandburg poeticized Lincoln, so this biography seemed, in the public mind, to have Lincolnized Carl Sandburg.

I have not read the six-volume *Abraham Lincoln,* but even in the one-volume edition, which I have read, the work seems to sprawl. It has the characteristic thinness that goes along with Sandburg's penchant for viewing everything at a distance, for making everything he writes about seem legendary, almost mythical. He was more omniscient than even an omniscient narrator is permitted to be. The feeling of falseness that results is not tempered by the heavily empurpled prose:

> He [the young Lincoln] was growing as inevitably as summer corn in Illinois loam. Leaning against the doorpost of a store to which few customers came he was growing, in silence, as corn grows.

Of Lincoln's courtship of Ann Rutledge:

> They were both young, with hope endless, and it could have been he had moments when the sky was to him a sheaf of blue dreams and the rise of the blood-gold red of a full moon in the evening was almost too much to live, see, and remember.

Sandburg developed a style that seems to call for slides to accompany it.

By the time Sandburg finished his Lincoln biography he was receiving between two hundred and four hundred fan letters a week, which he answered by using variants of thirteen different, rather folksy, form letters. He had more invitations for speaking engagements than he could hope to handle, yet he continued to accept a great many of them. Once, he needed these speaking engagements to keep his family afloat financially. "Without the platform work, of which the guitar and songs are a part," he told the critic Malcolm Cowley, who teased him about appearing before a Junior League audience, "I could not get by for a living while doing the sort of long-time books I am on." Yet as the People's Poet, Lincoln's Boswell, guru, general sage, and television personality, Sandburg also evidently derived genuine pleasure from his public appearances.

They were extraordinary performances. His was, as we nowadays say, a tight act. I caught it one night in the mid-1950s at the University of Illinois, where Sandburg easily filled the school's largest hall. Powerful applause greeted his appearance, thunderous applause his closing. One sensed that one was watching both a historical personage and a performer who was a pro. Sandburg wore a plain black suit and a string tie (if memory serves), and his face—high cheekbones, deep-set eyes—looked sufficiently historical to have come off the carving on the side of a mountain.

Sandburg began by reading a number of poems, offering brief commentaries upon each. He let fly short, haiku-like apothegms of a populist kind. And then he picked up his guitar and out came "John Henry" and other brass oldies. When he was done, there could not have been an unsatisfied customer in the house.

The magic was in the voice. Years before that night in Champaign-Urbana, Ben Hecht remembered: "It was a voice of pauses and undercurrents, with a hint of anger always in it, and a lilt of defiance in its quiet tones. It was a voice that made words sound fresh, and clothed the simplest of sentences with mysteries." That voice had become oiled and under even better control over the years. Sandburg worked his audience consummately.

Then there was his hair. Writers with a taste for cliché were not above referring to Sandburg as "the silver-thatched poet." Lank and clean and white, Sandburg's hair was easily the most impressive of his props. Robert Frost once remarked in a letter to a friend that Sandburg "was possibly hours in town and he spent one of those washing his white hair and toughening his expression for his public performance." Another time, Frost reportedly told someone that Sandburg was upstairs fixing his hair, "trying to get it in his eyes." I am reminded of the story of the journalist who was exasperated with Brendan Bracken, Churchill's minister of information. One day he told Bracken off: "Nothing about you is to be believed, nothing is as it seems. Even your hair, which looks so false—it turns out to be real."

What, Sandburg was once asked, was it like to be famous? "It's like a communicable disease," he replied, "nothing can be done about it." Certainly he himself did nothing about it, except to soak it up for what it was worth. Even the uncritical Miss Niven concedes:

> During the last decade of his life, [Sandburg] was a full-time celebrity, and only a part-time writer. Many people clamored for his attention, sought to superimpose his venerable image on television shows, advertisements, causes, prefaces to books, public occasions, motion pictures. His life was a public circus of entertainment and pilgrimages. . . .

The sententious garrulity that was always part of Sandburg's writing grew worse with age. When his verse came under attack by critics and fellow poets, the People's Poet looked to the people for self-justification. Modern poets, he averred, the sort of poets vaunted by his enemies the New Critics, were anti-democratic, writing not for the people but for each other. "I say to hell with the new poetry," was his view at seventy-five. Poets today "don't want poetry to say what it means. They have symbols and abstractions and a code amongst themselves—sometimes I think it's a series of ear wigglings." His own poetry, he concluded, because it had a wider audience, must have been better.

Sandburg died at the age of eighty-nine, wealthy, revered, easily the most famous living poet in America, and soon to be almost entirely, if not quite forgotten, unread. He had had a tremendous roll of the dice. Now his work is quite as inert as he. As a young man, in 1909, in a column for the *Milwaukee Journal,* Sandburg unconsciously wrote his own epitaph: "America has many businessmen but no poets. The reason for this is that we are a nation of hustlers and no poet can be a hustler." Funny, the things a man, over a long life, can forget.

Maurice Baring and
the Good Highbrow

I N *The Puppet Show of Memory,* his autobiography,
Maurice Baring mentions a cupboard set on the
landing between the first and second floors of the
country estate of his Russian friends the Benckendorffs, a cupboard filled with Tauchnitz novels of various ages and other
splendid books, so that, on the way to bed, in the darkness,
one could reach into the cupboard and always be certain of
finding something good to read. Would any of Maurice Baring's fifty-odd books have qualified for that wonderful cupboard? But perhaps an anterior, and more rudimentary, question
needs first to be asked, such as: Who was Maurice Baring?

Maurice Baring's is a name one generally meets connected
in a secondary or tertiary way with larger names. There he
stands in a photograph between his friends Chesterton and
Belloc. Here he is drawn as a caricature by Max Beerbohm
("Mr. Maurice Baring," the caption reads, "testing carefully
the Russian sense of humour," as a tall, stooped, mustachioed
man stares into the entirely uncomprehending face of a mou-
jik). There he pops up in the journals of A. C. Benson, Arnold
Bennett, Virginia Woolf, and Chips Channon. Here he is in
the letters of Evelyn Waugh and Lady Diana Cooper. There
he is as a minor figure in the Ann Thwaite biography of Edmund
Gosse. Here he is, on his own at last, in an admirable anthol-

ogy of his vast writings, *Maurice Baring Restored,* lovingly (it
does not go too far to say) edited and introduced by Paul Horgan. There he goes—gone, one might almost say, forever—in
a somewhat chilly essay of the 1960s by Edmund Wilson, "How
Not to Be Bored by Maurice Baring," the title of which makes
the problem sound perhaps more grueling than it in fact is.

In a letter written in 1859 from Berlin, where he was then a
student, Henry Adams writes of doing business with the Baring Brothers Bank. It was into this family of merchant bankers,
founded in 1740, that Maurice Baring was born in 1874, the
seventh of eight children. In her recent biography of Baring,
Emma Letley, who is his grandniece, makes plain how powerful a family the Barings were: "well established in the City,
at court, in European society." A Baring had served as viceroy
of India; another, a later, Baring was governor of Southern
Rhodesia and then governor of Kenya; yet another Baring, a
forceful man known for his statesmanship in Egypt, was called,
in a pun that was as inevitable as it was irresistible, "Over-
Baring." Only in a family of such furious achievers does Maurice Baring, with his continuous outpouring of books, seem
rather unambitious.

Anyone anticipating a dark side to the Baring family's record
of achievement will be disappointed. No devilish or besotted
father lurks in the foreground, no sly and heavily cozening
mother aft, venting her twisted frustrations on her children.
The Barings were not only rather eminent but by most accounts
quite nice Victorians. By his own account, Maurice Baring's
upbringing was as bracing as the best champagne and twice as
bubbly. He recalls his own boyhood as a fairyland. At Membland, one of the family's houses, there was a tennis court, a
yacht, a steam launch, a telegraph, lovely food, a nearly continuous flow of interesting relatives and friends. "Welcome ever
smiled at Membland," Maurice Baring wrote in *The Puppet
Show of Memory,* "and farewell went out with a sigh."

A many-servanted household, the Baring's, and Maurice's

early education came from a series of kindly governesses and servants. "I learned to read very quickly," he wrote, "in French first." His father spoke French, German, and Spanish, "not only easily, but naturally, without effort or affectation" (Maurice must have inherited his own facility with languages from him) and had much poetry by heart. His mother was musical. Culture was in the oxygen among the Barings. "I believe children absorb more *Kultur* from stray grown-up conversation they hear than they learn from books," wrote Baring, himself the recipient of vast quantities of such culture. Ronald Knox thought Maurice Baring seemed the least absorbed and the most retentive of readers. His nature, Knox wrote, "was one which constantly absorbed, as it constantly exuded, something which (for want of a less abused word) you can only label 'culture.' "

Maurice Baring, whose dates are 1874–1945, lived through a remarkable stretch of history, having been old enough to have met men who fought at Waterloo, to have had an aunt who played her harp for Lord Byron, to have had other relatives (intense verbal conservatives) who preferred to say cowcumbers instead of cucumbers, to have seen Sarah Bernhardt when she was in her prime, to have been a boy when *Treasure Island* was first published. With a generous father, a mother whose favorite he was said to have been, the best schooling, many natural gifts, not least among them a felicitous talent for friendship, Maurice Baring would seem to dispute Hemingway's dictum that the first requisite for a writer is an unhappy childhood.

And yet a shadow falls across some of the things that Maurice Baring wrote, as it seems to have fallen across his life, that makes one wonder if, in a reflective and largely spectatorial life, even all the advantages are sufficient. Not that Baring ever complained. Not from him do you hear the by now almost standard English literary rant about that absolute hell that was school days. Although not an athlete, Baring enjoyed Eton, as he wrote in an essay in *Lost Lectures,* "whole-heartedly and unreservedly: I enjoyed it all from the first to the last moment." The "tyranny of the intellect," as he referred to it, did not prevail at Eton; he claimed that "rule of the intellect is far severer than that of athletes." What did prevail was the freedom the school gave to its students to go off and do pretty much as they wished. Along with freedom went a sweet eccentricity, of the kind provided by such masters as Arthur C. Benson, who "would have preferred Shakespeare to have written novels" (it's an interesting notion), and the Vice Provost, F. W. Warre Cornish, who, as Baring would later write, "pulled some of the weeds, or did his best to, out of my mind and taught me things that were worth knowing in life." Baring won the Prince Consort Prize while at Eton for work in French. He was a lifelong champion of the school, and said of it that "Eton teaches those who teach themselves," which is, of course, the best that any school can hope to accomplish.

After Eton, Baring went off to Cambridge, where, Miss Letley says, "he was on the edge of the small intellectual world of the Society of Apostles." At Cambridge Baring kept his literary aspirations for the most part under wraps. When the Baring Brothers Bank suffered a serious reversal, the plan was for Maurice to enter the Diplomatic Service. This meant passing quite difficult examinations in a number of different subjects— among them mathematics of a fairly serious kind—as well as being questioned orally in French, German, and Italian. To prepare for these examinations, Baring went off to Germany and later availed himself of the services of crammers in London. He also spent two terms in Oxford toward the end of preparation for his Diplomatic Service examinations. Twice he failed and only succeeded on his third, which would have been his final, attempt at the Diplomatic Service. This was in 1898, when he was twenty-four years old.

But this is to make Baring seem a grind, which he was far

from being. His long days at the crammers were followed by long nights, "distracted and dislocated by many amusements," as he put it in *The Puppet Show of Memory*. These included theatrical evenings put on by Mrs. Patrick Campbell, Eleanora Duse, and Sarah Bernhardt (to whom he later became a friend). There were balls and races and, in the summer, long English country weekends, "where a constellation of beauty moved in muslin and straw hats and yellow roses on the lawns of gardens designed by Lenôtre, delicious with ripe peaches on old brick walls, with the smell of verbena, and sweet geranium." During these years, Baring seemed to live the kind of life about which Henry James wrote. Artistically, the cold-shower morality of Ibsen was alternated with the steamy drama of Wagner, both then much the fashion among young English intellectuals. Time, too, was made for foreign travel. "We bathed in the Nile and smoked hashish," he writes of a visit with a friend to his uncle in Cairo.

Maurice Baring was also developing a small but genuine reputation as a mild eccentric, English schoolboy division. He was from the beginning extravagant with money, perhaps owing to his having grown up with so much of it about the house. At Cambridge he edited a few issues of an undergraduate magazine to which he contributed topsy-turvy fairy tales he called *Immoral Stories for Children,* in which kindly children are punished, unpleasant ones rewarded, and cheaters come out winners. (Sounds, it will be argued, more like stark realism.) Lanky, shambling, with a thick brown mustache, not yet billiard-ball bald as he was later to become, the young Maurice Baring had blue eyes and a cackling laugh and easy erudition. His friend Eddie Marsh, with whom he was at Cambridge, wrote in his memoirs: "I don't think I ever saw Maurice actually reading a book—he would pick one up, peck at it like a thrush at a worm, and soon put it down again; but there must have been some process of 'inward penetration.'" Late in the pages of Baring's novel *Cat's Cradle,* a rather dim minor figure appears who, *mutatis mutandis,* seems reminiscent of the youthful Maurice Baring:

> Among the guests at Alton-Leigh there was a young man who had just come down from Oxford, called Horace Crane. He had been at Magdalen College and was a good scholar, but had not done as well as was expected. He had enjoyed life too much, and, although neither sporting nor athletic, he had had friends in both those camps, and in those camps only. He preferred them to the more serious or the more artistic. At the same time, he was a great reader. His friends suspected him of writing verse, in secret. He was untidy and short-sighted, and he had a round, good-natured face like the moon, and an infectious laugh.

Maurice Baring remained, as did so many Englishmen of his generation and after, something of a schoolboy for life. He corresponded his life long with one of his tutors in verse (in triolets, specifically). His whimsy, surely, was very much that of the schoolboy. When, for example, he was required to spell out his name for people over the telephone, he would exclaim: "B for Beastly, A for Apple, R for Rotten, I for England, N for Nothing, G for God." Eddie Marsh remembers him at a post office in Florence insisting that the stamps he purchase be "freschi" (fresh), since "they were for an invalid." (Non-sequiturial humor, to be sure, is not everyone's cup of claret.) As a university student, he partook in much throwing of food and wine; and, at Oxford, where he spent two terms after work at the crammer's, he and his friends used to buy wine that they referred to as "throwing port."

Later, working as an unpaid attaché at the British Embassy in Paris, Baring found himself engaged in what, in his book of essays *Lost Lectures,* he calls "the Battle of the Inkpots," in which he and a young third secretary threw every inkpot, black and red, they could find at each other, so that, at the battle's end, "not only were the staff drenched with ink, red and black, but so was the Chancery carpet, the staircase and the walls." He and the third secretary, who later went on to become an ambassador, "were sent for [by the Chancellor], and with terse acidity he told us we were nothing better than dirty little schoolboys." Not far off, perhaps.

Although Baring would hold minor diplomatic posts in Copenhagen and Rome, he soon enough discovered that the life of the diplomat was not for him. He had written smallish things through his youthful stint in the Diplomatic Service, and a part of him longed to be able to write full-time. Years before he had been encouraged by Edmund Gosse, the English man of letters, who praised an essay on Anatole France that Baring had written for *The Yellow Book,* telling him, in Baring's words, that "there was a unique opportunity for anyone who should make it his aim and business to write gracefully and delicately about beautiful and distinguished things, and that I could not do better than try to continue as I had begun." His love for Russia, too, contributed indirectly to his decision to give up the Diplomatic Service in favor of the writing life, for in Russia, which he first visited in 1901, staying with the diplomatist Count Benckendorff, everybody seemed "to live in such simplicity and without any paraphernalia at all," and in Russia, where the pace was deliciously slow, "there seemed to be no time." So smitten by his Russian visit was Baring that, as he would later note, "I resolved firstly to learn Russian, and, secondly, to go back there as soon as I could."

It was Baring's knowledge of the Russian language, which he acquired over the next few years, that permitted him to exit manfully from the Diplomatic Service into the literary life. While still a diplomat in Rome, he used to stroll in the Pincio garden with Violet Paget, who wrote under the name of Vernon Lee and who was once the friend of Henry James, where they "spoke of the past and the future and built castles in the air, or smoked what Balzac called enchanted cigarettes, that is to say, talked of books that never would be written." But now the cigarettes need not be enchanted, for Baring had the freedom and time to write real books.

As someone who had begun reading the Russians in Russian, Baring first proposed to publishers to translate Dostoevsky and Gogol into English. But the interest was not yet there. The Russians were still considered dark barbarians, coarse and more than a little mad. (As late as 1913, Max Beerbohm was still able to mock the vogue for Russian literature by creating an all-purpose Russian writer named Kolniyatsch, of whom Beerbohm wrote that "his burning faith in a personal Devil, his frank delight in earthquakes and pestilences, and his belief that every one but himself will be brought back to life in time to be frozen in the next glacial epoch, seem rather to stamp him as an optimist.") But when Baring returned to (then still) czarist Russia in 1904, he found a wonderfully fluid society, with "no barriers, no rules, no obstacles." He was an early devotee of Stanislavsky's Moscow Art Theatre, which made the reputation of Chekhov as a playwright. So natural was the acting in the Art Theatre that, on one occasion, Baring remembered, a member of the audience sitting in a box engaged one of the actors in conversation that led to an argument.

At his friend Count Benckendorff's recommendation, Baring signed on with the London *Morning Post* to cover the Russo-Japanese War in Manchuria. In the looser newspaper days of that era, the first piece that Baring sent the *Morning Post* was about the Moscow Art Theatre's production of Chekhov's *Uncle Vanya*. Baring wrote it on his way to Manchuria, the scene of the war, in the third-class carriage of a Russian train. Traveling third-class became part of Baring's modus operandi, for, as he remarks in *The Puppet Show of Memory:* "It was now, in this railway carriage, that I for the first time came into intimate contact with the Russian people, for in a third-class railway carriage the artificial barriers of life are broken down, and

everyone treats everyone else as an equal." Wellborn and perfectly at ease in the most luxe settings, Baring seems always to
have survived quite nicely under the roughest conditions, which
speaks to his impressively balanced disposition. It also speaks
to his equanimity, very useful in a writer, in accepting and
appreciating the world however he found it.

Baring also had a talent for discovering the best in people,
which is open only to the imaginative. In Manchuria, he found
good sense among the Chinese and good nature among the
Cossacks. But he could also be tough when the occasion required
it. Meek-looking man though he seemed, he apparently suffered not the least fear under gunfire. He took war for what it
was: a nightmare, a disaster, and a triumph of spirit. "I thought
war is to man," he wrote, "what motherhood is to woman—a
burden, a source of untold suffering, and yet a glory." To a
true writer, which Baring was, nothing is a total loss, not even
death itself. Here, for example, is Baring in Manchuria the
morning after a battle, surveying a corpse-strewn field in the
company of a Russian officer, who points out a dead Japanese
soldier to him:

> He was lying with brown eyes wide open and showing his white
> teeth. But there was nothing grim or ghastly in that smile. It
> was miraculously beautiful; it was not the smile of inscrutable
> content which we see on certain statues of sleeping warriors
> such as that of Gaston de Foix at Milan, or Guidarello Guidarelli
> at Ravenna, but a smile of radiant joy and surprise, as if he had
> suddenly met with a friend for whom he had longed, above all
> things, at a moment when of all others he had needed him. Near
> him a Russian boy was lying, fair and curly-headed, with his
> head resting on one arm, as if he had fallen asleep like a tired
> child overcome with insuperable weariness, and had opened his
> eyes to pray to be left at peace just a little longer.

One is right to sense a religious note in this portrait of the
sleeping dead, for it was written after Maurice Baring's con-

version, in 1909, to Roman Catholicism, which he later called "the only action in my life which I am quite certain I have never regretted." The religious note in Baring's writing is neither dominant nor crucial yet still significant. In *Maurice Baring: A Postscript,* Baring's friend Laura Lovat recounts his hearing, near the end of his life, that François Mauriac had told Robert Speaight that "what I most admire about Baring's work is the sense he gives you of the penetration of grace," and thrilling to think that he meant the word in its theological sense, which Mrs. Lovat assured him Mauriac did indeed.

But before Baring's conversion to Catholicism he had converted to Russophilism. As the *Morning Post*'s correspondent first in Moscow and then later in St. Petersburg, Baring met such figures as P. A. Stolypin, who attempted to derail the Russian Revolution before it began, and Prince D. S. Mirski, the literary critic, who as minister of the interior in 1905 ended newspaper censorship in Russia: "the opening of a small skylight," as Baring would later report, "into a darkened room." Baring's view of the political situation in Russia during the first decade of the century was that "an incompetent government was being opposed by an ineffectual revolution."

Baring was spared having to see Lenin's Soviet Union, which, in destroying all that he loved about Russia, could not have been other than noxious to him. His was instead the Russia of Tolstoy and Goncharov, Turgenev and Chekhov—the writer's Russia of beauteous nature contending with "dirt, squalor, misery, slovenliness, disorder, and the uninspiring wooden provincial towns, the dusty or sodden roads, the frequent grey skies, the long and heavy sameness." In such books as *The Russian People,* he recognized in the Russian character a firm realism that distrusted all that was abstract and metaphysical and that fought endlessly against a too-great malleability and weakness of will—"the hard kernel in the soft fruit," as Baring described it. Like many an observer before him, Baring in the end was left puzzled by the mixture of opposite qualities in the

Russian character, though he never doubted that "the Russian soul is filled with a human Christian charity which is warmer in kind and intenser in degree, and expressed with a greater simplicity and sincerity than is to be met with in any other people."

About Russia's literature Baring's understanding was not only prescient but nearly perfect. He understood that Tolstoy and Dostoevsky were greater writers than Turgenev. He called the former two writers "the two great columns which support the temple of Russian literature," while Turgenev's place was within the temple itself. Although he was no great devotee of the modern, he knew precisely wherein the power of Chekhov resided, which was to show the "Russian soul crying out in the desert." He knew, too, that Chekhov's importance was not only artistic but also political, even though politics was never mentioned in any of his plays. He sensed that Russian romanticism, as represented by such writers as Pushkin and Lermontov, had an impressive realism at its center. Of Pushkin, he wrote:

> His diction is the inseparable skin of the thought. You seem to hear him thinking. He was gifted with divine ease and unpremeditated spontaneity. His soul was sincere, noble, and open; he was frivolous, a child of the world and of his century; but if he was worldly, he was human; he was a citizen as well as a child of the world; and it is that which makes him the greatest of Russian poets.

Maurice Baring was one of those Englishmen happiest in other countries and cultures. He found amusement where it was available and seems never to have been put off by hardship. In Constantinople in 1909, he is not at all surprised that Turks mishandle rifles; after all, the Turks he has seen cannot even properly use an umbrella. He tells of the extreme politeness (*politesse de coeur*) of the Turks, one of whom, after taking and lighting a cigarette from an English officer, explains that his brother did not accept the cigarette offered him because he does not smoke, adding, "I do not either." Baring was attracted to the whimsical yet was himself far from frivolous. In *The Puppet Show of Memory*, he provides an account of a cholera epidemic in a suburb outside Constantinople, which he encountered while covering the Balkan War; it is chilling in its ghastliness and understates what must have been his own quiet heroic efforts in aiding the dying. Baring was of that generation of Englishmen possessed of the stiff upper lip; in his case this is sometimes forgotten, because that same lip would often collapse into a boyish smile.

Baring became something of a permanent transient, with headquarters in London, wandering from country to country, picking up new languages and friends. Edmund Gosse, writing in the *Sunday Times,* called Baring "A Citizen of Europe," remarking that "as no language presents any difficulty to him, he is able to pursue his own line of imaginative thought wherever he finds it." Gosse called Baring "a complete cosmopolitan," which may be another way of saying that he was a man not quite at home anywhere.

Baring never married. His taste in women tended to alternate, as his biographer Emma Letley points out, between beauties and Sapphists, the (socially) smart and the intellectually clever. Miss Letley remarks on his close friendship with Nan Herbert, the sister to his friend Auberon Herbert, going nowhere; there was once talk, too, of a relationship with a French woman in Copenhagen. But Miss Letley seems not greatly interested in such questions, or in penetrating the depths of Baring's character generally. Baring befriended women; he tended, one gathers, to have felt more genuinely comfortable around women than men, but inevitably backed off at the point where things threatened to go beyond friendship. Perhaps in his sensitivity about the fragility of human relationships—which is the central subject of the novels—he felt constrained to view all marriages as ultimately destined to fail.

When World War I began, Baring joined the nascent Royal Flying Corps, not as a flier but as an administrative aide to two of the leading figures in the RFC (predecessor of the RAF). He worked as an odd-jobs man, quite heedless of his own interests and relentless in his determination and ability always to get the job done, no matter how complicated or grindingly boring. Baring worked chiefly for Lord Trenchard, who originally had doubts about him, thinking him an indolent, rich literary man. Yet after Baring's death, he wrote in the *Times* that Baring was "the most unselfish man I have ever met or am likely to meet," and quoted Marshal Foch, who had earlier said that "there never was a staff officer in any country, in any nation, in any century like Major Maurice Baring." Baring was oddly without ego, never requiring much in the way of glory or praise generally—oddly for a writer, that is.

It was after the war that Maurice Baring became a writer full-time. His elder brother John, the fourth Earl of Revelstoke, had taken over the Baring Brothers Bank, setting it in good order, and had given Maurice an allowance, which freed him, for a time at least, of the need to make his own living. Although he had already published a number of books of various kinds—books of travel writing, poetry, studies of Russian literature, works of whimsy—he now began to write novels in great earnestness, having published his first novel, *Passing By,* in 1921 at the age of forty-seven. He continued to turn out a great many other belletristic works and do a good deal of journalism. Wherever he went he added to his already large stock of friends. As Eddie Marsh wrote in his memoirs: "I cannot but believe that at the General Resurrection Maurice Baring . . . will be the most warmly greeted by the greatest number and variety of his fellow-creatures from every country and continent, and from every walk of life. Russian peons, German students, old women in China, all the *beaux mondes* of Europe, writers, painters, actors, and musicians from all winds, men, women, and children who have known him for a week or for a lifetime will rise up and embrace him with individual affection."

At first glimpse, one might conclude that Maurice Baring was one of those fortunate writers favored both by talent and in life. He never appears to have felt the need to thrust himself forward. Certainly he seems to have been, if it be not oxymoronic to say so, impressively self-effacing. Yet for all his tranquillity, Ethel Smyth, the operatic singer who wrote an early biography of her friend Maurice Baring, concluded that "he can never have had one happy affair"; and Miss Letley remarks that "there is not one unqualifiedly happy affair in his fiction, and I am reasonably certain this is also true of his life." Anthony Powell, commenting on Baring's penchant for practical jokes, suggests that "there was something a bit uneasy in Baring's psychological make-up."

Anthony Powell speculates that Maurice Baring might have died a virgin. Technical evidence—what might it be?—on either side of the question isn't available. But there is something virginal that permeates Baring's writing. I do not mean by this that there is anything prissy about it, or secretly homosexual, but instead something distanced, something less than fully engaged by life, however much its author may be amused by life or even enamored of it, and Baring was both. The other side of this rare coin is the gift of perspective, about his own talents and much else. There seems not to have been the least competitive impulse in Baring. Whether his religion conferred this sweet passivity on Baring, or whether it was his stay against what he took to be life's hopelessness, cannot be known. The most generous explanation of Baring's extraordinary character is set out by Laura Lovat. "Perhaps one explanation," she writes, "was that with the maturity of much experience, the virtuosity of genius, the culture of great scholarship and the modesty of a saint, [Maurice] maintained, until the hour of his death, the mind of a child who walked through life's joys and sorrows with a deep conviction that he was always holding God's hand."

Reading Baring's novels, one sees the influence of the religious approach to life on literature, and discovers both its strengths and weaknesses. The first thing that must be noted about these novels, though, is their great flow. "Prose ought to be alive with rhythm," says a character in Baring's novel *C,* "however simple or complicated it may be." And Baring's novels are alive with rhythm, usually that provided by clear, clean, short declarative sentences. On they flow, onward, it sometimes seems, and a little beyond onward. Arnold Bennett, in his *Journal,* notes for Saturday, January 2, 1926: "I finished Baring's *Cat's Cradle* at 5:45 P.M. 720 big pages. It's curious fault is that it reads as if it really had happened: a report of actual events. It has taken me 14 days to read." Paul Horgan describes Baring's style well when he says that his prose has "the tone of a cultivated and sympathetically intelligent man talking gossip rapidly and evenly, in a level voice, with never a hesitation to choose between ways to say things, but simply running on to capture a sense of life because life—any life—is so important to catch before it is gone."

The fault Bennett points out is indeed a curious but also a true one. In one sense, Maurice Baring's novels are too much like life. The largish ones—*C, Cat's Cradle*—resemble life in presenting, so to say, just one damn thing after another. New characters can be introduced as late as page 650; characters crucial to plots inexplicably sicken and die. Baring can be deft and inept almost on the same page. Evelyn Waugh remarked, in a letter to Lady Diana Cooper, on Baring's carelessness in lapsing into clichés, which he thought "the curse of the polyglot." But just when one gets down on him, Baring can surprise by doing something brilliant in only a few strokes, such as the woman at a dinner party in *C*—and there are lots of dinner parties in Baring novels—who was "a middle-aged, hardened diner-out, [who] did not need to be talked to; she only wished to talk, and she never noticed if anyone listened or not." In his novels, Baring could kill more quickly than a cobra, and here, in *The Lonely Lady of Dulwich*, he does the job in one lively, lilting sentence, thus: "But just as she was ready to be taken out in London, Oliver Mostyn died of a cold caught at a race-meeting, much to the regret of a number of friends, especially those who played whist with him at his club, where he managed to lose everything except his temper." His novels are often nicely studded, too, with aphorisms of a high quality, as when he remarks, in the same novel, of male jealousy that "it is not what people do that makes men jealous, but what they are." A subsidiary character in *Cat's Cradle* remarks that "there is no such thing as a 'wonderful' woman. But men think there are, and that's just as well."

"A novel must not be too life-like," says another Baring character, "or else where does the artist come in?" He comes in, in Maurice Baring's case, in the larger vision. This vision, from one who was so generally pleasant in life, turns out to be rather dark. Paul Horgan, who is an excellent commentator upon Baring's work, notes that in his novels "love's image is linked to fatality, and never seems safe, as real things seem safe. Nothing is certain, except that love is equally a gift of the gods and a curse." Whether or not this is precisely so, it is a view that compelled Baring to write what are essentially love stories with unhappy endings. As the protagonist of *C* says, speaking, it seems safe here to say, for Baring:

> The point of life is—I think—its imperfection. The point of human beings to me is that they are full of faults and weaknesses and wickedness—it is because of all that that they are human, made up of a thousand things: defects, qualities, idiosyncrasies, tricks, habits, crotchets, hobbies, little roughnesses and queer pitfalls, unexpected quaintnesses: unexpected goodness, and unexpected badness; take all that away, and what is left? Nothing that I want to see again.

A character in *Cat's Cradle* finds "human life is *almost* intolerable, but not quite." The heroine of that novel tells a priest that "I don't feel strong enough, well-equipped enough to deal with life." To which he responds: "We none of us feel that, because we none of us are." "I'm human, Bernard," the same woman says later, "not reasonable." And neither, any serious reader of Baring's novels comes to understand, is life reasonable. Of another character in the same novel, his mother, seeing him about to make a terrible mistake, thinks: "He would have to go to the school of life like every one else. There was no escape from sorrow, misery, and pain; or, rather, man confined in those dungeons is forced to make his own rope-ladder, to climb the spiked walls, and with scarred and bleeding feet to reach 'lasting freedom.' " What constitutes "lasting freedom" in a Baring novel is not always clear. Sometimes it is easeful death; sometimes it is true faith, for those of Baring's characters who are settled in their Catholicism—and in his novels these are often minor characters—have an admirable serenity about them. Serenity, mind you, not happiness. Nor is true conversion open to all, even among those who seek it.

Much evidence exists that Baring himself died, not without pain, in serenity. Toward the end of his life he had Parkinson's disease (so much more vividly put in the French: *paralysie agitans*). When World War II began, owing to the fear of bombing, he had to leave his house in Rottingdean to stay—until death, as it turned out—with his friends the Lovats in Scotland. In her memoir, Laura Lovat speaks of his kindness to her children, to servants, to visiting servicemen, and to anyone else he encountered. He kept a bird, a blue budgerigar named Dempsey, which not infrequently perched on his quite bald head. He took immense pleasure from music, he worked at minor literary tasks, and he died eleven days before Christmas, in 1945, quietly and in his religion. His own was a happier ending than that provided by most of his novels.

Maurice Baring is today out of print, out of fashion, literarily out of luck. For those who have never read him, perhaps the best introduction is through Paul Horgan's *Maurice Baring*

Restored, a book of 1970 that is itself out of print but often found on the shelves of used-book stores. Mr. Horgan's well-selected volume gives an excellent sense of both Baring's quality and his extraordinary variety. (Perhaps it is the one book of Baring's that ought to go into Count Benckendorff's cupboard.) The only criticism that I would make about this admirable book is that Mr. Horgan, writing more than twenty years ago, predicted a modest surge in Baring's reputation. "A general restoration of Maurice Baring as a contributor to the continuing stream of literature in England seems not far off," Mr. Horgan wrote. Today it seems, if anything, rather farther off than it did in 1970.

In his lifetime, Baring's reputation was greater in France than in England. So at least Desmond MacCarthy once told Harold Nicolson, who quoted him in his diary apropos of Baring: "Desmond says, 'The English do not appreciate subtlety unless it is underlined. Maurice wrote so smoothly that the English swallowed him like junket, not realising how much flavor there really was. The French do not bolt things as we do; they keep the junket in their mouths for a while, and thus appreciate the flavor.' " Baring had other English appreciators: Max Beerbohm claimed to treasure all his books, with the exception of those about Russia, which he, Beerbohm, admitted may have been his own blind spot, and paid him the honor of a charming parody in his *Christmas Garland*. Evelyn Waugh gave Baring his due, saying that "what Maurice had was a haunting love of failure and sense of the inextricable intercalation of human lives which is impressive." In the United States, Edmund Wilson allowed that "Baring was a fine connoisseur of writing and an excellent guide to style."

And yet, for all that, reading and thinking about Maurice Baring, one cannot but conclude that everything about him seems, in the contemporary literary situation, quite impossible. To be sure, Baring had difficulties in his own day. He felt reviewers never grasped his point: "He is praising me for what isn't there," he told Laura Lovat about a misguided review, "I must explain." It wasn't always easy for him to get publishers for his books, though the firm of William Heinemann Ltd. did bring out a collected edition of his work in the 1930s. But the notion of a man of letters such as Baring setting out, as Edmund Gosse advised, to write "gracefully and delicately about beautiful and distinguished things," would seem laughable in our day if it were not so sad. (Imagine such a formulation of one's aim on the application for a Guggenheim Fellowship in 1992.) If Baring were alive today, publishers would have nothing to do with him; he would find no place in any university; it is doubtful that he could command the attention of even a few hundred readers.

In his essay "High Brows and Low Brows," Baring wrote: "I mean by the good high-brow, the man who is well educated and glad of the fact without thrusting it down other people's throats, who, without being ashamed of his knowledge, his intellectual or artistic superiority, or his gifts and aptitudes, does not use them as a rod to beat others with, and does not think that because he is the fortunate possessor of certain rare gifts or talents, he is therefore a better or a more useful man: such is the good high-brow." Baring continued: "My point is that the more of these there are the better for the nation, the better for all of us. When there shall be no more of them, it will mean the end of civilisation."

In this essay, Baring obviously could not have known that he was speaking not only precisely to the posthumous condition of his own writing, but, in a wider view, even more poignantly to the artistic and intellectual life of our own day. To put it in the cant language of environmentalism, when we talk about good high-brows of the kind Baring had in mind, we are no longer talking about an endangered but about an all-but-extinct species.

First Person Singular

T
HE BEST TIME to write one's autobiography, surely, is on one's deathbed. Leaving aside the technical problem of getting the job done—all those inter- ruptions from medicos, clergymen, florists, relatives—just before death, assuming one isn't squirming in pain, is likely to pro- vide one's best shot at understanding one's own life, if not, granted, life itself. Writing one's autobiography at the very close of one's life would also give the story a nice rounded-off qual- ity—a sense, as Dr. Kermode has it, of an ending. Before the end, after all, one is likely to have too much to defend and too much to hide, likely to be too worried about tact and about the tactics of one's own little career. But there, on one's death- bed, one can at last say—the hope is, with easeful breath—oh, screw it, let 'er rip, I shall tell the truth at last.

Until that time, though, truth about one's self and one's relationships with the people close to one is not usually freely expressed. Freud said that biographical truth was unavailable. Henry James thought that biography tended to flatten out life and make it thinner than in reality it is. And this, recall, is biography they were talking about. As for autobiography, Orwell, whose specialty was never that of putting things gently, said that "autobiography is only to be trusted when it reveals something disgraceful. A man who gives a good account of himself is probably lying, since any life when viewed from inside is simply a series of defeats."

Yet, theoretically, writing autobiography ought not to be so horrendously difficult. The autobiographer, as Leslie Stephen long ago pointed out, has "*ex officio* two qualifications of supreme importance in all literary work. He is writing about a topic in which he is keenly interested, and about a topic upon which he is the highest authority." Autobiography, according to Stephen, also allows one to give way to "an irresistible longing for confidential expansion," which was that very superior late Victorian's elegantly euphemistic way of referring to the pleasure of spilling the beans. True, not everyone has the same quantity of beans to spill, and then, too, not all beans are equally delectable. Yet the urge at some point to spill them doubtless resides in most of us. All this being so, one would think there would be a great deal of first-class autobiography around.

There isn't. Nor has there ever been. The problem of lying by way of moral self-aggrandizement that Orwell alluded to plays a role here. The knowledge that one has been a miserable failure, and probably a creep into the bargain, is not easily made public, and this is part of the problem. (All autobiographies, it has been noted, tend to grow dull at exactly the point where the autobiographer has achieved success.) Withholding evidence is a more serious part of the problem. But even this might be surmounted, or so one might think, if one didn't often withhold evidence even from oneself. Dostoevsky, that perpetual drag on optimism, put the matter with damnable perfection when he wrote:

> Every man has reminiscences which he would not tell to everyone, but only to his friends. He has other matters in his mind which he would not reveal even to his friends, but only to himself, and that in secret. But there are other things which a man is afraid to tell even himself, and every man has a number of such things in his mind.

As if this weren't troublesome enough, one recognizes that the cards dealt one in life present further obstacles on the Damascene road to truth. The cards I have in mind are called parents (face cards, those), one's sex (low clubs), social class (diamonds), religion, nationality, toss in geography within one's nationality (hearts all). Add to this the distinct prospect of getting one's own story confused with other people's stories, a prospect perhaps greater than at any other time in the past, since there appears to be a vast quantity of such stories afloat just now. By other people's stories I mean the competing stories put forth by psychoanalysis, Marxism, feminism, you name it, many of which are there to be adopted by the pliant-minded as their very own. Every psychoanalysand is, after all, merely a prone autobiographer, with the main themes of his story having already been foretold by that dogmatic, cigar-smoking gentleman from Vienna. Fresh stories of this generic kind are put into play with fair regularity. A psychiatrist of my acquaintance tells me that nowadays, owing to the publicity that child-abuse stories have received on television and in the press, a large number of patients under psychiatric care are combing their pasts searching for child abuse in their own lives. Surprise, surprise, with only a little stretch of the imagination, a little twist of personal history, not a few find it.

The cards one is dealt in life have a way of occluding, channeling, shaping the facts of one's life to the point where it is not always certain they can any longer be called facts. The potential motives for writing autobiography—ranging from the need for vengeance, to setting down for the record what a winsome fellow one is, to being a writer with nothing else in mind to write at the present time—are as great as those for going on with life itself. Alas, despite one's belief in objective truth, one has to allow the distinct possibility that there may be no autobiographical truth but only a handful of splendid autobiographies.

Odd, but very few of these really splendid autobiographies

have been written by novelists, poets, and playwrights. Saint Augustine, Cellini, Rousseau, Gibbon, Franklin, Mill, Alexander Herzen, Henry Adams, the men who wrote the monumental autobiographical works, were none of them primarily imaginative literary artists. Henry James, that consummate artist, botched his two volumes of autobiography, *A Small Boy and Others* and *Notes of a Son and Brother*—botched them insofar as they have no real standing as discrete works of art, but are of interest chiefly as Jamesian curiosities. How strange that Henry James, surely the greatest master of introspection the world has known, should fail at autobiography, which, at its best, is primarily the art of introspection.

Perhaps there is something about autobiography that discomfits literary artists. Literary artists, it has been said, use up their autobiographical experience, in more or less transmuted form, in their poems and plays, stories and novels. But the truth is that, in the use of experience, artists have been great recyclers long before the term recycling was invented. Why not run the same material through once more, this time non-fictionally or non-poetically, in one's autobiography? Many a literary artist has tried, but not generally with impressive results. Vladimir Nabokov's lovely autobiography, *Speak, Memory,* seems to me a notable exception, though it is a work driven by a deep nostalgic yearning for a lost country. But so overwhelmingly is this the case that one is inclined to think that perhaps autobiography and pure art are if not antithetical then less than compatible, and the better the artist the poorer the autobiographer he is likely to prove. To cite only two fairly recent examples, Anthony Powell, whose novels can be so greatly pleasing, wrote four volumes of autobiography that, for dullness, could bring sleep to an insomnia ward. Evelyn Waugh, who hadn't an uninteresting sentence in him, wrote, in *A Little Learning,* a single, most disappointing volume of autobiography.

My own two-cent theory holds that artists don't finally believe in autobiography; deep down they don't hold with it, as an earlier generation used to say, as a sufficiently worthy vessel of truth-telling. They don't hold with it principally because they sense, if they do not absolutely know, that there is a higher truth than that offered by the pedestrian but necessary factuality demanded by autobiography. Or, as Goethe wrote in *Fiction and Truth:* "A fact of our existence is of value not insofar as it is true, but insofar as it has something to signify." Only in art do all facts signify.

Not all but a fair part of the pleasure of reading autobiography is in catching the autobiographer out in suspicious reticences, self-serving misperceptions, cover-ups, and, of course, delightfully clever deceptions. What's he hiding, what's he withholding, why doesn't he talk about his first wife, who's he kidding leaving out his children, odd he never mentions money—such are the questions that roam randomly through the mind of your normally licentious reader of autobiography. An intelligent person reads autobiography for two things: for the facts and for the lies, knowing that the lies are often more interesting than the facts. From the other side, that of the writer, if you make yourself look good in your autobiography, you seem a hypocrite; own up to being a swine, you will have no difficulty finding people who will readily enough believe you. Not a game at which it is easy to win, autobiography.

This is not to say that the appetite for reading autobiography isn't very strong. Certainly it is with me, so much so that autobiography is the only kind of book I should rather read than write. (I have myself long ago decided never to write an autobiography, preferring to spend my own autobiography, in nickels and dimes, in essays, memoirs, and anecdotes.) The appetite for autobiography reaches quite across the brows, from high to appallingly low. Hence the vast sums laid out by publishers for the life stories—"self-biographies," Isaac D'Israeli called them—of such men and women far on the other side of the literary divide as Norman Schwartzkopf and Magic Johnson, Katharine Hepburn and the Mayflower Madame. Which reminds me that a friend of mine, who works on celebrity autobiographies, was simultaneously writing the autobiographies of Tip O'Neill, former Speaker of the House, and the Mayflower Madame, speaker of a house of another kind. I worried for him throughout these projects, fearful that he might mix up his galleys.

I have just read six autobiographies—one of these of two volumes, together running to more than 850 pages. Three of these are by Englishmen, three by very different sorts of Americans. One of the latter is a woman and two among them are Southerners and set in the South, which, one sometimes feels, is another country unto itself. I have the feeling that none of my six autobiographers would at all wish to spend much time in the company of any of the others. As a reader, I can say that all have stepped into my little confessional, and, having now heard them out, I don't know what penance ought to be assigned to them. A wise guy might say that it was I who served the penance, having to read all these pages filled with disdain, chagrin, outrage, and petty vengeance. Still, reading autobiography, while it does not increase one's hope for the race, does lend vast amusement in watching it all pass in review from the rail.

What also emerges—though perhaps my selection of autobiographies has an oddly skewed bias in this direction—is that one is never too old to express resentment against one's parents. Not many kind words for parents here; very few parents in these books come off at all handsomely; grandparents, too, take a few good shots. It's almost as if their authors all subscribed to Philip Larkin's view in "This Be the Verse," a version of which perhaps needs to be rewritten for parents:

> You tick them off, your son and daughter.
> You may not mean to, but you do.

> In old age and even death, expect from them no quarter,
> Nothing but resentment, and all aimed just at you.

National differences might be the best place to begin. Auberon Waugh offers an interesting throwaway sentence in his autobiography, *Will This Do?,* which seems to me nicely to distinguish the differences between English and American autobiography in our day. The sentence runs: "Of all the qualities of the British, this readiness to mock and subvert is the one that makes life in Britain preferable to life anywhere else." Whether the readiness to mock and subvert makes life better is arguable, but I think it is undoubtedly true that a tone of subversive mockery has been the reigning one in English intellectual life for a goodly while now, dominant in English plays, novels, and journalism. I think that this tone would, after a bit, become something of a strain on those who live by it; I have been around Englishmen whose tone it is and I can vouch that those who go in for it in a big way grow tiresome fairly quickly. When this tone came into being—one that implies in its very inflection, "No crap gets past me, Jack"—can be dated with unusual precision. It dates, precisely, from 1954, which is the publication date of Kingsley Amis's second novel, *Lucky Jim.* What Holden Caulfield did for a vast number of American adolescents—give them a strong distaste for phoniness—Jim Dixon did, much more wittily, for generations of English intellectuals, with the results still to be seen nearly forty years later.

And now Kingsley Amis, *Lucky Jim*'s inventor, once an angry young man now at the age of seventy turned corpulent curmudgeon, has come forth with an autobiography of his own. Contemplation of such a book must have caused the old con-detector in Amis to twist a bit in his sheets. But he has met the problem head on by pretty much straightaway avoiding it. In his preface Amis notes that he has decided in his *Memoirs* to "keep myself from center stage" and to "focus on others rather than myself." His chief reason for doing so, he continues, is that "to publish an account of my own intimate, domestic, sexual experiences would hurt a number of people who have emotional claims on me . . . and I have no desire to cause pain, or further pain, to them or myself." This makes Mr. Amis seem rather a more sensitive chap than he turns out to be, for there is bloodletting aplenty in the pages of his memoirs; it is mainly his apron that comes out clean at his book's close.

In defense of his not writing about himself, Amis claims that the professional life of the writer is intrinsically dull. "Who would want to read about the time I had thinking up and writing one book or another and what I felt about its reviews, sales, translation into Catalan, or about how I spent my summer holidays in 1959?" (This is exactly the subject of the second volume of the autobiography of Anthony Burgess, as we shall discover presently, who does all this quite interestingly.) Something I should not have minded reading about is Kingsley Amis's view of the strange curve of his career. For that career is one of those odd ones dominated by a single book, his second, the aforementioned one about fortunate James. Amis has never come close to writing another novel near so good. I continue to read Kingsley Amis's novels, always finding highly amusing bits in them, but all seem longueur-laden, at once too densely written and too relentlessly clever, so that the play of language and the spirit of put-down inevitably dominate plot or character. Even though Amis has had his share of the world's rewards—all of the usual literary prizes and, recently, a knighthood—to have labored nearly forty full years without quite hitting the gong a second time after clanging it resoundingly once cannot have been pleasing to contemplate, in life or in an autobiography.

As with his novels, so with this autobiography, Kingsley Amis is not much concerned with dark or very deep truths; he is only occasionally prepared to engage in candor, and generally ready to settle for honesty of a slashing kind, usually at the expense of others. Amis's very style, literary and psychological, his strong anti-nonsense approach to life, has made it all but impossible for him to write anything approaching a conventional autobiography. So instead he has told a number of anecdotes, blasted a few old enemies, made a few new ones, pulled down the flag early, and made off for the pub.

None of which is to say that there aren't charming things in the book. Amis has kind words for his friend Philip Larkin and tells funny stories about Robert Conquest. He writes that "one reason for the inferiority of women novelists to men, if indeed they are inferior, may well be that comparatively few of them shave with any regularity," for it is during shaving that novelists often get their best ideas, which is a shot with, as they say in the pool hall, lots of English on it. He is crushing on Dylan Thomas, Freudianism, Cyril Connolly, Philip Toynbee, & Co.; there is a standard bashing of George Steiner for his pretense to cultural omniscience and for his restrained hand as a host with booze. (A restrained hand at the liquor cabinet never earns Amis's gratitude.) A bit of candor we could have done well without crops up in a brief scene in which Amis and Malcolm Muggeridge drunkenly gang-bang a famous literary widow. He writes warmly about a journalist named George Gale, whom he describes as "a foe of bullshit." For Amis how one lines up in relation to bullshit turns out to be how he lines up his own friends or foes. As for what constitutes bullshit, for Amis the pretentious, the overblown, the obviously stupid, and the immitigably unreal chiefly qualify.

All this puts Kingsley Amis very much in the English commonsense tradition. So, of course, was his friend Philip Larkin. This quality is seen in highest relief in Amis's reaction to Larkin's poem "Aubade," the powerful poem about the man waking "at four to soundless dark," contemplating with terror the oblivion that awaits him in death. Of this poem, Amis says he regrets not having found a way of telling Larkin "that depression among the middle-aged and elderly is common in the early morning and activity disperses it, as you tell us in your last stanza, so if you feel as bad as you say then fucking get up, or if it's too early or something then put the light on and read Dick Francis."

Yet there is a softer side to Amis that does not disqualify the commonsensical streak in him but recognizes that common sense, though it is all we have, can only take one so far. Bloody human condition, you might say. Amis has seen his share of shrinks, he relates, for his own psychic system has had its share of jigeroos: he has suffered agoraphobia, marital problems, bouts of melancholia. He has valued his friends and seems to have enjoyed his enemies, but is now old enough to know that life is in good part about loss. The best of Kingsley Amis, which is not the characteristically public Kingsley Amis, comes through in the final words of his portrait in this book of Philip Larkin:

> My sorrow at his death and my abiding sense of loss is tinged with regret. He was my best friend and I never saw enough of him or knew him as well as I wanted to. If I had, I might have been able to tell him, among other things, that he was a wonderful poet whose work would last. But as it is I have to fall back on hoping he knew I thought so.

Amis likes America, and Americans generally, but thinks Americans do not really like literature for itself but for the generalizations that can be drawn from it. This causes us gringos, he believes, to go in for the balmy and the self-inflated, which in his opinion includes such cases of "literary elephantiasis" as Saul Bellow, James Dickey, Norman Mailer, and Allen Ginsberg. Like most English writers of his generation, he has a low view of the academic study of literature, and, given the turn that it has taken, one must add rightly so. Amis holds that Americans are "not much good at art, high art, fine art," but powerfully good at hybrids like jazz, movies, science fiction (at which he has himself dabbled). Where such English writers as

Anthony Powell and Iris Murdoch continue producing into old age, American writers, in his view, with their "fondness for size, for big books, for large statements, subjects, themes, a desire for greatness *now* rather than after a few decades of work," tend to go under, "destined to be or become stricken deer, misfits, assorted victims and freaks, drunks rather than mere drinkers, hermits, suicides." Something to it, I fear. Yet one wonders if the tradition of common sense, of the small bite, of which Kingsley Amis is at once proponent and exemplar, will itself any longer quite do. At just this moment in English literary life, for example, the novelists who seem to be stirring the most interest in England—V. S. Naipaul, Salman Rushdie, Kazui Ishiguro—tend to be non-Englishmen of English education.

No one would accuse Anthony Burgess of either common sense or taking the small bite. But then nor does Burgess, who has lived in tax-fleeing exile from England for many years now, seem, when one gets down to it, especially English. His lineage is Irish and Catholic, for one thing. His ambitions, for another, are extra- or para-English. His productivity, of which he has himself by now doubtless heard too much, doesn't feel particularly English either. "I have written much fiction and reviewed widely and unbrophianly [a reference to the book reviews intended to maim written by Brigid Brophy], and I was sneered at for over-production and reviled for compassionate blandness." Mr. Burgess is not a man to forget a bad review, many of which he quotes, rather like showing old scars, in his autobiography, and this, too, does not seem particularly English.

I have not myself had very good luck with Mr. Burgess's novels, only one of which, *Earthly Powers,* I have been able to read all the way through. As he puts it early in *You've Had Your Time,* the second volume of his autobiography: "I was, am, trying to be a kind of comic novelist playing with a few ideas." Fair enough, except that the ideas he has chosen to play with have not, somehow, seemed much to interest me. I do read his literary journalism, and am often impressed by his erudition, his extraordinary range, his facility—when invited to review a book, it is said of him, he generally answers the invitation by providing the finished review. Mr. Burgess's talent is not in doubt; nor is his seriousness. He is a writer I rather admire without necessarily longing to read.

One comes away from his two-volume autobiography in something of the same condition: rather admiring his accomplishment of having got so much work done, of having maintained his independence without toadying to anyone, of having survived at least eleven different kinds of hell—and yet without particularly liking him. Burgess speaks at one point of Orwell's "power to ensour things," but he himself can usually be relied upon to take the smile out of Christmas. He passes Orwell's own test for autobiography by recounting many disgraceful things about himself and by tending to view his own life as, for the most part, a series of defeats.

The first of Burgess's two autobiographical volumes deals with his birth and education and horrific first marriage, and ends with him being told that he has an inoperable brain tumor that will allow him at best a year to live. His second volume deals with his wife's death and his remarriage, but it has chiefly to do with the literary life. This second volume is impressive for, among other things, its sheer comprehensiveness. Anthony Burgess has been a literary man of all work, having not only written in all the standard literary forms—poems, novels, plays, criticism, journalism—but translation for the stage and for opera, libretti, movies, television scripts, everything short of subpoenas and health-food labels. "I had become," he notes at one point of his various literary jobs, "the least fatigable of hacks." He has come through all this neither a rich man nor a cheerful one, but he has come through with all that a writer can hope for, his skill and his integrity intact. No small victory.

Certain of us go through life acquiring large grievances, and live out our days attempting to collect claims on them that can never be repaid. Mr. Burgess began life with a most serious grievance and claim of this kind. His mother and older sister died, in the great influenza epidemic of 1919, when he was only two years old. Given his rather indifferent father, who remarried to an unfeeling woman, this left poor John Anthony Burgess Wilson (for such is his full name, later shortened by a publisher) immediately alone, emotionally chilled, bereft, a twentieth-century Dickensian character in a novel that would have no happy ending. "This boy," Burgess writes of himself, "nine, going on ten, was clearly abnormal. He needed a real mother, not a surrogate one, and a real-life male model, not a mostly absent drunk who called himself a father."

Setting aside the human consequences of this sadness, for a man whose entire life is literature, the literary consequences, too, have to be calculated. No one is better fit to do this than Mr. Burgess, who, in a striking passage of self-knowledge, writes of his upbringing:

> I was not in rags and I did not starve. I was permitted an education. But I regret the emotional coldness that was established then and which, apart from other faults, has marred my work. I read of family relationships in other people's books and I envy equally the tranquility and the turbulence. *Sons and Lovers* and *Fathers and Sons* are from an alien planet which I can visit only by stretching my imagination.

This unfortunate absence of family feeling in a novelist is not a minor defect; if one believes that love and the family are two of the great—perhaps the greatest—subjects of the novel, it might just be a major defect. At a minimum, it would tend to force such a novelist to fall back upon satire, upon the schematic, upon the ideational, upon the play of language in and for itself, all of which seems to have been the result in Mr. Burgess's case.

Burgess's two volumes press the question of how deep in detail one should go in the writing of autobiography. At times Burgess himself threatens to rival Borges's poor child Ireneo Funes, in his story "Funes the Memorius," who could not forget anything and died young of what we should today call information overload. Burgess telling us that he missed his comic books in the General Strike of 1926 seems a detail if not worth forgetting then probably worth failing to record. One can't fault Burgess for want of candor. He not only fills us in on all his and his wife's love affairs, but tells us of their giving each other crabs (initially acquired elsewhere) and remarks on his own youthful propensity for premature climax ("it sounds," he remarks, "like a damn critic's rebuke"), a problem he conquered by quoting to himself from Milton, *Paradise Lost,* Book Two. (The study of literature, it seems, has its uses after all.) Sex, as described by Burgess in these volumes, is never overly elegant.

After himself, the central figure in Burgess's autobiography is his first wife, Lynne, whose infidelities to him, and his to her, on two continents he recounts in a rather matter-of-fact way. Their marriage, in Burgess's present view of it, was a mistake from the start. It was not much aided by her being mugged by American GIs in London, causing her to abort her pregnancy and cutting off forever the chance of her having children. Instead the Burgesses substituted cats, at one point in Brunei, where he had a teaching job, having no fewer than twenty-five of them. She added gin to this recipe for family disaster, and more than once attempted suicide. Toss in jealousy, resentment, and rivalrousness and you have quite a domestic dish. "Lynne and I cautiously settled to a country life enlivened mostly with drunkenness and threats of suicide," Burgess writes, in a sentence of chillingly calm rhythm. Yet when Burgess's wife dies, not yet fifty, of alcoholism, he feels, yes, of course, luscious guilt, which he seems to have attempted to work off in this autobiography by demonstrating what a monstrous character she was. If raising a writer is not such a good idea, marrying one is not a less perilous proposition.

Burgess makes the most modest claims for himself as an artist in this autobiography. (Kingsley Amis, in his, makes no claims whatever.) "I do not boast about the quality of my work," he writes, "but I may be permitted to pride myself on the gift of steady application. . . . The gift of concentration stays with me, and it is perhaps my only gift." In fact, Anthony Burgess is an immensely gifted man. But one of the things that comes strongly through his autobiography is that he would have traded all his literary accomplishments for a career in serious musical composition. At one point, he refers to "the novel, the only literary genre for failed symphonists." In his first volume, he tells us that "at the age of thirteen I decided that I was to be a great composer, and I trained myself, pursuing an indulged hobby, to that end. It was an ambition that only really faded in my late thirties, and sometimes, in my late sixties, it is encouraged to re-emerge." In the 1980s, he composed a symphony that was played at the University of Iowa, and so a childhood dream was realized. It may well be that only music, in its abstraction and in its propensity to submerge to depths beneath the verbal, could have given true expression to Burgess's wounds.

The world has never been a pleasant place for Anthony Burgess, and he is not very intent on changing it—he is for the most part apolitical—or himself. He was, he reports, offered Lionel Trilling's job at Columbia, but turned it down. "Security for life, high status, the dignity of scholarship. I think, however, I made the right decision in refusing the honor. It was not really suited to one masochistically inclined to the hard knocks of the Grub Street life, not inclined to disdain vulgarity in the right place, one not averse to scandal." Liana, his second wife, he notes, "importuned me to make myself more simpatico, but I would not. Had Dante made himself simpatico?" Old mothers' wisdom impels one to reply, "Very well, but first be Dante."

Everything Anthony Burgess writes in this autobiography is believable. He cannot be accused of blowing his own tuba. There is a life-like, inexorable dreariness to his account of his own days, relieved by flashes of wit. (To the rumor that he was living in a *ménage à trois,* with his wife and a beautiful Ethiopian secretary in Manhattan, Burgess responds that the rumor was "only two-thirds true.") Yet is his finally the true perspective? Or is it instead that writers, who not only by the nature of their occupation but because of the depression that all too often seems to have sent them into this occupation to begin with, are the least qualified for telling us what their lives have been about? Under the enchantment of their words, one is almost ready to believe them, no matter how chilling their account. Then one remembers that the world abounds in beautiful children, music, lush landscapes, friends, delightful food, and more than enough artworks to divert the mind through a lifetime, and the words, like frost on a wintry windowpane, melt away.

I am in danger here of imitating Auberon Waugh, who, at the close of his autobiography, *Will This Do?,* remarks that "the only real wisdom I have acquired in fifty years of living is the banal, frequently made point that happiness requires no more than good food, good wine, laughter, and the presence of friends." Then, with a Wavian touch, he adds: "Even friends may not be altogether necessary." The comedy of viewing things, if not quite *sub specie aeternitatis,* then at a cool distance is the Waugh gift, passed down from father to son. Auberon Waugh, in a characteristic sentence, writes of an uncle: "Although keenly appreciative of the good things of life, Alick was primarily a philosopher, and this may have given him the strength necessary to face a life without work." That, too, is a sentence with a lot of English on it. Many such in Mr. Waugh's autobiography.

I see that I have written a full paragraph about Auberon Waugh without mentioning, by name, his father, Evelyn, a writer whose work has perhaps given as much pleasure to its

readers as any other in this century. Of all the world's blessings, surely the most mixed is that of having a famous parent
or—worse luck still—parents. To be the son or daughter of a
famous artist may well be the most thoroughly mixed blessing
of all. Nathan Asch, the novelist son of the (in his day) inter-
nationally best-selling novelist Sholem Asch, at the beginning
of an essay about himself and his father, once put the case
devastatingly: "Though it has not been written about much,
the children of famous artists do not have an easy time, nor do
they usually end up well. There is more apostasy, suicide,
homosexuality, fraud, and lying, as well as plain ne'er-do-well-
ism among them than among children of other kinds of people." To have an artist for a father is one thing; but if that artist
is Evelyn Waugh, whose nearly every utterance was barbed
with icy irony, madcap comedy, and occasional motiveless cruelty, then you are really playing the games spades double.

Auberon Waugh, his autobiography leads one to believe,
has beaten that game, at least to the extent that it is beatable.
In *Will This Do?* Mr. Waugh cites letters from his father about
himself and his brothers and sisters that even now cannot make
pleasant reading for him. "My children were much in evidence
and boring," Evelyn Waugh wrote in one such letter. He makes
jokes about favoring books over his son: "the truth is that a
child is easily replaced, while a book destroyed is utterly lost."
On another occasion, in his diary, he noted: "My children weary
me. I can only see them as defective adults: feckless, destructive, frivolous, sensual, humourless. . . ."

The lesson that Waugh's children had to learn—and it must
have been a ghastly difficult one—was not to take much of this
personally. Auberon Waugh reports: " 'Why do you expect me
to talk to this boring pig?' he [Evelyn Waugh] would suddenly
shout at his hostess about some guest. 'He is common, he is
ignorant and he is stupid, and he thinks Picasso is an important artist.' " Not much relief to be had, either, from Laura
Waugh, of whom her son Auberon writes that she loved the

cows she kept "as other women love their dogs or, as I have been told, their children." Of a later period in his life, when at seventeen he was allowed to go off to live for a spell by himself in Italy, with very little guidance from home, he writes of his parents: "But I would like to think that there was a streak of committed libertarianism in their make-up which harmonized with their natural inclination toward indifference." With such parents one either develops character or goes under. None of the Waugh children went under. Put that in your Dr. Spock and smoke it.

What Auberon Waugh seems to have done is, in the fullness of time, take his father's measure. He came to understand that there was a large streak of melancholia in Evelyn Waugh's nature, perhaps even what we nowadays term "clinical depression"; he came to learn how easily he was bored, and how almost palpably painful boredom was to him; he came to realize his father's limitations when, directly after the war, with fresh fruit still in short supply, he saw his father wolf down all three bananas allotted to his family, and "from that moment, I never treated anything he had to say on faith or morals very seriously"; he came, as he grew older, to appreciate his father's light-handed and often good-hearted whimsy; and, not long after he, Auberon, was badly wounded in a machine-gun accident while serving in the British army in Cyprus, he came "to be quite fond of my father, never having liked him much in childhood or early youth"; and in the end, he came to love him, writing of him after his death:

> But he still projected an immensely powerful presence. Just as school holidays had been happier and more carefree when he was away, so his death lifted a great brooding awareness not only from the house but from the whole of existence. Papa possessed to an unusual degree the power of making other people want to please him. . . . Nothing ever happened to me while he was alive but I mentally subedited it into a report which would

be sent to him in my next letter. . . . It was many years before I
could break the habit of viewing every event with half an eye to
the bulletin I would send to my father. Even now, I find when
I hear a funny story about someone in whom he would have
been interested—the child of a friend, perhaps, or some gran-
dee—I mentally store it away to repeat to him. There always
follows a pang of bereavement when I remember that he is no
longer around to hear it.

Having so famous a father has to be the overriding fact in
one's life, and so it has been in Auberon Waugh's. Mr. Waugh
is candid and evenhanded in toting up the debits and credits
of this fact as it bore on his career: the doors that opened to
him because he was his father's son, the enemies that came to
him ready made for the same reason, the expectations the name
Waugh aroused, and the rest of it. Although Mr. Waugh has
been on his own since the age of twenty, earning his own way
as a journalist in a very competitive English field, although he
raised a large family, wrote five youthful novels, is the principal
editor of a journal (*Literary Review*), although he is himself
now an entirely established figure in English intellectual life
and even by now a grandfather, he remains, for better *and*
worse, the son of Evelyn Waugh. The plain truth is that, in
this generally agreeable autobiography, far and away the most
interesting passages of the book have to do with Evelyn Waugh,
a dominating presence even in death. Auberon Waugh is very
good at what he does—and what he does, as he himself allows,
is practice the vituperative arts through journalism; he claims,
rightly, to have a small gift "for making the comment, at any
given time, which people like least to hear." Yet there is a sense
in which without his father he could not be said to exist. Unfair
though it is, one cannot, even now, read him without comparing him to his father; even when he is very good, one tends to
think his father might have done it better. Not a light burden,
this. In English public schools, when two brothers are at the

school together, they are distinguished, older from younger, by the designation of major and minor. Luck of the draw, poor Auberon Waugh, not a brother but a son, is condemned always to be Waugh minor.

Ben Sonnenberg has drawn not one but two difficult cards. He, too, has had a less but still a famous enough father—also named Ben Sonnenberg, an art collector and a self-advertised genius at public relations, work he once likened to "making giant plinths for little men to stand on." Sonnenberg's second tough card has been his health; he was hit with the poisoned dart of multiple sclerosis, the degenerative disease that he first learned he had at the age of thirty-four and that by his late forties left him so weakened that he could no longer turn the pages of the magazine, *Grand Street,* which he had founded and loved to edit. Rotten luck.

With Ben Sonnenberg's *Memoirs and Confessions of a Bad Boy* we move from English to American autobiography, though, to be sure, Mr. Sonnenberg is not the kid next door who had the paper route and won the state tournament by sinking two free throws in overtime. (Long before he might have been doing such things, he was upstairs in his parents' antique-stuffed mansion on Gramercy Park trying to *schtupp* one of the maids.) Americans write autobiography very differently than do the English. They tend to bring a heavier freight to the task: of grudges against parents, of distaste for their country, of anger at life for not working out. Americans do not, when writing autobiography, allow themselves much distance. The air in which they work is dense, the emotions intense. Although bits of humor are allowed, the general atmosphere is grim. Thus turn to almost any page in Ben Sonnenberg's autobiography and you hear the gnip-gnop of that endless Ping-Pong match of *Sturm* versus *Drang.*

Why, one wonders, does it scarcely ever occur to an American to write an amusing autobiography? Auberon Waugh's is an amusing book; so, too, allowing for a certain acid content, is Kingsley Amis's. Ben Sonnenberg's might have been; the freedom that his family money made available to him gave him a privileged seat at the human masquerade carried on in some of its most sumptuous and absurd costumes. Mr. Sonnenberg has, moreover, taste and literary style; he has read widely and is, in almost every wise, no dope. Rather than writing an amusing autobiography, he has written one that prefers instead to show what a wild screw-up he has been. But the reasons for his screwing up are perhaps less fascinating than he thinks them. It is also, in his rendering of it, a story with something like a partially happy ending: notorious screw-up finds redemption through editing a highbrow little magazine that is "an insolent reflection of only one man's taste," which is "admired by those I admired."

Ben Sonnenberg's story is by now not so uncommon a one as he might think. It is the story of a family going, in three generations, from a Russian Jewish immigrant selling clothes out of a pushcart on the Lower East Side in New York to a grandson editing a modish, left-wing little magazine called *Grand Street,* considerably more uptown in every way. But Mr. Sonnenberg's is finally a story that might appear under the rubric of My Hate Belongs to Daddy. Although Mr. Sonnenberg is busily banging nails into his father's coffin in this book, his father manages to emerge—not, to be sure, from the coffin but from the book—as rather attractive nonetheless. A man whose snobbery took an Anglophiliac turn, Ben Sonnenberg, Sr., went everywhere and knew everyone: "I know the difference between Irving Berlin and Isaiah Berlin," he once told an interviewer, "and I know them both." It was not uncommon for Orson Welles to pop into a restaurant and ask Sonnenberg, Sr., what the hell he was doing there. He was, as his son notes, especially artful at the secondary name-drop. When he was asked if he knew George Gershwin, Sonnenberg *père* replied, "*Know* him? I used to play gin rummy with his mother."

One of the most troublesome things about having a power-ful father is that he is likely to leave an endlessly lingering doubt that one is not the man one's father was. (A powerful mother is no easier, leaving the even more troubling doubt that one is not the man one's mother was.) Mr. Sonnenberg seems to have grown up almost entirely in reaction to his father. When his father bought the house at 20 Gramercy Park next to his man-sion at 19 Gramercy Park and evicted the tenants, one of whom was Norman Thomas, young Ben instantly became a socialist. He used all the standard modern rich boy's vengeance gam-bits: getting kicked out of lots of schools, racking up debts, clocking heavy therapy time—the desperation of a young man who, however truly desperate he may be, in his heart knows he is working with a golden net under him. Sonnenberg, Jr., grew enormously fat—turned into a bulimic without the vom-iting part. As he grew older, his tastes in dissipation changed but not the main project, which seemed to be wasting his life. "Reading books, buying art, writing unproduced plays, seduc-ing women," he notes, "not much of a life."

It would have remained such had not Sonnenberg, at age forty-three, his multiple sclerosis confining him increasingly to a wheelchair, begun his magazine, *Grand Street,* modeled on Cyril Connolly's *Horizon. Grand Street* was, under Mr. Son-nenberg's editorship, literary and leftist, and better when it was the former than the latter. As a subscriber to the magazine for most of its ten-year life, I thought it often filled with good things, and I miss it now that it has been passed on to another editor, Jean Stein, who has very different, rather depressing notions about what constitutes an interesting magazine. *Grand Street* was an achievement, a thing built out of nothing, and Mr. Sonnenberg, after a life of more than four decades of "fas-tidious disengagement," of specializing in non-achievement, is justly proud of it. "At last," he writes, "I was doing something my father would have liked: which would have spoiled it for me, instantly." Fathers and sons, sons and fathers, Turgenev, apparently, didn't know the half of it.

Let us not speak of fathers and daughters, except that a remarkable autobiography entitled *The Bookmaker's Daughter* by Shirley Abbott takes up this relationship in a most interesting way that compels me to do so. Miss Abbott is a writer of my generation—she is in her middle fifties—until now unknown to me. She has written one earlier book, *Womenfolks: Growing Up Down South,* which I have not read but whose title suggests that it might be what I have come to think of as a gender-bender—that is, one of those books that twists and crushes all experience to tell yet another story of relentless oppression. I hope I am quite wrong about this, though what leads me to think I may not be is the occasional shot of feminudging that shows up in *The Bookmaker's Daughter:* Miss Abbott notes that there were few books by female authors in her father's library or that women didn't seem to make out so well in the fairy tales read to her as a child. In the current intellectual climate, it takes, I suppose, real character to resist such silliness, and Miss Abbott isn't always able to do so.

Shirley Abbott is much better than this. She is a writer of wit and penetration; she has a style and can do splendid things with it. She has sensed, too, that the conditions of her upbringing, as the daughter of a cash-out man in an elaborate bookie operation in Hot Springs, Arkansas, a town that shared both a traditional Southern ethos and corruption of a kind that was only to be met in the city of Chicago during its palmier days and in a few other sin cities of the South, make for rich material of an autobiographical kind. Miss Abbott grew up a daddy's girl in a marriage that was generally civil but, in her view, finally and sadly loveless. She was an only child. Her mother was never other than good to her, but her father, she early sensed, had a true stake in her.

One can grow up with a steady belief in goodness and then go on to be progressively shocked by the corruption inherent in life; or one can grow up believing in the corruption inherent in life and then go on to be fairly regularly surprised by how much goodness there is in the world. As someone who grew up in the second way, I tend to agree with Miss Abbott's father, who, when she was a child, gave her, as the Jews say, the *emess,* or the real lowdown: "Life is not led according to the civics books. Life is not Sunday school. Life is two-thirds con." Her father, known to his confreres as Hat Abbott, also told his daughter, "That's how people are, darling—never satisfied. Always wanting more."

Living in Hot Springs, the child Shirley—named, she tells us, after Shirley Temple—would have had to have been morally dyslexic to have read life any other way. Hot Springs was in those days what was known as a wide-open town. It had the Southern Club, where one could place bets, a racetrack, hookers at the ready, a historical tradition that included such luminaries among its visitors as the Younger Brothers, the James Brothers (not, distinctly, William and Henry), and the Capone Brothers. At the center of the town was a health spa, the baths, where people with various complaints, from arthritis to impotence, sought surcease from physical anguish in the putatively magical properties of hot spring water. Available, too, was surcease from boredom in the form of gambling of all sorts and women of one sort. When I was a boy in Chicago, old sports used to take their girlfriends and cufflinks down to Hot Springs for the racing season in February, stay at the Arlington Hotel, take the baths and live it up. Las Vegas and regular air travel put a serious crimp in the action at Hot Springs, which, after the early 1950s, never quite revived.

With deft strokes, Miss Abbott limns her parents' lives in Hot Springs. She does the same for her paternal grandparents, who lived with her parents during the early years of her childhood and who, in their grotesquerie, would have made a fine subject for the photography of Diane Arbus. But it was her father who took Miss Abbott's education in hand, explaining to her the etymology of the phrase "C-note" and turning her loose in his unexpectedly good—for a bookie who had no education beyond high school—library: it included Casanova (her introduction to sex), Gibbon (whom, with his subtext that corruption had been around for a long while, her father loved), Oscar Wilde, Dickens, Somerset Maugham, and much more. "I want you to read," her father told her. She did, and it turned her, in time, into a girl on whom not much was lost. He convinced her that she was extraordinary, and of course there is nothing easier for a child to believe than that.

Miss Abbott is very good at establishing the mildly exotic town of Hot Springs and quite as good at reviving a period, the late forties and early fifties, when, in small towns, prudery prevailed alongside corruption. As an adolescent, she worked in a drugstore, and she reminds us that, in those days, "just coming into a drugstore seemed to embarrass people, seemed always to expose some bodily function or shortcoming or physical need." (How different from today, when one calmly asks for a packet of condoms and shamefacedly requests a packet of cigarettes!) The status importance of clothes and cars is not lost to her. She recalls, too, how much everyone's dream life was connected to the movies. She had herself a crush on Cornel Wilde, though in a touch of retrospective feminudging she recalls admiration for Lauren Bacall. "No crocheted bedspreads for Lauren Bacall," she notes. "There was room for me, I concluded, in this man-getting game."

Only when she became a young woman did Miss Abbott's father begin sorely to let her down. Stirred by his encouragements, she was always an excellent student, which made her an oddity among her classmates, and thought of going to Radcliffe, though her parents, chiefly her father, insisted she stay closer to home, which meant going to Texas State College for Women at Denton. There she became, in his own words, even "weirder—a dingo among poodles." After college, when she wanted to go off to live in New York, her father opposed her all the way. The struggles between them grew fiercer. Her father, who had taught her never to depend on a man, now instructed her that every woman needs a husband. Her elegant, intelligent daddy could not learn that most difficult of parental arts, that of letting go. He became a nuisance and an embarrassment, a drag in every way. They met only to argue. "My romance with my father," she notes, after recounting his rather hard-line position on racial segregation in the South, "was definitely over."

Miss Abbott is very hard on her father in his last years. She saves all the virtuous sides of their arguments for herself. In their family drama, she is the queen of the enlightenment, he the prince of damn-near darkness. As he falls into decay, becoming toothless and snarly, she, now free and living in New York ("north toward home," Willie Morris, another Southerner, long ago called Manhattan), hasn't much tolerance for him. "This hateful, sick old bastard who abused my mother was somebody else"—somebody else besides her father, she means. Or is she only saying that, in her freedom, and through the struggle with all it entailed, she has lost all daughterly feeling?

"Daughter," Miss Abbott writes toward the end of her book, "is not a lifelong assignment." I am not sure that she is right about that; son and daughter may be an assignment that continues even after one's parents are dead. Maybe it picks up again especially after death. For proof of this, I put on exhibit Miss Abbott's book with its filial title; without her father, no book. His life made possible this book, which may well be the best thing she ever writes. Oh, Dad, Poor Dad, Someone's Put You in Her Autobiography and I'm Feeling So Sad.

If Miss Abbott's upbringing was lower-middle class, threatening to drop lower when her father lost his job owing to a reform candidate running for governor of Arkansas or the Baptists going on a virtue rampage, that of Tim McLaurin, author of *Keeper of the Moon,* was Southern white working-class, in rural to small-town North Carolina, and proud of it. McLaurin's people, as they say down South, drove for bakeries, worked construction, ran hardscrabble farms, sold Coca-Cola and Pepsi, and not in suits either but off the truck. Mr. McLaurin, though young to be writing an autobiography, has already, in his thirties, shored up experience out of proportion to his years. In particular, he has the experience all of us who have not gone through it fear: that of cancer. He has had multiple myeloma, a virulent form of cancer of the blood that involved him in the excruciating medical torture called marrow transplant. As Mr. McLaurin's book ends, it is not clear whether he will survive, though the ordeal he has gone through has given him the perspective that only living on close terms with death gives.

Mr. McLaurin's illness takes up only a small portion of his autobiography, which for much the better part is about growing up in the South at slightly below what might be called the K-Mart level of culture, among "hard living people," as he nicely puts it, "who had seen life from all angles except the top." Describing the scenery of his boyhood, Mr. McLaurin writes: "A jet howls overhead, her rockets churning clouds as she lifts and flies to one of those picture places like New York or Paris. It might as well be the moon." McLaurin's turf is a long way from, say, a party at George Plimpton's.

Tim McLaurin grew up in the Southern tradition of the good ole boy, on a small farm that his father worked when not driving a bakery truck. Difficult not to be impressed with the pervasiveness of violence described in McLaurin's pages. Lots of hard drinking and not much small talk in his life. Waylon Jennings, Porter Waggoner, Emmylou Harris playing on the radio in the pickup truck. No shortage of women who "had been backhanded once too often" and seen much pain and sadness.

Coon and deer hunting and fishing are the local sports; but so, too, are cockfights and setting pit bulldogs against each other; and let us not forget, just to work out the kinks, crunching barfights. Many men seem to die of lung cancer—all those unfiltered Camels with all those tall cool Buds—or heart attack in their fifties; many others go under in brawls or car accidents; and suicides aren't all that uncommon.

Tim McLaurin has written two novels, which means that he has escaped his environment—as in good part did Miss Abbott—through the magic carpet of the word. "Everyone I loved," he writes, "seemed to go on forever wishing and wanting and waiting and waiting. . . . At the ends of their lives, they held on to two or three items of pride and dismissed every other ambition as wishful thinking, nothing more than a dream." Not, somehow, this, for him. A pretty wild ole boy—a collector of snakes, a Marine, a man who likes his booze—he has nonetheless, as he allows, lived under a self-control that many another Southern man of his social class has chosen not to recognize. Where this comes from, he does not know. He was wild but not insane. And then, not long after discovering he had a knack for "stringing words together," he further discovered writing fiction, "a world where I was God, the one in control, where actions and results occurred on my timetable with my results."

McLaurin's autobiography is not without its flaws. He not infrequently lapses into sentimentality, which is often the obverse side of brutality; his book wants pace; it is, in patches, overwritten; and at other places padded. But for all this, it feels real and true. This is doubtless owing in good part to the fact that McLaurin is not an intellectual, with that species' gift for distancing itself from reality in favor of ideas; and to the additional fact that, though McLaurin felt the need to escape from the short, often dark lives of the people with whom he grew up, he respects these people and hasn't the least whiff of self-hatred for his origins and never sets himself above them.

Although not everyone's notion of paradise, the South where he still lives is a land he continues to love, and his book, which both begins and ends on descriptions of Southern landscape, is a homage to the region in its beautiful, brutal reality. Reality, he reminds us, is "Southern working-class men, expected to hammer out a paycheck, produce children, and hold [their] liquor." Reality is also cancer, and death waiting in the next room. As McLaurin has had to learn before the age of forty, reality also compels us to take life, with all its brutality and injustice, without complaint and make the most of it.

I don't mean to suggest that Tim McLaurin has written a classic autobiography—he hasn't—only that this younger, much less worldly man has written a book propelled by a greater love of life than writers older and more sophisticated than he. He has nothing of Kingsley Amis's spirit of put-down; he is far from anywhere near registering the disgust with life that Anthony Burgess has so long lived with; he has had none of the advantages (and disadvantages) of Auberon Waugh's birth; he feels nothing of Ben Sonnenberg's need to kill all over again the dead father; he does not put himself, as does Shirley Abbott, in the position of writing above, and therefore looking down upon, the culture that made him. Through his not yet completed bout with cancer, he has had the unwanted opportunity to look death long in the eye, an experience that, for the right person, can go a long way toward separating the trivial from the significant in life. His book, compared with those of our other autobiographers, is a strong reminder that there is often a vast difference between being well equipped and being well qualified to write about one's life—and that being well qualified is better.

Remembering Sidney Hook

ALTHOUGH Sidney Hook, who died in 1989 at the age of eighty-six, contributed a number of important articles to the *American Scholar,* the magazine I edit; although we corresponded fairly frequently and would speak by telephone every so often; and although we met on two separate occasions, I am reasonably certain that, had we passed on the street, Sidney would not have recognized me.

One of those two occasions was the evening of October 30, 1982, at a dinner given to honor Sidney on his eightieth birthday. The other was in 1985 at a different dinner, also in New York. On the second of these occasions Sidney made it clear that he could not have remembered our earlier meeting, for as we shook hands he told me that he had expected me to be a fatter man. When I asked why fatter, he said that he found a lot of what I wrote amusing and that in his subconscious he must have thought of amusing people as fat. "You know," he added, "like Falstaff." Something very Sidney about that.

I had seen Sidney in the flesh one earlier time. This was in the winter of 1964, when he was one of four panelists who met under the auspices of *Commentary* to discuss the subject of "Liberalism and the Negro." It was an event of the kind that I had come to New York in my middle twenties to witness. Owing to the topic under discussion, some of the chief figures in the civil-rights movement of the day were present: the earnest and immensely dignified Roy Wilkins; the burly Whitney Young, looking like a highly cerebral NFL linebacker; the elegant Bayard Rustin. The audience was by invitation only, but there must have been three hundred people in the room. This was the first time I had ever seen the now much-written-about New York intellectuals foregathered. Their presence was not altogether, to put it gently, illusioning. As I looked across the aisle one among them rather delicately crossed a leg to reveal a sock embossed with the figure of Donald Duck. One could work one's way backward from a single detail like that to discover a whole way of life.

When the transcript of "Liberalism and the Negro" appeared in an edited version in *Commentary* (March 1964) it bore the subtitle "A Round-Table Discussion." Forgive my pedantry, but it is pertinent here to point out that the actual table at which the discussion took place was not round but rectangular. As the moderator, Norman Podhoretz, the editor of *Commentary*, sat in the middle of this table, and to his left, sharing a microphone, were the sociologist Nathan Glazer and the economist Gunnar Myrdal; to his right, sharing another microphone, were Sidney Hook and the writer James Baldwin. I was in the audience, on the aisle four or five rows back, next to a handsome woman of very good posture. Luck of the draw, I had one of the best seats in the house, for all the real action took place on my side of the room, where Hook and Baldwin were positioned.

I had seen dust-jacket photographs of Sidney Hook before, but I was impressed, if I may put it so, at how much like himself he looked. In 1964, he was sixty-two years old. He seemed remarkably fit—not athletically but intellectually fit. He was smallish and wiry but solid; no fat on *him*. He dressed neatly but nondescriptly, eschewing the two chief options in academic dress: the bohemian and the Ivy League Anglophile. From his clothes one might have taken him for an insurance salesman or a small-scale manufacturer of gaskets or other appliance parts.

This plainness of dress may have owed something to the puritanism of Sidney's socialist youth and young manhood. In larger part, though, it may have reflected his simple lack of interest in clothes as a medium of style or a form of snobbery. My guess is that he just did not care about life lived at what one might call the Tom Wolfe level of culture. In later years, a photograph of Sidney smiling and wearing a beret would sometimes appear alongside a review of one of his books or an article about him. I disliked this photograph, chiefly because the beret reminded me of the one Groucho Marx wore after he had begun to hoist the yellow flag of senility. Sidney lived longer than Groucho, but as one of his editors I have reason to know that he kept his mental acuity right up to the end.

Sidney had a strong, crowded face. Notable upon it were an ample nose, glasses, a substantially receded hairline, good-sized ears, and a mustache—above all, a mustache. George Balanchine, in an interview he gave not long before his death, remarked that in the latter half of the twentieth century, unlike in his father's generation, beards were not only bad style but, their historical moment having passed, quite fake. I think he would have said something similar about mustaches, but he would surely have excepted Sidney's, which seemed one of the last authentic mustaches around, not an afterthought or a piece of pathetic male vanity but a permanent and prominent and perfectly natural feature. It was part of his dignity, a slight formality of the kind adopted by men of his generation, even rather old-shoe men like Sidney. The name Sidney had something of that same formality. I never heard anyone refer to him as "Sid," or as "Sid Hook." Bertrand Russell addressed him as "Hook," but that was an upper-class English mannerism. He was always "Sidney" to people who knew and admired him, "Sidney Hook"—last name pronounced with a slight snarl—to enemies.

James Baldwin in those days did not go in for fancy dress, either. He had not yet begun to wear the heavy jewelry and flamboyant duds of his later years. That afternoon he wore a plain dark blue suit, a white shirt, and a black knit tie, the effect of which was slightly ministerial. Then there was his extraordinary face—the same face that appeared on the Beacon Press paperback edition of *Notes of a Native Son*, his best book. With its bulging eyes, its wide nose, its somewhat flattened head, it was the face of a black frog. But once Baldwin spoke, you sensed immediately the prince inside. He had the kind of control over his face that only a superior actor can command. He could make a dramatic event out of smoking a cigarette, he could kill with a pause. He was beautifully well-spoken, and that afternoon he spoke beautifully well indeed.

In the discussion, each of the panelists began with a talk of ten minutes or so, first Hook, then Baldwin, then Glazer, then Myrdal. Although Glazer, as a working sociologist and the co-author of *Beyond the Melting Pot,* and Myrdal, whose *An American Dilemma* was at that time considered the definitive work on race relations in this country, had wider knowledge of the subject than either Hook or Baldwin, Baldwin did have—no small thing—actual experience: as a black from Harlem, he had been there. Hook had only his principles. As Norman Podhoretz remarked, throwing things open for discussion, "Mr. Hook, while you may not be an expert on race relations, you are most certainly an expert on the principles of liberalism. . . ." Because the proceedings immediately took a moral turn—they were to be almost entirely about principles and ethics—Hook and Baldwin dominated them, with the former pointing out what the ethics of democracy demanded in race relations and the latter insisting that, so long as they were talking about the United States, they were not talking about an ethical society at all.

The transcript of the discussion printed in *Commentary,* though accurate on all that was said, cannot give a sense of the atmosphere in the room. I, for example, thought Baldwin scored heavily, though less on the points he made than on what I think of as his stage mastery, which did not come across in print. A certain amount of byplay had of course to be excluded from the published version. Hook and Baldwin shared a microphone, as I have mentioned, and on more than one occasion Hook would lean in, grab at the mike, and half-interrupt Baldwin. "Sidney, Sidney," said the woman seated next to me, in a loud stage-prompter's whisper, "Sidney, let him finish, let him speak." She was, I soon realized, Mrs. Hook. At one point, in a question from the audience following the general discussion, there was a terrible moment when the black social scientist Kenneth B. Clark accused Hook from the floor of putting Baldwin on the defensive, adding that Hook's only experience of Negroes was probably through his cook. "Oh, I've never had a cook," sputtered Sidney as Clark angrily sat back down.

Well, no point in attempting to recapitulate that interesting afternoon on East 56th Street except to say that Sidney Hook then struck me as the heavy and the patsy of the proceedings, and that when I read them now I see that he was in reality their hero. Although, as Norman Podhoretz indicated, Sidney probably did not know much about race relations in any particularity, his principles nonetheless stood him in damn fine stead. Of the five people on that panel, it was Sidney who said the best and most penetrating things that afternoon, a few of them, sadly, prophetic.

While allowing that a "temporary" program to aid underclass and other blacks in difficulty would be useful, Sidney added that he "would consider a program which would lower the standards of *achievement* for Negroes as tantamount to regarding them as second-class citizens." He considered it important not to gainsay such progress as had actually been made in race relations and in the condition of blacks in America, and felt that "a good deal of the discussion concerning the Negro problem these days [was] very rhetorical and unnecessarily inflammatory; much of it puts obstacles in the way of progress." He insisted that "the conception of democracy—which, as I keep repeating, is fundamentally an ethical conception—is that we can live peacefully together with *differences*." He chided Baldwin for doing a disservice, in his writings, "to the whole cause of liberalism"; for, while stressing the responsibility of white liberals, neglecting to ask about "the responsibility of the Negro intellectual"; and for aiding in the development of a "myth of collective guilt," from which blacks had themselves suffered. "There's a difference between collective guilt for the past and collective responsibility in the present," said Sidney, "for such responsibility can ultimately be brought to each individual's door."

Even grabbing the microphone ("Sidney, Sidney, let him speak"), I now understand, was not the boorish act of an intellectual ruffian but an expression of Sidney's inveterate disgust for and impatience with lies, falsity, people saying the thing that was patently not so. Throughout his life Sidney spent a good deal of time writing letters to newspapers, magazines, individuals, pointing out errors in fact, logic, and principle. To have Sidney pounce upon you could not have been an altogether pleasant experience. "He was not, in our experience at least, a terribly nice man," wrote Martin Peretz, editor-in-chief of the *New Republic,* after Sidney's death. "In recent years he'd periodically send us letters correcting, reproaching, hectoring. We were wrong on this, wrong on that, and often he was right. But he was not only right about small things. He was right on the big things."

Let me jump in quickly to say that, in my experience, Sidney Hook was a terribly nice man. But before enlarging upon that, I should emphasize that it was on what Peretz calls "the big things" that Sidney taught a great many people, myself among them. I first came across him in the pages of *Partisan Review, Commentary,* and *Encounter,* which I began to read at twenty or so, near the close of my formal education. I was more interested in literary than political matters, and had not yet any notion of how the two frequently intertwined to the point of inseparability. Around this time, though, I was also attempting to gain the rudiments of a political education, until now virgin territory for me, a Chicago boy who knew how to bribe a policeman but could not tell you the definition of realpolitik.

In his contributions to these magazines, Sidney invariably wrote on political subjects and he inevitably did so with more authority than any other American intellectual. Others might cite Marx, Lenin, Trotsky, but never with Sidney's certitude. In part, this was owing to his unadorned, no-nonsense prose, with its confident cadences. But in greater part it was owing to the fact that Sidney had pored over, struggled with, and mastered the entire literature of revolution, so that he not only knew it but knew its every interior weakness, in the intimate way a television repairman knows the weakness of last year's diodes.

In 1958, in the pages of the *New Leader,* Sidney took on Bertrand Russell, a philosopher he much admired—he was one of his intellectual heroes—in a debate over the question of whether the West ought to be prepared to enter into war with the Soviet Union even at the risk of extinction, or would do better to disarm unilaterally even at the risk of Communist domination. This was the "Better-Red-Than-Dead" question, as it was known at the time. Russell had one of the most lucid and sharpest minds of the century, and was everywhere conceded to be one of the toughest opponents in argument. He once debated Mortimer J. Adler at the University of Chicago on the subject of education, and it was said that Adler might have won but the victory wasn't worth it. "One cannot but admire the rough-hewn simplicity of Dr. Adler's argument," Russell's initial rejoinder supposedly began.

Against Russell, Sidney took the position that, yes, the risk even of extinction was worth it: he held, as he put it in an epigraph to the book in which the debate was later republished, that "it is better to be a live jackal than a dead lion—for jackals, not men; and that those who are prepared to live like men and, if necessary, die like men, have the best prospect of surviving as free men and escaping the fate of jackals and lions." In the actual debate, which took place over the course of three issues of the *New Leader,* Sidney ripped, roasted, and fricasseed Bertrand Russell, making his position seem mean, ruinous, and cowardly. It was a most impressive performance, and one that helped stiffen intellectual resistance to the advances of the Soviet Union during a difficult time.

The first book by Sidney I ever read was a closely printed, tightly argued collection of essays entitled *Political Power and Personal Freedom.* I remember tackling it, with my shirt off, during a number of scorching afternoons in a furnished, un-air-conditioned studio apartment in Little Rock, Arkansas, during the summer of 1959, in a lather brought on by a combination of Southern humidity and intellectual excitement. The book is a catechism, a *vade mecum,* of democratic theory; it not only sets out the strongest explanation of and justification for democracy that I have ever encountered, but along the way establishes a guide for distinguishing those governments whose claims to be democratic are true from those that are specious— a guide that would prove to be especially useful over the next thirty years. This may sound like dry stuff, but it didn't in the least seem so to me, who, with the lingering habits of a student, underlined roughly two-thirds of the book for future reference.

It was a book written with evident passion, and the passion derived in good part from Sidney's own passionate belief in reason. He did not, like some bush-league Rousseau, believe that all men were inherently reasonable and only education and other institutions of society made them stupid, but he did believe that reason remained the best weapon available in the fight to improve social and political conditions and to defeat those who would make things worse. In an essay in *Political Power and Personal Freedom* entitled "The Justifications of Democracy," he wrote: "It is noteworthy that, in an age not conspicuous for its appeal to reason, few will give assent to doctrines which they admit to be demonstrably false or out of line with verifiable fact."

It is remarkable how frequently the word "fight" appears in the pages of this book. ("The truth is that the amount of freedom and democracy in the present and future depends as much upon human willingness to fight for them as upon anything else.") Sidney was himself all his life a battler. He knew that people often lied and cheated and operated out of motives that were sometimes tangled and perverse; that political intellectuals not uncommonly rewrote their own personal histories to ensure self-portraits of virtuousness. Somewhere along the line, however, he determined not to let them get away with it.

The three strong philosophical influences on Sidney were Morris Raphael Cohen, Bertrand Russell, and John Dewey, and of the three Dewey, both philosophically and personally, was the man he admired most. Admire him greatly though he did, by temperament Sidney was unable to emulate Dewey, whom he once described as "naturally shy, reticent, and undemonstrative in manner." Nobody would have applied such words to Sidney. ("Sidney, Sidney, let him speak.") But Dewey did, according to Sidney, appreciate "passion, enthusiasm, color, and originality in others." John Dewey must have found all those things in Sidney Hook, while Sidney Hook found in John Dewey a towering standard of intellectual honesty, probity, and above all a complex philosophy—that of pragmatism—which Sidney seemed able to express better than Dewey himself. "When I read you," Dewey once told him, "I understand myself better."

Sidney felt a lifelong sense of obligation to Dewey and an allegiance of similar duration to pragmatism, which, in his view, had acquired an entirely false popular reputation as little more than a philosophy of usefulness, itself so useful to the American spirit of opportunity and the cult of success. In Sidney's reading of it, pragmatism was a "method of clarifying ideas and therefore preeminently a method of criticism." The only truly American contribution to philosophy, pragmatism—whose proponents before John Dewey were Charles Peirce and William James—attempted to clarify ideas by testing their consequences in the behavior of human beings. According to Sidney, in his essay "Pragmatism and the Tragic Sense of Life," pragmatism also taught "a temper of mind toward the vital options which men confront when they become aware of what alternative proposals commit them to."

> It [pragmatism] stressed the efficacy of human ideals and actions and at the same time their inescapable limitations. It forswore the promise of total solutions and wholesale salvation for piecemeal gains. Yet far from embracing easy formulae of the ultimate reconciliation of conflicting interests and values, it acknowledged the reality of piecemeal losses even when we risk our lives to achieve the gains.

"Philosophies," said John Dewey, "are different ways of construing life," and Sidney construed pragmatism not as a struggle for personal salvation but as the pursuit of understanding of a kind useful to a philosopher. In due course such understanding would be useful in influencing the life of one's time, through providing ideas that advanced the general human enterprise and through criticizing other ideas that retarded it. Sidney referred to this function of philosophy as "normative social inquiry" and made plain that it dealt with "the problems of man."

Sidney's was very much a worldly, as opposed to an otherworldly, philosophy. For him what gave life its tragic quality was not the presence of evil in the world, or that human beings grow old, sicken, and die—such things he regarded as among

themselves to criticism and abuse. I remember his once telling me, too, how stalwart Melvin Lasky (the editor of *Encounter*) could be in situations calling for physical courage, and that he much admired Lasky's fighting heart. His letters to me were filled with kind words for such academic colleagues as Edward Shils, Lewis Feuer, Richard Rorty, and others. He dispensed praise—which Thomas Mann, in his diaries, used to refer to as Vitamin P—wonderfully well, but he was impatient when it was dispensed to him. Whenever I told him that something he had written was extremely good, he would change the subject. "I want to tell you," I wrote in one of my early letters to him, "how proud I am to have a hand in publishing your work in the *American Scholar*. I think you are an extraordinary man— and a man to whom I and a great many other people owe a considerable intellectual debt." I am pleased that I wrote that sentence, though he never responded to it.

It was at his eightieth-birthday celebration that Sidney reported on one of the most intellectually gratifying moments in his life. A professor had informed him that he had written his dissertation on a political thinker whom Sidney had long ago thoroughly attacked in print, but whose case Sidney had presented so fairly as to excite a then-young academic's curiosity. Sidney greatly valued fairness, honesty, playing the game by the agreed-upon rules. "I am old-fashioned enough to believe," he wrote to me when I had asked him to review one of Malcolm Cowley's later, quite self-serving books, "one can and should be fair even to someone who is unfair to others."

Although Sidney was in many quarters hated, he was not himself much of a hater. A tough and terrible opponent, yes, but not a true hater. I happen to be a pretty fair country hater myself, and I never saw any of the requisite qualities in Sidney. Your good hater is obsessive about his enemies; he tends to make enmity personal; he does not merely dislike his opponents but detests, despises, loathes them. Nothing of this personal intensity ever crept into Sidney's judgments. Instead he seemed always freshly surprised, amazed, astonished at the atrocious behavior of his own enemies. When the *New York Times Book Review* passed up reviewing four of Sidney's books in a row, he reported this outrageous fact to me not with the sense of outrage it deserved but with an air of someone amazed that an editor could get away with something like that. He would recount the false political past that a prominent literary critic had invented for himself as if to say, "Wild, isn't it?" I do not mean to imply that Sidney was a naïf—he had fought too many political battles for that—but meanness and dishonesty nonetheless seemed a little crazy to him. They did not quite make sense. Something of this quality of honest puzzlement in Sidney came through to me recently in a remark attributed to the biologist Max Delbrück: "If you cheat in science you are simply missing the point."

In the realm of politics, Sidney took on the burdensome role of reminding people what the point was. He was forever correcting historical error owing to political bias, jumping in to remind people of what actually happened, straightening out people on the lessons they had long ago learned but chosen to forget. These efforts, needless to say, were not warmly appreciated. Sidney took a good pounding from those who did not wish to be corrected, reminded, straightened out. For a long stretch—from the early 1960s to the middle of the 1970s, when anti-anti-Communism was riding high among political intellectuals—the mere mention of Sidney Hook, whose name was synonymous with anti-Communism, drew fire and spit. But even after the hatred of Sidney had let up some, he himself did not in the least let up. No untruth that came his way was too minute to respond to; a lie was a lie, no matter how obscure its provenance or backwoods its venue. And when Sidney discovered a lie he had to point it out, tear it down, correct it. He would fire off a letter to the *New York Times* or to a student newspaper with equal ardor. "At a time when age and achievement had earned him the right to retire from active political life, he devoted all his energies and most of his husbanded hours of leisure to the fight for freedom, from which many of his younger colleagues turned away." Sidney wrote that about John Dewey, and of course it was quite as true of him, who at the time of his death was enmeshed in writing about the curriculum controversy at Stanford.

Not that Sidney's entire life was a battle. I used to imagine him during his summers in Vermont, walking the New England countryside discussing the old philosophical questions with his dear friend Ernest Nagel, who died a few years before he did. (Did one or the other of them, I wonder, ever trot out the problem of good?) My distant sense is that his family life was rich and satisfying: *Pragmatism and the Tragic Sense of Life* is dedicated to his four grandsons and their generation; *Out of Step* to his wife Ann, "unfailing source of strength and joy." His health in his last years was wretched, but his conscience (I should imagine) clear and his mind in splendid working order. Listening to him talk, I sometimes thought that Sidney had the reverse of Alzheimer's disease—he remembered everything. The last piece he wrote for the *American Scholar* was a strong but by no means hostile criticism of Allan Bloom's *The Closing of the American Mind*. That piece, and the response he had to it, turned Sidney to thinking once more about the questions, issues, and problems of education. Rosinante to the road again.

Nowadays it is acknowledged that a scientist may be altogether unscientific in the daily conduct of his life, a poet a fool, a novelist a perfect pig of vanity. But a philosopher one somehow still expects to live like a philosopher: the life and the work influencing each other and both devoted to the pursuit of wisdom. One is usually disappointed in this expectation, but not in the case of Sidney Hook, in whom man and philosopher were one.

After the tributes made to him at his eightieth-birthday celebration, Sidney rose and spoke: humorously, modestly, seriously, profoundly. Walking from the room after the standing ovation given to him, I felt an exhilaration and lightness of step, and my sense is that nearly everyone else there that night felt something similar. I, for one, have only known such feelings at the conclusion of some extraordinary artistic performance. Sidney's life was, I think, such a performance. He made fighting for one's beliefs—if those beliefs be sound—seem not merely an honorable, but the only honorable, way to live. To have done it for so long, so relentlessly, so fairly as Sidney did constitutes its own kind of greatness. Sidney, of course, would have rejected the assertion that he was in any way a great man. But, take it from one who beat him in argument, Sidney would have been wrong.